**W9-BEV-002**

# NEW
# COUNTRY&
# FARMHOUSE
# HOME PLANS

CREATIVE HOMEOWNER®, Upper Saddle River, New Jersey

Vice President and Publisher: Timothy O. Bakke
Production Director: Kimberly H. Vivas

Home Plans Editor: Kenneth D. Stuts, CPBD
Home Plans Designer Liaison: Timothy Mulligan

Design and Layout: Arrowhead Direct (David Kroha, Cindy DiPierdomenico, Judith Kroha); Maureen Mulligan

Cover Design: David Geer

Current Printing (last digit)
10 9 8 7 6 5

New Country & Farmhouse Home Plans,
Library of Congress Control Number: 2007921257
ISBN-10: 1-58011-358-3
ISBN-13: 978-1-58011-358-8

CREATIVE HOMEOWNER®
A Division of Federal Marketing Corp.
24 Park Way
Upper Saddle River, NJ 07458
**www.creativehomeowner.com**

*Note: The homes as shown in the photographs and renderings in this book may differ from the actual blueprints. When studying the house of your choice, please check the floor plans carefully.*

**Front cover:** *main plan* 181151, page 206; *left to right:* plan 161024, page 163; plan 161061, page 342; plan 131029, page 332; plan 131029, page 332 **page 1:** plan 121014, page 145 **page 3:** *top to bottom* plan 401039, page 192; plan 331002, page 213; plan 311005, page 219 **page 4:** plan 181094, page 217 **page 5:** plan 331001, page 152 **page 6:** *top to bottom plan 521040, page 115; plan 321041, page 257* **page 7:** plan 111026, page 260 **page 66:** Alan Shortall Photography **page 67:** *top* Mark Lohman; *center* Leonard Lammi, design: Cheryl Casey Ross; *bottom* Philip Clayton-Thompson, design: Nancy Setterquist **page 68:** *top and top inset* Jessie Walker, design: Claire Golan; *bottom* courtesy of York Wallcoverings **page 69:** Leonard Lammi, design: Cheryl Casey Ross **page 70:** *top* Tria Giovan; *bottom* Mark Lohman **pages 72–73:** *top center and top right center* Brian Vanden Brink, design: Atlantic Kitchens; *top right* Mark Samu; *bottom right* Phillip Clayton Thompson; *bottom center* Mark Lohman; *bottom left center* courtesy of American Olean; *bottom left* Brian Vanden Brink, design: Atlantic Kitchens; *top left* Mark Samu **page 132:** Mark Lohman **page 133:** *both* Bob Greenspan, stylist: Susan Andrews **page 134:** Mark Lohman **page 135:** Tria Giovan **page 136:** Todd Caverly **page 137:** *top* Mark Lohman; *bottom* Tria Giovan **page 138:** *top* Mark Lohman; *bottom* Paul Johnson, design: Austin Interiors **page 139:** *top* Mark Lohman; *bottom* Bill Rothschild **page 198:** courtesy of Osram Sylvania **page 199:** courtesy of Maine Cottage Furniture **page 200:** *left* courtesy of Kraftmaid Cabinetry; *right* courtesy of Maine Cottage Furniture **page 201:** courtesy of Sharp Electronics Corp. **page 202–205:** *all* George Ross/CH, designer: Lyn Peterson **pages 264–271:** *all* illustrations Steve Buchanan **page 334:** Jessie Walker **pages 335–337:** *all* courtesy of Hostetler Patio Enclosures, Inc. **page 338:** illustrations Mario Ferro **page 339:** Roger Bruhn **page 340:** *top left* Jessie Walker; *top right* Jessie Walker, design: Adele Lampert/Interiors II; *bottom* Roger Holmes **page 341:** Jessie Walker **page 373:** plan 121112, page 98 **page 377:** *top to bottom* plan 151490, page 108; plan 141026, page 111; plan 141024, page 128 **page 384:** *top to bottom* plan 151029, page 289; plan 461092, page 295; plan 331003, page 322 **back cover:** *top plan* 161061, page 342; *left to right:* plan 181151, page 206; plan 151035, page 64; plan 151035, page 64

# Contents

# Getting Started

Maybe you can't wait to bang the first nail. Or you may be just as happy leaving town until the windows are cleaned. The extent of your involvement with the construction phase is up to you. Your time, interests, and abilities can help you decide how to get the project from lines on paper to reality. But building a house requires more than putting pieces together. Whoever is in charge of the process must competently manage people as well as supplies, materials, and construction. He or she will have to

- Make a project schedule to plan the orderly progress of the work. This can be a bar chart that shows the time period of activity by each trade.
- Establish a budget for each category of work, such as foundation, framing, and finish carpentry.
- Arrange for a source of construction financing.
- Get a building permit and post it conspicuously at the construction site.
- Line up supply sources and order materials.
- Find subcontractors and negotiate their contracts.
- Coordinate the work so that it progresses smoothly with the fewest conflicts.
- Notify inspectors at the appropriate milestones.
- Make payments to suppliers and subcontractors.

## You as the Builder

You'll have to take care of every logistical detail yourself if you decide to act as your own builder or general contractor. But along with the responsibilities of managing the project, you gain the flexibility to do as much of your own work as you want and subcontract out the rest. Before taking this path, however, be sure you have the time and capabilities. Do you also have the time and ability to schedule the work, hire and coordinate subs, order materials, and keep ahead of the accounting required to manage the project successfully? If you do, you stand to save the amount that a general contractor would charge to take on these responsibilities, normally 15 to 30 percent of the construction cost. If you take this responsibility on but mismanage the project, the potential savings will erode and may even cost you more than if you had hired a builder in the first place. A subcontractor might charge extra for hav-

**Acting as the builder,** above, requires the ability to hire and manage subcontractors.

**Building a home,** opposite, includes the need to schedule building inspections at the appropriate milestones.

ing to return to the site to complete work that was originally scheduled for an earlier date. Or perhaps because you didn't order the windows at the beginning, you now have to pay for a recent cost increase. (If you had hired a builder in the first place he or she would absorb the increase.)

## Hiring a Builder to Handle Construction

A builder or general contractor will manage every aspect of the construction process. Your role after signing the construction contract will be to make regular progress payments and ensure that the work for which you are paying has been completed. You will also consult with the builder and agree to any changes that may have to be made along the way.

Leads for finding builders might come from friends or neighbors who have had contractors build, remodel, or add to their homes. Real-estate agents and bankers may have some names handy but are more likely familiar with the builder's ability to complete projects on time and budget than the quality of the work itself.

The next step is to narrow your list of candidates to three or four who you think can do a quality job and work harmoniously with you. Phone each builder to see whether he or she is interested in being considered for your project. If so, invite the builder to an interview at your home. The meeting will serve two purposes. You'll be able to ask the candidate about his or her experience, and you'll be able to see whether or not your personalities are compatible. Go over the plans with the builder to make certain that he or she understands the scope of the project. Ask if they have constructed similar houses. Get references, and check the builder's standing with the Better Business Bureau. Develop a short list of builders, say three, and ask them to submit bids for the project.

## Contracts

### Lump-Sum Contracts

A lump-sum, or fixed-fee, contract lets you know from the beginning just what the project will cost, barring any changes made because of your requests or unforeseen conditions. This form works well for projects that promise few surprises and are well defined from the outset by a complete set of contract documents. You can enter into a fixed-price contract by negotiating with a single builder on your short list or by obtaining bids from three or four builders. If you go the latter route, give each bidder a set of documents and allow at least two weeks for them to submit their bids. When you get the bids, decide who you want and call the others to thank them for their efforts. You don't have to accept the lowest bid, but it probably makes sense to do so since you have already honed the list to builders you trust. Inform this builder of your intentions to finalize a contract.

### Cost-Plus-Fee Contracts

Under a cost-plus-fee contract, you agree to pay the builder for the costs of labor and materials, as verified by receipts, plus a fee that represents the builder's overhead and profit. This arrangement is sometimes referred to as "time and materials." The fee can range between 15 and 30 percent of the incurred costs. Because you ultimately pick up the tab—whatever the costs—the contractor is never at risk, as he is with a lump-sum contract. You won't know the final total cost of a cost-plus-fee contract until the project is built and paid for. If you can live with that uncertainty, there are offsetting advantages. First, this form allows you to accommodate unknown conditions much more easily than does a lump-sum contract. And rather than being tied down by the project documents, you will be free to make changes at any point along the way. This can be a trap, though. Watching the project take shape will spark the desire to add something or do something differently. Each change costs more, and the accumulation can easily exceed your budget. Because of the uncertainty of the final tab and the built-in advantage to the contractor, you should think twice before entering into this form of contract.

### Contract Content

The conditions of your agreement should be spelled out thoroughly in writing and signed by both parties, whatever contractual arrangement you make with your builder. Your contract should include provisions for the following:

- The names and addresses of the owner and builder.
- A description of the work to be included ("As described in the plans and specifications dated . . .").
- The date that the work will be completed if time is of the essence.
- The contract price for lump-sum contracts and the builder's allowed profit and overhead costs for changes.
- The builder's fee for cost-plus-fee contracts and the method of accounting and requesting payment.
- The criteria for progress payments (monthly, by project milestones) and the conditions of final payment.
- A list of each drawing and specification section that is to be included as part of the contract.
- Requirements for guarantees. (One year is the standard period for which contractors guarantee the entire project, but you may require specific guarantees on

**When submitting bids,** all of the builders should base their estimates on the same specifications. Once the work begins, communicate with your builder to keep the work proceeding smoothly.

**Inspect your newly built home,** if possible, before the builder closes it up and finishes it.

certain parts of the project, such as a 20-year guarantee on the roofing.)
- Provisions for insurance.
- A description of how changes in the work orders will be handled.

The builder may have a standard contract that you can tailor to the specifics of your project. These contain complete specific conditions with blanks that you can fill in to fit your project and a set of "general conditions" that cover a host of issues from insurance to termination provisions. It's always a good idea to have an attorney review the draft of your completed contract before signing it.

## Working with Your Builder

The construction phase officially begins when you have a signed copy of the contract and copies of any insurance required from the builder. It's not unheard of for a builder to request an initial payment of 10 to 20 percent of the total cost to cover mobilization costs, those costs associated with obtaining permits and getting set up to begin the actual construction. If you agree to this, keep a careful eye on the progress of the work to ensure that the total paid out at any one time doesn't get too far out of sync with the actual work completed.

What about changes? From here on, it's up to you and your builder to proceed in good faith and to keep the channels of communication open. Even so, changes of one sort or another beset every project, and they usually add to its cost.

### Light at the End of the Tunnel.

The builder's request for a final inspection marks the end of the construction phase—almost. At the final inspection meeting, you and the builder will inspect the work, noting any defects or incomplete items on a "punch list." When the builder tidies up the punch list items, you should reinspect. Sometimes, builders go on to another job and take forever to clean up the last few details, so only after all items on the list have been completed satisfactorily should you release the final payment, which often accounts for the builder's profit.

## Some Final Words

Having a positive attitude is important when undertaking a project as large as building a home. A positive attitude can help you ride out the rigors and stress of the construction process.

**Stay Flexible.** Expect problems, because they certainly will occur. Weather can upset the schedule you have established for sub-contractors. A supplier may get behind on deliveries, which also affects the schedule. An unexpected pipe may surprise you during excavation. Just as certain, every problem that comes along has a solution if you are open to it.

**Be Patient.** The extra days it may take to resolve a construction problem will be forgotten once the project is completed.

**Express Yourself.** If what you see isn't exactly what you thought you were getting, don't be afraid to look into changing it. Or you may spot an unforeseen opportunity for an improvement. Changes usually cost more money, though, so don't make frivolous decisions.

Finally, watching your home go up is exciting, so stay upbeat. Get away from your project from time to time. Dine out. Take time to relax. A positive attitude will make for smoother relations with your builder. An optimistic outlook will yield better-quality work if you are doing your own construction. And though the project might seem endless while it is under way, keep in mind that all the planning and construction will fade to a faint memory at some time in the future, and you will be getting a lifetime of pleasure from a home that is just right for you.

## Plan #131014

**Dimensions:** 48' W x 43'4" D
**Levels:** 1
**Square Footage:** 1,380
**Bedrooms:** 3
**Bathrooms:** 2
**Foundation:** Crawl space, slab, or basement
**Materials List Available:** Yes
**Price Category:** C

CAD FILE AVAILABLE

Living Room

The exterior of this home looks formal, thanks to its twin dormers, gables, and the bay windows that flank the columned porch, but the inside is contemporary in both design and features.

### Features:

• **Great Room:** Centrally located, this great room has a 10-ft. ceiling. A fireplace, built-in cabinets, and windows that overlook the rear covered porch make it as practical as it is attractive.

• **Dining Room:** A bay window adds to the charm of this versatile room.

• **Kitchen:** This U-shaped room is designed to make cooking and cleaning jobs efficient.

• **Master Suite:** With a bay window, a walk-in closet, and a private bath with an oval tub, the master suite may be your favorite area.

• **Additional Bedrooms:** Located on the opposite side of the house from the master suite, these rooms share a full bath in the hall.

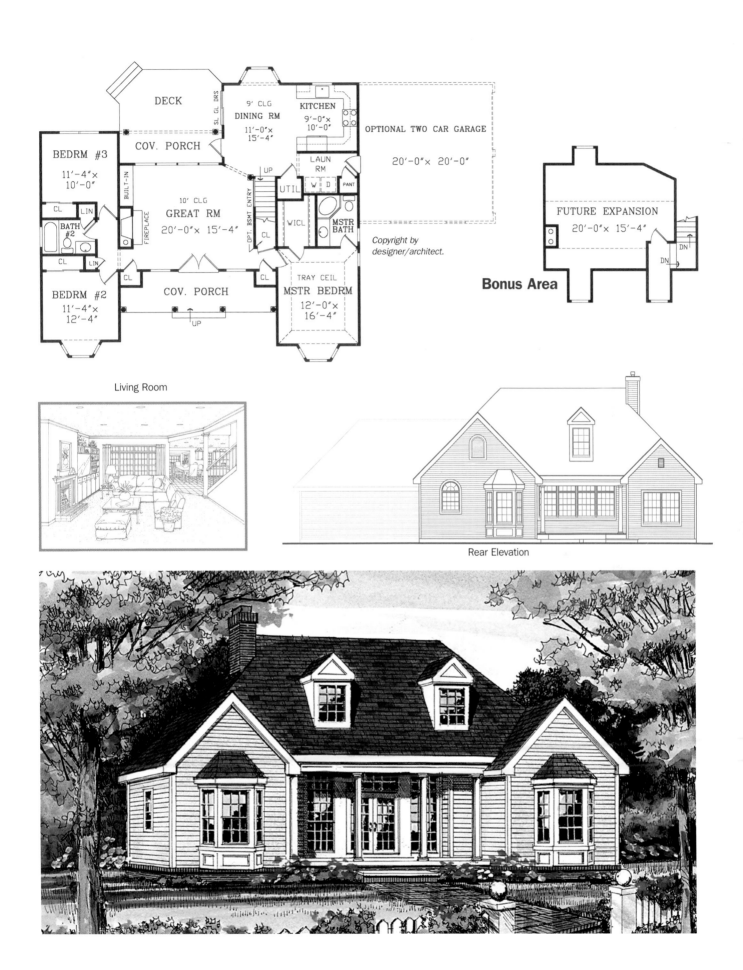

DECK

9' CLG
DINING RM
11'-0"x
15'-4"

KITCHEN
9'-0"x
10'-0"

OPTIONAL TWO CAR GARAGE

20'-0"x 20'-0"

COV. PORCH

BEDRM #3
11'-4"x
10'-0"

BUILT-IN

CL  LIN

BATH
#2

CL  LIN

LAUN
RM

UTIL  W  D  PANT

UP

10' CLG
GREAT RM
20'-0"x 15'-4"

FIREPLACE

OPT. BSMT ENTRY

CL

WICL

MSTR
BATH

Copyright by
designer/architect.

BEDRM #2
11'-4"x
12'-4"

CL

COV. PORCH

CL

UP

TRAY CEIL
MSTR BEDRM
12'-0"x
16'-4"

SL. GL. DRS

FUTURE EXPANSION
20'-0"x 15'-4"

DN

DN

**Bonus Area**

Living Room

Rear Elevation

## Plan #651026

**Dimensions:** 40' W x 36' D

**Levels:** 1

**Square Footage:** 1,145

**Bedrooms:** 3

**Bathrooms:** 2

**Foundation:** Slab

**Materials List Available:** No

**Price Category:** B

CAD FILE AVAILABLE · CAD

You'll love this design if you're looking for a compact home with amenities usually found in much larger designs.

**Features:**

• Master Suite: The coffered master bedroom area leads to a walk-in closet and private bath area.

• Kitchen: This open kitchen design connects to the dining area, making it perfect for easily bringing meals to the table.

• Family Area: Relax or entertain in this large family area, with easy accessibility to the kitchen and dining areas.

• Secondary Bedrooms: These two bedrooms are wonderful for siblings, or to turn into a home office or library.

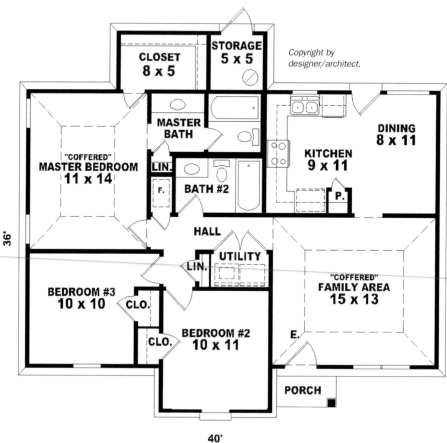

CLOSET 8 x 5

STORAGE 5 x 5

MASTER BATH

"COFFERED" MASTER BEDROOM 11 x 14

LIN.

F.

BATH #2

DINING 8 x 11

KITCHEN 9 x 11

P.

HALL

UTILITY

LIN.

BEDROOM #3 10 x 10

CLO.

CLO.

BEDROOM #2 10 x 11

"COFFERED" FAMILY AREA 15 x 13

E.

PORCH

36'

40'

## Plan #401031

**Dimensions:** 42' W x 52' D

**Levels:** 1

**Square Footage:** 1,260

**Bedrooms:** 3

**Bathrooms:** 2

**Foundation:** Basement

**Materials List Available:** Yes

**Price Category:** B

*Images provided by designer/architect.*

This economical-to-build bungalow works well as a small family home or a retirement cottage. The covered porch leads to a vaulted living room with a fireplace.

**Features:**

• Kitchen: This L-shaped space with a walk-in pantry and an island with a utility sink. An attached breakfast nook has sliding glass doors to a rear patio.

• Master Suite: The master bedroom has a private full bathroom with bright skylight.

• Bedrooms: There are three bedrooms, each with a roomy wall closet, that share a main bathroom with skylight.

• Garage: A two-car garage sits at the front of the plan to protect the bedrooms from street noise.

CAD FILE
**CAD**
AVAILABLE

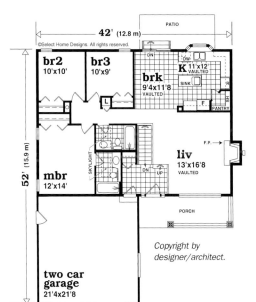

*Copyright by designer/architect.*

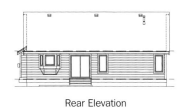

Rear Elevation

Right Side Elevation

Left Side Elevation

## Plan #131034

**Dimensions:** 40' W x 32' D
**Levels:** 2 (upper unfinished)
**Square Footage:** 1,040
**Bedrooms:** 5 or 4
**Bathrooms:** 2½
**Foundation:** Crawl space, slab, basement; walk out for fee
**Materials List Available:** Yes
**Price Category:** C

You'll love the versatility this expandable ranch-style home gives, with its unfinished, second story that you can transform into two bedrooms and a bath if you need the space.

**Features:**

• **Porch:** Decorate this country-style porch to accentuate the charm of this warm home.

• **Living Room:** This formal room features a wide, dramatic archway that opens to the kitchen and the dining room.

• **Kitchen:** The angled shape of this kitchen gives it character, while the convenient island and well-designed floor plan make cooking and cleaning tasks unusually efficient.

• **Bedrooms:** Use the design option in the blue-prints of this home to substitute one of the bedrooms into an expansion of the master bedroom, which features an amenity-laden, private bathroom for total luxury.

*Images provided by designer/architect.*

### Optional Main Level Floor Plan

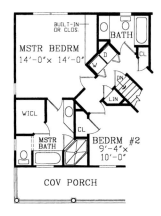

### Main Level Floor Plan

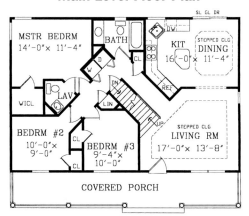

Kitchen

### Optional Upper Level Floor Plan

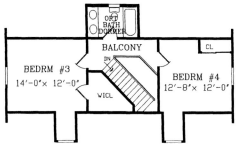

*Copyright by designer/architect.*

## Plan #121056

**Dimensions:** 48' W x 50' D
**Levels:** 1
**Square Footage:** 1,479
**Bedrooms:** 2
**Bathrooms:** 2
**Foundation:** Basement
**Materials List Available:** Yes
**Price Category:** B

This home is ideal if the size of your live-in family is increasing with the addition of a baby, or if it's decreasing as children leave the nest.

**Features:**

• Entry: This entry gives you a long view into the great room that it opens into.

• Great Room: An 11-ft. ceiling and a fireplace framed by transom-topped windows make this room comfortable in every season and any time of day or night.

• Den: French doors open to this den, with its picturesque window. This room would also make a lovely third bedroom.

• Kitchen: This kitchen has an island that can double as a snack bar, a pantry, and a door into the backyard.

• Master Suite: A large walk-in closet gives a practical touch; you'll find a sunlit whirlpool tub, dual lavatories, and a separate shower in the bath.

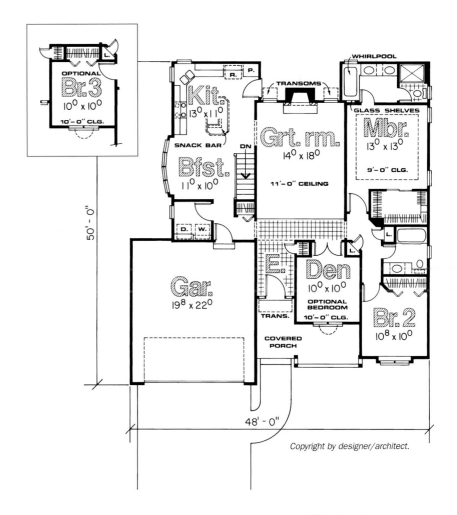

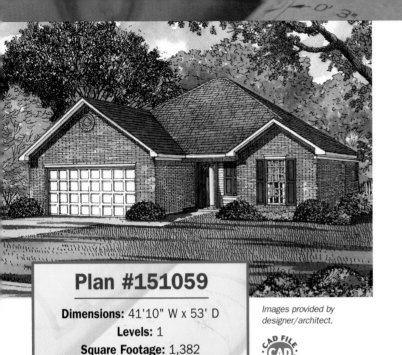

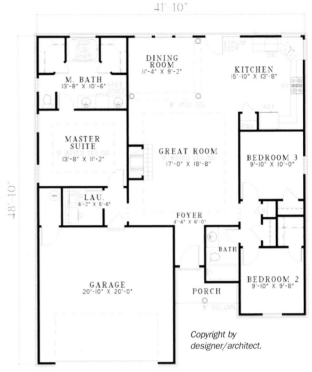

Images provided by designer/architect.

CAD FILE AVAILABLE

## Plan #151059

**Dimensions:** 41'10" W x 53' D

**Levels:** 1

**Square Footage:** 1,382

**Bedrooms:** 3

**Bathrooms:** 2

**Foundation:** Crawl space, slab; basement for fee

**CompleteCost List Available:** Yes

**Price Category:** B

Copyright by designer/architect.

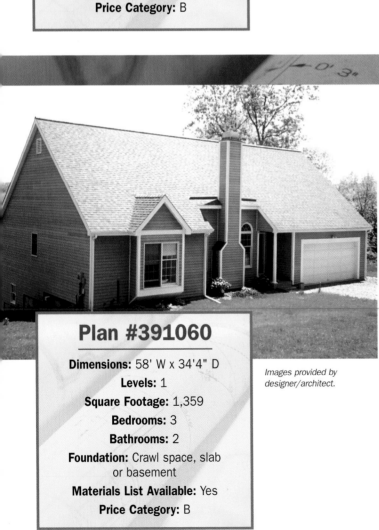

Images provided by designer/architect.

Copyright by designer/architect.

## Plan #391060

**Dimensions:** 58' W x 34'4" D

**Levels:** 1

**Square Footage:** 1,359

**Bedrooms:** 3

**Bathrooms:** 2

**Foundation:** Crawl space, slab or basement

**Materials List Available:** Yes

**Price Category:** B

Rear View

# Plan #381048

**Dimensions:** 32' W x 40' D

**Levels:** 1

**Square Footage:** 895

**Bedrooms:** 2

**Bathrooms:** 1

**Foundation:** Crawl space or basement

**Material List Available:** Yes

**Price Category:** A

*Images provided by designer/architect.*

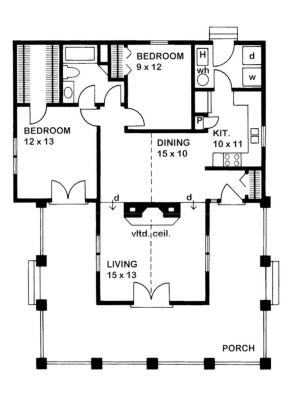

*Copyright by designer/architect.*

# Plan #381045

**Dimensions:** 36' W x 44' D

**Levels:** 1

**Square Footage:** 1,015

**Bedrooms:** 2

**Bathrooms:** 1

**Foundation:** Crawl space

**Material List Available:** Yes

**Price Category:** B

*Images provided by designer/architect.*

*Copyright by designer/architect.*

## Plan #121035

**Dimensions:** 45'4" W x 38' D

**Levels:** 2

**Square Footage:** 1,471

**Main Level Sq. Ft.:** 716

**Upper Level Sq. Ft.:** 755

**Bedrooms:** 3

**Bathrooms:** 2½

**Foundation:** Basement

**Materials List Available:** Yes

**Price Category:** B

*Images provided by designer/architect.*

This convenient and elegant home is designed to expand as the family does.

**Features:**

- Ceiling Height: 8 ft. unless otherwise noted.

- Family Room: An open staircase to the second level visually expands this room where a built-in entertainment center maximizes the floor space. The whole family will be drawn to the warmth from the handsome fireplace.

- Kitchen: Cooking will be a pleasure in this

bright and efficient kitchen that features a corner pantry. A snack bar offers a convenient spot for informal family meals.

- Dining Area: This lovely bayed area adjoins the kitchen.

- Room to Expand: Upstairs is 258 sq. ft. of unfinished area offering plenty of space for expansion as the family grows.

- Garage: This two-bay garage offers plenty of storage space in addition to parking for cars.

**CAD FILE AVAILABLE**

### Main Level Floor Plan

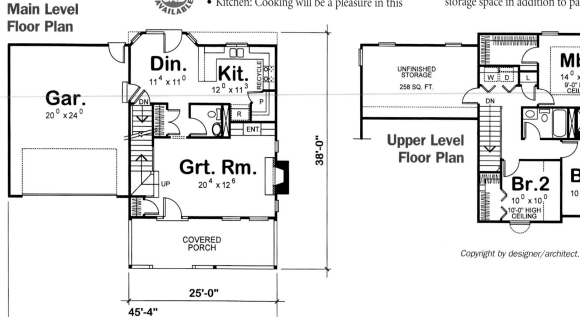

*Copyright by designer/architect.*

## Plan #131017

**Dimensions:** 69'8" W x 39'4" D
**Levels:** 1
**Square Footage:** 1,480
**Bedrooms:** 3
**Bathrooms:** 2
**Foundation:** Crawl space, slab, or basement
**Materials List Available:** Yes
**Price Category:** C

This fully accessible home is designed for wheelchair access to every area, giving everyone true enjoyment and freedom of movement.

**Features:**

• Great Room: Facing towards the rear, this great room features a volume ceiling that adds to the spacious feeling of the room.

• Kitchen: Designed for total convenience and easy work patterns, this kitchen also offers a view out to the covered front porch.

• Master Bedroom: Enjoy the quiet in this room which is sure to become your favorite place to relax at the end of the day.

• Additional Bedrooms: Both rooms have easy access to a full bath and feature nicely sized closet spaces.

• Garage: Use the extra space in this attached garage for storage.

*Images provided by designer/architect.*

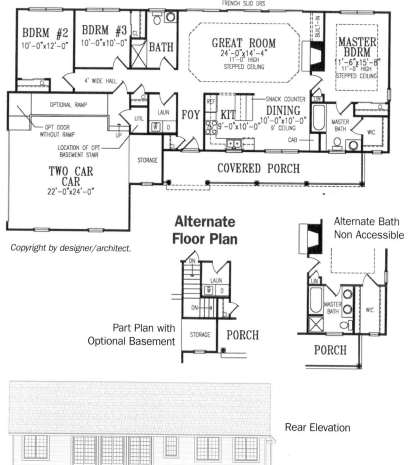

*Copyright by designer/architect.*

**Alternate Floor Plan**

Part Plan with Optional Basement

**Alternate Bath Non Accessible**

Rear Elevation

## Plan #131004

**Dimensions:** 59'4" W x 35'8" D

**Levels:** 1

**Square Footage:** 1,097

**Bedrooms:** 3

**Bathrooms:** 2

**Foundation:** Crawl space, slab, or basement

**Materials List Available:** Yes

**Price Category:** C

You'll love the extra features you'll find in this charming but easy-to-build ranch home.

**Features:**

- **Porch:** This full-width porch is graced with impressive round columns, decorative railings, and ornamental moldings.

- **Living Room:** Just beyond the front door, the living room entrance has a railing that creates the illusion of a hallway. The 10-ft. tray ceiling makes this room feel spacious.

- **Dining Room:** Flowing from the living room, this room has a 9-ft.-high stepped ceiling and leads to sliding glass doors that open to the large rear patio.

- **Kitchen:** This kitchen is adjacent to the dining room for convenience and has a large island for efficient work patterns.

- **Master Suite:** Enjoy the privacy in this bedroom with its private bathroom.

*This home, as shown in the photograph, may differ from the actual blueprints. For more detailed information, please check the floor plans carefully.*

*Images provided by designer/architect.*

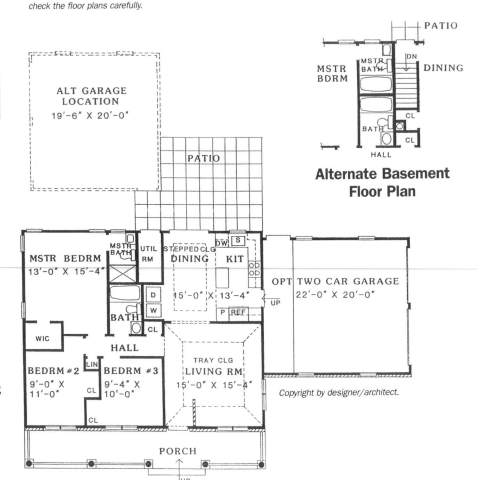

**Alternate Basement Floor Plan**

*Copyright by designer/architect.*

## Plan #341100

**Dimensions:** 43'4" W x 34'4" D

**Levels:** 1

**Square Footage:** 1,207

**Bedrooms:** 3

**Bathrooms:** 2

**Foundation:** Crawl space, slab, basement or walkout

**Material List Available:** No

**Price Category:** B

This cozy Country-style home boasts a charming brick-and-wood exterior.

### Features:

- Entry: This covered front entry invites visitors and residents into the home.

- Living Room: This generously sized living room allows you and your family space to spread out and relax. Its location provides easy access to the other rooms in the home.

- Kitchen and Dining Room: Conveniently conjoined, these two rooms accent each other perfectly. Entertain dinner guests with ease, and enjoy conversation while preparing a meal.

- Master Suite: Privacy and spaciousness are two appealing elements of this design. Set up a dressing corner and entertainment center in the comfortable bedroom. Enjoy a morning routine filled with ease and comfort thanks to the large bath.

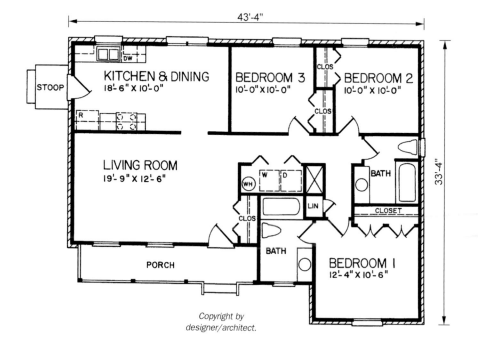

*Copyright by designer/architect.*

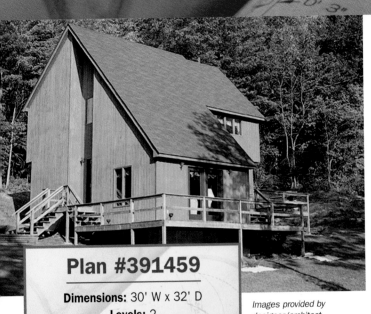

## Plan #391459

**Dimensions:** 30' W x 32' D
**Levels:** 2
**Square Footage:** 1,341
**Main Level Sq. Ft.:** 769
**Upper Level Sq. Ft.:** 572
**Bedrooms:** 3
**Bathrooms:** 2
**Foundation:** Basement
**Material List Available:** Yes
**Price Category:** B

*Images provided by designer/architect.*

**Main Level Floor Plan**

**Upper Level Floor Plan**

*Copyright by designer/architect.*

---

## Plan #181050

**Dimensions:** 31'8" W x 24' D
**Levels:** 2
**Square Footage:** 1,297
**Main Level Sq. Ft.:** 670
**Upper Level Sq. Ft.:** 627
**Bedrooms:** 2
**Bathrooms:** 1½
**Foundation:** Basement
**Material List Available:** Yes
**Price Category:** B

*Images provided by designer/architect.*

**Main Level Floor Plan**

**Upper Level Floor Plan**

*Copyright by designer/architect.*

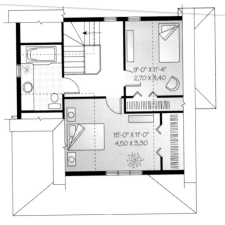

## Plan #211016

**Dimensions:** 44'6" W x 59' D

**Levels:** 1

**Square Footage:** 1,191

**Bedrooms:** 3

**Bathrooms:** 2

**Foundation:** Slab

**Materials List Available:** Yes

**Price Category:** B

*Images provided by designer/architect.*

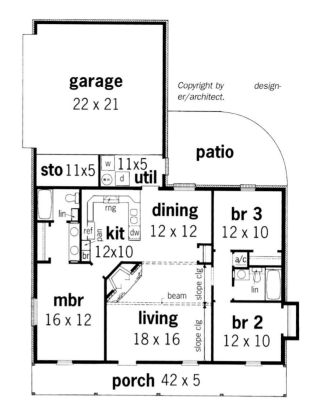

*Copyright by designer/architect.*

garage 22 x 21

patio

sto 11x5

w 11x5 d
util

dining 12 x 12

br 3 12 x 10

rng

kit 12x10

ref pan dw

a/c

lin

mbr 16 x 12

beam

slope clg

living 18 x 16

slope clg

br 2 12 x 10

**porch** 42 x 5

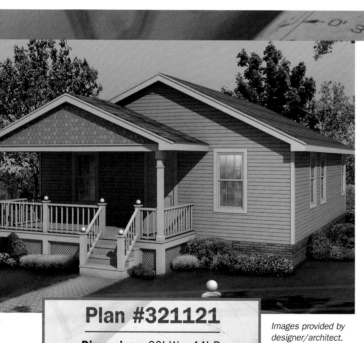

## Plan #321121

**Dimensions:** 30' W x 44' D

**Levels:** 1

**Square Footage:** 1,320

**Bedrooms:** 3

**Bathrooms:** 2

**Foundation:** Crawl space

**Material List Available:** Yes

**Price Category:** B

*Images provided by designer/architect.*

CAD FILE AVAILABLE

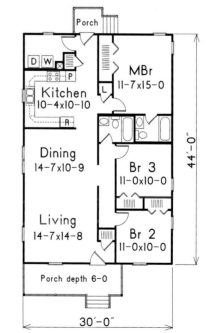

Porch

D W P

Kitchen 10-4x10-10

MBr 11-7x15-0

L

R

Dining 14-7x10-9

Br 3 11-0x10-0

Living 14-7x14-8

Br 2 11-0x10-0

44'-0"

Porch depth 6-0

30'-0"

**Main Level Floor Plan**

*Copyright by designer/architect.*

## Plan #121036

**Dimensions:** 42' W x 43' D

**Levels:** 2

**Square Footage:** 1,297

**Main Level Sq. Ft.:** 603

**Upper Level Sq. Ft.:** 694

**Bedrooms:** 3

**Bathrooms:** 2½

**Foundation:** Basement

**Materials List Available:** Yes

**Price Category:** B

*Images provided by designer/architect.*

This bright and cheery home offers the growing family plenty of room to expand.

**Features:**

• Ceiling Height: 8 ft. unless otherwise noted.

• Living Room: Family and friends will be drawn to this delightful living room. A double window at the front and windows framing the fireplace bring lots of sunlight that adds to the appeal.

• Dining Room: From the living room, you'll usher guests into this large and inviting dining room.

• Kitchen: A center island is the highlight of this attractive and well-designed kitchen.

• Three-Season Porch: This appealing enclosed porch is accessible from the dining room.

• Master Bedroom: A dramatic angled ceiling highlights a picturesque window in this bedroom.

• Bonus Area: With 354 sq. ft. of unfinished area, you'll never run out of space to expand.

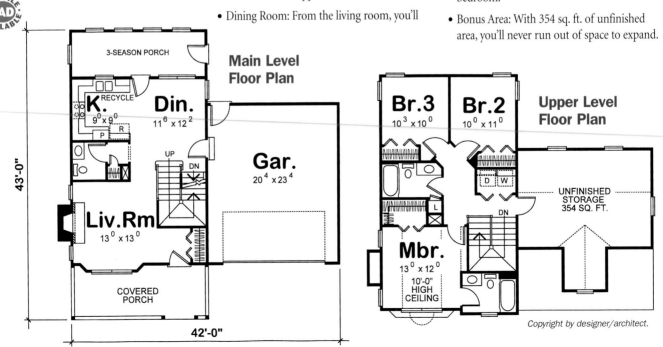

*Copyright by designer/architect.*

# Plan #251001

**Dimensions:** 61'3" W x 40'6" D

**Levels:** 1

**Square Footage:** 1,253

**Bedrooms:** 3

**Bathrooms:** 2

**Foundation:** Crawl space or slab

**Materials List Available:** Yes

**Price Category:** B

*Images provided by designer/architect.*

This charming country home has a classic full front porch for enjoying summertime breezes.

**Features:**

• Ceiling Height: 8 ft.

• Foyer: Guests will walk through the front porch into this foyer, which opens to the family room.

• Screened Porch: A second porch is screened and is located at the rear of the home off the dining room, so your guests can step out for a bit of fresh air after dinner.

• Family Room: Family and friends will be drawn to this large open space, with its handsome fireplace and sloped ceiling.

• Kitchen: This open and airy kitchen is a pleasure in which to work. It has ample counter space and a pantry.

• Master Bedroom: This master bedroom features a large walk-in closet. It has its own master bath with a single vanity, a tub, and a walk-in shower.

• Garage: This attached garage provides plenty of extra storage space, as well as parking for two cars.

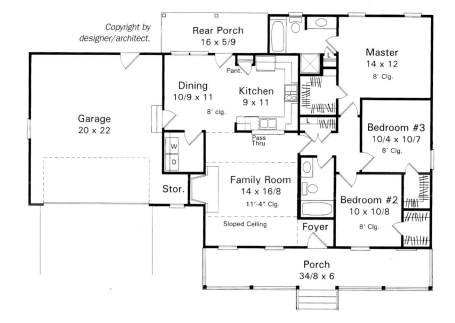

# Plan #351009

**Dimensions:** 54' W x 47' D

**Levels:** 1

**Square Footage:** 1,400

**Bedrooms:** 3

**Bathrooms:** 2

**Foundation:** Crawl space, slab, or basement

**Materials List Available:** Yes

**Price Category:** B

This design offers a great value in space planning by using the open concept, with split bedrooms, in a layout that is easy to build.

**Features:**

- Ceilings: All ceilings are a minimum of 9-ft. high.

- Great Room: This large gathering area provides room for family activities as well as being open to the kitchen and dining area.

- Master Suite: This oversized private area provides a great bathroom arrangement for busy couples as well as a large walk-in closet.

- Bedrooms: The split bedroom layout provides zoned privacy and improved noise control.

- Patio: This area is the perfect place to enjoy the afternoons grilling out or relaxing with friends and family.

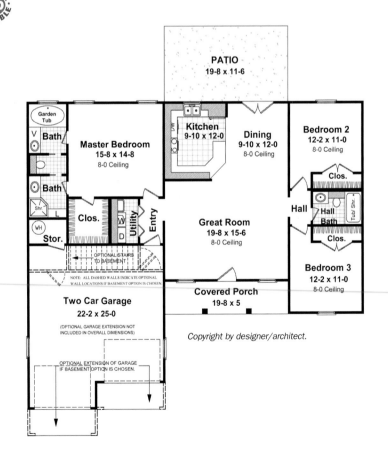

## Plan #181218

**Dimensions:** 38' W x 28'8" D

**Levels:** 1

**Square Footage:** 946

**Bedrooms:** 2

**Bathrooms:** 1

**Foundation:** Basement

**Materials List Available:** Yes

**Price Category:** A

With a showcase front porch trimmed by quaint railings and carved brackets, this design uses all of its space beautifully and practically.

**Features:**

- Living room: This company-loving room waits just inside the entrance.

- Kitchen: This creative U-shaped kitchen has a bounty of counter and cabinet space as well as a breakfast counter that stretches into the dining area and doubles as a serving board.

- Utility Areas: The full bathroom is paired with the laundry area, and a side door near the kitchen leads to a smaller covered porch.

- Bedrooms: Two spacious bedrooms sit comfortably beside each other.

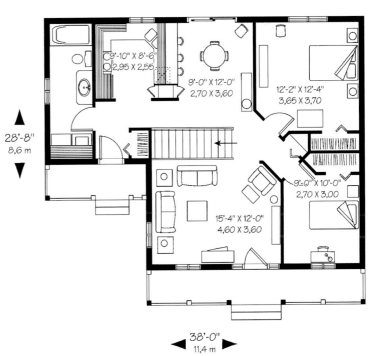

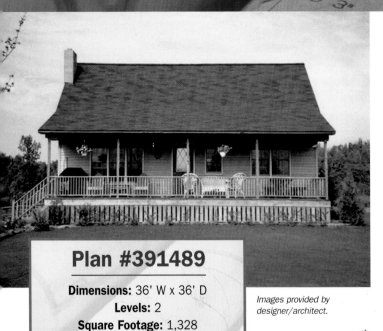

## Main Level Floor Plan

Kitchen & Dining
17-4 x 10-8

Br 2
12-0 x 10-4
8' Flat Clg

16'-3" Flat Clg

Living Rm
19-4 x 16-8

Br 3
12-0 x 13-0
8' Flat Clg

UP

Porch

## Plan #391489

**Dimensions:** 36' W x 36' D

**Levels:** 2

**Square Footage:** 1,328

**Main Level Sq. Ft.:** 1,013

**Upper Level Sq. Ft.:** 315

**Bedrooms:** 3

**Bathrooms:** 2

**Foundation:** Crawl space, slab or basement

**Material List Available:** Yes

**Price Category:** B

*Images provided by designer/architect.*

Rear Elevation

Master Br
12-0 x 13-4

Flat Clg @ 7'-6"

DN

### Upper Level Floor Plan

---

## Plan #181262

**Dimensions:** 26' W x 32' D

**Levels:** 2

**Square Footage:** 1,226

**Main Level Sq. Ft.:** 443

**Upper Level Sq. Ft.:** 783

**Bedrooms:** 2

**Bathrooms:** 2

**Foundation:** Basement

**Materials List Available:** Yes

**Price Category:** B

*Images provided by designer/architect.*

CAD FILE AVAILABLE

12'-0" X 12'-0"
3,60 X 3,60

12'-2" X 14'-4"
3,65 X 4,30

12'-6" X 15'-0"
3,75 X 4,50

32'-0"
9,6 m

### Main Level Floor Plan

26'-0"
7,8 m

14'-8" X 12'-0"
4,40 X 3,60

11'-0" X 11'-0"
3,30 X 3,30

### Upper Level Floor Plan

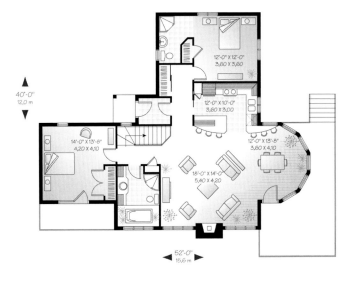

## Plan #181146

**Dimensions:** 52' W x 40' D

**Levels:** 1

**Square Footage:** 1,314

**Bedrooms:** 2

**Bathrooms:** 2

**Foundation:** Walkout

**Material List Available:** Yes

**Price Category:** B

*Images provided by designer/architect.*

CAD FILE AVAILABLE

*Copyright by designer/architect.*

## Plan #341028

**Dimensions:** 40' W x 32' D

**Levels:** 1

**Square Footage:** 1,248

**Bedrooms:** 3

**Bathrooms:** 2

**Foundation:** Crawl space, slab, or basement

**Materials List Available:** Yes

**Price Category:** B

*Images provided by designer/architect.*

CAD FILE AVAILABLE

*Copyright by designer/architect.*

## Plan #121012

**Dimensions:** 40' W x 48'8" D
**Levels:** 1
**Square Footage:** 1,195
**Bedrooms:** 3
**Bathrooms:** 2
**Foundation:** Basement
**Materials List Available:** Yes
**Price Category:** B

*This home, as shown in the photograph, may differ from the actual blueprints. For more detailed information, please check the floor plans carefully.*

**CAD FILE AVAILABLE**

*Images provided by designer/architect.*

This compact one-level home uses an open plan to make the most of its square footage.

### Features:

- Ceiling Height: 8 ft.

- Covered Porch: This delightful area, located off the kitchen, provides a private spot to enjoy some fresh air.

- Open Plan: The family room, dining area and kitchen share a big open

space to provide a sense of spaciousness. Moving so easily between these interrelated areas provides the convenience demanded by a busy lifestyle.

- Master Suite: An open plan is convenient, but it is still important for everyone to have their private space. The master suite enjoys its own bath and walk-in closet. The secondary bedrooms share a nearby bath.

- Garage: Here you will find parking for two cars and plenty of extra storage space as well.

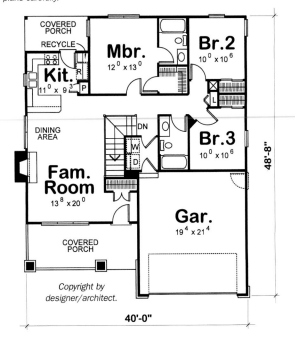

COVERED PORCH
RECYCLE
**Kit.** 11⁰ x 9³
**Mbr.** 12⁰ x 13⁰
**Br.2** 10⁰ x 10⁶
DINING AREA
DN
**Br.3** 10⁰ x 10⁶
**Fam. Room** 13⁸ x 20⁰
**Gar.** 19⁴ x 21⁴
COVERED PORCH
48'-8"
40'-0"

*Copyright by designer/architect.*

*Rendering reflects floor plan*

## Plan #351020

**Dimensions:** 54' W x 48' D

**Levels:** 1

**Square Footage:** 1,488

**Bedrooms:** 3

**Bathrooms:** 2

**Foundation:** Crawl space, slab, or basement

**Materials List Available:** Yes

**Price Category:** C

*Images provided by designer/architect.*

This is a lot of house for its size and is an excellent example of the popular split bedroom layout.

**Features:**

- Great Room: This large room is open to the dining room.

- Kitchen: This fully equipped kitchen has a peninsula counter and is open into the dining room.

- Master Suite: This private area, located on the other side of the home from the secondary bedrooms, features large walk-in closets and bath areas.

- Bedrooms: The two secondary bedrooms have large closets and share a hall bathroom.

*Copyright by designer/architect.*

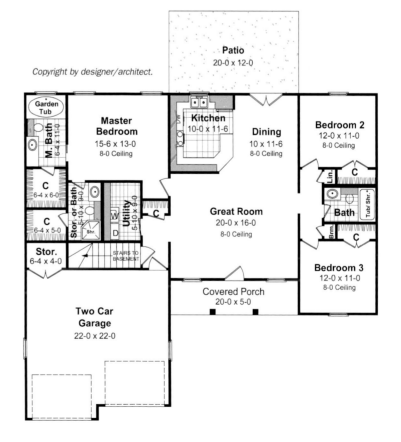

## Plan #181120

**Dimensions:** 32' W x 40' D

**Levels:** 2

**Square Footage:** 1,480

**Main Level Sq. Ft.:** 1,024

**Upper Level Sq. Ft.:** 456

**Bedrooms:** 2

**Bathrooms:** 2

**Foundation:** basement

**Material List Available:** Yes

**Price Category:** C

Escape to this charming all-season vacation home with lots of view-capturing windows.

*Images provided by designer/architect.*

**Features:**

- Ceiling Height: 8 ft. unless otherwise noted.

- Living/Dining Area: The covered back porch opens into this large, inviting combined area. Its high ceiling adds to the sense of spaciousness.

- Family Room: After relaxing in front of the fireplace that warms this family room, family and guests can move outside onto the porch to watch the sun set.

- Kitchen: Light streams through a triple window in this well-designed kitchen. It's conveniently located next to the dining area and features a center island with a breakfast bar and double sinks.

- Master Suite: This first floor suite is located in the front of the house and is enhanced by its large walk-through closet and the adjoining private bath.

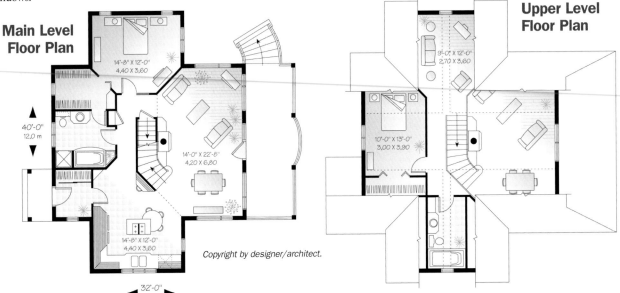

**Main Level Floor Plan**

14'-8" X 12'-0"
4,40 X 3,60

40'-0"
12,0 m

14'-0" X 22'-8"
4,20 X 6,80

14'-8" X 12'-0"
4,40 X 3,60

32'-0"
9,6 m

**Upper Level Floor Plan**

9'-0" X 12'-0"
2,70 X 3,60

10'-0" X 13'-0"
3,00 X 3,90

*Copyright by designer/architect.*

# Plan #151413

**Dimensions:** 32' W x 42' D
**Levels:** 1.5
**Square Footage:** 1,400
**Main Level Sq. Ft.:** 948
**Upper Level Sq. Ft.:** 452
**Bedrooms:** 2
**Bathrooms:** 2
**Foundation:** Crawl space or slab
**CompleteCost List Available:** Yes
**Price Category:** B

*Images provided by designer/architect.*

Relax on the front porch of this lovely little cottage. It's a great starter home or a weekend getaway.

**Features:**

- **Great Room:** Enter from the front porch into this large room, with its vaulted ceiling and stone fireplace.

- **Kitchen:** This large kitchen has plenty of cabinets and counter space; there is even a raised bar.

- **Grilling Porch:** Just off the kitchen is this porch. Bedroom 1 has access to this area as well.

- **Upper Level:** Located on this level are a loft area, a full bathroom, and a bedroom.

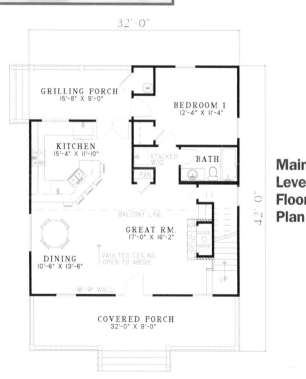

**Main Level Floor Plan**

**Upper Level Floor Plan**

*Copyright by designer/architect.*

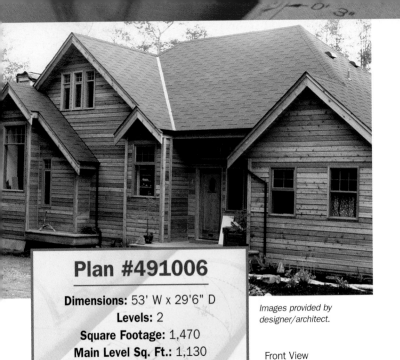

## Main Level Floor Plan

SUNDECK

DINING
14' x 12'
16'11" VAULTED CLG.

BR.
11' x 12'4"
10' VAULTED CLG.

LIVING
16' x 15'
16'11" VAULTED CLG.

FOYER

SEAT

SITTING

COVERED PORCH

LDR

10'-0"

29'-6"

53'-0"

4'-0"

# Plan #491006

**Dimensions:** 53' W x 29'6" D
**Levels:** 2
**Square Footage:** 1,470
**Main Level Sq. Ft.:** 1,130
**Upper Level Sq. Ft.:** 340
**Bedrooms:** 2
**Bathrooms:** 2
**Foundation:** Crawl space
**Material List Available:** Yes
**Price Category:** B

*Images provided by designer/architect.*

Front View

BALCONY

BR.
12'2" x 10'
10' VAULTED CLG.

LOFT
VAULTED

OPEN TO BELOW

RAILING

PLANT LEDGE

OPEN

DN

## Upper Level Floor Plan

*Copyright by designer/architect.*

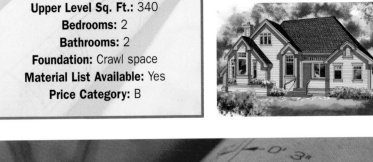

30'-0"

14'-6"

4'-0"

30'-0"

26'-0"

DINING ROOM
13'-0" x 11'-0"

LIVING ROOM
13'-0" x 13'-0"

GARAGE (OPTION)
13'-6" x 22'-0"

## Main Level Floor Plan

# Plan #571027

**Dimensions:** 30' W x 26' D
**Levels:** 2
**Square Footage:** 1,376
**Main Level Sq. Ft.:** 724
**Upper Level Sq. Ft.:** 652
**Bedrooms:** 3
**Bathrooms:** 1½
**Foundation:** Basement
**Material List Available:** Yes
**Price Category:** B

*Images provided by designer/architect.*

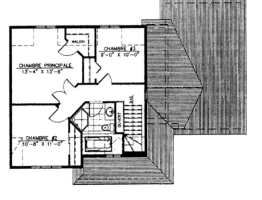

WALKIN

CHAMBRE PRINCIPALE
13'-4" x 13'-8"

CHAMBRE #3
9'-0" x 10'-0"

CHAMBRE #2
10'-8" x 11'-0"

## Upper Level Floor Plan

*Copyright by designer/architect.*

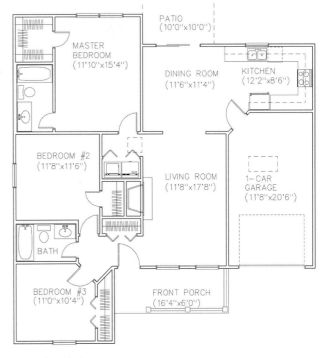

## Plan #521063

**Dimensions:** 42' W x 50' D

**Levels:** 1

**Square Footage:** 1,229

**Bedrooms:** 3

**Bathrooms:** 2

**Foundation:** Slab

**Material List Available:** No

**Price Category:** B

*Images provided by designer/architect.*

*Copyright by designer/architect.*

---

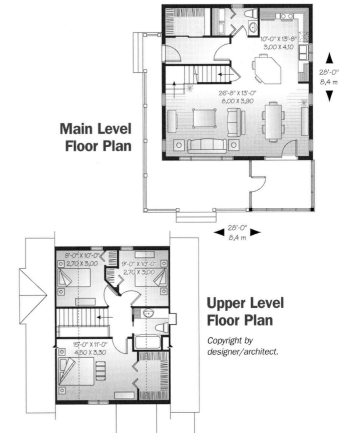

## Plan #181244

**Dimensions:** 28' W x 28' D

**Levels:** 2

**Square Footage:** 1,381

**Main Level Sq. Ft.:** 784

**Upper Level Sq. Ft.:** 597

**Bedrooms:** 3

**Bathrooms:** 1½

**Foundation:** Basement

**Materials List Available:** Yes

**Price Category:** B

*Images provided by designer/architect.*

**Main Level Floor Plan**

**Upper Level Floor Plan**

*Copyright by designer/architect.*

## Plan #121216

**Dimensions:** 40' W x 47'8" D

**Levels:** 1

**Square Footage:** 1,205

**Bedrooms:** 2

**Bathrooms:** 2

**Foundation:** Basement; crawl space or slab for fee

**Material List Available:** Yes

**Price Category:** B

This home boasts a beautiful arched entry.

**Features:**

• Great Room: Enter this large gathering area from the foyer; the warmth of the fireplace welcomes you home. The 10-ft.-high ceiling gives the area an open feeling.

• Kitchen: Family and friends will enjoy gathering in this cozy kitchen, with its attached breakfast room. The area provides access to a future rear patio. The garage and laundry area are just a few steps away.

• Master Suite: This private area features a stepped ceiling in the sleeping area and a large window for backyard views. The master bath boasts a whirlpool bathtub, a separate shower, and dual vanities.

• Secondary Bedroom: A large front window brings light into this comfortable bedroom. A full bathroom is located nearby.

*Images provided by designer/architect.*

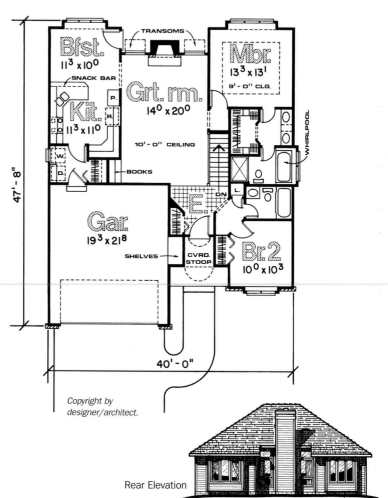

*Copyright by designer/architect.*

Rear Elevation

## Plan #371030

**Dimensions:** 38'10" W x 64'4" D

**Levels:** 1

**Square Footage:** 1,434

**Bedrooms:** 3

**Bathrooms:** 2

**Foundation:** Slab

**Materials List Available:** No

**Price Category:** B

*Images provided by designer/architect.*

The stylish front of this country home conceals a charming floor plan. This is the perfect home for a young family.

**Features:**

- Living Room: Entertaining is a snap in this large, open room with a bookcase and a fireplace.

- Kitchen: This kitchen has a raised bar, a pantry, and breakfast nook.

- Master Suite: This large suite has a luxurious master bathroom with two walk-in closets.

- Bedrooms: The two additional bedrooms share a convenient bathroom with a dressing room.

*Copyright by designer/architect.*

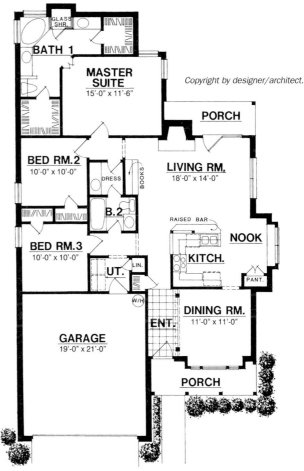

## Plan #341110

**Dimensions:** 48' W x 56'8" D

**Levels:** 1

**Square Footage:** 1,454

**Bedrooms:** 3

**Bathrooms:** 2

**Foundation:** Crawl space, slab, basement or walkout

**Material List Available:** No

**Price Category:** B

*Images provided by designer/architect.*

The attention paid to practical and pleasing features both inside and outside ensures a winning three-bedroom home design.

### Features:

- **Foyer:** A neighborly front porch shelters this front entry. Decorative columns enhance the transition between this foyer and the family room.

- **Kitchen:** This kitchen/dining room, which has a pantry and lots of counter and cabinet space, offers informal dining with views of the front porch and yard.

- **Master Suite:** A short hallway leads to this master bedroom suite, which includes a large walk-in closet and a private bathroom.

- **Secondary Bedrooms:** Another full bathroom lies between two bedrooms on the opposite end of the house from the master suite.

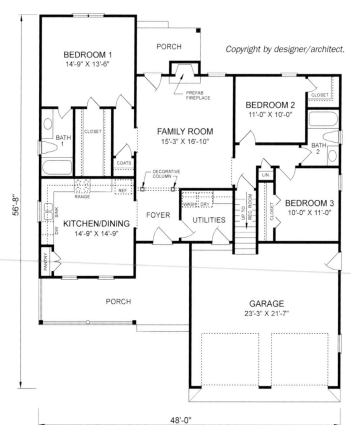

*Copyright by designer/architect.*

# Plan #121144

**Dimensions:** 40' W x 48'8" D

**Levels:** 1

**Square Footage:** 1,195

**Bedrooms:** 3

**Bathrooms:** 2

**Foundation:** Basement; crawl space for fee

**Material List Available:** Yes

**Price Category:** B

*Images provided by designer/architect.*

CAD FILE CAD AVAILABLE

This is the right design if you want a home that will be easy to expand as your family grows.

**Features:**

- Front Porch: Hang baskets of plants from the roof of this porch, which is just the right size for a couple of comfortable rocking chairs and a side table.

- Family Room: This family room welcomes you as you enter the home. A crackling fire enhances the ambiance of the room.

- Kitchen: This intelligently designed kitchen has an efficient U-shape layout. A serving bar open to the dining area is a feature that makes entertaining easier.

- Master Suite: This is a compact space that is designed to feel large, and it includes a walk-in closet. The master bath is an added bonus.

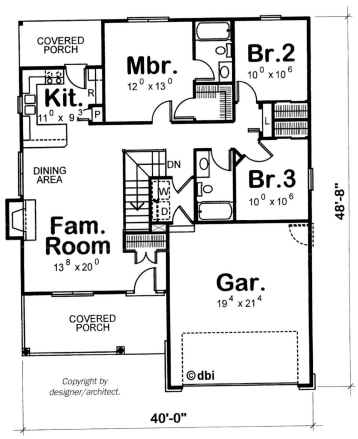

DECK
10'-0" X 10'-0"

GARDEN TUB

BATH 1

CABINET ABOVE

WASH DRY

SHWR

WH

SHELVES

SINK

DW

RANGE

REF.

KITCHEN/DINING
15'-9" X 12'-3"

CLOSET

LINENS

BEDROOM 3
10'-0" X 11'-6"

BATH 2

CLOSET

CLOSET

VAULTED CEILING

FAMILY ROOM
15'-9" X 15'-7"

BEDROOM 2
11'-0" X 11'-0"

MASTER SUITE
13'-3" X 17'-5"

TRAY CEILING

PORCH

34'-0"

44'-0"

*Images provided by designer/architect.*

CAD FILE AVAILABLE

*Copyright by designer/architect.*

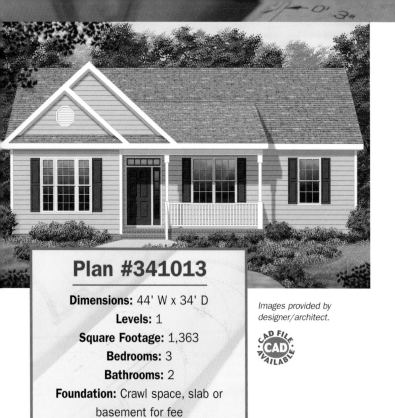

# Plan #341013

**Dimensions:** 44' W x 34' D

**Levels:** 1

**Square Footage:** 1,363

**Bedrooms:** 3

**Bathrooms:** 2

**Foundation:** Crawl space, slab or basement for fee

**Material List Available:** Yes

**Price Category:** B

## Main Level Floor Plan

*Copyright by designer/architect.*

48'-0"
14,4 m

10'-0" X 11'-0"
3,00 X 3,30

14'-4" X 10'-0"
4,30 X 3,00

12'-0" X 12'-8"
3,60 X 3,80

12'-8" X 11'-6"
3,80 X 3,45

14'-0" X 11'-6"
4,20 X 3,45

26'-0"
7,8 m

14'-4" X 11'-0"
4,30 X 3,30

14'-4" X 12'-6"
4,30 X 3,75

## Upper Level Floor Plan

# Plan #181172

**Dimensions:** 26' W x 48' D

**Levels:** 1

**Square Footage:** 1,484

**Main Level Sq. Ft.:** 908

**Upper Level Sq. Ft.:** 578

**Bedrooms:** 3

**Bathrooms:** 2

**Foundation:** Walkout

**Material List Available:** Yes

**Price Category:** B

*Images provided by designer/architect.*

CAD FILE AVAILABLE

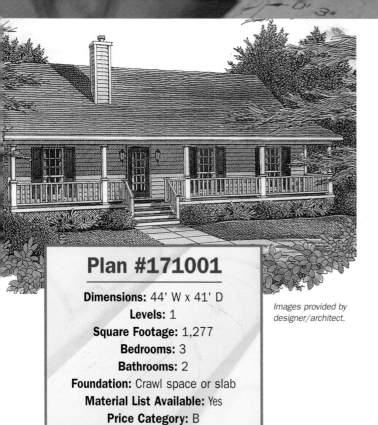

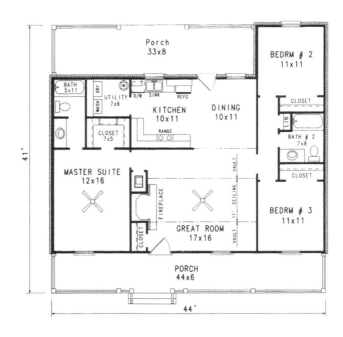

# Plan #171001

**Dimensions:** 44' W x 41' D

**Levels:** 1

**Square Footage:** 1,277

**Bedrooms:** 3

**Bathrooms:** 2

**Foundation:** Crawl space or slab

**Material List Available:** Yes

**Price Category:** B

*Images provided by designer/architect.*

*Copyright by designer/architect.*

# Plan #501593

**Dimensions:** 58' W x 61' D

**Levels:** 1

**Square Footage:** 1,490

**Bedrooms:** 3

**Bathrooms:** 2

**Foundation:** Basement

**Material List Available:** Yes

**Price Category:** B

*Images provided by designer/architect.*

CAD FILE AVAILABLE

*Copyright by designer/architect.*

## Plan #391211

**Dimensions:** 58' W x 40' D
**Levels:** 1
**Square Footage:** 1,461
**Bedrooms:** 3
**Bathrooms:** 2
**Foundation:** Basement
**Material List Available:** Yes
**Price Category:** B

*Images provided by designer/architect.*

This gorgeous, traditionally styled home borrows Victorian ideas to attain its flair.

### Features:

- Living Room: Brightly lit, with massive sky lights and access to an outdoor deck, this living room is sure to be a cheery gathering place for your family

- Kitchen: This outstanding area of the home features a sunny breakfast nook and the added charm of a hearth room. Enjoy quiet breakfasts beside a blazing fire.

- Master Suite: A vaulted ceiling accents the bathtub in the suite, adding a spa-like feel to the room. The bedroom itself is spacious and beautiful.

- Secondary Bedrooms: Three more bedrooms surround the upstairs balcony, and two full baths alleviate the morning rush.

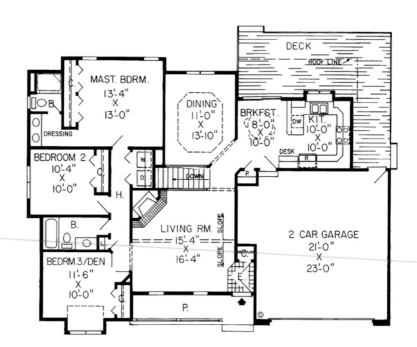

*Copyright by designer/architect.*

## Plan #401047

**Dimensions:** 38' W x 34' D

**Levels:** 1

**Square Footage:** 1,064

**Bedrooms:** 2

**Bathrooms:** 1

**Foundation:** Crawl space or basement

**Materials List Available:** Yes

**Price Category:** B

This farmhouse squeezes space-efficient features into its compact plan. Twin dormer windows flood the vaulted interior with natural light and accentuate the high ceilings.

*Images provided by designer/architect.*

**Features:**

- **Porch:** This cozy front porch opens into a vaulted great room and its adjoining dining room.

- **Great Room:** A warm hearth in this gathering place for the family adds to its coziness.

- **Kitchen:** This U-shaped kitchen has a breakfast bar open to the dining room and a sink overlooking a flower box. Nearby side-door access is found in the handy laundry room.

- **Bedrooms:** Vaulted bedrooms are positioned along the back of the plan. They contain wall closets and share a full bathroom with a soaking tub.

- **Future Expansion:** An open-rail staircase leads to the basement, which can be developed into living or sleeping space at a later time, if needed.

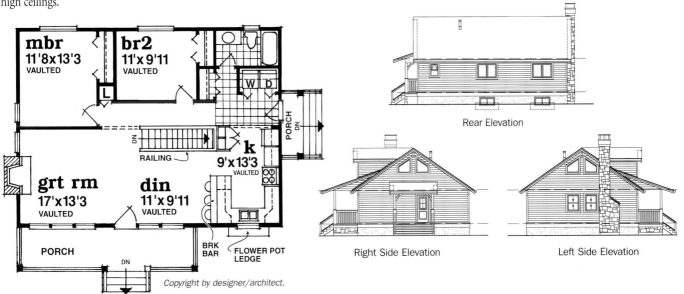

Rear Elevation

Right Side Elevation

Left Side Elevation

*Copyright by designer/architect.*

## Plan #191030

**Dimensions:** 33' W x 36' D

**Levels:** 1

**Square Footage:** 864

**Bedrooms:** 2

**Bathrooms:** 1

**Foundation:** Crawl space or slab

**Materials List Available:** No

**Price Category:** A

*Images provided by designer/architect.*

Enjoy the view from the spacious front porch of this cozy cottage, which is ideal for a retirement home, vacation retreat, or starter home.

**Features:**

- **Porch:** This 6-ft.-wide porch, which runs the length of the home, gives you plenty of space to set up a couple of rockers next to a potted herb garden.

- **Living/Dining Room:** This huge living and dining area gives you many options for design. The snack bar that it shares with the kitchen is a practical touch.

- **Kitchen:** The first thing you'll notice in this well-planned kitchen is how much counter and storage space it offers.

- **Laundry Room:** Opening to the backyard, this room also features ample storage space.

- **Bedrooms:** Both rooms have good closet space and easy access to the large, luxurious bath.

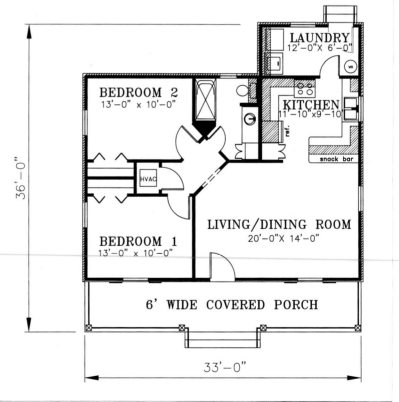

LAUNDRY
12'-0" X 6'-0"

BEDROOM 2
13'-0" X 10'-0"

KITCHEN
11'-10" X 9'-10"

snack bar

HVAC

BEDROOM 1
13'-0" X 10'-0"

LIVING/DINING ROOM
20'-0" X 14'-0"

36'-0"

6' WIDE COVERED PORCH

33'-0"

*Copyright by designer/architect.*

## Plan #181021

**Dimensions:** 37' W x 44' D

**Levels:** 1

**Square Footage:** 1,124

**Bedrooms:** 2

**Bathrooms:** 1

**Foundation:** Basement

**Materials List Available:** Yes

**Price Category:** B

*Images provided by designer/architect.*

This cozy country cottage is enhanced by lattice trim details over the porch and garage.

### Features:

- Ceiling Height: 8 ft.

- Living Room: This living room gets extra architectural interest from a sunken floor. The room, located directly to the left of the entry hall, has plenty of space for entertaining.

- Dining Room: This dining room is located in center of the home. It's adjacent to the kitchen to make it easy to serve meals.

- Kitchen: This bright and efficient kitchen is a real pleasure in which to work. It includes a pantry and double sinks. There's a breakfast bar that will see plenty of informal meals for families on the go.

- Covered Porch: This is the perfect place to which to retire after dinner on a warm summer evening.

- Bedrooms: Each of the two bedrooms has its own closet. They share a full bathroom.

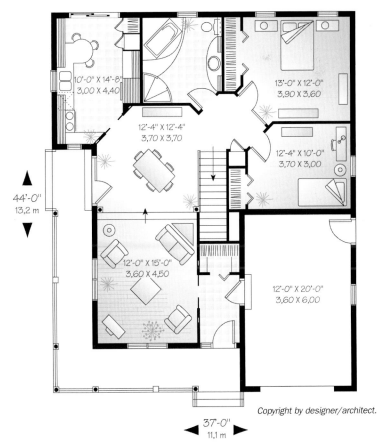

*Copyright by designer/architect.*

## Plan #521056

**Dimensions:** 36'8" W x 41' D

**Levels:** 2

**Square Footage:** 1,400

**Main Level Sq. Ft.:** 953

**Upper Level Sq. Ft.:** 447

**Bedrooms:** 3

**Bathrooms:** 2½

**Foundation:** Crawl space

**Material List Available:** No

**Price Category:** B

*Images provided by designer/architect.*

CAD FILE AVAILABLE / CAD

**Main Level Floor Plan**

SIDE PORCH

MASTER BEDROOM (12'4"x11'8")

DINING AREA (11'4"x10'0")

LIVING ROOM (16'4"x16'10")

KITCHEN (9'0"x10'0")

ENTRY

FRONT PORCH

**Upper Level Floor Plan**

*Copyright by designer/architect.*

ATTIC STORAGE

BEDROOM #2 (10'0"x11'8")

BEDROOM #3 (10'0"x11'6")

**Front View**

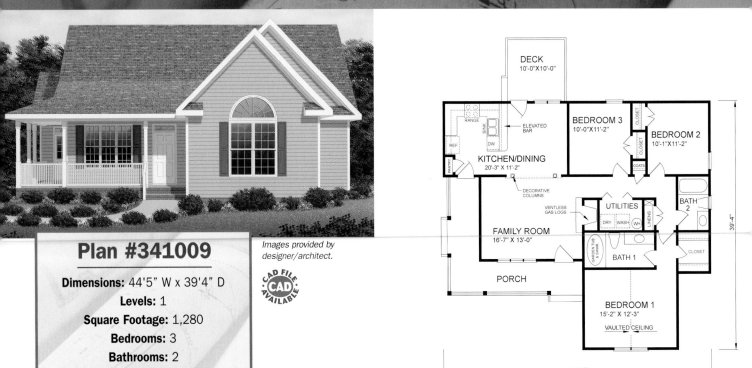

## Plan #341009

**Dimensions:** 44'5" W x 39'4" D

**Levels:** 1

**Square Footage:** 1,280

**Bedrooms:** 3

**Bathrooms:** 2

**Foundation:** Crawl space; slab or basemene for fee

**Material List Available:** Yes

**Price Category:** B

*Images provided by designer/architect.*

CAD FILE AVAILABLE / CAD

DECK 10'-0"X10'-0"

RANGE

SINK

DW

ELEVATED BAR

REF

PANTRY

KITCHEN/DINING 20'-3" X 11'-2"

DECORATIVE COLUMNS

VENTLESS GAS LOGS

FAMILY ROOM 16'-7" X 13'-0"

PORCH

BEDROOM 3 10'-0"X11'-2"

CLOSET

BEDROOM 2 10'-1"X11'-2"

CLOSET

COATS

UTILITIES

DRY / WASH / WH

LINENS

BATH 2

GARDEN TUB & SHWR

BATH 1

CLOSET

BEDROOM 1 15'-2" X 12'-3"

VAULTED CEILING

39'-4"

44'-5"

*Copyright by designer/architect.*

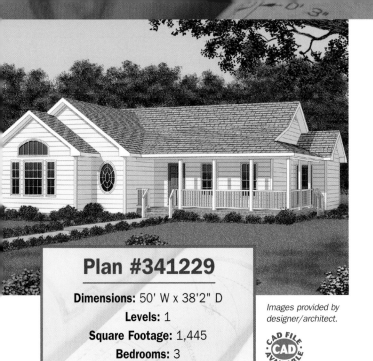

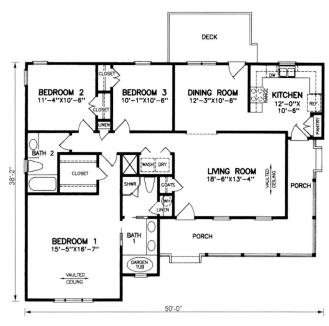

## Plan #341229

**Dimensions:** 50' W x 38'2" D

**Levels:** 1

**Square Footage:** 1,445

**Bedrooms:** 3

**Bathrooms:** 2

**Foundation:** Crawl space, slab, basement, or walkout

**Materials List Available:** Yes

**Price Category:** B

*Images provided by designer/architect.*

**CAD FILE AVAILABLE**

DECK

BEDROOM 2
11'-4"X10'-6"

BEDROOM 3
10'-1"X10'-6"

DINING ROOM
12'-3"X10'-6"

KITCHEN
12'-0"X 10'-6"

CLOSET

PANTRY

BATH 2

CLOSET

WASH DRY

COATS

LIVING ROOM
18'-6"X13'-4"

VAULTED CEILING

PORCH

SHWR

LINEN

WH

BEDROOM 1
15'-5"X16'-7"

BATH 1

PORCH

GARDEN TUB

VAULTED CEILING

38'-2"

50'-0"

*Copyright by designer/architect.*

---

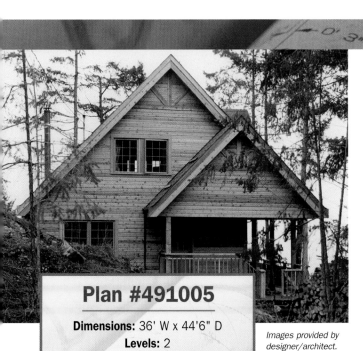

## Plan #491005

**Dimensions:** 36' W x 44'6" D

**Levels:** 2

**Square Footage:** 1,333

**Main Level Sq. Ft.:** 768

**Upper Level Sq. Ft.:** 565

**Bedrooms:** 2

**Bathrooms:** 2

**Foundation:** Crawl space

**Material List Available:** Yes

**Price Category:** B

*Images provided by designer/architect.*

**Main Level Floor Plan**

6'-0"    24'-0"    6'-0"

8'-0"

16' VAULTED CLG.

GREAT ROOM
23' x 10'2" x& 16'6"

WOOD STOVE

KIT
8'6" x 8'

32'-0"

GUEST
10'8" x 11'

W D

41'-6"

**Upper Level Floor Plan**

*Copyright by designer/architect.*

RAILING

OPEN

STUDIO
15'4" x13'4"
13' VAULTED CLG.

DN

BED RM.
15' x 11'
10' VAULTED CLG.

Rear View

## Plan #251003

**Dimensions:** 42' W x 42' D

**Levels:** 1

**Square Footage:** 1,393

**Bedrooms:** 3

**Bathrooms:** 2

**Foundation:** Crawl space or slab

**Materials List Available:** Yes

**Price Category:** B

*Images provided by designer/architect.*

Come home to this three-bedroom home with front porch and unattached garage.

**Features:**

- Family Room: This room feels large and warm, with its high ceiling and cozy fireplace.

- Kitchen: This island kitchen with dining area has plenty of cabinet space.

- Master Bedroom: This large master bedroom features a walk-in closet and a view of the backyard.

- Master Bath: Located in the rear of the home, this master bath features a soaking tub and a separate shower.

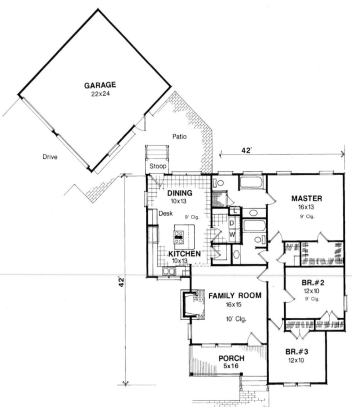

*Copyright by designer/architect.*

## Plan #351012

**Dimensions:** 30' W x 32' D

**Levels:** 1

**Square Footage:** 600

**Bedrooms:** 1

**Bathrooms:** 1

**Foundation:** Crawl space, slab, or basement

**Materials List Available:** Yes

**Price Category:** A

This home is designed for the woods, the lake, or the beach for a weekend getaway. It is the perfect house to relax in all summer or winter long.

**Features:**

- Living Room: Just off the entry porch is this open living room with fireplace.

- Kitchen: This nice-size kitchen, with a raised bar into the living room, has plenty of cabinet space.

- Rear Porch: This rear porch is located just off the kitchen.

- Storage: A wonderful 12 x 30-ft. attic storage space, floored for all the "stuff" you need, is 8 ft. tall in the middle.

*Images provided by designer/architect.*

Rear Elevation

### Optional Floor Plan for Basement

*Copyright by designer/architect.*

## Plan #341064

**Dimensions:** 58'6" W x 36'9" D

**Levels:** 1

**Square Footage:** 1,418

**Bedrooms:** 3

**Bathrooms:** 2

**Foundation:** Crawl space, slab, basement, or walkout

**Materials List Available:** Yes

**Price Category:** B

*Images provided by designer/architect.*

This sweet starter home has many of the amenities of a larger home.

### Features:

- Family Room: Already equipped with gas fireplace, all this room needs is some entertainment options and comfy furniture to welcome guests into the warmth of your home and out of the cold.

- Dining Room: This versatile space can be used for formal dinners or for barbecues that have been cooked on the deck.

- Kitchen: This efficiently designed space features a large pantry and an elevated bar for informal meals on the run. Or use the bar as a serving or buffet area for hosting dinner parties.

- Master Suite: A cozy retreat, this main bedroom features two walk-in closets and a full master bath with a garden tub.

DECK

BEDROOM 3
10'-0" X 11'-5"

BATH 2

KITCHEN
10'-4" X 11'-5"

DINING
11'-1" X 11'-5"

BEDROOM 2
10'-0" X 10'-1"

GARAGE
13'-7" X 23'-3"

FAMILY ROOM
17'-3" X 15'-5"

PREFAB GAS LOG
FIREPLACE

36'-9"

BEDROOM 1
14'-9" X 13'-8"

BATH 1

PORCH

GARDEN
TUB

58'-6"

*Copyright by designer/architect.*

## Plan #251002

**Dimensions:** 55'6" W x 64'3" D
**Levels:** 1
**Square Footage:** 1,333
**Bedrooms:** 3
**Bathrooms:** 2
**Foundation:** Crawl space, slab
**Materials List Available:** Yes
**Price Category:** B

*Images provided by designer/architect.*

Although compact, this farmhouse has all the amenities for comfortable modern living.

**Features:**

- Ceiling Height: 8 ft. unless otherwise noted.

- Foyer: This gracious and welcoming foyer opens to the family room.

- Family Room: This inviting family room is designed to accommodate all kinds of family activities. It features a 9-ft. ceiling and a handsome, warming fireplace.

- Kitchen: Cooking in this kitchen is a real pleasure. It includes a center island, so you'll never run out of counter space for food preparation.

- Master Bedroom: This master bedroom features a large walk-in closet and an elegant 9-ft. recessed ceiling.

- Master Bath: This master bath offers a double vanity, a tub, and a walk-in shower.

- Garage: This attached garage provides plenty of extra storage space, as well as parking for two cars.

## SMARTtip

### Arts and Crafts Style

The heart of this style rests in its earthy connection. The more you can bring nature into it, the more authentic it will be. An easy way to do this is with plants. A bonus is that plants naturally thrive in the bathroom, where they enjoy the humid environment.

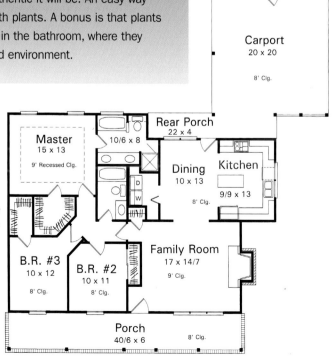

*Copyright by designer/architect.*

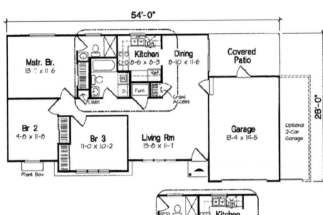

*Images provided by designer/architect.*

## Plan #391328

**Dimensions:** 54' W x 28' D

**Levels:** 1

**Square Footage:** 988

**Bedrooms:** 3

**Bathrooms:** 2

**Foundation:** Crawl space or basement

**Material List Available:** Yes

**Price Category:** A

**Optional Main Level Floor Plan for Basement Stairs**

*Copyright by designer/architect.*

## Plan #571029

**Dimensions:** 26' W x 32' D

**Levels:** 1

**Square Footage:** 844

**Bedrooms:** 2

**Bathrooms:** 1

**Foundation:** Basement

**Material List Available:** Yes

**Price Category:** A

*Images provided by designer/architect.*

*Copyright by designer/architect.*

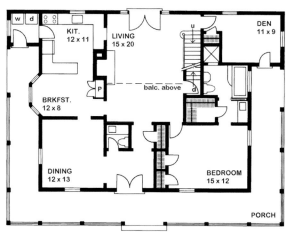

**Main Level Floor Plan**

*Images provided by designer/architect.*

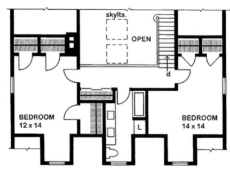

**Upper Level Floor Plan**

*Copyright by designer/architect.*

## Plan #381131

**Dimensions:** 53' W x 40' D
**Levels:** 1.5
**Square Footage:** 2,190
**Main Level Sq. Ft.:** 1,460
**Upper Level Sq. Ft.:** 730
**Bedrooms:** 3
**Bathrooms:** 2½
**Foundation:** Crawl space or basement
**Material List Available:** Yes
**Price Category:** D

*Images provided by designer/architect.*

## Plan #211024

**Dimensions:** 61' W x 44' D
**Levels:** 1
**Square Footage:** 1,418
**Bedrooms:** 3
**Bathrooms:** 2
**Foundation:** Slab
**Materials List Available:** Yes
**Price Category:** B

*Copyright by designer/architect.*

## Plan #311024

**Dimensions:** 56' W x 45' D
**Levels:** 1
**Square Footage:** 1,492
**Bedrooms:** 3
**Bathrooms:** 2
**Foundation:** Crawl space, slab, or basement
**Materials List Available:** Yes
**Price Category:** B

With its uncomplicated layout, this charming, traditional house is a perfect starter or retirement home.

### Features:

- **Porches:** Front and back covered porches allow you to enjoy the outdoors without leaving home. Sit out on warm summer evenings, enjoying the breeze and greeting passersby.

- **Kitchen:** This efficient layout includes a snack bar, which can act as a transition or buffet for the adjacent formal dining room.

- **Master Suite:** Enjoy a private entry to the porch, a walk-in closet, and a large master bath with his and her vanities, a large whirlpool tub, and a separate shower.

- **Secondary Bedrooms:** Two additional bedrooms have ample closet space and access to a shared bathroom, all tucked away from the main area of the home.

Porch 31-4x7-8 9' ceiling

Master Bedroom 16-6x13-2 9' ceiling

Closet 6-6x8-0

Bedroom 11-4x11-4 9' ceiling

Kitchen/Dining 19-11x11-4 9' ceiling

M.Bath 12-4x11-0 9' ceiling

Laundry 6-7x5-10

Snack Bar

Bath

Greatroom 16-11x19-0 11' ceiling

Garage 21-3x19-2 9' ceiling

Storage

Bedroom 11-4x11-4 9' Ceiling

Porch 32-0x5-4 9' ceiling

Rear View

### Bonus Area Floor Plan

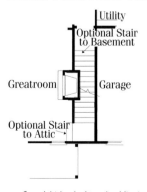

Utility

Optional Stair to Basement

Greatroom

Garage

Optional Stair to Attic

## Plan #371049

**Dimensions:** 52' W x 45' D

**Levels:** 1

**Square Footage:** 1,440

**Bedrooms:** 3

**Bathrooms:** 2

**Foundation:** Slab

**Materials List Available:** No

**Price Category:** B

*Images provided by designer/architect.*

This country classic is sure to please. It has three bedrooms and is perfect for any-size family.

**Features:**

- Living Room: This large room with 10-foot-high ceiling is just off the entry. Bookcases surround the inviting fireplace here.

- Dining Room: The living room flows into this large room, which features a beautiful bay window.

- Kitchen: This fully functional kitchen is perfect for any chef. The garage is accessible through the adjoining utility room.

- Master Suite: This private area boasts a luxurious master bath with a marble tub, glass shower, and his and her walk-in closets.

- Bedrooms: The two large additional bedrooms share a convenient bath.

*Copyright by designer/architect.*

## Plan #161116

**Dimensions:** 52'8" W x 45' D

**Levels:** 1

**Square Footage:** 1,442

**Bedrooms:** 3

**Bathrooms:** 2

**Foundation:** Basement

**Material List Available:** Yes

**Price Category:** B

This delightful home offers space-saving convenience and functional living space.

*Images provided by designer/architect.*

**Features:**

- Great Room: This gathering area features an over-11-foot-tall ceiling and a corner gas fireplace. A few steps out the back door, and you are on the rear deck.

- Kitchen: This fully equipped kitchen offers a counter with seating, dishwasher, and built-in microwave. The garage and laundry areas are conveniently a few steps away.

- Master Suite: Split bedrooms offer privacy to this elegant area, which enjoys a 9-ft. ceiling height and large walk-in closet. The master bath boasts a double-bowl vanity and compartmented lavatory and shower area.

- Bedrooms: Two secondary bedrooms are located just off the great room and share the second bathroom.

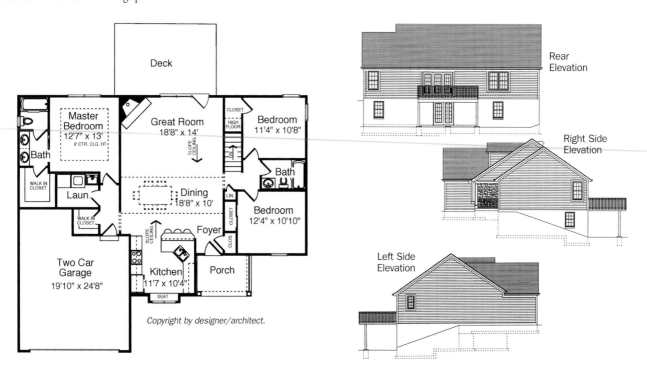

*Copyright by designer/architect.*

## Plan #351014

**Dimensions:** 30' W x 38'4" D

**Levels:** 1

**Square Footage:** 1,000

**Bedrooms:** 2

**Bathrooms:** 2

**Foundation:** Crawl space or slab

**Materials List Available:** Yes

**Price Category:** D

*Images provided by designer/architect.*

This small home has many great features.

**Features:**

- **Living Room:** This gathering area boasts a fireplace with gas logs and plenty of built-ins.

- **Kitchen:** This large kitchen features a raised bar that's open to the living room and another raised bar that's open to the breakfast area.

- **Bedrooms:** These two bedrooms are much larger than you would expect for a home of this size.

- **Bathrooms:** The main bath, with access from bedroom 1, has a 42 x 60-in. jetted tub. The second bath is located off the hall near bedroom 2.

*Copyright by designer/architect.*

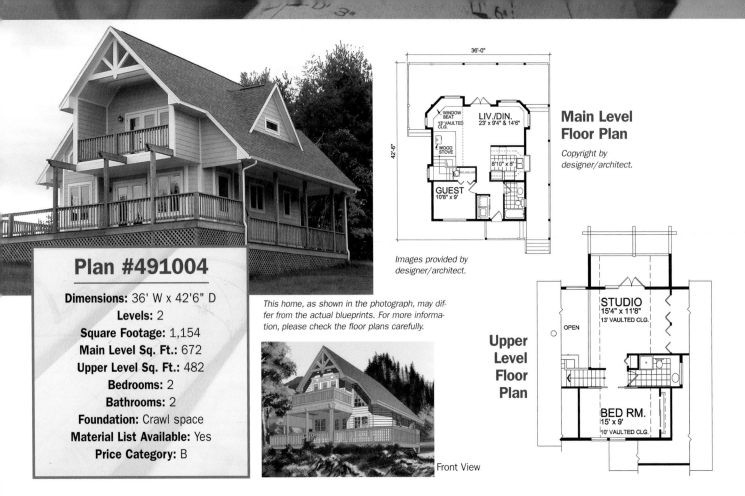

# Plan #491004

**Dimensions:** 36' W x 42'6" D
**Levels:** 2
**Square Footage:** 1,154
**Main Level Sq. Ft.:** 672
**Upper Level Sq. Ft.:** 482
**Bedrooms:** 2
**Bathrooms:** 2
**Foundation:** Crawl space
**Material List Available:** Yes
**Price Category:** B

## Main Level Floor Plan

*Copyright by designer/architect.*

*Images provided by designer/architect.*

This home, as shown in the photograph, may differ from the actual blueprints. For more information, please check the floor plans carefully.

Front View

## Upper Level Floor Plan

36'-0"

42'-6"

WINDOW SEAT
13' VAULTED CLG.

LIV./DIN.
23' x 9'4" & 14'6"

WOOD STOVE

8'10" x 8'

GUEST
10'8" x 9'

STUDIO
15'4" x 11'8"
13' VAULTED CLG.

OPEN

BED RM.
15' x 9'
10' VAULTED CLG.

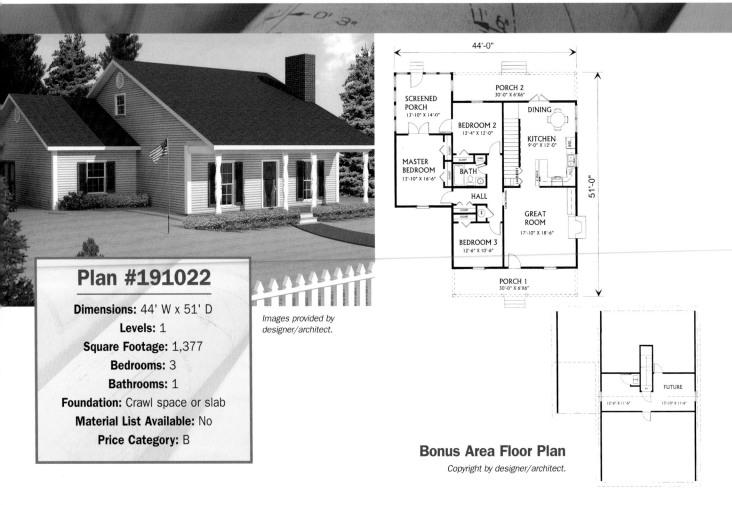

# Plan #191022

**Dimensions:** 44' W x 51' D
**Levels:** 1
**Square Footage:** 1,377
**Bedrooms:** 3
**Bathrooms:** 1
**Foundation:** Crawl space or slab
**Material List Available:** No
**Price Category:** B

*Images provided by designer/architect.*

44'-0"

51'-0"

SCREENED PORCH
13'-10" X 14'-0"

PORCH 2
30'-0" X 6'X6"

DINING

BEDROOM 2
12'-4" X 12'-0"

KITCHEN
9'-0" X 12'-0"

MASTER BEDROOM
13'-10" X 16'-6"

BATH

CLOSET

LINEN

LAUNDRY

HALL

CLOSET

GREAT ROOM
17'-10" X 18'-6"

BEDROOM 3
12'-6" X 10'-6"

PORCH 1
30'-0" X 6'X6"

## Bonus Area Floor Plan

*Copyright by designer/architect.*

FUTURE

12'-6" X 11'-6"

13'-10" X 11'-6"

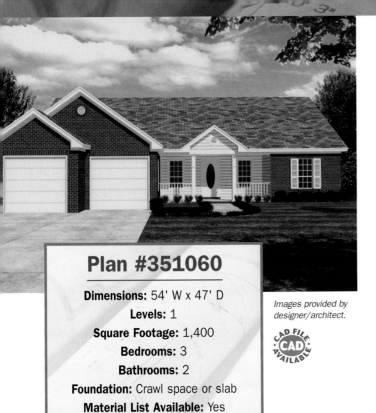

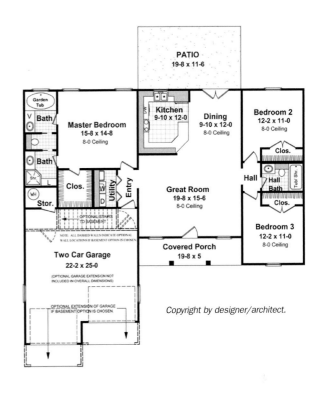

Images provided by
designer/architect.

Copyright by designer/architect.

## Plan #351060

**Dimensions:** 54' W x 47' D

**Levels:** 1

**Square Footage:** 1,400

**Bedrooms:** 3

**Bathrooms:** 2

**Foundation:** Crawl space or slab

**Material List Available:** Yes

**Price Category:** D

CAD FILE AVAILABLE • CAD

Copyright by designer/architect.

Images provided by
designer/architect.

## Plan #181345

**Dimensions:** 34' W x 34' D

**Levels:** 1

**Square Footage:** 1,079

**Bedrooms:** 2

**Bathrooms:** 1

**Foundation:** Basement; crawl space
or slab for fee

**Materials List Available:** Yes

**Price Category:** B

CAD FILE AVAILABLE • CAD

## SMARTtip

### Hydro-seeding

An alternative to traditional seeding is hydro-seeding.
In this process, a slurry of grass seed, wood fibers,
and fertilizer is spray-applied in one step. Hydro-seeding is relatively inexpensive. Compared with seeding
by hand, hydro-seeding is also very fast.

# Plan #351016

**Dimensions:** 52' W x 38'4" D

**Levels:** 1

**Square Footage:** 1,002

**Bedrooms:** 2

**Bathrooms:** 2

**Foundation:** Crawl space or slab

**Materials List Available:** Yes

**Price Category:** D

CAD FILE AVAILABLE

*Images provided by designer/architect.*

This design includes many popular features, including a two-car garage.

**Features:**

- **Living Room:** This room welcomes you into the cozy home. It features a gas fireplace with built-in shelves on each side.

- **Kitchen:** This kitchen boasts two raised bars. One is open to the breakfast area and the other is open to the living room.

- **Bedrooms:** These two bedrooms have large closets, and bedroom 1 has direct access to the bathroom, which features a jetted tub.

- **Garage:** This two-car garage has a storage area, plus room for two nice-sized cars.

*Copyright by designer/architect.*

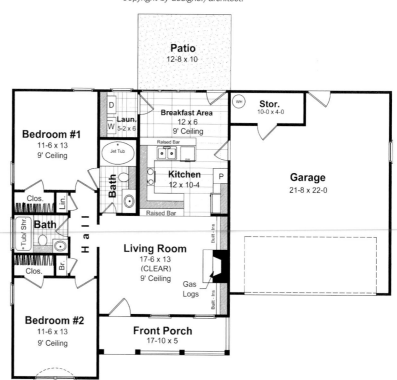

## Plan #131013

**Dimensions:** 50' W x 41'8" D
**Levels:** 1
**Square Footage:** 1,489
**Bedrooms:** 3
**Bathrooms:** 2
**Foundation:** Crawl space, slab or basement
**Materials List Available:** Yes
**Price Category:** C

You'll love the Victorian details on the exterior of this charming ranch-style home.

**Features:**

- Front Porch: This porch is large enough so that you can sit out on warm summer nights to catch a breeze or create a garden of potted ornamentals.

- Great Room: Running from the front of the house to the rear, this great room is bathed in natural light from both directions. The volume ceiling adds a luxurious feeling to it, and the fireplace creates a cozy place on chilly afternoons.

- Kitchen: Cooking will be a pleasure in this kitchen, thanks to the thoughtful layout and well-designed work areas.

- Master Suite: Enjoy the quiet in this room, where it will be easy to relax and unwind, no matter what the time of day. The walk-in closet gives you plenty of storage space, and you're sure to appreciate both the privacy and large size of the master bath.

*Images provided by designer/architect.*

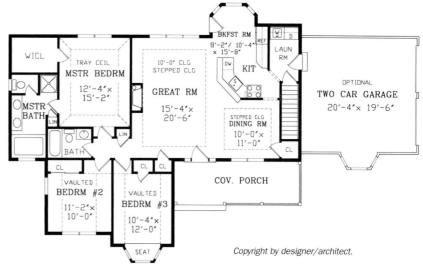

*Copyright by designer/architect.*

**Rear Elevation**

## Plan #401024

**Dimensions:** 70' W x 36' D

**Levels:** 1

**Square Footage:** 1,365

**Bedrooms:** 3

**Bathrooms:** 2

**Foundation:** Basement

**Materials List Available:** Yes

**Price Category:** B

CAD FILE AVAILABLE

*Images provided by designer/architect.*

A front veranda, ceader lattice, and a solid-stone chimney enhance the appeal of this one-story country-style home,

**Features:**

• Great Room: The open plan begins with this great room, which includes a fireplace and a plant ledgeover the wall seperating the living space from the country kitchen.

• Kitchen: This U-shaped kitchen provides an island work counter and sliding glass doors to the rear deck and screened porch.

• Master Suite: This area has a wal closet and a private bath with window seat.

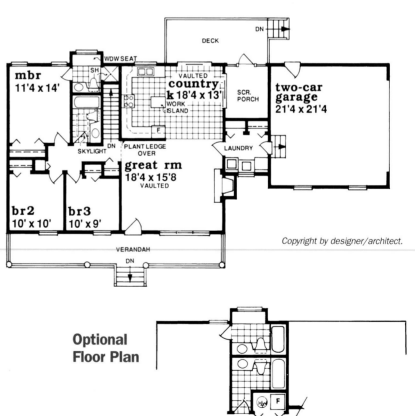

*Copyright by designer/architect.*

**Optional Floor Plan**

## Plan #351019

**Dimensions:** 54' W x 47' D

**Levels:** 1

**Square Footage:** 1,427

**Bedrooms:** 3

**Bathrooms:** 3

**Foundation:** Crawl space or slab; basement for fee

**Materials List Available:** Yes

**Price Category:** D

*Images provided by designer/architect.*

This fine three-bedroom home, with its open floor plan, may be just what you have been looking for.

**Features:**

• Great Room: This large room is open to the dining room.

• Kitchen: This fully equipped kitchen has a peninsula counter and is open into the dining room.

• Master Suite: This private area, located on the other side of the home from the secondary bedrooms, features large walk-in closets and bath areas.

• Bedrooms: Two secondary bedrooms have large closets and share a hall bathroom.

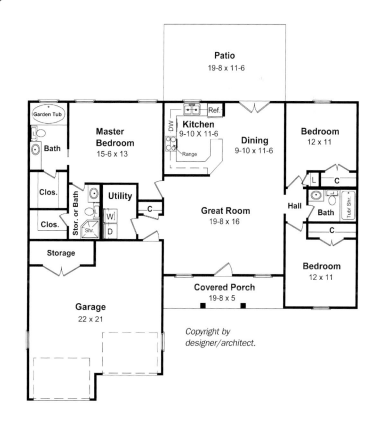

## Plan #361340

**Dimensions:** 24' W x 32' D

**Levels:** 2

**Square Footage:** 1,331

**Main Level Sq. Ft.:** 658

**Upper Level Sq. Ft.:** 673

**Bedrooms:** 3

**Bathrooms:** 2½

**Foundation:** Crawl space or basement

**Material List Available:** No

**Price Category:** B

*Images provided by designer/architect.*

CAD FILE AVAILABLE

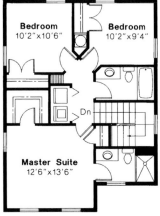

**Main Level Floor Plan**

Covered Patio

Kitchen 11'x11'4"

Dining 10'10"x13'6"

Up

Foyer

Living 13'6"x14'2"

Entry Porch

Bedroom 10'2"x10'6"

Bedroom 10'2"x9'4"

Dn

**Upper Level Floor Plan**

*Copyright by designer/architect.*

Master Suite 12'6"x13'6"

---

## Plan #391026

**Dimensions:** 35' W x 42' D

**Levels:** 2

**Square Footage:** 1,470

**Main Level Sq. Ft.:** 1,035

**Upper Level Sq. Ft.:** 435

**Bedrooms:** 3

**Bathrooms:** 2

**Foundation:** Crawl space, slab, or basement

**Materials List Available:** Yes

**Price Category:** B

*Images provided by designer/architect.*

**Main Level Floor Plan**

Deck

Brkfst 9-0 x 6-0

Flat clg.

Kit. 11-6 x 9-8

Utility

Foyer Flat clg.

UP

DN

Br #2 12-2 x 9-11

Living Rm 18-11 x 12-11

Br #3 12-2 x 9-3

Porch

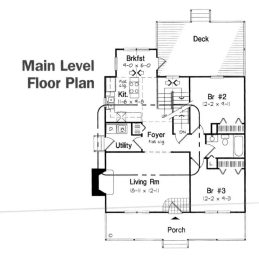

**Upper Level Floor Plan**

*Copyright by designer/architect.*

DN

Master Br 14-3 x 12-11

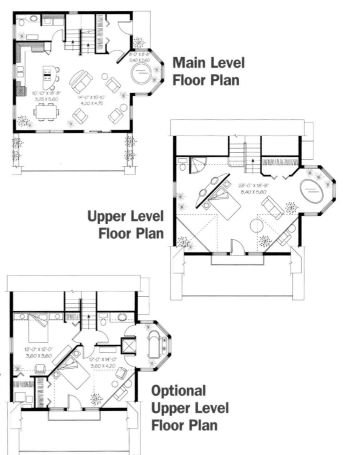

**Main Level Floor Plan**

**Upper Level Floor Plan**

*Images provided by designer/architect.*

CAD FILE AVAILABLE

*Copyright by designer/architect.*

**Optional Upper Level Floor Plan**

## Plan #181232

**Dimensions:** 33' W x 26' D

**Levels:** 2

**Square Footage:** 1,325

**Main Level Sq. Ft.:** 741

**Upper Level Sq. Ft.:** 584

**Bedrooms:** 2

**Bathrooms:** 1½

**Foundation:** Basement or walkout

**Materials List Available:** Yes

**Price Category:** B

---

**Main Level Floor Plan**

DINING 10 x 10

KIT. 8 x 10

w/d

LIVING 13 x 15

BEDROOM 11 x 15

PORCH

**Upper Level Floor Plan**

storage

skylt.

BEDROOM 10 x 10

BEDROOM 11 x 14

stor.

*Images provided by designer/architect.*

*Copyright by designer/architect.*

## Plan #381029

**Dimensions:** 28' W x 32' D

**Levels:** 2

**Square Footage:** 1,200

**Main Level Sq. Ft.:** 730

**Upper Level Sq. Ft.:** 470

**Bedrooms:** 3

**Bathrooms:** 2

**Foundation:** Crawl space or basement

**Material List Available:** Yes

**Price Category:** B

## Plan #151035

**Dimensions:** 37'8" W x 38'4" D

**Levels:** 1.5

**Square Footage:** 1,451

**Main Level Sq. Ft.:** 868

**Upper Level Sq. Ft:** 583

**Bedrooms:** 3

**Bathrooms:** 2

**Foundation:** Crawl space or slab

**CompleteCost List Available:** Yes

**Price Category:** B

*Images provided by designer/architect.*

**Features:**

• Den: The large stone fireplace is the focal point in this gathering area. Located just off the entry porch, the area welcomes you home.

• Kitchen: This efficiently designed kitchen has an abundance of cabinets and counter space. The eat-at counter, open to the den, adds extra space for family and friends.

• Grilling Porch: On nice days, overflow your dinner guests onto this rear covered grilling porch. From the relaxing area you can watch the kids play in the backyard.

• Upper Level: Two bedrooms, with large closets, and a full bathroom occupy this level. The dormers in each of the bedrooms add more space to these rooms.

Kitchen/Den

Country living meets the modern day family in this well designed home.

Porch

Kitchen

Master Bedroom

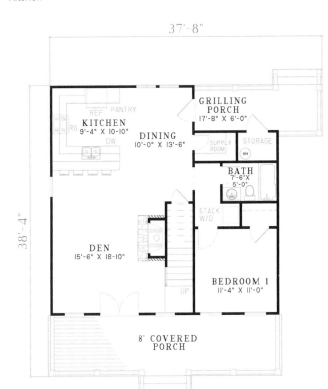

**Main Level Floor Plan**

Den

**Upper Level Floor Plan**

*Images provided by designer/architect.*

Dining Room

the ^new^ Smart Approach to
# kids'
# rooms

CREATIVE
HOMEOWNER®

This article was reprinted from *The New Smart Approach to Kids' Rooms* (Creative Homeowner 2005).

# Bathrooms Designed for Kids

**B**athing is a key part in everyone's life, and children are no exception. The bathroom, therefore, is an important environment that deserves particular attention. One that is designed around a child's smaller size enables him to move most effortlessly into taking charge of his own personal hygiene. Special safety concerns should always take precedence over other design elements. If you share a bathroom with your child, take prudent steps to accommodate his size and needs in addition to your own.

Most newer homes contain a second bath, which is often designated for the children in the family. What should be included in it depends on the ages and number of children who will use it. If your child is lucky enough to have the room all to herself, plan it for her growing and changing needs. Anticipate the storage and lighting requirements of a teenage girl's grooming habits, for example. If more than one child will share the bath, consider their genders, and whether they will use the room at the same time. How many lavatories do they need? At least two. The best designs for shared bathrooms include compartmentalized spaces—one for the toilet, one for bathing (with a separate shower, if space permits), and one for grooming. A double-bowl vanity would be most practical. At least try to set the toilet apart from the bathing area—even a half wall will help.

There are fixtures on the market that are tailored for a child's use, but you may not want to make the investment in something that will have to be replaced once your child matures or leaves home. As always, it's a matter of choice. If you want to make the room appealing to the younger set but your funds are limited, look into wallpaper

A **rubber mat** will prevent slipping, left.

**Avoid accidents** by installing antiscalding devices on faucets, above.

**Make the room accessible** for children, below.

patterns that have a juvenile theme and use lively, kid-friendly colors and accessories.

## Sensible and Basic

There are lots of things you can do to make any bathroom practical, comfortable, and safe for family members of all ages. When you're planning to build a bath that will be used by a child, careful consideration should be given to both of you, but pay particular attention to the age-specific needs of the youngster.

### Caring for Baby

The baby's bathroom should be a warm, draft-free environment. You should organize this space around your needs for bathing the baby. You'll want everything right at hand so you can keep a constant vigil. Remember: a child can drown in less than 2 inches of water in a baby tub or toilet, or even in a bucket filled with water.

Appropriate furnishings include a comfortable seating area where you can dry the baby or towel a toddler, a convenient place to house the baby bath, perhaps a changing table, and ample storage for the baby's bath toiletries and linens, diapers, bath toys, a hamper, and a diaper pail.

Consider your own comfort when positioning the baby bath. Counter height will probably be most comfortable, or you may consider a freestanding bathing unit. Install an anti-scald faucet, which contains a device that keeps water temperate. Because a child's skin is thinner and more tender than an adult's, it can be burned within 3 seconds after coming into contact with water that's over 120 degrees Fahrenheit. Fixtures equipped with a pressure-balancing feature will maintain the same degree of hotness even when cold-

water flow is reduced (when you flush the toilet, for example). Style-wise, a single-lever faucet, as opposed to two separate valves, is much easier for a child to use when regulating water flow and temperature. You can present some of them, as well.

A hand-held shower device that allows you to position the showerhead at a convenient level can be retrofitted onto a con-

**Special hand-painted tile** looks charming, above, in this one-of-a-kind boys' bathroom.

ventional showerhead or installed separately. Look for one that's been designed for children to handle.

Once you start to bathe the baby in the tub, you'll want to make it slip-resistant. A textured surface helps. You can easily add this with antislip decals and mats. Install soft covers over the faucet and spout so that a little one can't be bruised. Parents can protect themselves by using a mat that extends over the side of the tub to cushion their arms while holding up and bathing the baby. Part of the mat also rests on the floor to pad adult knees.

It's a good idea to install easy-care wallcovering and flooring. From the first moment a toddler learns to splash, all claims to toughness are tested. Classic selections include tiles, waterproof wallcovering that has a built-in

mildewcide, solid-surfacing material or a fiberglass tub surround, and gloss or semi-gloss paint, with a mildewcide.

A one-piece toilet hugs closer to the wall and has an elongated bowl that makes toilet training a little easier. Because it sits lower than a two-piece model, this type is better-scaled for a child yet comfortable for an adult.

## Helping Preschoolers

Toilet training and the beginning of self-grooming mark this stage, necessitating a few changes in the way your child will use the bathroom. Tubs and toys seem to go together here. You'll need more room for toy storage; gear it to something your child can access himself, such as a plastic basket that can be kept inside a vanity cabinet or on the floor of the linen closet. You'll also need a place to keep a small step stool when it's not in use as a booster in front of the lav. If you're renovating or building a new bathroom for a child, consider installing a lav into a vanity or countertop that is built at a lower height.

Because the standard rule of thumb is to install a mirror 8 inches above a standard-height vanity countertop (to avoid splatters), you may want to include a standing mirror or one that extends from the wall at a proper height to suit your child. To encourage neatness, a towel rack that is within a child's reach is another good idea. A low freestanding rack works well, too.

## Accommodating School-Age Kids

Socializing skills in school reinforce the needs for individual identity at home, including specific grooming styles as a child gets older. Storage niches once devoted to bathtub toys can be used for hair ribbons, special soaps and shampoos, or other toiletries. Keep electrical appliances, such as hair dryers and steam rollers, or electric shavers out of the room until your child is old enough to handle them responsibly and understand the hazards posed by electricity and water.

**More About Shared Spaces.** The crunch starts when kids begin toilet training and continues through the school years when everybody has to get bathed, dressed, and out of the house at the same time. To cope with the increased demands, create private areas within the room, such as the separate bathing, grooming, and toilet areas suggested earlier. Color-code towels and accessories so that everyone can clearly see

**Hang a deep basket** from a peg, above, and tuck bath toys or small laundry items into it.

**Here's a stylish way** to make sure everyone has his or her own bath towel, left.

## Bathroom Safety

Here's a list of things that you should have on hand at all times to make sure any bathroom
that is intended for a child's use is safe and comfortable.

**Tub & Shower Areas**

· Safety glazing on glass doors

· Doors that are hinged to swing out into the room

· Grab bars at adult and child heights

· A shower seat

**Toilets & Water Closets**

· No lock on the water-closet door

· Locked toilet lid

· Tip-resistant training step stool

· Toilet-paper holder installed within the child's reach

**Plumbing**

· Water valves within easy reach

· Single-lever controls

· Anti-scald and pressure-balanced faucets

· Adjustable child-size hand shower

**Electric**

· Ground-fault circuit interrupters (GFCIs) on all outlets

· Covered receptacles

· Vapor-proof light fixtures installed out of the child's reach

· Low-voltage task lighting

· Night light

**Cabinet & Counter Surfaces**

· Small doors that can be easily opened

· Childproof locks

· Locked medicine cabinet

· No more than 8-inch-deep cabinets installed over the toilet

· Rounded corners and edges

· Seating for drying off and dressing

**Flooring**

· Nonslip surface

· Water-resistant surface

· Anchors for area rugs and mats

**Windows & Doors**

· Doors that swing into the room

· Door locks that can be opened from the outside

· Safety bars on all windows

---

what belongs to each person who uses the room into a vanity or countertop that is built at a lower height.

Finally, move certain activities to other rooms. Dressing and grooming can be done in the bedroom, for example. Whether your home has one small bathroom that is shared by all or a separate bathroom for each member of the family, there are steps you can take to make space more efficient.

**Step One: Plan storage.** If you don't have a linen closet or large cabinet in the room, add shelving to hold extra towels, bars of soap, and other necessities. Small storage niches created between the wall studs make handy spots for shampoo and toiletries. Mount hooks or pegged racks to the wall or behind the door for hanging extra towels or robes. New medicine cabinets come with extra deep shelves that are large enough to hold rolls of toilet paper or bulky hair dryers.

**Step Two: Consider a better way to use space.**
Cramped floor space? Replace the bathroom door with a pocket door to free up floor space that might allow you to create a separate shower stall or a double vanity.

**Step Three: Light it properly.** Besides general lighting, plan adequate task lighting at the sink and mirror for grooming. Avoid locating lights above the mirror where they create glare and shadows. A better choice is to place lights down the sides of the vanity mirror. This arrangement eliminates glare.

**Step Four: Keep the air clear.** Invest in a good exhaust fan to make the room's air quality healthier and surfaces less slick. It will also deter water build up and mildew, which can damage surfaces and materials.

1. Rounded edges are gentle on kids.
2. Here's one way to keep towels neat.
3. A spacious vanity and lots of storage are important when kids share a bathroom.
4. Kids can help pick out cute accessories for their bathroom.
5. A shower seat is a safety feature that should be included in every bathroom.
6. Secure all rugs with a nonskid backing.
7. A handheld sprayer in the bath makes it easy to rinse shampoo out of hair.
8. Kids can personalize the space by painting their own designs in the room.

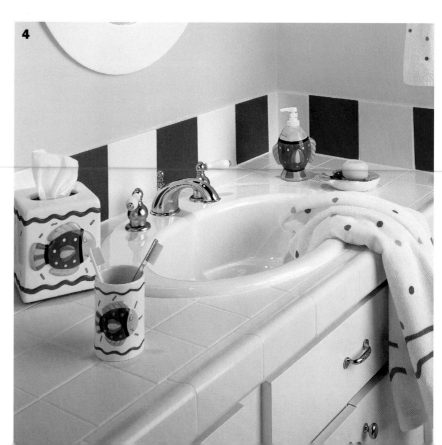

# Design Ideas for Kids' Baths

## Plan #161001

**Dimensions:** 67'2" W x 47' D

**Levels:** 1

**Square Footage:** 1,782

**Bedrooms:** 3

**Bathrooms:** 2

**Foundation:** Basement

**Materials List Available:** Yes

**Price Category:** C

An all-brick exterior displays the solid strength that characterizes this gracious home.

### Features:

- **Great Room:** A feeling of spaciousness permeates the gathering area created by the foyer, great room, and dining room. Multiple windows provide natural light that dances along a sloped ceiling, spilling onto decorative columns and a fireplace.

- **Breakfast Area:** A continuation of the sloped ceiling leads to the breakfast area where French doors open to a screened porch.

- **Kitchen:** An abundance of cabinets and counter space are the hallmarks of this large kitchen with its easy access to a spacious laundry room and storage area.

- **Master Suite:** A tray ceiling and spacious walk-in closet in the master bedroom, along with a whirlpool tub and double-bowl vanity in the bathroom, enable you to pamper yourself.

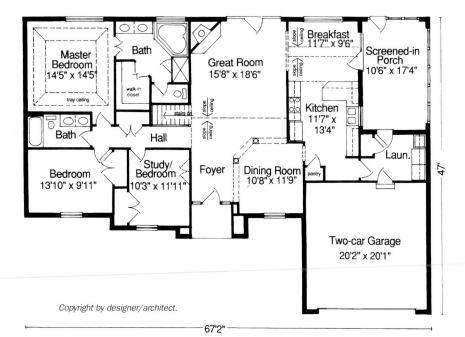

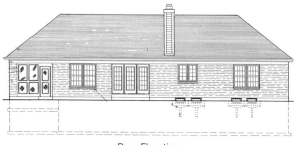

Rear Elevation

Left Side Elevation

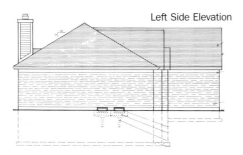

Right Side Elevation

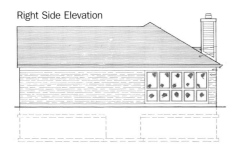

Front View

Great Room / Foyer

## Plan #441032

**Dimensions:** 45' W x 55' D
**Levels:** 2
**Square Footage:** 1,944
**Main Level Sq. Ft.:** 1,514
**Upper Level Sq. Ft.:** 430
**Bedrooms:** 3
**Bathrooms:** 2½
**Foundation:** Crawl space; slab or basement available for fee
**Materials List Available:** Yes
**Price Category:** D

Images provided by designer/architect.

It's the little things—decorative eave vents, wooden shutters, a porch column, and multiple-pane windows—that create the initial impression of this home.

**Features:**

- Great Design: The master suite is on the main level, while family bedrooms are upstairs, creating convenient separation and allowing full livability of the main level for empty nesters.

- Kitchen: This kitchen features an island work area and has the use of a walk-in pantry just around the corner.

- Master Suite: Don't overlook amenities in this suite: a large walk-in closet, a fully appointed bath, and a lovely wide window with views of the backyard.

- Garage: This garage holds extra space that can become a workshop, if you choose, or a place for those coveted big-boy toys.

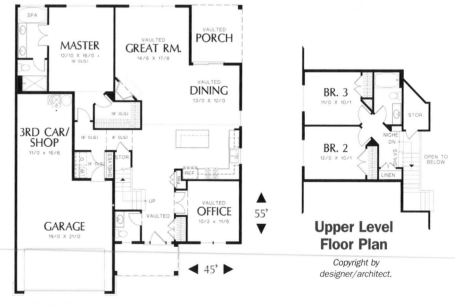

**Main Level Floor Plan**

**Upper Level Floor Plan**

*Copyright by designer/architect.*

Rear Elevation

*Images provided by designer/architect.*

# Plan #401044

**Dimensions:** 34' W x 48' D

**Levels:** 2

**Square Footage:** 1,568

**Main Level Sq. Ft.:** 1,012

**Upper Level Sq. Ft.:** 556

**Bedrooms:** 3

**Bathrooms:** 2½

**Foundation:** Basement

**Materials List Available:** Yes

**Price Category:** C

Country comes home to this plan with details such as a metal roof, horizontal siding, multi-pane double-hung windows, and front and rear porches.

**CAD FILE AVAILABLE**

**Features:**

- Entry: This recessed front entry leads to the great room, flanked by a breakfast bar and formal dining room with access to both the front and rear porches.

- Great Room: This room is warmed by a fireplace and features a two-story ceiling.

- Master Suite: Located the first level, this sweet retreat has a private bath and walk-in closet.

- Bedrooms: Upstairs, two more bedrooms and a full bathroom complete the plan.

**Main Level Floor Plan**

PORCH

**mbr** 12'4x12'8

**din** 12'x10'

**k** 8'4x10'

W D

CABINETS

DN

UP

BREAKFAST BAR

**great rm** 17'x13'6

PORCH

Right Side Elevation

Left Side Elevation

**br2** 12'4x12'8

**br3** 10'x10'
OR OPTIONAL LOFT

3'6 RAILING

DN

OPEN TO BELOW

**Upper Level Floor Plan**

*Copyright by designer/architect.*

Rear Elevation

# Plan #101005

**Dimensions:** 63' W x 57'2" D

**Levels:** 1

**Square Footage:** 1,992

**Bedrooms:** 3

**Bathrooms:** 2½

**Foundation:** Crawl space, slab, or basement

**Materials List Available:** Yes

**Price Category:** D

CAD FILE AVAILABLE

Rear View

This midsized ranch is accented with Palladian windows and inviting front porch.

**Features:**

- Ceiling Height: 9 ft. unless otherwise noted.

- Special Ceilings: Tray or vaulted ceilings adorn the living room, family room, dining room, and master suite.

- Kitchen: This bright and airy kitchen is designed to be a pleasure in which to work. It shares a big bay window with the contiguous breakfast room.

- Breakfast Room: The light streaming in from the bay window makes this the perfect place to linger with coffee and the Sunday paper.

- Master Suite: This lovely suite is exceptional, with its sitting area and direct access to the deck, as well as a full-featured bath, and spacious walk-in closet.

- Secondary Bedrooms: The other bedrooms each measure about 13 ft. x 11 ft. They have walk-in closets and share a "Jack-and-Jill" bath.

*Copyright by designer/architect.*

## Plan #121045

**Dimensions:** 40' W x 48' D

**Levels:** 2

**Square Footage:** 1,575

**Main Level Sq. Ft.:** 787

**Upper Level Sq. Ft.:** 788

**Bedrooms:** 3

**Bathrooms:** 2½

**Foundation:** Basement

**Materials List Available:** Yes

**Price Category:** C

*This home, as shown in the photograph, may differ from the actual blueprints. For more detailed information, please check the floor plans carefully.* *Images provided by designer/architect.*

This home is carefully laid out to provide the convenience demanded by busy family life.

**Features:**

• Ceiling Height: 8 ft.

• Family Room: This charming family room, with its fireplace and built-in cabinetry, will become the central gathering place for family and friends.

• Kitchen: This kitchen offers a central island that makes food preparation more convenient and doubles

as a snack bar for a quick bite on the run. The breakfast area features a pantry and planning desk.

• Computer Loft: The second-floor landing includes this loft designed to accommodate the family computer.

• Room to Grow: Also on the second-floor landing you will find a large unfinished area waiting to accommodate the growing family.

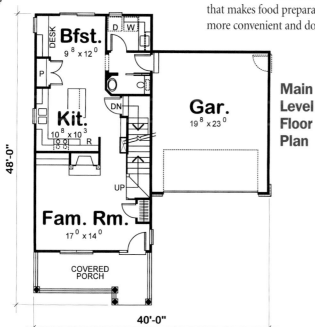

**Main Level Floor Plan**

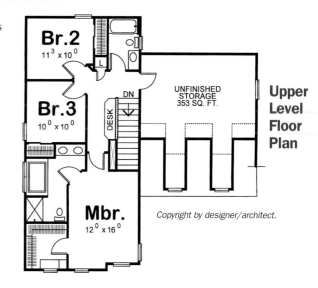

**Upper Level Floor Plan**

*Copyright by designer/architect.*

## Plan #521036

**Dimensions:** 36' W x 43'8" D

**Levels:** 2

**Square Footage:** 1,578

**Main Level Sq. Ft.:** 1,080

**Upper Level Sq. Ft.:** 498

**Bedrooms:** 3

**Bathrooms:** 2½

**Foundation:** Crawl space

**Material List Available:** No

**Price Category:** C

*Images provided by designer/architect.*

**CAD FILE AVAILABLE**

### Main Level Floor Plan

SCREENED PORCH (10'0"x10'0")
MASTER BEDROOM (16'4"x12'0")
DINING AREA (10'0"x14'8")
KITCHEN (12'8"x9'0")
LAUNDRY
LIVING ROOM (18'0"x13'8")
FRONT WRAP AROUND PORCH

### Upper Level Floor Plan

*Copyright by designer/architect.*

BEDROOM #2 (11'4"x10'0")
BEDROOM #3 (11'8"x10'0")

---

## Plan #391373

**Dimensions:** 50' W x 40' D

**Levels:** 2

**Square Footage:** 1,554

**Main Level Sq. Ft.:** 806

**Upper Level Sq. Ft.:** 748

**Bedrooms:** 3

**Bathrooms:** 2½

**Foundation:** Crawl space, slab, or basement

**Material List Available:** Yes

**Price Category:** C

*Images provided by designer/architect.*

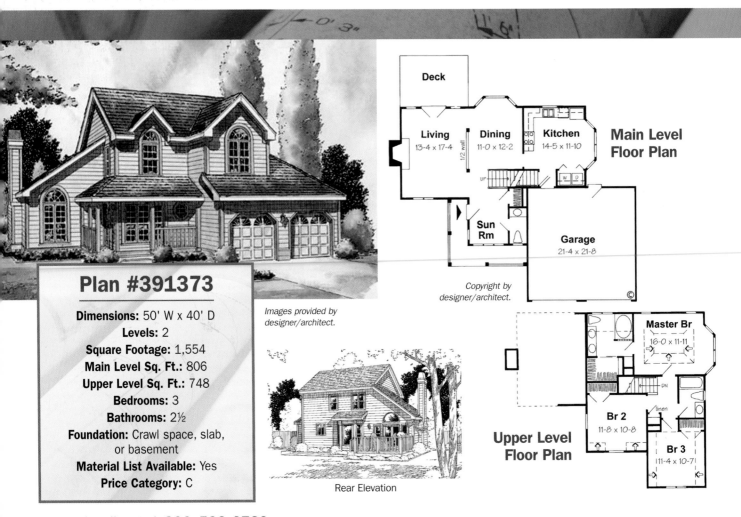

Rear Elevation

### Main Level Floor Plan

Deck
Living 13-4 x 17-4
1/2 wall
Dining 11-0 x 12-2
Kitchen 14-5 x 11-10
UP
W D
Sun Rm
Garage 21-4 x 21-8

*Copyright by designer/architect.*

### Upper Level Floor Plan

Master Br 16-0 x 11-11
DN
Br 2 11-8 x 10-8
linen
Br 3 11-4 x 10-7

## Plan #281018

**Dimensions:** 50' W x 52'6" D

**Levels:** 1

**Square Footage:** 1,565

**Bedrooms:** 3

**Bathrooms:** 2

**Foundation:** Basement

**Materials List Available:** Yes

**Price Category:** C

*Images provided by designer/architect.*

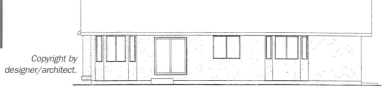

*Copyright by designer/architect.*

Rear Elevation

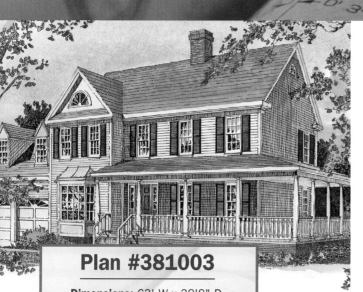

## Plan #381003

**Dimensions:** 63' W x 38'8" D

**Levels:** 2

**Square Footage:** 1,925

**Main Level Sq. Ft.:** 1,000

**Upper Level Sq. Ft.:** 925

**Bedrooms:** 3

**Bathrooms:** 2½

**Foundation:** Basement, crawl space

**Materials List Available:** Yes

**Price Category:** D

*Images provided by designer/architect.*

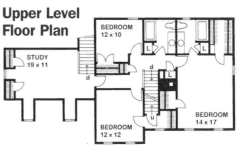

**Main Level Floor Plan**

**Upper Level Floor Plan**

*Copyright by designer/architect.*

## Plan #281015

**Dimensions:** 32' W x 48' D
**Levels:** 2
**Square Footage:** 1,660
**Main Level Sq. Ft.:** 964
**Upper Level Sq. Ft.:** 696
**Bedrooms:** 4
**Bathrooms:** 2½
**Foundation:** Basement
**Materials List Available:** Yes
**Price Category:** C

You'll love the gracious features and amenities in this charming home, which is meant for a narrow lot.

### Features:

- **Foyer:** This two-story foyer opens into the spacious living room.

- **Living Room:** The large bay window in this room makes a perfect setting for quiet times alone or entertaining guests.

- **Dining Room:** The open flow between this room and the living room adds to the airy feeling.

- **Family Room:** With a handsome fireplace and a door to the rear patio, this room will be the heart of your home.

- **Kitchen:** The U-shaped layout, pantry, and greenhouse window make this room a joy.

- **Master Suite:** The bay window, large walk-in closet, and private bath make this second-floor room a true retreat.

*Images provided by designer/architect.*

**Main Level Floor Plan**

**Upper Level Floor Plan**

*Copyright by designer/architect.*

Rear Elevation

Left Side Elevation

Right Side Elevation

## Plan #401008

**Dimensions:** 87' W x 44' D

**Levels:** 1

**Square Footage:** 1,541

**Bedrooms:** 3

**Bathrooms:** 2

**Foundation:** Basement

**Materials List Available:** Yes

**Price Category:** C

This popular design begins with a wraparound covered porch made even more charming by turned wood spindles.

**Features:**

- Great Room: The entry opens directly into this great room, which is warmed by a woodstove.

- Dining Room: This room offers access to a screened porch for outdoor after-dinner leisure.

- Kitchen: This country kitchen features a center island and a breakfast bay for casual meals.

- Bedrooms: Family bedrooms share a full bath that includes a soaking tub.

*Images provided by designer/architect.*

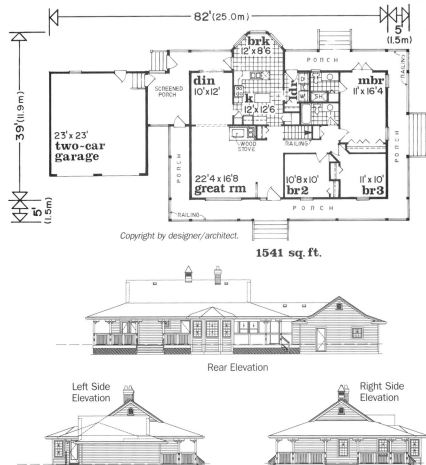

*Copyright by designer/architect.*

**1541 sq. ft.**

Rear Elevation

Left Side Elevation

Right Side Elevation

# Plan #391068

**Dimensions:** 40' W x 27' D
**Levels:** 2
**Square Footage:** 1,855
**Main Level Sq. Ft.:** 913
**Upper Level Sq. Ft.:** 516
**Basement Level Sq. Ft.:** 426
**Bedrooms:** 3
**Bathrooms:** 2
**Foundation:** Basement
**Materials List Available:** No
**Price Category:** D

*Images provided by designer/architect.*

Wide windows on multiple levels infuse this home with the beauty of natural light.

**Features:**

- Great Room: This room with fireplace extends to the dining room, joining the camaraderie of an open kitchen.

- Master Suite: This suite with walk-in closet features a master bath with double vanities, a shower, and access to a terrace.

- Bedrooms: The second-floor loft embraces these two additional bedrooms and full bathroom as it overlooks the downstairs.

- Recreation Room: This fun area is located on the lower level with access to the lower patio. Close by is the mechanical room and an unfinished area for storage.

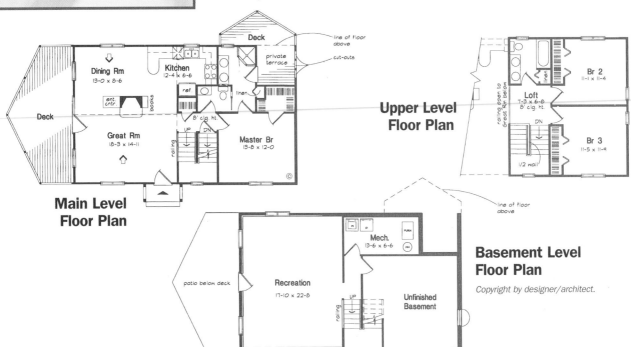

**Main Level Floor Plan**

**Upper Level Floor Plan**

**Basement Level Floor Plan**

*Copyright by designer/architect.*

## Plan #381010

**Dimensions:** 62' W x 87'6" D

**Levels:** 1

**Square Footage:** 1,905

**Bedrooms:** 3

**Bathrooms:** 2

**Foundation:** Crawl space

**Materials List Available:** Yes

**Price Category:** E

*Images provided by designer/architect.*

This home has all the features that are important to today's discerning homebuyer.

**Features:**

- **Porches:** The side porch serves as the everyday entry as it ushers visitors directly to the spacious kitchen. The front porch maintains its distinction as the formal entrance to the home.

- **Great Room:** The dining and living rooms are combined into this colossal great room. The room features a stone fireplace and a soaring vaulted ceiling with exposed beams. A circular stairway ascends to the loft.

- **Kitchen:** A vaulted ceiling, abundant cabinets, an island counter, and a dining room pass-through are all part of this very functional kitchen. An adjoining oversized utility room contains a coat closet and a pantry, and it offers access to the three-car garage.

- **Master Suite:** This master suite boasts a vaulted ceiling, a large walk-in closet, and a private bath.

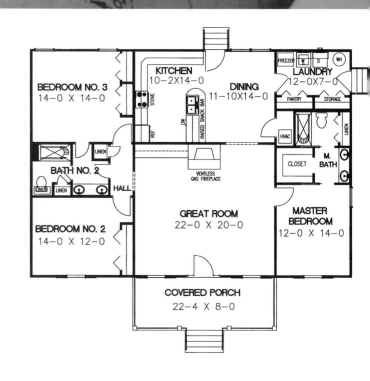

KITCHEN
10-2X14-0

BEDROOM NO. 3
14-0 X 14-0

DINING
11-10X14-0

FREEZER

LAUNDRY
12-0X7-0

PANTRY    STORAGE

STOVE    DW    RAISED SNACK BAR

REF

BATH NO. 2

LINEN

HVAC

LINEN

LINEN    LINEN

HALL

VENTLESS
GAS FIREPLACE

CLOSET

M.
BATH

BEDROOM NO. 2
14-0 X 12-0

GREAT ROOM
22-0 X 20-0

MASTER
BEDROOM
12-0 X 14-0

COVERED PORCH
22-4 X 8-0

## Plan #191024

**Dimensions:** 50' W x 42' D

**Levels:** 1

**Square Footage:** 1,700

**Bedrooms:** 3

**Bathrooms:** 2

**Foundation:** Crawl space, slab or basement

**Materials List Available:** No

**Price Category:** C

*Images provided by designer/architect.*

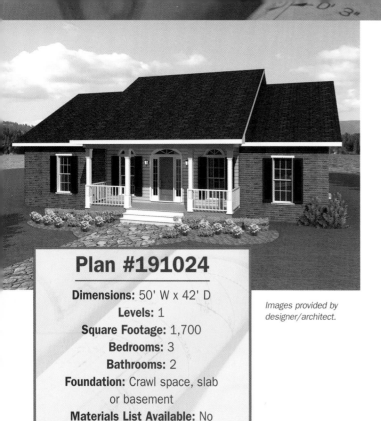

35'-0"

PORCH

FAMILY
ROOM
18'-0"x19'-6"

MORNING
ROOM
8'-0"x11'-6"

KITCHEN
10'-0"x11'-6"

DINING
ROOM
13'-9"x14'-4"

FAMILY
ENTRY

VAULTED CEILING

FP

DN

PANTRY

LAUNDRY
W D

44'-0"

DN

LAV.

UP

ENTRY
FOYER

LIVING
ROOM
13'-9"x18'-6"

TWO-CAR GARAGE
23'-4"x23'-2"

PORCH

**Main Level
Floor Plan**

58'-0"

**Upper Level Floor Plan**

BEDROOM
13'-0"x8'-10"

WIC

BEDROOM
12'-8"x11'-0"

LIN

BATH

DN

UPPER HALL

MASTER
BATH

BEDROOM
12'-0"x11'-0"

WIC

32'-0"

MASTER
BEDROOM
13'-9"x14'-2"

35'-0"

## Plan #291012

**Dimensions:** 58' W x 44' D

**Levels:** 2

**Square Footage:** 1,898

**Main Level Sq. Ft.:** 1,182

**Upper Level Sq. Ft.:** 716

**Bedrooms:** 4

**Bathrooms:** 2½

**Foundation:** Basement

**Materials List Available:** No

**Price Category:** D

*Images provided by designer/architect.*

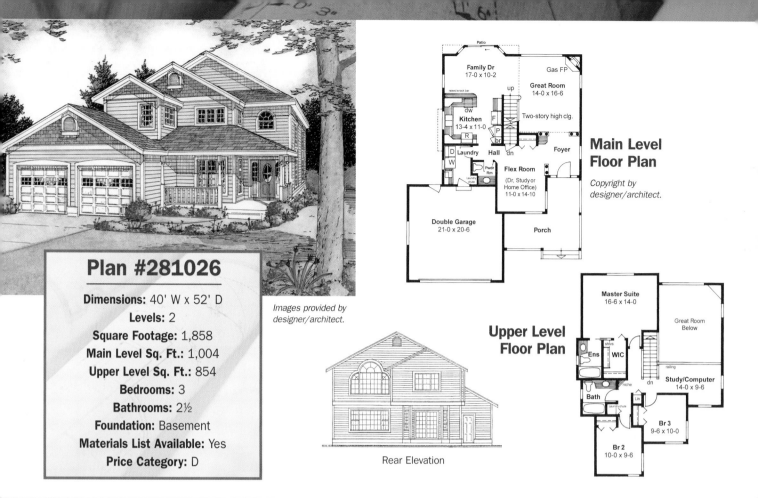

## Plan #281026

**Dimensions:** 40' W x 52' D
**Levels:** 2
**Square Footage:** 1,858
**Main Level Sq. Ft.:** 1,004
**Upper Level Sq. Ft.:** 854
**Bedrooms:** 3
**Bathrooms:** 2½
**Foundation:** Basement
**Materials List Available:** Yes
**Price Category:** D

Images provided by designer/architect.

**Main Level Floor Plan**

Copyright by designer/architect.

**Upper Level Floor Plan**

Rear Elevation

## Plan #241026

**Dimensions:** 59'11" W x 50'2" D
**Levels:** 1
**Square Footage:** 1,660
**Bedrooms:** 3
**Bathrooms:** 2
**Foundation:** Slab
**Materials List Available:** No
**Price Category:** C

Images provided by designer/architect.

Copyright by designer/architect.

**Bonus Area Floor Plan**

## Plan #281016

**Dimensions:** 46' W x 44' D

**Levels:** 2

**Square Footage:** 1,945

**Main Level Sq. Ft.:** 1,211

**Upper Level Sq. Ft.:** 734

**Bedrooms:** 3

**Bathrooms:** 3

**Foundation:** Combination basement/slab

**Materials List Available:** Yes

**Price Category:** D

*Images provided by designer/architect.*

The fabulous window shapes on this Tudor-style home give just a hint of the beautiful interior design.

**Features:**

• **Living Room:** A vaulted ceiling in this raised room adds to its spectacular good looks.

• **Dining Room:** Between the lovely bay window and the convenient door to the covered sundeck, this room is an entertainer's delight.

• **Family Room:** A sunken floor, cozy fireplace, and door to the patio make this room special.

• **Study:** Just off the family room, this quiet spot can be a true retreat away from the crowd.

• **Kitchen:** The family cooks will be delighted by the ample counter and storage space here.

• **Master Suite:** A large walk-in closet, huge picture window, and private bath add luxurious touches to this second-floor retreat.

**Main Level Floor Plan**

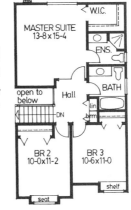

**Upper Level Floor Plan**

*Copyright by designer/architect.*

Rear Elevation

Left Side Elevation

Right Side Elevation

# Plan #351108

**Dimensions:** 65' W x 60'8" D

**Levels:** 1

**Square Footage:** 1,816

**Bedrooms:** 3

**Bathrooms:** 2

**Foundation:** Basement

**Material List Available:** Yes

**Price Category:** E

*Images provided by designer/architect.*

This beautiful country home presents a pleasing exterior that includes a welcoming porch and eye-catching gables.

**CAD FILE AVAILABLE**

**Features:**

- Entry: This front porch, with regal white columns and curved brick steps, adds an upscale tone to the home.

- Flex Space: Located just off of the foyer, the use of this area is open to your creativity. Make it into a home office or a hobby room.

- Great Room: Enjoy the warmth of the gas fireplace in this lush great room. Impressive vaulted ceilings add to the elegant aura of the space.

- Kitchen and Breakfast Nook: This large kitchen boasts an eating bar and island, ideal for everyday tasks and quick snacking. The breakfast nook features 9-ft.-high ceilings and space for a built-in benches and a table.

- Master Suite: Perhaps the most appealing of the rooms in the home, this master bedroom features 10-ft.-high ceilings and a massive walk-in closet. A jet-tub, two sinks, and a separate shower grace the luxurious bath.

### Main Level Floor Plan

*Copyright by designer/architect.*

Rear Elevation

**Bonus Area Floor Plan**

## Plan #181544

**Dimensions:** 48' W x 41'2" D
**Levels:** 2
**Square Footage:** 1,846
**Main Level Sq. Ft.:** 958
**Upper Level Sq. Ft.:** 888
**Bedrooms:** 4
**Bathrooms:** 2½
**Foundation:** Basement
**Material List Available:** Yes
**Price Category:** D

*Images provided by designer/architect.*

This noble home, with its handsome exterior and well-planned interior, would be a welcome addition to any neighborhood.

**CAD FILE AVAILABLE**

**Features:**

- Living Room: Flanked by windows and a fireplace, this spacious area is great for entertaining guests or just hanging out with the family.

- Kitchen: This U-shape kitchen surrounds the family cook with workspace and storage. It's nestled among a sunny breakfast room, back porch, and formal dining room, so you'll have plenty of choices at mealtime.

- Office: This space provides a quiet retreat for working at home or just working on the household bills and schedule.

- Master Suite: This master bedroom features a bay of windows that will fill the room with moonlight to aid sleep and sunlight to help waking. The space also includes ample closet space and a full bath with separate tub and shower.

- Secondary Bedrooms: Two additional bedrooms have access to a nearby full bathroom and a sitting room, perfect for family or guests.

Rear Elevation

*Copyright by designer/architect.*

**Main Level Floor Plan**

**Upper Level Floor Plan**

## Plan #181159

**Dimensions:** 37' W x 31' D

**Levels:** 1

**Square Footage:** 1,992

**Main Level Sq. Ft.:** 996

**Lower Level Sq. Ft.:** 996

**Bedrooms:** 3

**Bathrooms:** 2

**Foundation:** Walkout basement

**Materials List Available:** Yes

**Price Category:** D

Ideal for the family who loves the outdoors, this charmer features a wraparound porch that creates a covered pavilion and roofed terrace.

**Features:**

- Ceiling Height: 9-ft. ceilings enhance the airy feeling given by the many windows here.

- Family Rooms: These family rooms (one on each floor) allow a busy family adequate space for entertaining a crowd.

- Kitchen: Designed for efficient work patterns, this kitchen features ample work and storage space, as well as an island that can double as a

- Bedrooms: Each bedroom features a large, walk-in closet and easy access to a large, amenity-filled bathroom with a double vanity, tub, enclosed shower, and a private toilet.

- Porch: Enjoy the panoramic view from this spacious covered porch at any time of day.

**CAD FILE AVAILABLE**

This home, as shown in the photograph, may differ from the actual blueprints. For more detailed information, please check the floor plans carefully.

*Images provided by designer/architect.*

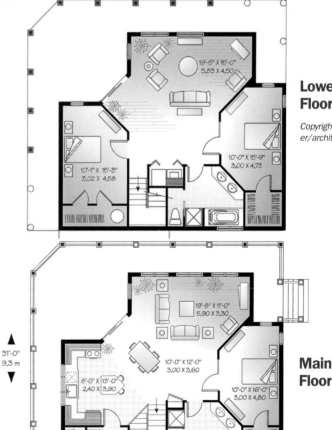

**Lower Level Floor Plan**

*Copyright by designer/architect.*

**Main Level Floor Plan**

## Plan #391070

**Dimensions:** 52' W x 31' D

**Levels:** 2

**Square Footage:** 1,960

**Main Level Sq. Ft.:** 1,005

**Upper Level Sq. Ft.:** 955

**Bedrooms:** 4

**Bathrooms:** 2½

**Foundation:** Crawl space, slab, or basement

**Material List Available:** Yes

**Price Category:** D

*Images provided by designer/architect.*

**Main Level Floor Plan**

**Crawl Space/Slab Option**

**Upper Level Floor Plan**

*Copyright by designer/architect.*

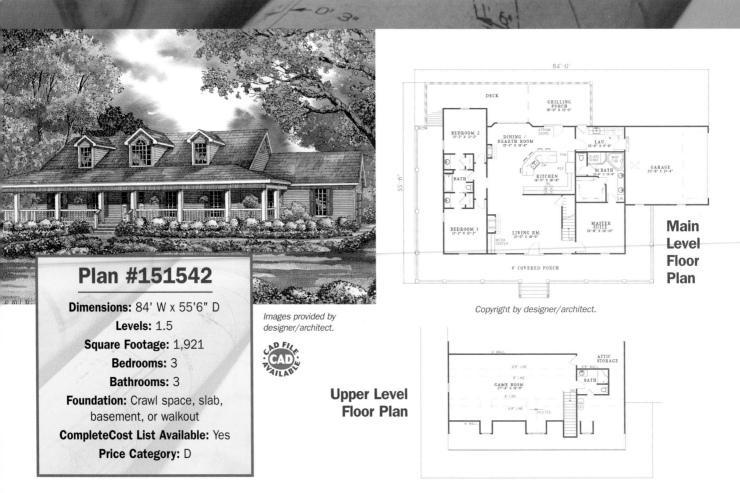

## Plan #151542

**Dimensions:** 84' W x 55'6" D

**Levels:** 1.5

**Square Footage:** 1,921

**Bedrooms:** 3

**Bathrooms:** 3

**Foundation:** Crawl space, slab, basement, or walkout

**CompleteCost List Available:** Yes

**Price Category:** D

*Images provided by designer/architect.*

**CAD FILE AVAILABLE**

**Main Level Floor Plan**

*Copyright by designer/architect.*

**Upper Level Floor Plan**

## Upper Level Floor Plan

VAULTED MASTER
12/2 X 14/10

BONUS / BR.3
17/6 X 12/6

LINEN

BR. 2
11/2 X 11/6

DN.

## Main Level Floor Plan

*Copyright by designer/architect.*

DINING
11/8 X 11/6
(9' CLG.)

DEN/BR. 4
10/8 X 10/0
(9' CLG.)

GARAGE
11/0 X 17/0

VAULTED GREAT RM.
17/2 X 15/0
(TO ISLAND)

PAN.

GARAGE
21/0 X 22/0

FOYER

UP

44'-6"

50'

*Images provided by designer/architect.*

**CAD FILE AVAILABLE**

## Plan #441021

**Dimensions:** 50' W x 44'6" D
**Levels:** 2
**Square Footage:** 1,760
**Main Level Sq. Ft.:** 941
**Upper Level Sq. Ft.:** 819
**Bedrooms:** 4
**Bathrooms:** 3
**Foundation:** Crawl space; slab
or basement for fee
**Material List Available:** No
**Price Category:** C

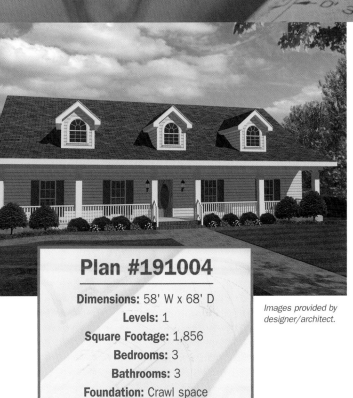

## Plan #191004

**Dimensions:** 58' W x 68' D
**Levels:** 1
**Square Footage:** 1,856
**Bedrooms:** 3
**Bathrooms:** 3
**Foundation:** Crawl space
**Material List Available:** No
**Price Category:** D

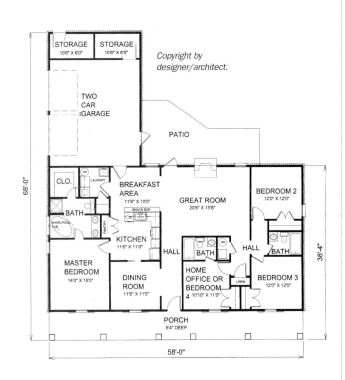

*Copyright by designer/architect.*

STORAGE
10'6" X 6'0"

STORAGE
10'6" X 6'0"

TWO CAR GARAGE

PATIO

68'-0"

CLO.

LAUNDRY

BREAKFAST AREA
11'6" X 10'0"

GREAT ROOM
20'6" X 15'8"

BEDROOM 2
12'0" X 12'0"

BATH

WHIRLPOOL TUB

SNACK BAR

KITCHEN
11'6" X 11'0"

HALL

BATH

HALL

BATH

MASTER BEDROOM
14'0" X 16'0"

DINING ROOM
11'6" X 11'0"

HOME OFFICE OR BEDROOM 4
10'10" X 11'0"

LINEN

BEDROOM 3
12'0" X 12'0"

38'-4"

PORCH
6'4" DEEP

58'-0"

*Images provided by designer/architect.*

# Plan #121064

**Dimensions:** 44' W x 40' D
**Levels:** 2
**Square Footage:** 1,846
**Main Level Sq. Ft.:** 919
**Upper Level Sq. Ft.:** 927
**Bedrooms:** 4
**Bathrooms:** 2½
**Foundation:** Basement
**Materials List Available:** Yes
**Price Category:** D

*Images provided by designer/architect.*

You'll love the features and design in this compact but amenity-filled home.

**Features:**

- **Entry:** A balcony overlooks this two-story entry, where a plant shelf tops the coat closet.

- **Great Room:** A trio of tall windows points up the large dimensions of this room, which is sure to be the hub of your home. Arrange the furniture to create a cozy space around the fireplace, or leave it open to the room.

- **Kitchen:** You'll love to work in this well-designed kitchen area.

- **Master Suite:** On the second floor, this master suite features a tiered ceiling and two walk-in closets. In the bath, you'll find a double vanity, whirlpool tub, and separate shower.

## Main Level Floor Plan

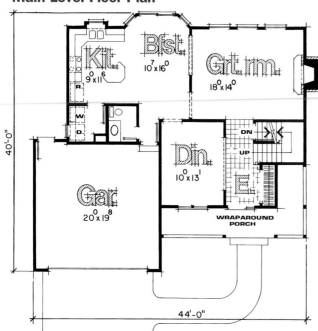

## Upper Level Floor Plan

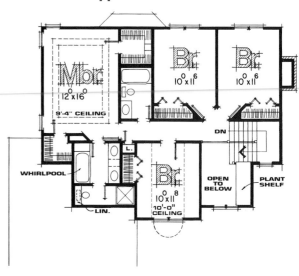

*Copyright by designer/architect.*

# Plan #341071

**Dimensions:** 72'7" W x 38'6" D

**Levels:** 1

**Square Footage:** 1,500

**Bedrooms:** 3

**Bathrooms:** 2

**Foundation:** Crawl space, slab, basement, or walkout

**Materials List Available:** Yes

**Price Category:** C

*Images provided by designer/architect.*

A contemporary ranch design with classic features and country charm, this home promises a relaxing environment that is sure to please.

**Features:**

- **Vaulted Ceilings:** The living room and dining room feature vaulted ceilings, giving these rooms the feeling of spaciousness.

- **Master Suite:** This private area is located toward the rear of the home to add to its seclusion. The walk-in closet has an abundance of space. The master bath boasts dual vanities and a garden tub.

- **Secondary Bedrooms:** Bedroom 2 makes the perfect child's room and is in close proximity to the second full bathroom. Bedroom 3 has built-in bookshelves and a light well for natural illumination.

- **Garage:** A front-loading two-car garage has easy access to the pantry in the kitchen, making grocery unloading simple. The washer and dryer are also close by.

*Copyright by designer/architect.*

*Images provided by designer/architect.*

## Plan #191037

**Dimensions:** 57'4" W x 65' D
**Levels:** 1
**Square Footage:** 1,575
**Bedrooms:** 3
**Bathrooms:** 2
**Foundation:** Crawl space, slab
**Materials List Available:** No
**Price Category:** C

This home seems to expand from the inside out and has everything the growing family needs.

### Features:

- **Great Room:** Gather with guests around the fireplace for conversation or relax with the family in front of the television in this welcoming space.

- **Kitchen:** This area is surrounded by storage and workspace, which includes a center island. Transition easily from the kitchen to the dining room or patio for meals.

- **Master Suite:** A window-flanked whirlpool tub, dual sinks, standing shower, and walk-in closet all make for a relaxing atmosphere in the master bath.

- **Secondary Bedrooms:** Two additional bedrooms are separated from the rest of the house by a small hallway. A compartmentalized full bathroom is shared between the two.

- **Garage:** This two-car garage has extra storage areas, one accessible from the inside, the other accessible from the outside.

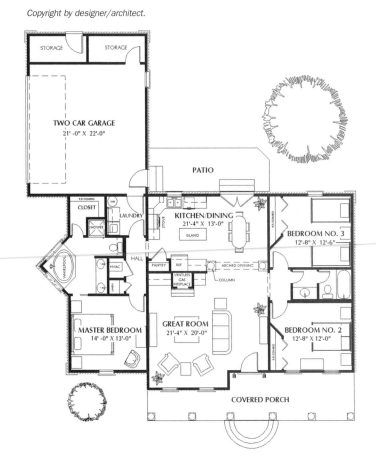

## Plan #171023

**Dimensions:** 74' W x 41' D
**Levels:** 1
**Square Footage:** 1,684
**Bedrooms:** 3
**Bathrooms:** 2
**Foundation:** Crawl space, slab
**Materials List Available:** Yes
**Price Category:** C

*Images provided by designer/architect.*

This house's open and inviting floor plan is wonderful for entertaining or having guests over.

**Features:**

• Master Suite: Located away from the living areas of this home, this private master suite features a large walk-in closet, a garden tub, and a large bedroom area.

• Great Room: You and your guests will love this beautiful room's corner fireplace, location to the dining room and kitchen, and door to the rear porch, great for extending your entertaining outdoors.

• Kitchen: This well-located kitchen features plenty of counter space and easy accessibility to the entertainment areas of the home.

• Secondary Bedrooms: Two additional bedrooms are perfect for the children, or if guests or family stay over.

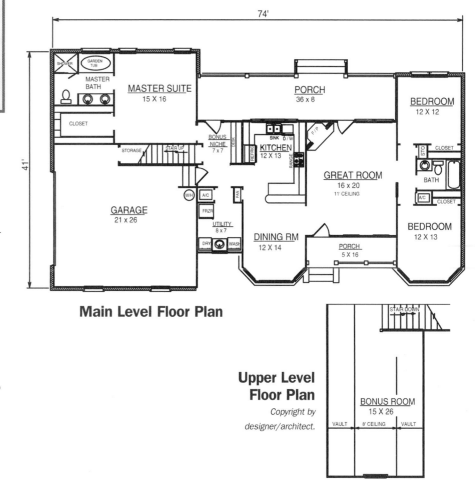

**Main Level Floor Plan**

**Upper Level Floor Plan**
*Copyright by designer/architect.*

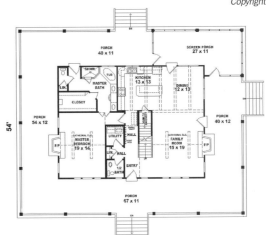

Main Level Floor Plan

Copyright by designer/architect.

## Plan #651079

**Dimensions:** 68' W x 55' D
**Levels:** 1.5
**Square Footage:** 2,207
**Main Level Sq. Ft.:** 1,466
**Upper Level Sq. Ft.:** 741
**Bedrooms:** 3
**Bathrooms:** 2½
**Foundation:** Crawl space or basement
**Materials List Available:** No
**Price Category:** E

*Images provided by designer/architect.*

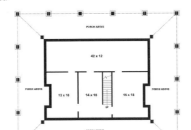

### Lower Level Floor Plan

### Upper Level Floor Pla

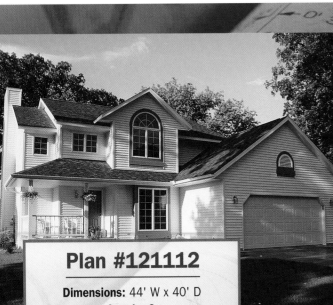

**Upper Level Floor Plan**

**Main Level Floor Plan**

## Plan #121112

**Dimensions:** 44' W x 40' D
**Levels:** 2
**Square Footage:** 1,650
**Main Level Sq. Ft.:** 891
**Upper Level Sq. Ft.:** 759
**Bedrooms:** 3
**Bathrooms:** 2½
**Foundation:** Basement;
crawl space for fee
**Material List Available:** Yes
**Price Category:** C

*Images provided by designer/architect.*

Copyright by designer/architect.

# Plan #511012

**Dimensions:** 50' W x 57'8" D

**Levels:** 1

**Square Footage:** 1,573

**Bedrooms:** 3

**Bathrooms:** 2

**Foundation:** Crawl space or slab

**Material List Available:** No

**Price Category:** C

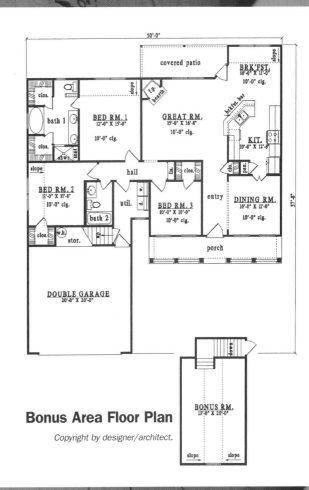

*Images provided by designer/architect.*

covered patio

BRK'FST.
10'-8" X clg.

BED RM. 1
12'-0" X 15'-0"
10'-0" clg.

GREAT RM.
15'-4" X 16'-8"
10'-0" clg.

bath 1

KIT.
10'-0" X 12'-8"

BED RM. 2
13'-0" X 11'-8"
10'-0" clg.

hall

entry

BED RM. 3
10'-0" X 10'-0"
10'-0" clg.

DINING RM.
10'-0" X 11'-0"
10'-0" clg.

util.

bath 2

stor.

porch

DOUBLE GARAGE
20'-0" X 20'-0"

50'-0"

57'-8"

## Bonus Area Floor Plan

BONUS RM.
13'-0" X 20'-0"

slope

slope

*Copyright by designer/architect.*

---

# Plan #181724

**Dimensions:** 55'4"W x 58' D

**Levels:** 1

**Square Footage:** 1,808

**Bedrooms:** 3

**Bathrooms:** 2

**Foundation:** Basement

**Material List Available:** Yes

**Price Category:** D

*Images provided by designer/architect.*

14'-0" X 12'-4"
4,20 X 3,70

14'-0" X 13'-0"
4,20 X 3,90

14'-0" / 17'-8" X 14'-6"
4,20 / 5,30 X 4,35

15'-4" X 19'-0"
4,60 X 5,70

20'-8" X 20'-2"
6,20 X 6,05

10'-0" X 11'-4"
3,00 X 3,40

10'-0" X 11'-4"
3,00 X 3,40

58'-0"
17,4 m

55'-4"
16,6 m

*Copyright by designer/architect.*

## Plan #211070

**Dimensions:** 46' W x 68' D

**Levels:** 2

**Square Footage:** 1,700

**Main Level Sq. Ft.:** 1,160

**Upper Level Sq. Ft.:** 540

**Bedrooms:** 3

**Bathrooms:** 2½

**Foundation:** Crawl space or slab;
basement option for fee

**Materials List Available:** Yes

**Price Category:** C

You'll be charmed by the three roof dormers and the full-width covered porch on this traditional home.

*Images provided by designer/architect.*

**Features:**

• Living Room: With 9-ft. ceilings throughout the living room, dining room, and kitchen merge to maximize usable space and create a spacious, airy feeling in this home. You'll find a fireplace here and three pairs of French doors.

• Dining Room: Walk through this room to the rear covered porch beyond that connects the house to the garage.

• Kitchen: Designed for convenience, this kitchen features a wet bar that is centrally located so that it can easily serve both the living and dining rooms.

• Master Suite: A sloped ceiling with a skylight and French doors leading to the front porch make this area luxurious. The bath includes a raised marble tub, dual-sink vanity, and walk-in closet.

**Main Level Floor Plan**

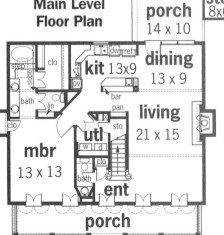

carport
22 x 22

ATTIC STAIRS

porch
14 x 10

sto
8x6

kit 13x9

dining
13 x 9

living
21 x 15

utl

mbr
13 x 13

ent

porch

**Upper Level Floor Plan**

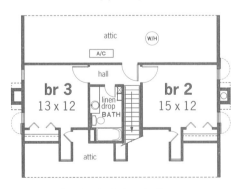

attic

W/H

A/C

hall

br 3
13 x 12

linen drop
BATH

br 2
15 x 12

attic

*Copyright by designer/architect.*

## Plan #151528

**Dimensions:** 41'4" W x 84'2" D

**Levels:** 1

**Square Footage:** 1,747

**Bedrooms:** 2

**Bathrooms:** 2

**Foundation:** Crawl space or slab

**CompleteCost List Available:** Yes

**Price Category:** C

This Craftsman-inspired design combines a rustic exterior with an elegant interior. The 10-ft.-high ceilings and abundance of windows enhance the family areas with plenty of natural lighting.

**CAD FILE AVAILABLE**

**Features:**

- **Great Room:** Featuring a fireplace and built-in computer center, this central gathering area is open to the breakfast room and has access to the rear covered porch.

- **Kitchen:** This combination kitchen and break fast room enjoys a bar counter for additional seating. Note the large laundry room with pantry, which is located between the kitchen and the garage.

- **Master Suite:** You'll spend many luxurious hours in this beautiful suite, with its 10-ft.-high boxed ceiling, his and her walk-in closets, and large bath with glass shower, whirlpool tub, and double vanity.

- **Bedrooms:** On the same side of the home as the master suite are these two other bedrooms, which have large closets and an adjoining bath room between them.

Front View

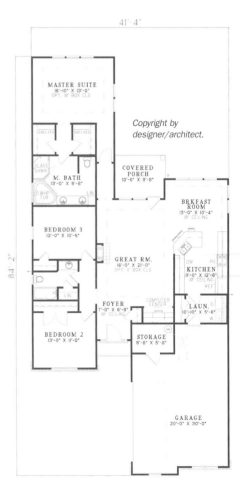

## Plan #121153

**Dimensions:** 62' W x 42'6" D
**Levels:** 1.5
**Square Footage:** 1,984
**Main Level Sq. Ft.:** 1,487
**Upper Level Sq. Ft.:** 497
**Bedrooms:** 3
**Bathrooms:** 2½
**Foundation:** Slab; basement for fee
**Material List Available:** Yes
**Price Category:** D

*Images provided by designer/architect.*

**Features:**

- Living Room: This two-story gathering area is available for family and friends. The fireplace adds a focal point to the room.
- Kitchen: This peninsula kitchen features a raised bar open to the breakfast area. The breakfast area boasts French doors that lead to the future rear deck.

- Master Suite: Residing on the main level is this beautiful retreat, which boasts a tray ceiling. The master bath features dual vanities, whirlpool tub, and a separate toilet area.
- Upper Level: Two secondary bedrooms are found on this level. A large full bathroom is centrally located for easy access.

A stone and stucco exterior give this home an elegant look.

## Main Level Floor Plan

## Upper Level Floor Plan

*Copyright by designer/architect.*

# Plan #391478

**Dimensions:** 70' W x 46' D

**Levels:** 1

**Square Footage:** 1,583

**Bedrooms:** 3

**Bathrooms:** 2

**Foundation:** Crawl space, slab or basement

**Material List Available:** Yes

**Price Category:** C

Tastefully designed, this Country-style home has chic appeal.

## Features:

- Living Room: Charming and spacious, this living room is centrally located.

- Kitchen: The unique design of this kitchen features plenty of room to prepare elegant meals and an octagon-shaped breakfast nook.

- Master Suite: Roomy and beautiful, this master suite features skylights and a compart-mentalized bath.

- Secondary Bedrooms: Enjoy the option of converting one of these two secondary bed-rooms into a den or study. The flexibility of the home's design is appealing and practical.

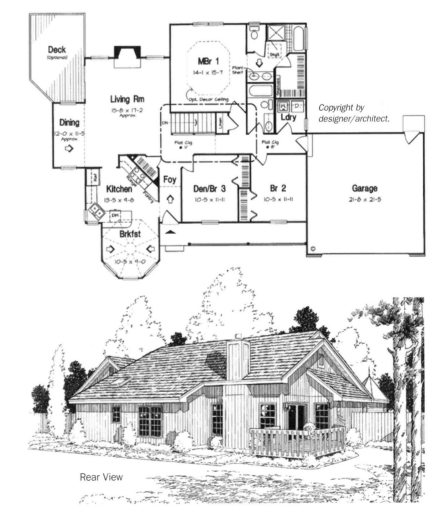

Rear View

## Plan #371007

**Dimensions:** 72'10" W x 48'4½" D

**Levels:** 1

**Square Footage:** 1,944

**Bedrooms:** 4

**Bathrooms:** 2

**Foundation:** Crawl space, slab, or basement

**Materials List Available:** No

**Price Category:** D

*Images provided by designer/architect.*

NOOK 11'-8" x 8'-0" — 9'-0" CEILING

PORCH

STORAGE

UTIL.

STOR.

W/H

RAISED BAR

KITCH. 13' x 13' — ISLAND CABINET

D.W.

OVEN

12'-0" HIGH CEILING FAMILY RM. 15'-0" x 19'-0"

9'-0" HIGH CEILING

GARAGE 20'-8" x 21'-6"

STEP UP CEILING DINING RM. 11'-0" x 12'-0"

ENTRY

STEP UP CEILING MASTER SUITE 12'-0" x 15'-6"

BOXED WINDOW

W.I.C.

B.1

SEAT

SHR.

W.I.C.

9'-0" CLG.

LIN.

B.2

LINEN

DRESS.

STOR.

9'-0" HIGH CEILING BED RM. 4 10'-0" x 10'-6"

W/H

LINEN

DESK

9'-0" HIGH CEILING BED RM. 2 11'-0" x 11'-6"

9'-0" HIGH CEILING BED RM. 3 10'-0" x 11'-0"

PORCH

BOXED WINDOW

---

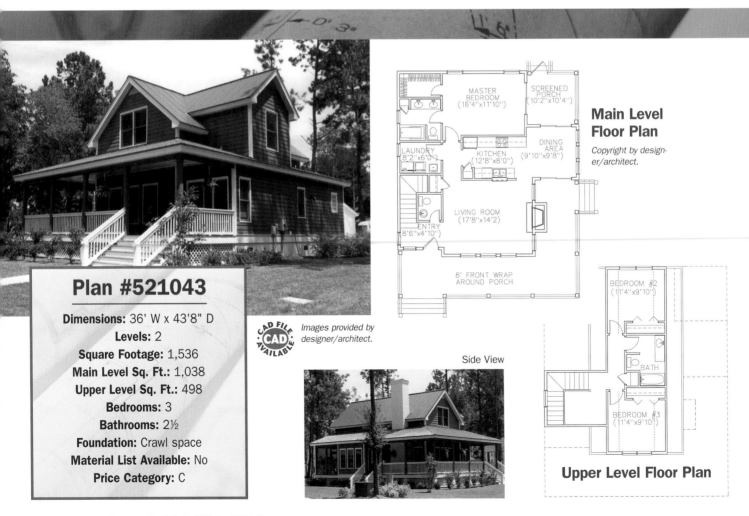

## Plan #521043

**Dimensions:** 36' W x 43'8" D

**Levels:** 2

**Square Footage:** 1,536

**Main Level Sq. Ft.:** 1,038

**Upper Level Sq. Ft.:** 498

**Bedrooms:** 3

**Bathrooms:** 2½

**Foundation:** Crawl space

**Material List Available:** No

**Price Category:** C

*Images provided by designer/architect.*

**Main Level Floor Plan**

*Copyright by designer/architect.*

MASTER BEDROOM (16'4"x11'10")

SCREENED PORCH (10'2"x10'4")

LAUNDRY 8'2"x6'0"

KITCHEN (12'8"x8'0")

DINING AREA (9'10"x9'8")

LIVING ROOM (17'8"x14'2)

ENTRY 8'6"x4'10")

8' FRONT WRAP AROUND PORCH

*Side View*

BEDROOM #2 (11'4"x9'10")

BATH

BEDROOM #3 (11'4"x9'10")

**Upper Level Floor Plan**

**Main Level Floor Plan**

GARAGE
23'-0" x 23'-0"

PORCH

KITCH.
9'-6" x 12'-0"

DINING RM.
11'-0" x 14'-0"

REF.

RAISED BAR

D.W.

UTIL.

W/H

STOR.

BATH 1

WALK IN CLOSET

POWDER ROOM

LIN.

STOR.

LIVING RM.
20'-6" x 16'-0"

STOR. UNDER STAIR

STAIR UP

MASTER SUITE
17'-0" x 12'-6"

WD. RAIL

ENT.

PORCH

CAD FILE AVAILABLE

## Plan #371004

**Dimensions:** 49'10" W x 53'6" D

**Levels:** 2

**Square Footage:** 1,815

**Main Level Sq. Ft.:** 1,245

**Upper Level Sq. Ft.:** 570

**Bedrooms:** 3

**Bathrooms:** 2

**Foundation:** Slab; crawl space for fee

**Materials List Available:** No

**Price Category:** D

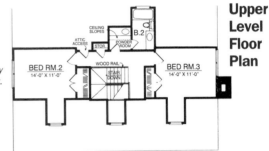

**Upper Level Floor Plan**

CEILING SLOPES

B.2

ATTIC ACCESS

STOR.

POWDER ROOM

BED RM.2
14'-0" X 11'-0"

WOOD RAIL

STAIR DOWN

BED RM.3
14'-0" X 11'-0"

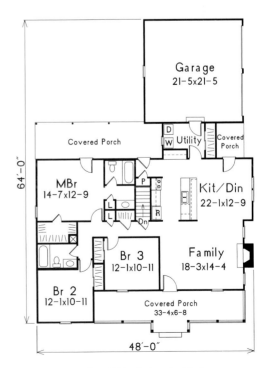

Garage
21-5x21-5

Covered Porch

D

W

Utility

Covered Porch

64'-0"

MBr
14-7x12-9

P

L

R

L

Dn

Kit/Din
22-1x12-9

Br 3
12-1x10-11

Family
18-3x14-4

Br 2
12-1x10-11

Covered Porch
33-4x6-8

48'-0"

## Plan #321015

**Dimensions:** 48' W x 64' D

**Levels:** 1

**Square Footage:** 1,501

**Bedrooms:** 3

**Bathrooms:** 2

**Foundation:** Crawl space, slab, or basement

**Materials List Available:** Yes

**Price Category:** C

CAD FILE AVAILABLE

# Plan #131024

**Dimensions:** 36' W by 54'4" D
**Levels:** 2
**Square Footage:** 1,635
**Main Level Sq. Ft.:** 880
**Upper Level Sq. Ft.:** 755
**Bedrooms:** 3
**Bathrooms:** 2½
**Foundation:** Crawl space, slab, or basement
**Materials List Available:** Yes
**Price Category:** D

*Images provided by designer/architect.*

You'll love the combination of early-American detailing on the outside and the contemporary, open layout of the interior.

**Features:**

• Ceiling Height: 8 ft.

• Front Porch: Use this wraparound front porch as an extra room when the weather's fine.

• Living Room: Separated only by columns, the open arrangement of the living and dining rooms enhances the spacious feeling in this home.

• Family Room/Kitchen: This combination family room/country kitchen includes a large work island and snack bar for convenience.

• Master Suite: A tray ceiling creates a contemporary look in the spacious master bedroom, and three closets make it practical. A compartmented full bath completes the suite.

• Bedrooms: Two additional bedrooms share a second full bath.

• Attic: Finish the attic space that's over the garage for even more living space.

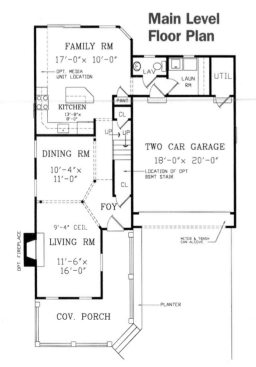

**Main Level Floor Plan**

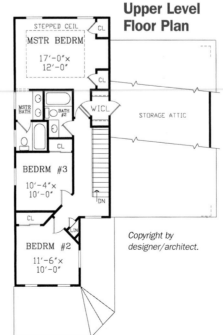

**Upper Level Floor Plan**

*Copyright by designer/architect.*

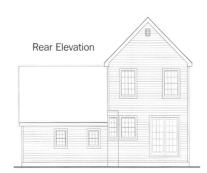

Rear Elevation

# Plan #181644

**Dimensions:** 30' W x 36' D

**Levels:** 2

**Square Footage:** 1,692

**Main Level Sq. Ft.:** 760

**Upper Level Sq. Ft.:** 932

**Bedrooms:** 3

**Bathrooms:** 2½

**Foundation:** Basement

**Material List Available:** Yes

**Price Category:** C

*Images provided by designer/architect.*

A stately mixture of brick and siding create an elegant exterior while the interior has contemporary design in mind.

**Features:**

• Living Room: This large room has plenty of space for guests or lounging family members. French doors separate it from the rest of the main level to maintain different activities in different areas.

• Kitchen: This uniquely designed kitchen features lots of workspace, a walk-in pantry, and a curvaceous snack bar.

• Second Level: Relax with a good book by the fireplace in the spacious master bedroom. A large walk-in closet simplifies morning wardrobe decisions. This and two additional bedrooms share access to two full bathrooms. The larger of the two reduces morning confusion with its dual vanities and separate tub and shower.

**Main Level Floor Plan**

**Upper Level Floor Plan**

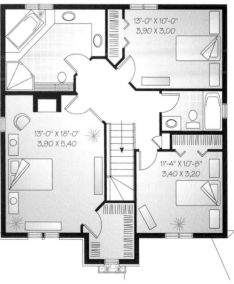

*Copyright by designer/architect.*

# Plan #151490

**Dimensions:** 52' W x 69'6" D

**Levels:** 1

**Square Footage:** 1,869

**Bedrooms:** 3

**Bathrooms:** 2

**Foundation:** Crawl space or slab

**CompleteCost List Available:** Yes

**Price Category:** D

Beautiful brick and wood siding impart warmth to this French Country design.

**Features:**

- Open Plan: Elegance is achieved in this home by using boxed columns and 10-ft.-high ceilings. The foyer and dining room are lined with columns and adjoin the great room, all with high ceilings.

- Kitchen: This combined kitchen and breakfast room is great for entertaining and has access to the grilling porch.

- Master Suite: The split-bedroom plan features this suite, with its large walk-in closet, whirlpool tub, shower, and private area.

- Bedrooms: The two bedrooms and a large bathroom are located on the other side of the great room, giving privacy to the entire family.

*Images provided by designer/architect.*

**Bonus Area Floor Plan**

BONUS ROOM
12'-10" X 20'-4"

4' WALL
8' LINE
4' WALL

52'-0"

OPTIONAL GRILLING PORCH
15'-10" X 10'-0"

BEDROOM 3
11'-8" X 11'-2"

GREAT RM.
10' BOXED CEILING
15'-0" X 19'-2"

BREAKFAST ROOM
10'-0" X 10'-0"

MASTER SUITE
12' BOXED CEILING
13'-6" X 14'-0"

KITCHEN
9'-8" X 10'-9"

BATH

FOYER
10' CEILING
6'-4" X 9'-6"

DINING ROOM
10' CEILING
11'-10" X 11'-0"

LAU.

M. BATH
9'-8" X 13'-0"

BEDROOM 2
11'-8" X 14'-0"

COVERED PORCH

STORAGE
19'-6" X 4'-4"

GARAGE
20'-8" X 20'-4"

69'-6"

*Copyright by designer/architect.*

## Plan #121044

**Dimensions:** 40' W x 55'8" D

**Levels:** 2

**Square Footage:** 1,923

**Main Level Sq. Ft.:** 1,351

**Upper Level Sq. Ft.:** 572

**Bedrooms:** 3

**Bathrooms:** 3

**Foundation:** Basement

**Materials List Available:** Yes

**Price Category:** D

*Images provided by designer/architect.*

The layout of this gracious home is designed with the contemporary family in mind.

**Features:**

• Ceiling Height: 8 ft. unless otherwise noted.

• Foyer: This elegant entry is graced with an open stairway that enhances the sense of spaciousness.

• Kitchen: Located just beyond the entry, this convenient kitchen features a center island that doubles as a snack bar.

• Breakfast Area: A sloped ceiling unites this area with the family room. Here you will find a planning desk for compiling menus and shopping lists.

• Master Bedroom: This bedroom has a distinctively contemporary appeal, with its cathedral ceiling and triple window.

• Computer Loft: Designed to house a computer, this loft overlooks the family room.

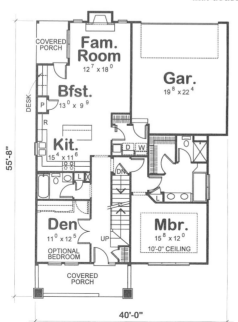

Main Level Floor Plan

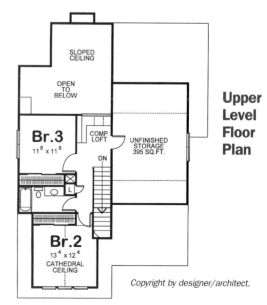

Upper Level Floor Plan

*Copyright by designer/architect.*

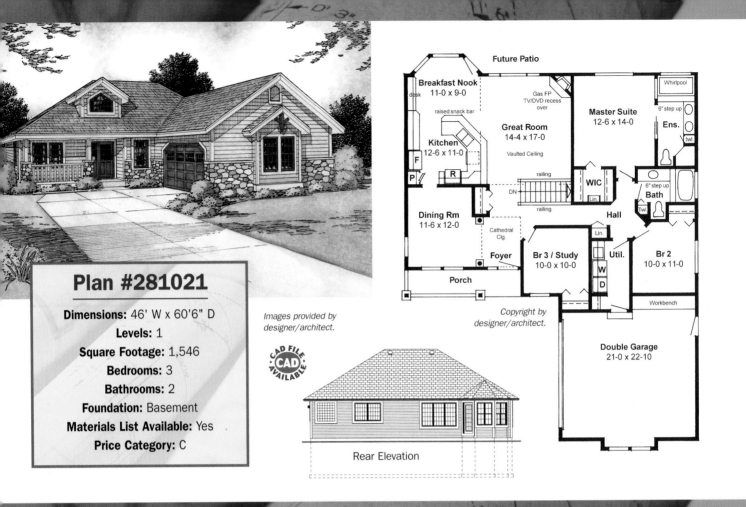

## Plan #281021

**Dimensions:** 46' W x 60'6" D

**Levels:** 1

**Square Footage:** 1,546

**Bedrooms:** 3

**Bathrooms:** 2

**Foundation:** Basement

**Materials List Available:** Yes

**Price Category:** C

*Images provided by designer/architect.*

Rear Elevation

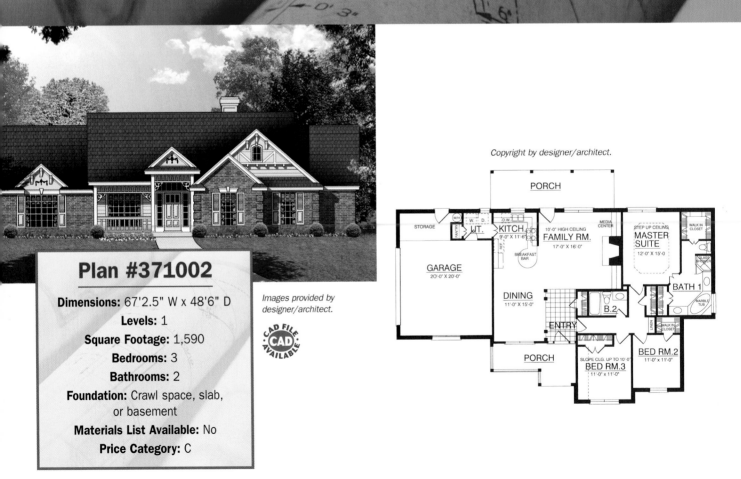

## Plan #371002

**Dimensions:** 67'2.5" W x 48'6" D

**Levels:** 1

**Square Footage:** 1,590

**Bedrooms:** 3

**Bathrooms:** 2

**Foundation:** Crawl space, slab, or basement

**Materials List Available:** No

**Price Category:** C

*Images provided by designer/architect.*

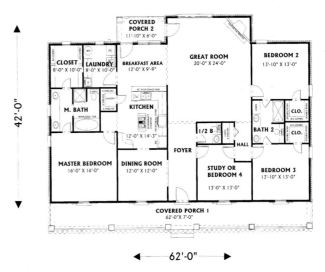

*Images provided by designer/architect.*

## Plan #191027

**Dimensions:** 62' W x 42' D

**Levels:** 1

**Square Footage:** 2,354

**Bedrooms:** 4

**Bathrooms:** 2½

**Foundation:** Crawl space or slab

**Materials List Available:** No

**Price Category:** E

*Copyright by designer/architect.*

---

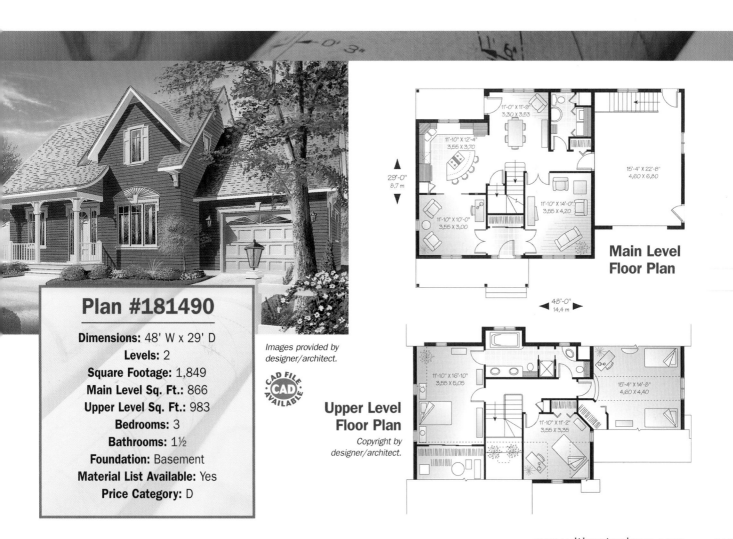

**Main Level Floor Plan**

**Upper Level Floor Plan**

*Images provided by designer/architect.*

CAD FILE AVAILABLE

*Copyright by designer/architect.*

## Plan #181490

**Dimensions:** 48' W x 29' D

**Levels:** 2

**Square Footage:** 1,849

**Main Level Sq. Ft.:** 866

**Upper Level Sq. Ft.:** 983

**Bedrooms:** 3

**Bathrooms:** 1½

**Foundation:** Basement

**Material List Available:** Yes

**Price Category:** D

## Plan #211069

**Dimensions:** 58' W x 42' D
**Levels:** 1.5
**Square Footage:** 1,600
**Main Level Sq. Ft.:** 1,136
**Upper Level Sq. Ft.:** 464
**Bedrooms:** 3
**Bathrooms:** 2
**Foundation:** Crawl space
**Materials List Available:** Yes
**Price Category:** C

Enjoy the large front porch on this traditionally styled home when it's too sunny for the bugs, and use the screened back porch at dusk and dawn.

**Features:**

• Living Room: Call this the family room if you wish, but no matter what you call it, expect friends and family to gather here, especially when the fireplace gives welcome warmth.

• Kitchen: You'll love the practical layout that pleases everyone from gourmet chefs to beginning cooks.

• Master Suite: Positioned on the main floor to give it privacy, this suite has two entrances for convenience. You'll find a large walk-in closet here as well as a dressing room that includes a separate vanity and mirror makeup counter.

• Storage Space: The 462-sq.-ft. garage is roomy enough to hold two cars and still have space to store tools, out-of-season clothing, or whatever else that needs a dry, protected spot.

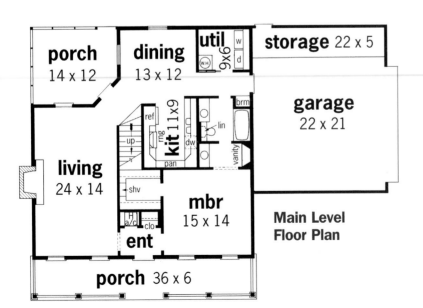

**Main Level Floor Plan**

porch 14 x 12
dining 13 x 12
util 9x6
storage 22 x 5
garage 22 x 21
ref
rng
kit 11x9
dw
pan
brm
lin
vanity
living 24 x 14
up
shv
mbr 15 x 14
a/c
clo
ent
porch 36 x 6

## Upper Level Floor Plan

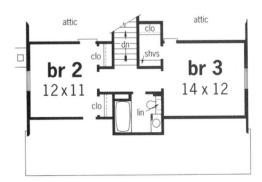

attic
clo
dn
shvs
attic
br 2 12 x 11
clo
clo
br 3 14 x 12
clo
lin

## Plan #181242

**Dimensions:** 48' W x 35'4" D

**Levels:** 2

**Square Footage:** 1,826

**Main Level Sq. Ft.:** 918

**Upper Level Sq. Ft.:** 908

**Bedrooms:** 3

**Bathrooms:** 2

**Foundation:** Basement

**Materials List Available:** Yes

**Price Category:** D

*Images provided by designer/architect.*

This charming home has room for everyone.

**Features:**

• Foyer: This closed entry space will work as an "air-lock" to help keep heating and cooling costs down.

• Kitchen: L-shaped, with an eat-in design, this kitchen has a lunch counter for added seating space.

• Family Room: This relaxing area has a cozy fireplace and a large window looking onto the front yard.

• Master Bedroom: A his-and-her walk-in closet graces this large bedroom.

• Bedrooms: The two secondary bedrooms have large closets, and each has a unique nook.

## Main Level Floor Plan

*Copyright by designer/architect.*

## Upper Level Floor Plan

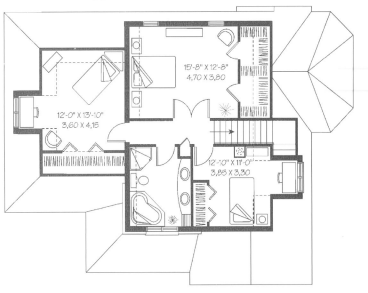

## Plan #181217

**Dimensions:** 38' W x 35' D

**Levels:** 2

**Square Footage:** 1,588

**Main Level Sq. Ft.:** 778

**Upper Level Sq. Ft.:** 810

**Bedrooms:** 3

**Bathrooms:** 1½

**Foundation:** Basement

**Materials List Available:** Yes

**Price Category:** C

*Images provided by designer/architect.*

Growing families will embrace all the charm and comfort of this Victorian-style three-bedroom home.

**Features:**

• Style: Timeless exterior styling begins with a covered front porch and beautiful windows, including a bright bay.

• Entry: Double windows in the closed front entrance infuse this space with cheerful natural light.

• Kitchen: A circular lunch counter rounds off this U-shaped kitchen, which has a nearby laundry and half bath.

• Bathroom: This upstairs full bath features a separate shower and tub for bathing in beauty and luxurious comfort.

*Copyright by designer/architect.*

**Main Level Floor Plan**

**Upper Level Floor Plan**

Copyright by designer/architect.

## Plan #521040

**Dimensions:** 42'2" W x 57' D
**Levels:** 1
**Square Footage:** 1,555
**Bedrooms:** 3
**Bathrooms:** 2½
**Foundation:** Slab
**Material List Available:** No
**Price Category:** C

Beautifully and intelligently designed, this house has everything you want and everything you need.

*CAD FILE AVAILABLE*

### Features:

• **Porches:** The front porch provides a covered entry while still being open to the sights and sounds of the outdoors, ideal for sitting outside on a lovely evening. On the opposite end

of the house is a screened-in porch that opens into the master suite, the living room, and the deck. It is perfect for keeping out unwanted pests and bringing in the breeze. Next to that is the deck, great for soaking up the sun and barbecuing.

• **Living Room:** With light from the dining-area windows and the deck and warmth from the fireplace, this room can become anything you want it to be: warm and cozy or light and airy.

• **Kitchen:** This working area has a walk-in pantry and plenty of workspace and storage, and it opens freely into the dining room. As the busiest part of any home, the kitchen is

perfect for gatherings or simple family dinners, making the transition between preparing and serving simple.

• **Master Suite:** A spacious full bath, a large walk-in closet, and a direct entrance to the screened porch make this the ideal place to rest and relax. It is truly a master's bedroom.

• **Bedrooms:** The secondary bedrooms each have their highlights. Bedroom No. 2 has a wide closet and lots of light from its three extended windows while being a short distance from the second full bathroom. Bedroom No. 3 has a direct connection with the bathroom and a small walk-in closet. Both are also a short distance from the large laundry room.

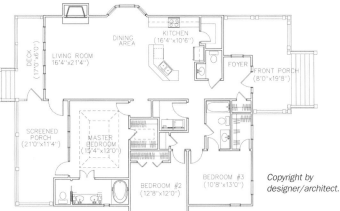

Copyright by designer/architect.

Front View

Rear View

*This home, as shown in the photographs, may differ from the actual blueprints. For more detailed information, please check the floor plans carefully.*

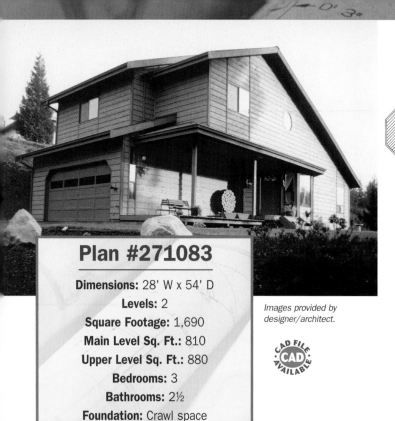

## Plan #271083

**Dimensions:** 28' W x 54' D

**Levels:** 2

**Square Footage:** 1,690

**Main Level Sq. Ft.:** 810

**Upper Level Sq. Ft.:** 880

**Bedrooms:** 3

**Bathrooms:** 2½

**Foundation:** Crawl space

**Materials List Available:** Yes

**Price Category:** C

*Images provided by designer/architect.*

**CAD FILE AVAILABLE**

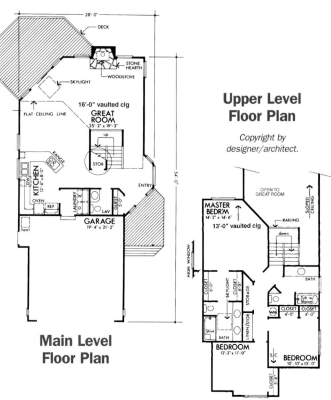

**Upper Level Floor Plan**

*Copyright by designer/architect.*

**Main Level Floor Plan**

## Plan #111046

**Dimensions:** 37' W x 57' D

**Levels:** 2

**Square Footage:** 1,768

**Main Level Sq. Ft.:** 1,247

**Upper Level Sq. Ft.:** 521

**Bedrooms:** 3

**Bathrooms:** 2½

**Foundation:** Crawl space

**Materials List Available:** No

**Price Category:** D

*Images provided by designer/architect.*

**Main Level Floor Plan**

**Upper Level Floor Plan**

*Copyright by designer/architect.*

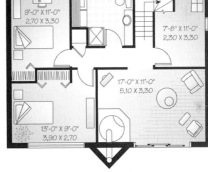

## Plan #241015

**Dimensions:** 67'2" W x 46'10" D

**Levels:** 1

**Square Footage:** 1,609

**Bedrooms:** 3

**Bathrooms:** 2

**Foundation:** Slab

**Material List Available:** No

**Price Category:** C

*Images provided by designer/architect.*

*Copyright by designer/architect.*

**Lower Level Floor Plan**

**Main Level Floor Plan**

## Plan #181106

**Dimensions:** 32'4" W x 25'6" D

**Levels:** 1

**Square Footage:** 1,648

**Main Level Sq. Ft.:** 824

**Lower Level Sq. Ft.:** 824

**Bedrooms:** 3

**Bathrooms:** 2

**Foundation:** Basement or walkout

**Materials List Available:** Yes

**Price Category:** C

*Images provided by designer/architect.*

*Copyright by designer/architect.*

## Plan #271030

**Dimensions:** 55'8" W x 45' D

**Levels:** 2

**Square Footage:** 1,926

**Main Level Sq. Ft.:** 1,490

**Upper Level Sq. Ft.:** 436

**Bedrooms:** 3

**Bathrooms:** 2½

**Foundation:** Crawl space or basement

**Materials List Available:** Yes

**Price Category:** D

*Images provided by designer/architect.*

This traditional home's main-floor master suite is hard to resist, with its inviting window seat and delightful bath.

**Features:**

• Master Suite: Just off from the entry foyer, this luxurious oasis is entered through double doors, and offers an airy vaulted ceiling, plus a private bath that includes a separate tub and shower, dual-sink vanity, and walk-in closet.

• Great Room: This space does it all in style, with a breathtaking wall of windows and a charming fireplace.

• Kitchen: A cooktop island makes dinnertime tasks a breeze. You'll also love the roomy pantry. The adjoining breakfast room, with its deck access and built-in desk, is sure to be a popular hangout for the teens.

• Secondary Bedrooms: Two additional bedrooms reside on the upper floor and allow the younger family members a measure of desired—and necessary—privacy.

**CAD FILE AVAILABLE**

## Main Level Floor Plan

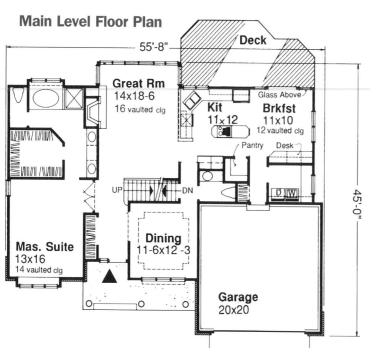

## Upper Level Floor Plan

*Copyright by designer/architect.*

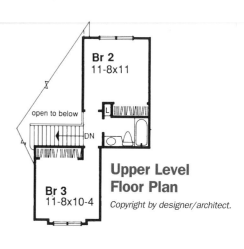

## Plan #211030

**Dimensions:** 75' W x 37' D

**Levels:** 1

**Square Footage:** 1,600

**Bedrooms:** 3

**Bathrooms:** 2

**Foundation:** Slab

**Materials List Available:** Yes

**Price Category:** C

You'll love the way your family can make use of the well-designed living space in this home.

*Images provided by designer/architect.*

**Features:**

- Living Room: The exposed beams in the 16-ft. tall vaulted ceiling, stone hearth for the fireplace, and 6-in. sunken floor add up to pure luxury.

- Dining Room: A divider sets off this room, but even so, it feels open to the other areas.

- Kitchen: A built-in snack bar separates this room from the dining room. A large pantry closet and amply counter area make it a cook's delight.

- Sewing Room: Set between the kitchen and the laundry room, this area is ideal for the sewer.

- Master Suite: A sunken floor and sitting room are luxurious amenities to add to the walk-in closet and bath with separate tub and shower.

- Storage Room: Just off the garage, this large room has open space and built-in shelves.

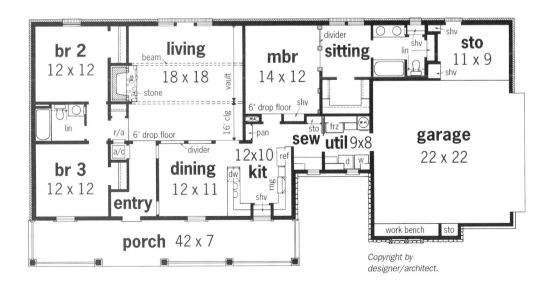

*Copyright by designer/architect.*

# Plan #571078

**Dimensions:** 30' W x 32' D
**Levels:** 2
**Square Footage:** 1,870
**Main Level Sq. Ft.:** 935
**Upper Level Sq. Ft.:** 935
**Bedrooms:** 3
**Bathrooms:** 2½
**Foundation:** Basement
**Material List Available:** Yes
**Price Category:** D

This sweet home, country in style, is the perfect haven for your growing family.

*Copyright by designer/architect.*

*Images provided by designer/architect.*

**Features:**

• Entry: Enter through a beautiful front porch with ornamental spindles and plenty of space for rocking chairs.

• Living Room: This capacious living area features the option of an added fireplace for warmth and comfort.

• Master Suite: This conglomeration of bed and bath is at the height of luxury. With dual vanity sinks, a whirlpool tub, and walk-in closet, the rooms are sure to be a wonderful retreat from everyday stresses.

• Home Theater: Entertain the option of converting this optional space into a home theater, with a large-screened TV and top-notch sound system for a quality experience.

Rear Elevation

**Main Level Floor Plan**

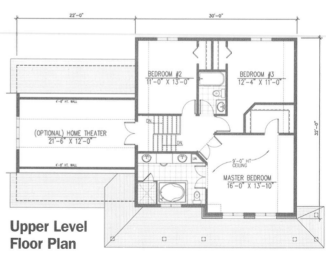

**Upper Level Floor Plan**

## Plan #121027

**Dimensions:** 46' W x 48' D

**Levels:** 2

**Square Footage:** 1,660

**Main Level Sq. Ft.:** 1,265

**Upper Level Sq. Ft.:** 395

**Bedrooms:** 3

**Bathrooms:** 2½

**Foundation:** Basement

**Materials List Available:** Yes

**Price Category:** C

*Images provided by designer/architect.*

This elegant home is designed for architectural interest and gracious living.

**Features:**

• Ceiling Height: 8 ft. unless otherwise noted.

• Great Room: Family and guests will be drawn to this inviting, sun-filled room with its 13-ft. ceiling and raised-hearth fireplace.

• Formal Dining Room: An angled ceiling lends architectural interest to this elegant room. Alternately, this room can be used as a parlor.

• Master Suite: Corner windows are designed to ease furniture placement. The sunlit whirlpool bath invites you to take time to luxuriate and rejuvenate. There's a double vanity, separate shower, and a walk-in closet.

• Garage: This two bay garage offers plenty of space for storage in addition to parking.

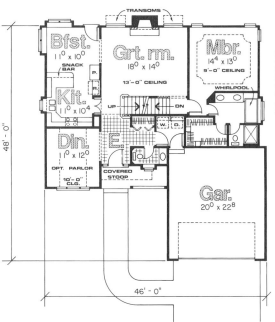

**Main Level Floor Plan**

**Upper Level Floor Plan**

*Copyright by designer/architect.*

## Plan #571056

**Dimensions:** 26' W x 34' D

**Levels:** 2

**Square Footage:** 1,559

**Main Level Sq. Ft.:** 799

**Upper Level Sq. Ft.:** 760

**Bedrooms:** 3

**Bathrooms:** 1½

**Foundation:** Basement

**Material List Available:** Yes

**Price Category:** C

**Main Level Floor Plan**

*Images provided by designer/architect.*

*Copyright by designer/architect.*

Rear Elevation

**Upper Level Floor Plan**

## Plan #521030

**Dimensions:** 41'8" W x 41' D

**Levels:** 2

**Square Footage:** 1,660

**Main Level Sq. Ft.:** 1,034

**Upper Level Sq. Ft.:** 626

**Bedrooms:** 4

**Bathrooms:** 2½

**Foundation:** Crawl space

**Materials List Available:** No

**Price Category:** C

*Images provided by designer/architect.*

**Main Level Floor Plan**

**Upper Level Floor Plan**

*Copyright by designer/architect.*

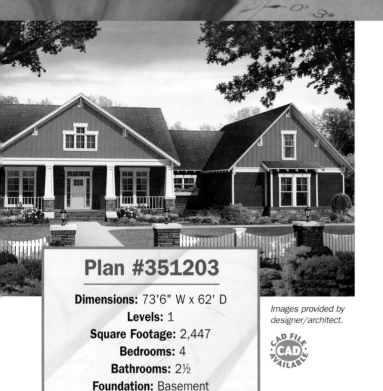

## Plan #351203

**Dimensions:** 73'6" W x 62' D
**Levels:** 1
**Square Footage:** 2,447
**Bedrooms:** 4
**Bathrooms:** 2½
**Foundation:** Basement
**Material List Available:** Yes
**Price Category:** E

*Images provided by designer/architect.*

**CAD FILE AVAILABLE** CAD

**Main Level Floor Plan**

**Bonus Level Floor Plan**

*Copyright by designer/architect.*

## Plan #311032

**Dimensions:** 69' W x 67'4" D
**Levels:** 1
**Square Footage:** 2,127
**Bedrooms:** 3
**Bathrooms:** 2½
**Foundation:** Basement
**Material List Available:** Yes
**Price Category:** D

*Images provided by designer/architect.*

Rear Elevation

**Main Level Floor Plan**

*Copyright by designer/architect.*

**Bonus Level Floor Plan**

## Plan #121094

**Dimensions:** 40'8" W x 46' D
**Levels:** 2
**Square Footage:** 1,768
**Main Level Sq. Ft.:** 905
**Upper Level Sq. Ft.:** 863
**Bedrooms:** 3
**Bathrooms:** 2½
**Foundation:** Basement
**Materials List Available:** Yes
**Price Category:** C

*Images provided by designer/architect.*

You'll love this design if you're looking for a home to complement a site with a lovely rear view.

**Features:**

- Great Room: A trio of lovely windows looks out to the rear entry of this home. The French doors in this room open to the breakfast area for everyone's convenience.

- Kitchen: Designed to suit a gourmet cook, this kitchen includes a roomy pantry and an island with a snack bar.

- Breakfast Area: The boxed window here is perfect for houseplants or a collection of culinary herbs. A door leads to the rear porch, where you'll love to dine in good weather.

- Master Suite: On the upper level, the bedroom features a cathedral ceiling, two walk-in closets, and a window seat. The bath also has a cathedral ceiling and includes dual lavatories, a large dressing area, and a sunlit whirlpool tub.

### Main Level Floor Plan

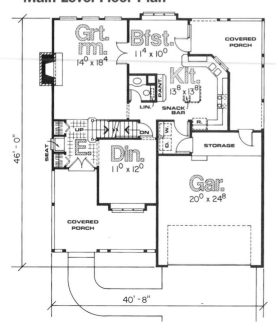

### Upper Level Floor Plan

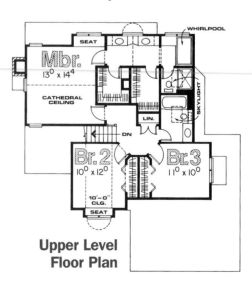

*Copyright by designer/architect.*

# Plan #401036

**Dimensions:** 42' W x 38' D
**Levels:** 2
**Square Footage:** 1,583
**Main Level Sq. Ft.:** 1,050
**Upper Level Sq. Ft.:** 533
**Bedrooms:** 3
**Bathrooms:** 2
**Foundation:** Basement
**Materials List Available:** Yes
**Price Category:** C

What a combination — a charming turn-of-the-century exterior with a contemporary interior! A wraparound railed porch and rear deck expand the living space to outdoor entertaining.

## Features:

- **High Ceilings:** Vaulted ceilings throughout the great room and dining room add spaciousness, while a fireplace warms the area.

- **Master Suite:** Located on the first floor for privacy and convenience, this suite boasts a roomy walk-in closet and private bathroom with a whirlpool tub, separate shower, and dual vanities.

- **Bedrooms:** Two vaulted family bedrooms on the second floor share a full bathroom. Note the loft area and extra storage space.

*Images provided by designer/architect.*

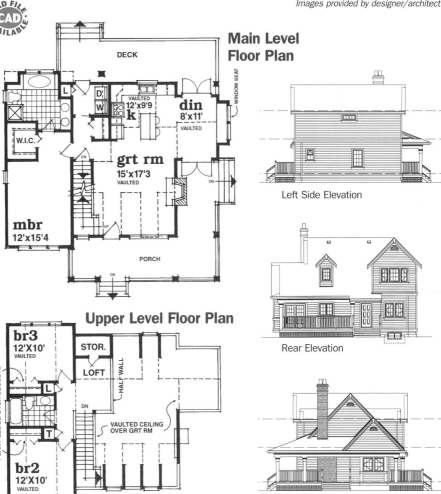

**Main Level Floor Plan**

**Upper Level Floor Plan**

Left Side Elevation

Rear Elevation

Right Side Elevation

*Copyright by designer/architect.*

## Plan #351005

**Dimensions:** 61' W x 47'4" D

**Levels:** 1

**Square Footage:** 1,501

**Bedrooms:** 3

**Bathrooms:** 2

**Foundation:** Crawl space, slab, or basement

**Materials List Available:** Yes

**Price Category:** E

*Images provided by designer/architect.*

This home provides a very functional split-floor-plan layout with many of the features that your family desires.

**Features:**

- Porches: Enjoy the beautiful weather on one of your porches, front and rear.

- Great Room: This large room, with its vaulted ceiling and gas log fireplace, is perfect for entertaining.

- Kitchen: With plenty of counter space for that growing family, this kitchen has an open layout.

- Master Suite: This expansive master bedroom and bathroom area has plenty of storage space in the separate walk-in closets.

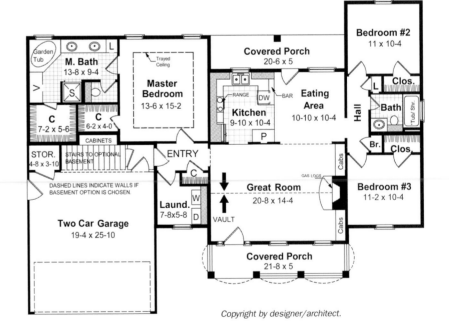

*Copyright by designer/architect.*

# Plan #441004

**Dimensions:** 55' W x 48' D

**Levels:** 1

**Square Footage:** 1,728

**Bedrooms:** 2

**Bathrooms:** 2

**Foundation:** Crawl space; slab or basement for fee

**Materials List Available:** Yes

**Price Category:** C

Empty nesters and first-time homeowners will adore the comfort within this charming home. Rooms benefit from the many windows, which welcome light into the home.

**Features:**

- **Great Room:** This vaulted room is equipped with a media center and fireplace. Windows span across the back of the room and the adjoining dining room, extending the perceived area and offering access to the covered patio.

- **Kitchen:** Taking advantage of corner space, this kitchen provides ample cabinets and countertops to store goods and prepare meals. Every chef will appreciate the extra space afforded by the pantry.

- **Master Suite:** This luxurious escape has a large sleeping area with views of the backyard. The master bath features a spa tub, dual vanities, and a walk-in closet.

- **Garage:** This front-loading two-car garage has a shop area located in the rear.

*Images provided by designer/architect.*

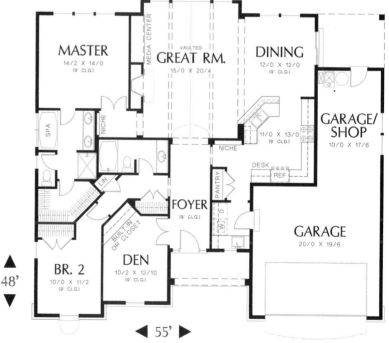

*Copyright by designer/architect.*

Rear Elevation

## Plan #571077

**Dimensions:** 30' W x 34' D
**Levels:** 2
**Square Footage:** 1,945
**Main Level Sq. Ft.:** 979
**Upper Level Sq. Ft.:** 966
**Bedrooms:** 3
**Bathrooms:** 2½
**Foundation:** Basement
**Material List Available:** Yes
**Price Category:** D

*Images provided by designer/architect.*

### Main Level Floor Plan

### Upper Level Floor Plan

*Copyright by designer/architect.*

---

## Plan #631065

**Dimensions:** 78'8" W x 39'8" D
**Levels:** 1
**Square Footage:** 1,682
**Bedrooms:** 3
**Bathrooms:** 2
**Foundation:** Basement
**Materials List Available:** Yes
**Price Category:** C

*Images provided by designer/architect.*

CAD FILE AVAILABLE

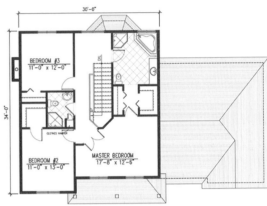

### Main Level Floor Plan

*Copyright by designer/architect.*

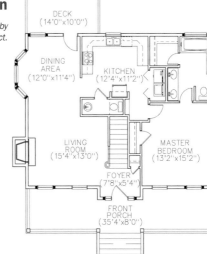

## Main Level Floor Plan

*Copyright by designer/architect.*

DECK (14'0"x10'0")

DINING AREA (12'0"x11'4")

KITCHEN (12'4"x11'2")

LIVING ROOM (15'4"x13'0")

MASTER BEDROOM (13'2"x15'2")

FOYER (7'8"x5'4")

FRONT PORCH (35'4"x8'0")

*Images provided by designer/architect.*

CAD FILE AVAILABLE

## Plan #521042

**Dimensions:** 37'8" W x 46' D
**Levels:** 2
**Square Footage:** 1,552
**Main Level Sq. Ft.:** 1,020
**Upper Level Sq. Ft.:** 532
**Bedrooms:** 3
**Bathrooms:** 2½
**Foundation:** Crawl space
**Material List Available:** No
**Price Category:** C

BATH

BEDROOM #2 (12'8"x13'4")

BEDROOM #3 (13'0"x13'4")

## Upper Level Floor Plan

patio

porch 12 x 6

sto 9x5

sto 9x5

eating 12 x 10

living 20 x 20 flat clg

mbr 16 x 13

garage 22 x 22

kit 12x10

dining 12 x 11

entry

br 3 14 x 12

br 2 14 x 12

porch 46 x 6

*Copyright by designer/architect.*

*Images provided by designer/architect.*

CAD FILE AVAILABLE

## Plan #211036

**Dimensions:** 80' W x 40' D
**Levels:** 1
**Square Footage:** 1,800
**Bedrooms:** 3
**Bathrooms:** 2
**Foundation:** Slab
**Materials List Available:** Yes
**Price Category:** D

## SMARTtip

## Dimmer Switches

You can dim lights just slightly to extend lamp life and save energy, and there will be very little perceptible change in light level. For instance, dimming the light to 50 percent will be perceived as though the light were only dimmed to 70 percent. Therefore, there is no dramatic dilation or constriction of the eye due to light level change.

# Plan #101022

**Dimensions:** 66'2" W x 62' D

**Levels:** 1

**Square Footage:** 1,992

**Bedrooms:** 3

**Bathrooms:** 3

**Foundation:** Crawl space, slab, or basement

**Materials List Available:** Yes

**Price Category:** D

*Images provided by designer/architect.*

The exterior of this lovely home is traditional, but the unusually shaped rooms and amenities are contemporary.

**Features:**

- **Foyer:** This two-story foyer is open to the family room, but columns divide it from the dining room.

- **Family Room:** A gas fireplace and TV niche, flanked by doors to the covered porch, sit at the rear of this seven-sided, spacious room.

- **Breakfast Room:** Set off from the family room by columns, this area shares a snack bar with the kitchen and has windows looking over the porch.

- **Bedroom 3:** Use this room as a living room if you wish, and transform the guest room to a media room or a family bedroom.

- **Master Suite:** The bedroom features a tray ceiling, has his and her dressing areas, and opens to the porch. The bath has a large corner tub, separate shower, linen closet, and two vanities.

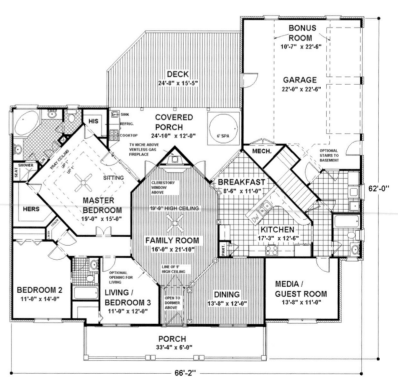

*Copyright by designer/architect.*

Kitchen

Living Room

Dining Room

Family Room

Master Bedroom

Master Bath

# Window Treatments for Kitchens & Family rooms

**K**itchens and family rooms are the busiest rooms of your home, the spaces where the real day-to-day living takes place—preparing and sharing meals and snacks, catching up on paperwork or homework, enjoying all kinds of home entertainment, working on projects, and even doing the laundry.

You'll want these rooms to be warm, welcoming, informal places where family and friends can kick back and truly feel at home. Simple, functional, easy-care window treatments will be most comfortable to live with in these hardworking rooms, but that doesn't mean you can't incorporate charm, style, or even drama.

**The combination of blue and yellow plaids** infuses this bow-trimmed valance with French-country charm, opposite.

**Fruit prints** are perfect for a kitchen. Tone down a bold print by using it for valances, combined with plain café curtains, tabbed and banded with a coordinating plaid, above.

**Choose wooden shutters** for a clean window treatment that lets your table take center stage, left.

## Country Style

Country styles remain the all-time most popular choices for kitchens and family rooms—for good reasons. They're comforting because they evoke the past in a gentle, homey, unpretentious way. In kitchens, where food is the focus, country style serves as a reminder of the origins of the ingredients you're using to prepare a favorite family recipe. The materials of country styles are inexpensive and easy to maintain. Simple cottons, such as muslin, gingham, calico, ticking, homespun, and plain linens wash easily and age well, actually looking better over time. Shutters and blinds wipe clean easily and open wide to expel odors and let in fresh air.

**Use a gathered valance** to maximize light from a small bay window, left. Matching it to the sofa helps unify this relaxed family room.
**Choose natural linen** in softly tailored styles, below, to evoke understated French elegance.

**Use unbleached muslin** for tied-back curtains to create an iconic American farmhouse look, above.

**Use casually pinned-up panels** to suggest traditional-style draperies, opposite top. Weight the edges of lightweight fabric with heavier bands to help them fall gracefully.

**These valances have been gathered** and tacked up at the top corners of the windows in a style that was first popular in the early twentieth century, opposite bottom.

**Choose a ruffled valance,** right, for a cheerful, straightforward look, and hang matchstick blinds beneath to control light.

**Bright prints** on dark backgrounds, below, are commonly used on windows in Mediterranean homes to keep rooms cool and shady.

**These simple, graceful valances** are just straight lengths of fabric, pleated and held by wooden holdbacks, opposite top.

**Use classic chintz** in subdued colors, opposite bottom, to bring English country-house decorum to your kitchen.

# Plan #131007

**Dimensions:** 59'10" W x 47'8" D

**Levels:** 1

**Square Footage:** 1,595

**Bedrooms:** 3

**Bathrooms:** 2

**Foundation:** Crawl space, slab, basement, or walkout

**Materials List Available:** Yes

**Price Category:** D

Imagine living in this home, with its traditional country comfort and individual brand of charm.

**Features:**

- Exterior elements: The mixture of a front porch with a cameo front door, decorative posts, bay windows, and dormers will delight you.

- Great Room: A tray ceiling gives distinction to this large room, and a wet bar eases entertaining.

- Screened Porch: At dusk and dawn, this porch is sure to be your favorite outdoor spot.

- Kitchen: Eat any meal in this large kitchen for a touch of homey charm.

- Dining Room: Perfect for hosting a formal dinner, this bayed dining room can increase your enjoyment of simple family meals.

- Master Bedroom: For the sake of privacy, this room is somewhat secluded. Decorate to emphasize the elegant tray ceiling.

*Images provided by designer/architect.*

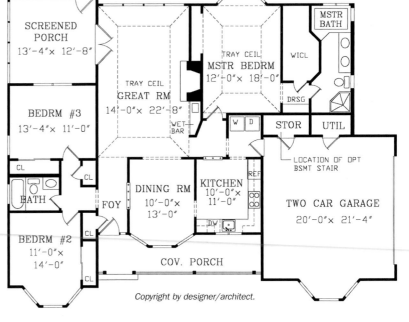

*Copyright by designer/architect.*

Rear Elevation

Alternate Front View

Foyer / Dining Room

Great Room

## Add the Extras

Simple or plain, it's the little conveniences and miscellaneous touches that push the dining experience to perfection. Here are some extra things to think about.

- You can never have too many serving trays when you entertain outside. For carrying food or drinks from the kitchen or the grill, trays are indispensable.

- A serving cart on wheels makes a perfect movable outdoor bar and provides an additional serving surface. Look for one at yard sales or buy one new.

- Chances are you won't have a sideboard, but a few small tables to hold excess items are great substitutes for one. They're also easier to position in the different places where you need them.

- For cooler weather or even a summer's evening with a bit of nip in the air, nothing beats an outdoor fireplace for comfort. You could build one into the house, but various types of stand-alone units are sold in home centers. To add a Southwest ambiance, consider a chiminea, a clay fireplace. Try burning some piñon pine, and you'll feel as if you're in Santa Fe. Be sure to follow manufacturers' instructions when using these fireplaces. You might also have to store them during the winter.

- Pots of fragrant plants—lavender, scented geraniums, flowering tobacco, or jasmine—provide a sensual aroma. Flowers such as roses climbing up an arbor or trellis are beautiful, evoke a romantic feeling, and lend a delicate scent to the atmosphere as well.

Nothing adds romance and intrigue to an evening soiree as candlelight does. Include just a few candles for an intimate dinner. Use more for a larger gathering, placing one or more on each table. Scatter luminaries around the yard. As the beautiful evening dusk begins, light candles, a few at a time, so your eyes can adjust to the dimming light. Not only do the candles illuminate the night in a magical way but they can also keep bugs at bay.

## Plan #181074

**Dimensions:** 42' W x 40' D
**Levels:** 2
**Square Footage:** 1,760
**Main Level Sq. Ft.:** 880
**Upper Level Sq. Ft.:** 880
**Bedrooms:** 3
**Full Baths:** 2½
**Foundation:** Basement; crawl space, slab and walkout for fee
**Materials List Available:** Yes
**Price Category:** D

A front porch and a standing-seam metal roof add to the country charm of this home.

**CAD FILE AVAILABLE**

*Images provided by designer/architect.*

**Features:**

- **Great Room:** Imagine coming home from a hard day of working or chauffeuring the kids and being welcomed by comfy couch and warm fire. This is the perfect room to help you unwind.

- **Kitchen:** From culinary expert to family cook, everyone will find this kitchen's workspaces and storage just what they need to create special meals. A sun-drenched family area shares the space and opens onto the future patio.

- **Second Floor:** For a restful atmosphere, the bedrooms are separated from the hum of daily life. The spacious master bedroom receives light from the bay windows. The area features a walk-in closet and a private bathroom. The two additional bedrooms share access to a Jack-and-Jill bathroom.

- **Garage:** A single-car garage adds convenience to this plan. It can be used as additional storage space.

**Main Level Floor Plan**

**Upper Level Floor Plan**

*Copyright by designer/architect.*

# Plan #101009

**Dimensions:** 70'2" W x 59' D

**Levels:** 1

**Square Footage:** 2,097

**Bedrooms:** 3

**Bathrooms:** 3

**Foundation:** Crawl space, slab or basement

**Materials List Available:** Yes

**Price Category:** E

*Images provided by designer/architect.*

Round columns enhance this country porch design, which will nestle into any neighborhood.

### Features:

• Ceiling Height: 9 ft. unless otherwise noted.

• Family Room: This large family room seems even more spacious, thanks to the vaulted ceiling. It's the perfect spot for all kinds of family activities.

• Dining Room: This elegant dining room is adorned with a decorative round column and a tray ceiling.

• Kitchen: You'll love the convenience of this enormous 14-ft.-3-in. x 22-ft.-6-in. country kitchen, which is open to the family room.

• Screened Porch: A French door leads to this breezy porch, with its vaulted ceiling.

• Master Suite: This sumptuous suite includes a double tray ceiling, a sitting area, a large walk-in closet, and a luxurious bath.

• Patio or Deck: This area is accessible from both the screened porch and master suite.

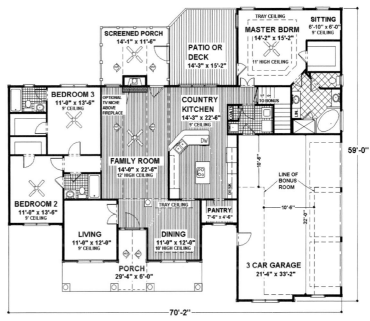

*Copyright by designer/architect.*

## SMARTtip

### Single-Level Decks

A single-level deck can use a strong vertical element, such as a pergola or a gazebo, to make it interesting. A simple and less-expensive option is a potted conical shrub or a clematis growing on a trellis.

## Plan #221015

**Dimensions:** 69'8" W x 46' D

**Levels:** 1

**Square Footage:** 1,926

**Bedrooms:** 3

**Bathrooms:** 2½

**Foundation:** Basement; crawl space or slab for fee

**Materials List Available:** No

**Price Category:** D

CAD FILE CAD AVAILABLE

You'll love the open plan in this lovely ranch and admire its many features, which are usually reserved for much larger homes.

**Features:**

- Ceiling Height: 8 ft.

- Great Room: A vaulted ceiling and tall windows surrounding the centrally located fireplace give distinction to this handsome room.

- Dining Room: Positioned just off the entry, this formal room makes a lovely spot for quiet dinner parties.

- Dining Nook: This nook sits between the kitchen and the great room. Central doors in the bayed area open to the backyard.

- Kitchen: An island will invite visitors while you cook in this well-planned kitchen, with its corner pantry and ample counter space.

- Master Suite: A tray ceiling, bay window, walk-in closet, and bath with whirlpool tub, dual-sink vanity, and standing shower pamper you here.

Rear Elevation

Copyright by designer/architect.

## Plan #121014

**Dimensions:** 52' W x 47'4" D

**Levels:** 2

**Square Footage:** 1,869

**Main Level Sq. Ft.:** 1,421

**Upper Level Sq. Ft.:** 448

**Bedrooms:** 3

**Bathrooms:** 2½

**Foundation:** Basement; crawl space or slab for fee

**Materials List Available:** Yes

**Price Category:** D

*Images provided by designer/architect.*

This compact home is packed with all the amenities you'll need for a gracious lifestyle.

### Features:

- Ceiling Height: 8 ft. except as noted.

- Great Room: A soaring ceiling and six tall transom-topped windows make this a light and airy spot for entertaining.

- Formal Dining Room: This elegant room is ideal for entertaining dinner guests.

- Breakfast Area: This sunny area shares a see-through fireplace with the great room. It's the perfect place to start the day.

- Master Suite: Here are all the features you expect to find in large luxury homes. Wake up to tall, sloped ceilings, and enjoy the corner whirlpool, separate shower, and vanity. A large walk-in closet provides plenty of wardrobe storage.

- Attached Garage: The garage provides two bays of parking plus plenty of storage space.

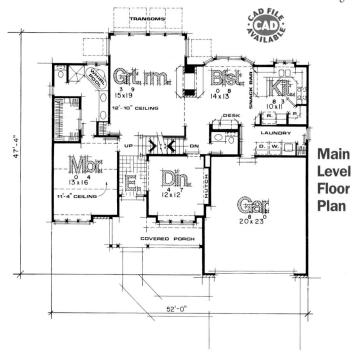

**Main Level Floor Plan**

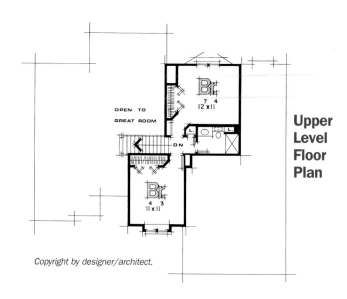

**Upper Level Floor Plan**

*Copyright by designer/architect.*

## Plan #281022

**Dimensions:** 48' W x 58' D

**Levels:** 1

**Square Footage:** 1,506

**Bedrooms:** 3

**Bathrooms:** 2

**Foundation:** Basement

**Materials List Available:** Yes

**Price Category:** C

*Images provided by designer/architect.*

*Copyright by designer/architect.*

Rear Elevation

## Plan #391504

**Dimensions:** 48' W x 44' D

**Levels:** 2

**Square Footage:** 1,763

**Main Level Sq. Ft.:** 909

**Upper Level Sq. Ft.:** 854

**Bedrooms:** 3

**Bathrooms:** 2½

**Foundation:** Crawl space, slab or basement

**Material List Available:** Yes

**Price Category:** C

*Images provided by designer/architect.*

Rear View

*Copyright by designer/architect.*

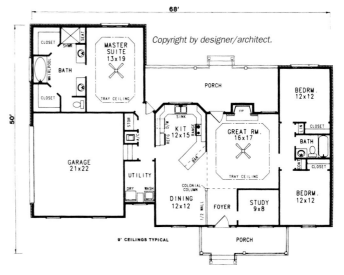

Copyright by designer/architect.

Images provided by designer/architect.

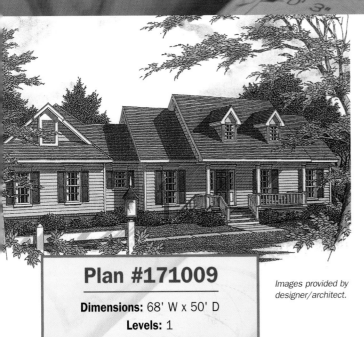

## Plan #171009

**Dimensions:** 68' W x 50' D

**Levels:** 1

**Square Footage:** 1,771

**Bedrooms:** 3

**Bathrooms:** 2

**Foundation:** Crawl space, slab

**Materials List Available:** Yes

**Price Category:** C

## SMARTtip

### Deck Awnings

Awnings come in bright colors. As light filters through, it will cast a hue to anything under the deck. Warm colors, such as red or pink, will create a rosy glow; cool colors, such blues or greens, will enhance the shade.

Copyright by designer/architect.

## Plan #121176

**Dimensions:** 67' W x 52' D

**Levels:** 1

**Square Footage:** 2,144

**Bedrooms:** 4

**Bathrooms:** 2

**Foundation:** Slab; basement for fee

**Materials List Available:** Yes

**Price Category:** D

Images provided by designer/architect.

## Plan #221020

**Dimensions:** 69'8" W x 43' D

**Levels:** 1

**Square Footage:** 1,859

**Bedrooms:** 3

**Bathrooms:** 2½

**Foundation:** Basement

**Materials List Available:** No

**Price Category:** D

*Images provided by designer/architect.*

You'll love this design if you're looking for a compact home with amenities usually found in much larger designs.

**Features:**

- Ceiling Height: 8 ft.

- Living Room: A vaulted ceiling gives an elegant feeling, and a bank of windows lets natural light pour in during the daytime.

- Dining Room: Located just off the entry for the convenience of your guests, this room is ideal for intimate family meals or formal dinner parties.

- Kitchen: Just across from the dining room, this kitchen is distinguished by its ample counter space. The adjacent nook is large enough to use as a casual dining area, and it features access to the backyard.

- Master Suite: The large bay window lends interest to this room, and you'll love the walk-in closet and private bath, with its whirlpool tub, standing shower, and dual-sink vanity.

Rear Elevation

*Copyright by designer/architect.*

## Plan #151196

**Dimensions:** 89' W x 49'4" D
**Levels:** 1
**Square Footage:** 1,800
**Bedrooms:** 3
**Bathrooms:** 2
**Foundation:** Crawl space or slab; basement for fee
**CompleteCost List Available:** Yes
**Price Category:** C

This charming home, with its wide front porch, is perfect on a little piece of land or a quiet suburban street.

### Features:

- **Screened Porch:** This screened-in porch creates extra living space where you can enjoy warm summer breezes in a bug-free atmosphere.

- **Great Room:** Make a "great" first impression by welcoming guests into this spacious, firelight-illuminated great room.

- **Kitchen:** This efficient area is surrounded on all sides by workspace and storage. A snack bar, adjacent dining room, and attached grilling porch create plenty of mealtime options.

- **Master Suite:** This master suite creates a stress-free environment with its, large walk-in closet, whirlpool tub, standing shower, and his and her vanities.

*Images provided by designer/architect.*

*Copyright by designer/architect.*

## Plan #321008

**Dimensions:** 57' W x 52'2" D

**Levels:** 1

**Square Footage:** 1,761

**Bedrooms:** 4

**Bathrooms:** 2

**Foundation:** Basement

**Materials List Available:** Yes

**Price Category:** C

One look at the roof dormers and planter boxes that grace the outside of this ranch, and you'll know that the interior is planned for comfortable family living.

**Features:**

- Great Room: A vaulted ceiling in this room points up its generous dimensions. Put a grouping of chairs near the fireplace to take advantage of the cozy spot it creates in chilly weather.

- Kitchen: Open to the great room, this kitchen has been planned for convenience. It features a pass-through to the dining area for easy serving when you've got a crowd to feed.

- Master Bedroom: A vaulted ceiling here makes you feel especially pampered, and the walk-in closet and amenity-filled bath add to that feeling.

- Additional Bedrooms: Great closet space characterizes all the rooms in this home, making it easy for children of any age to keep it organized and tidy.

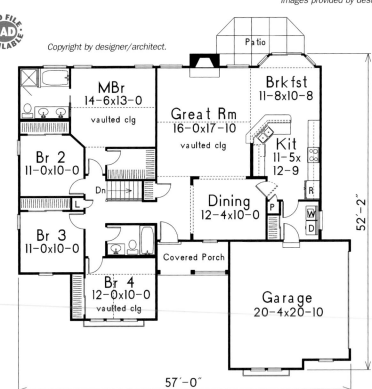

## SMARTtip

### Hanging Wallpaper

Use liner paper to smooth out a damaged wall and to provide uniform support for expensive paper.

## Plan #101004

**Dimensions:** 55'8" W x 56'6" D

**Levels:** 1

**Square Footage:** 1,787

**Bedrooms:** 3

**Bathrooms:** 2

**Foundation:** Crawl space, slab, or basement

**Materials List Available:** Yes

**Price Category:** D

This carefully designed ranch provides the feel and features of a much larger home.

### Features:

- Ceiling Height: 9 ft. unless otherwise noted.

- Entry: Guests will step up onto the inviting front porch and into this entry, with its impressive 11-ft. ceiling.

- Dining Room: Open to the entry and to its left is this elegant dining room, perfect for entertaining or informal family gatherings.

- Family Room: This family gathering place features an 11-ft. ceiling to enhance its sense of spaciousness.

- Kitchen: This intelligently designed kitchen has an open plan. A breakfast bar and a serving bar are features that add to its convenience.

- Master Suite: This suite is loaded with amenities, including a double-step tray ceiling, direct access to the screened porch, a sitting room, deluxe bath, and his and her walk-in closets.

*Images provided by designer/architect.*

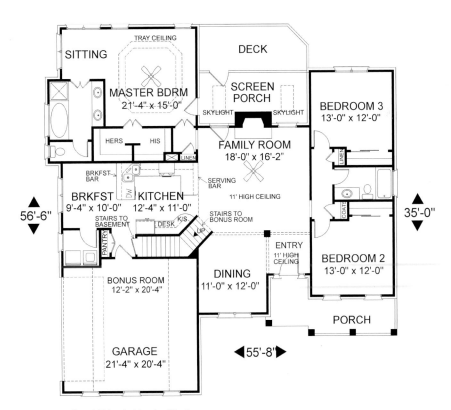

*Copyright by designer/architect.*

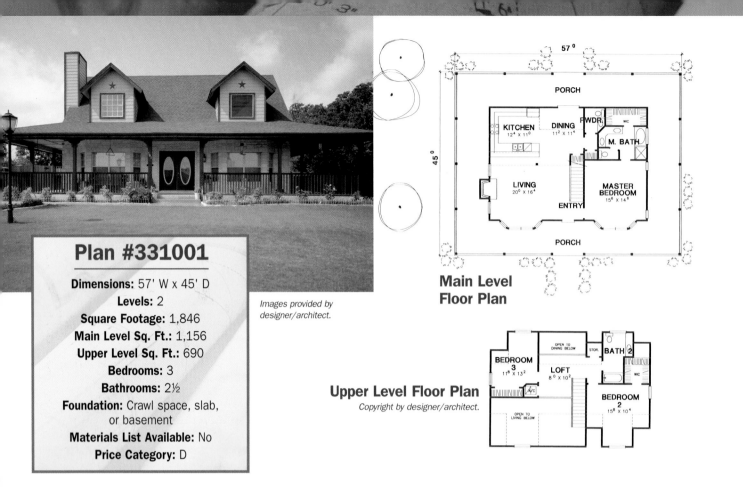

## Plan #331001

**Dimensions:** 57' W x 45' D

**Levels:** 2

**Square Footage:** 1,846

**Main Level Sq. Ft.:** 1,156

**Upper Level Sq. Ft.:** 690

**Bedrooms:** 3

**Bathrooms:** 2½

**Foundation:** Crawl space, slab, or basement

**Materials List Available:** No

**Price Category:** D

*Images provided by designer/architect.*

**Main Level Floor Plan**

**Upper Level Floor Plan**
*Copyright by designer/architect.*

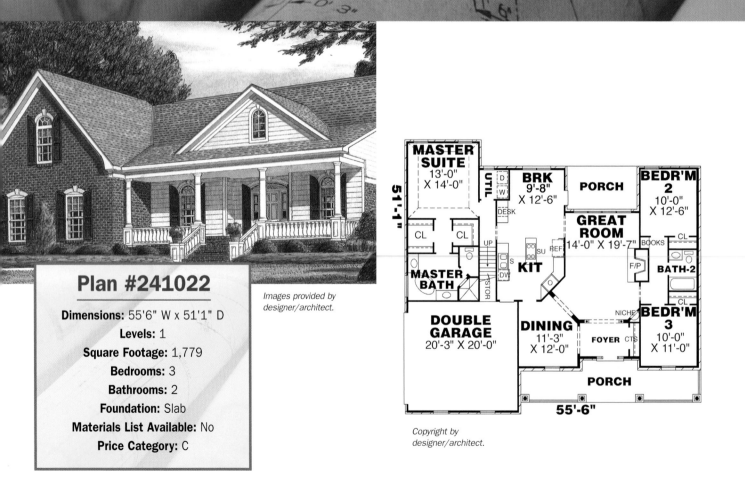

## Plan #241022

**Dimensions:** 55'6" W x 51'1" D

**Levels:** 1

**Square Footage:** 1,779

**Bedrooms:** 3

**Bathrooms:** 2

**Foundation:** Slab

**Materials List Available:** No

**Price Category:** C

*Images provided by designer/architect.*

*Copyright by designer/architect.*

# Plan #431002

**Dimensions:** 40' W x 49'4" D

**Levels:** 2

**Square Footage:** 1,680

**Main Level Sq. Ft.:** 900

**Upper Level Sq. Ft.:** 780

**Bedrooms:** 3

**Bathrooms:** 2½

**Foundation:** Crawl space, slab or basement

**Material List Available:** Yes

**Price Category:** C

*Images provided by designer/architect.*

**Main Level Floor Plan**

**Upper Level Floor Plan**

*Copyright by designer/architect.*

# Plan #351003

**Dimensions:** 64' W x 45'10" D

**Levels:** 1

**Square Footage:** 1,751

**Bedrooms:** 3

**Bathrooms:** 2

**Foundation:** Crawl space, slab, or basement

**Materials List Available:** Yes

**Price Category:** D

*Images provided by designer/architect.*

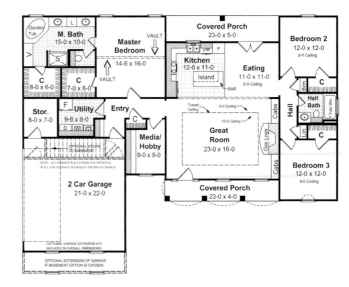

*Copyright by designer/architect.*

## Plan #131041

**Dimensions:** 42' W x 45' D
**Levels:** 2
**Square Footage:** 1,679
**Main Level Sq. Ft.:** 1,134
**Upper Level Sq. Ft.:** 545
**Bedrooms:** 3
**Bathrooms:** 2½
**Foundation:** Crawl space, slab, or basement
**Materials List Available:** Yes
**Price Category:** D

*Images provided by designer/architect.*

This rustic-looking two-story cottage includes contemporary amenities for your total comfort.

**Features:**

- **Great Room:** With a 9-ft.-4-in.-high ceiling, this large room makes everyone feel at home. A fireplace with raised hearth and built-in niche for a TV will encourage the whole family to gather here on cool evenings, and sliding glass doors leading to

the rear covered porch make it an ideal entertaining area in mild weather.

- **Kitchen:** When people aren't in the great room, you're likely to find them here, because the convenient serving bar welcomes casual dining, and this room also opens to the p porch.

- **Master Suite:** Relax at the end of the day in this room, with its 9-ft.-4-in.-high ceiling and walk-in closet, or luxuriate in the private bath with whirlpool tub and dual-sink vanity.

- **Optional Basement:** This area can include a tuck-under two-car garage if you desire it.

**Main Level Floor Plan**

```
UP

COVERED PORCH
37'-0" x 10'-0"

KITCHEN
12'-8" x 14'-6"

MUD RM

MSTR BEDRM
12'-0" x 16'-0"

CLOS W/O BSMT

CLOS OR BUILT-IN

9'-4" HIGH STEP'D CEIL

OPT. GARAGE BELOW

GREAT ROOM
14'/18'-0" x 26'-4"

CL

BUILT-IN FOR T.V.

9'-4" HI CEIL

WICL

MSTR BATH

HIGH WINDOW

VAULTED FOYER

LAV

COVERED PORCH
37'-0" x 8'-0"

UP
```

*Copyright by designer/architect.*

**Upper Level Floor Plan**

```
BATH

LIN

BEDRM #3
12'-0" x 11'-0"

DN

BALC.

CL

BEDRM #2
16'-4" x 11'-0"

CL
```

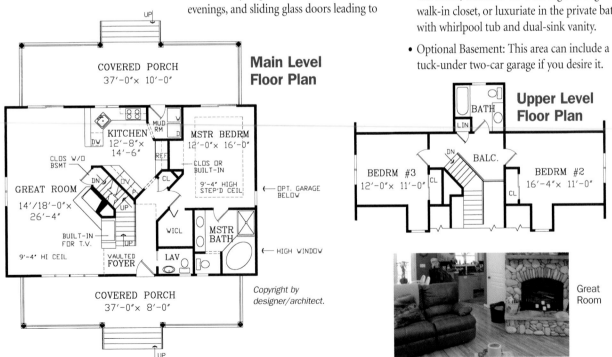

Great Room

# Plan #101014

**Dimensions:** 52' W x 28' D

**Levels:** 2

**Square Footage:** 1,598

**Main Level Sq. Ft.:** 812

**Upper Level Sq. Ft.:** 786

**Bedrooms:** 3

**Bathrooms:** 2½

**Foundation:** Crawl space, slab

**Materials List Available:** No

**Price Category:** D

This lovely Victorian home has a perfect balance of ornamental features and modern amenities.

**Features:**

• Ceiling Height: 8 ft. unless otherwise noted.

• Foyer: An impressive beveled glass-front door invites you into this roomy foyer.

• Kitchen: This bright and open kitchen offers an abundance of counter space to make cooking a pleasure.

• Breakfast Room: You'll enjoy plenty of informal family meals in this sunny and open spot next to the kitchen.

• Family Room: The whole family will be attracted to this handsome room. A full-width bay window adds to the Victorian charm.

• Master Suite: This dramatic suite features a multi-faceted vaulted ceiling and his and her closets and vanities. A separate shower and 6-ft. garden tub complete the lavish appointments.

**Main Level Floor Plan**

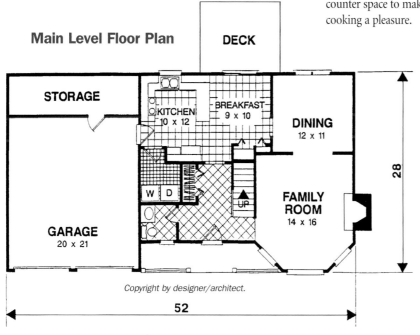

**Upper Level Floor Plan**

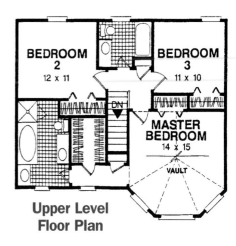

# Plan #121006

**Dimensions:** 46' W x 58' D

**Levels:** 1

**Square Footage:** 1,762

**Bedrooms:** 3

**Bathrooms:** 2

**Foundation:** Slab

**Materials List Available:** Yes

**Price Category:** C

*Images provided by designer/architect.*

The entry has a trio of arched openings that leads you to other areas of this amenity-packed home.

## Features:

- Ceiling Height: 8 ft. except as noted.

- Eating Bar: Conveniently located between the kitchen and family room, this is sure to be a favorite spot for informal entertaining and family gatherings.

- Family room: A wall of windows, a fireplace, and a vaulted ceiling stretching to 11 ft. work together to make this a bright and warm room.

- Kitchen: There's no shortage of counter space in this well-planned kitchen that features a center island in addition to the eating bar.

- Master Suite: Luxuriate at the end of the day in this large bedroom with its decorative tray ceiling and walk-in closet. Enjoy the pampering bath with its sunlit corner whirlpool flanked by vanities.

- Garage: Two bays provide room for cars and plenty of storage as well.

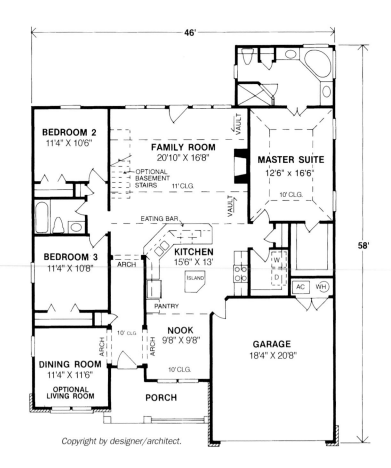

*Copyright by designer/architect.*

## Plan #151016

**Dimensions:** 60'2" W x 39'10" D
**Levels:** 2
**Square Footage:** 1,783;
2,107 with bonus
**Main Level Sq. Ft.:** 1,124
**Upper Level Sq. Ft.:** 659
**Bonus Room Sq. Ft.:** 324
**Bedrooms:** 3
**Bathrooms:** 2½
**Foundation:** Crawl space, slab,
or basement
**CompleteCost List Available:** Yes
**Price Category:** C

*Images provided by designer/architect.*

**Features:**

- Great Room: Enjoy the fireplace in this spacious, versatile room.
- Dining Room: Entertaining is easy, thanks to the open design with the kitchen.
- Master Suite: Luxury surrounds you in this suite, with its large walk-in closet, double vanities, and a bathroom with a whirlpool tub and separate shower.

- Upper Bedrooms: Window seats make wonderful spots for reading or relaxing, and a nook between the windows of these rooms is a ready-made play area.
- Bonus Area: Located over the garage, this space could be converted to a home office, a studio, or a game room for the kids.
- Attic: There's plenty of storage space here.

An open design characterizes this spacious home built for family life and entertaining.

### Bonus Room Above Garage

*Copyright by designer/architect.*

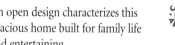

**Main Level Floor Plan**

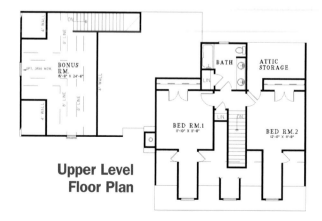

**Upper Level Floor Plan**

# Plan #351021

**Dimensions:** 61' W x 47'4" D

**Levels:** 1

**Square Footage:** 1,500

**Bedrooms:** 3

**Bathrooms:** 2

**Foundation:** Crawl space, slab, or basement

**Materials List Available:** Yes

**Price Category:** *E*

*Images provided by designer/architect.*

**CAD FILE AVAILABLE**

*Copyright by designer/architect.*

**Main Level Floor Plan**

**Upper Level Floor Plan**

*Copyright by designer/architect.*

# Plan #421005

**Dimensions:** 51' W x 50'9" D

**Levels:** 2

**Square Footage:** 1,784

**Main Level Sq. Ft.:** 1,112

**Upper Level Sq. Ft.:** 672

**Bedrooms:** 3

**Bathrooms:** 2½

**Foundation:** Crawl space, slab, or basement

**Materials List Available:** Yes

**Price Category:** *C*

*Images provided by designer/architect.*

**CAD FILE AVAILABLE**

## Plan #151169

**Dimensions:** 51'6" W x 49'10" D

**Levels:** 1

**Square Footage:** 1,525

**Bedrooms:** 3

**Bathrooms:** 2

**Foundation:** crawl space, slab, basement, or daylight basement

**CompleteCost List Available:** Yes

**Price Category:** C

*Images provided by designer/architect.*

*Copyright by designer/architect.*

Rear Elevation

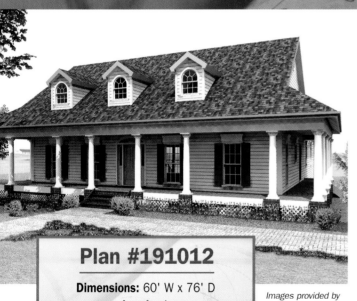

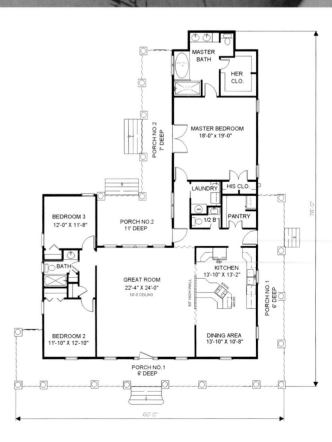

## Plan #191012

**Dimensions:** 60' W x 76' D

**Levels:** 1

**Square Footage:** 2,123

**Bedrooms:** 3

**Bathrooms:** 2½

**Foundation:** Crawl space or slab

**Materials List Available:** No

**Price Category:** D

*Images provided by designer/architect.*

*Copyright by designer/architect.*

## Plan #131016

**Dimensions:** 75' W x 45' D
**Levels:** 1
**Square Footage:** 1,902
**Bedrooms:** 3
**Bathrooms:** 2
**Foundation:** Crawl space, slab, or basement
**Materials List Available:** Yes
**Price Category:** E

*Images provided by designer/architect.*

If traditional country looks appeal to you, you'll be delighted by the wraparound covered porch that forms the entryway to this comfortable home.

### Features:

• Great Room: Sit by the fireplace in this room with feature walls so large that they'll suit a home theater or large media center.

• Kitchen: Overlooking the great room, this well-designed kitchen has great cabinets and ample counter space to make all your cooking and cleaning a pleasure.

• Master Suite: A large bay window makes the bedroom in this private suite sophisticated, and two walk-in closets make it practical. You'll love to relax in the master bath, whether in the whirlpool tub or the separate shower. A dual-sink vanity completes the amenities in this room.

• Garage: Find extra storage space in this two-bayed, attached garage.

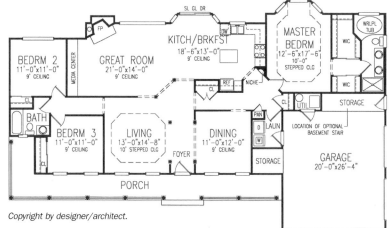

*Copyright by designer/architect.*

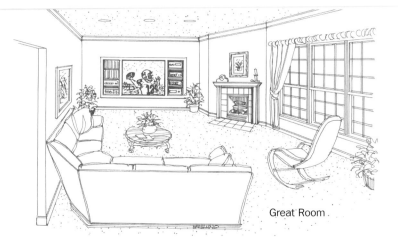

Great Room

## Plan #131002

**Dimensions:** 70'1" W x 60'7" D
**Levels:** 1
**Square Footage:** 1,709
**Bedrooms:** 3
**Bathrooms:** 2½
**Foundation:** Slab or basement
**Materials List Available:** Yes
**Price Category:** D

*Images provided by designer/architect.*

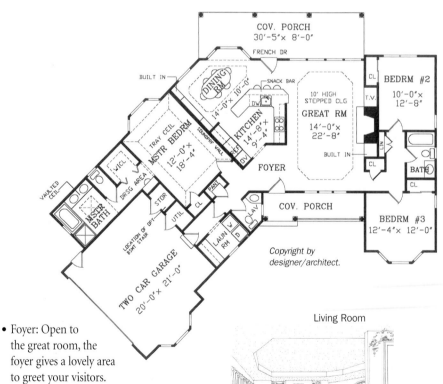

COV. PORCH
30'-5"x 8'-0"

FRENCH DR

BUILT IN

DINING RM
14'-0"x 10'-0"

SNACK BAR

KITCHEN
14'-8"x
9'-4"

10' HIGH
STEPPED CLG

GREAT RM
14'-0"x
22'-8"

BEDRM #2
10'-0"x
12'-8"

CL

T.V.

TRAY CEIL

MSTR BEDRM
12'-0"x
18'-4"

SOUNDPRF WALL

REF

DW

LIN

BUILT IN

FOYER

CL

WICL

VAULTED CEIL

DRSG AREA

MSTR BATH

STOR

PAN

CL

BATH

CL

COV. PORCH

LOCATION OF OPT. BSMT STAIR

UTIL

LAV

LAUN RM

W D

BEDRM #3
12'-4"x 12'-0"

TWO CAR GARAGE
20'-0"x 21'-0"

*Copyright by designer/architect.*

Rear View

You'll love the way this angled ranch brings out the best in a corner lot or on a slope.

### Features:

- Ceiling Height: 8 ft.

- Front Porch: Hang baskets of plants from the roof of this porch, which is just the right size for a couple of rockers and a side table.

- Dining Room: Well-placed windows flood this room with sunlight during the day and a built-in cabinet gives ample storage space for all your china, linens, and collectables.

- Foyer: Open to the great room, the foyer gives a lovely area to greet your visitors.

- Great Room: A built-in media center surrounds the fireplace where friends and family are sure to gather.

- Master Suite: You'll love the privacy of this somewhat isolated but easily accessed room. Decorate to show off the large bay window and tray ceiling, and enjoy the luxury of a separate toilet room.

Living Room

## Plan #151089

**Dimensions:** 84' W x 55'6" D
**Levels:** 1
**Square Footage:** 1,921
**Bedrooms:** 3
**Bathrooms:** 3
**Foundation:** Crawl space, slab, basement or walk out
**CompleteCost List Available:** Yes
**Price Category:** E

*Images provided by designer/architect.*

If your family loves to combine indoor and outdoor living, this home's fabulous porches and deck space make it perfect.

**Features:**

- Porches: A huge wraparound front porch, sizable rear porch, and deck that joins them give you space for entertaining or simply lounging.

- Living Room: A fireplace and built-in media center could be the focal points in this large room.

- Hearth Room: Open to both the living room and kitchen, this hearth room also features a fireplace.

- Kitchen: This step-saving kitchen includes ample storage and work space, as well as an angled bar it shares with the hearth room. Atrium doors lead to the rear porch.

- Bonus Upper Level: A large game room and a full bath make this area a favorite with the children.

*Copyright by designer/architect.*

**Bonus Area Floor Plan**

## Plan #161024

**Dimensions:** 54'4" W x 26'8" D
**Levels:** 2
**Square Footage:** 1,698
**Main Level Sq. Ft.:** 868
**Upper Level Sq. Ft.:** 830
**Bonus Space Sq. Ft.:** 269
**Bedrooms:** 3
**Bathrooms:** 2½
**Foundation:** Basement
**Materials List Available:** No
**Price Category:** C

*This home, as shown in the photograph, may differ from the actual blueprints. For more detailed information, please check the floor plans carefully.* *Images provided by designer/architect.*

The covered porch, dormers, and center gable that grace the exterior let you know how comfortable your family will be in this home.

**Features:**

- **Great Room:** Walk from windows overlooking the front porch to a door into the rear yard in this spacious room, which runs the width of the house.

- **Dining Room:** Adjacent to the great room, the dining area gives your family space to spread out and makes it easy to entertain a large group.

- **Kitchen:** Designed for efficiency, the kitchen area includes a large pantry.

- **Master Suite:** Tucked away on the second floor, the master suite features a walk-in closet in the bedroom and a luxurious attached bathroom.

- **Bonus Room:** Finish the 269-sq.-ft. area over the 2-bay garage as a guest room, study, or getaway for the kids.

*Copyright by designer/architect.*

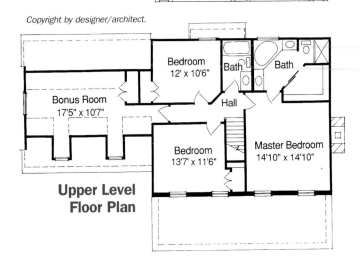

**GARAGE**
20'-0" X 20'-6"

**NOOK**
10'-0" X 10'-0"

**KITCH.**
10'-0" X 12'-0"

**PORCH**

**STEP UP CLG.**
**MASTER SUITE**
12'-0" X 15'-0"

10' CEILING
**LIVING RM.**
14'-0" X 18'-0"

**PANTRY**

REF.

UT.
6' X 8'

STORAGE

10' CEILING
**DINING**
11'-8" X 14'-6"

**BATH 1**

**ENTRY**

**PORCH**
9' CEILING

**BED RM. 3**
11'-0" X 11'-0"

**BED RM. 2**
11'-0" X 11'-0"

77'-6"

39'-9"

LINE OF ROOF OVER HANG

*Images provided by designer/architect.*

CAD FILE AVAILABLE

*Copyright by designer/architect.*

## Plan #371125

**Dimensions:** 77'6" W x 39'9" D

**Levels:** 1

**Square Footage:** 1,746

**Bedrooms:** 3

**Bathrooms:** 2

**Foundation:** Crawl space or slab

**Material List Available:** No

**Price Category:** C

---

**Deck**
16' x 10'

**Vaulted Master Suite**
12' x 17'

**Vaulted Great Room**
15' x 17'

**Vaulted Dining**
11' x 11'

**Garage**
20'8" x 22'4"

**Vaulted Entry**

**Kitchen**

**Vaulted Nook**
10'6" x 9'4"

**Bedroom**
10'10" x 10'

**Bedroom**
10'10" x 12'6"

**Covered Porch**

*Images provided by designer/architect.*

CAD FILE AVAILABLE

*Copyright by designer/architect.*

## Plan #361448

**Dimensions:** 68' W x 40' D

**Levels:** 1

**Square Footage:** 1,634

**Bedrooms:** 3

**Bathrooms:** 2

**Foundation:** Crawl space or basement

**Material List Available:** No

**Price Category:** C

# Plan #151181

**Dimensions:** 76'10" W x 59'2" D

**Levels:** 1.5

**Square Footage:** 2,373

**Bedrooms:** 4

**Bathrooms:** 3

**Foundation:** Crawl space or slab; basement or walkout for fee

**CompleteCost List Available:** Yes

**Price Category:** E

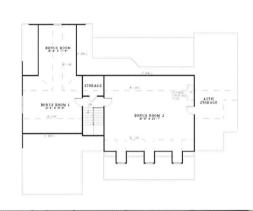

**Main Level Floor Plan**

*Images provided by designer/architect.*

**Bonus Level Floor Plan**

*Copyright by designer/architect.*

# Plan #441003

**Dimensions:** 50' W x 48' D

**Levels:** 1

**Square Footage:** 1,580

**Bedrooms:** 3

**Bathrooms:** 2½

**Foundation:** Crawl space; slab or basement available for fee

**Materials List Available:** Yes

**Price Category:** C

*Images provided by designer/architect.*

*Copyright by designer/architect.*

Rear Elevation

## Plan #121040

**Dimensions:** 50' W x 48' D
**Levels:** 2
**Square Footage:** 1,818
**Main Level Sq. Ft.:** 1,302
**Upper Level Sq. Ft.:** 516
**Bedrooms:** 3
**Bathrooms:** 2½
**Foundation:** Basement
**Materials List Available:** Yes
**Price Category:** D

*Images provided by designer/architect.*

Offering plenty of architectural style, this home is designed with the busy modern lifestyle in mind.

**Features:**

- Ceiling Height: 8 ft. unless otherwise noted.
- Great Room: This is sure to be the central gathering place of the home with its volume ceiling, abundance of windows, and its handsome fireplace.
- Kitchen: This convenient and attractive kitchen includes a snack bar that will get lots of use for impromptu family meals.
- Breakfast Area: Joined to the kitchen by the snack bar, this breakfast area will invite you to linger over morning coffee. It includes a pantry and access to the backyard.

*Copyright by designer/architect.*

**CAD FILE AVAILABLE**

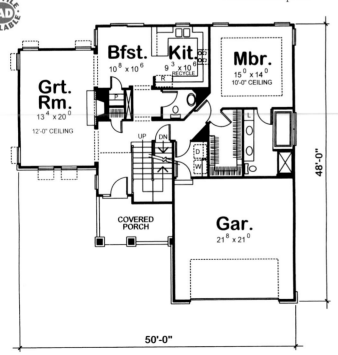

**Main Level Floor Plan**

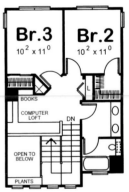

**Upper Level Floor Plan**

- Master Bedroom: This private retreat offers the convenience of a walk-in closet and the luxury of its own whirlpool bath and shower.
- Computer Loft: Designed with the family computer in mind, this loft overlooks a two-story entry.

## Plan #401037

**Dimensions:** 53' W x 44' D

**Levels:** 2

**Square Footage:** 1,924

**Main Level Sq. Ft.:** 1,007

**Upper Level Sq. Ft.:** 917

**Bedrooms:** 3

**Bathrooms:** 2½

**Foundation:** Basement

**Materials List Available:** Yes

**Price Category:** D

*Images provided by designer/architect.*

This charming country exterior conceals an elegant interior, starting with formal living and dining rooms, each with a bay window. Decorative columns help define an elegant dining room.

**CAD FILE AVAILABLE**

**Features:**

- **Kitchen:** This gourmet kitchen features a work island and a breakfast area with its own bay window.

- **Family Room:** A fireplace warms this room, which opens to the rear porch through French doors.

- **Master Suite:** Located on the second floor, this area boasts a vaulted ceiling, a walk-in closet, and a tiled bath.

- **Bedrooms:** Upstairs, two family bedrooms share a full bath and a gallery hall with a balcony overlook to the foyer.

**Main Level Floor Plan**

Left Side Elevation

Right Side Elevation

Upper Level Floor Plan

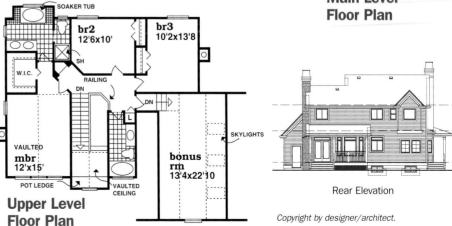

Rear Elevation

*Copyright by designer/architect.*

## Plan #351004

**Dimensions:** 78' W x 49'6" D
**Levels:** 1
**Square Footage:** 1,852
**Bedrooms:** 3
**Bathrooms:** 2½
**Foundation:** Crawl space, slab, or basement
**Materials List Available:** Yes
**Price Category:** D

You'll love this design if you've been looking for a one-story home large enough for both a busy family life and lots of entertaining.

**Features:**

- Great Room: A vaulted ceiling, substantial corner fireplace, and door to the rear porch give character to this sizable, airy room.

- Dining Room: This well-positioned room, lit by a wall of windows, can comfortably hold a crowd.

- Kitchen: The center island and deep pantry add efficiency to this well-planned kitchen, which also features a raised snack bar.

- Master Suite: Two walk-in closets and a bath with jet tub and separate shower complement the spacious bedroom here.

- Garage Storage: Barn doors make it easy to store yard equipment and tools here. Finish the optional area at the rear of the garage or overhead for a home office or media room.

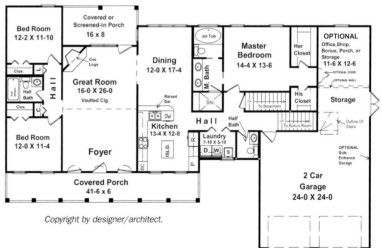

Copyright by designer/architect.

Rear Elevation

**Bonus Room**

## Plan #121099

**Dimensions:** 40' W x 47'8" D

**Levels:** 2

**Square Footage:** 1,699

**Main Level Sq. Ft.:** 1,268

**Upper Level Sq. Ft.:** 431

**Bedrooms:** 3

**Bathrooms:** 2½

**Foundation:** Basement

**Materials List Available:** Yes

**Price Category:** C

*This home, as shown in the photograph, may differ from the actual blueprints. For more detailed information, please check the floor plans carefully.*

**CAD FILE AVAILABLE**

You'll love the open, spacious design of the living areas in this home, as well as the privacy you'll find in the bedrooms.

**Features:**

- Den: French doors just off the entry lead to this private den, which could easily serve as a home-office area.

- Living Area: At the rear of the home, you'll find this open living area. Decorate to emphasize the flow from one spot to another or to create a secluded nook or two.

- Kitchen: An island with space for a snack bar and a pantry combine to add convenience to this well-designed kitchen area.

- Master Suite: A boxed ceiling and triple window give this private area an elegant feeling, and the bath has a whirlpool tub, shower, and vanity.

- Upper Level: A computer area here is centrally located, and bedroom 3 features a walk-in closet.

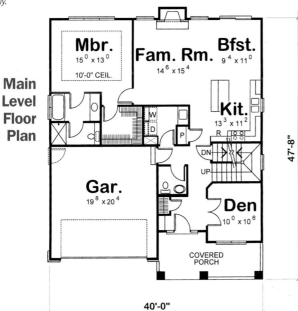

**Main Level Floor Plan**

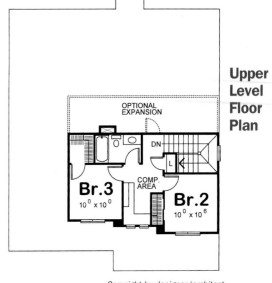

**Upper Level Floor Plan**

## Plan #441002

**Dimensions:** 70' W x 51' D
**Levels:** 1
**Square Footage:** 1,873
**Bedrooms:** 3
**Bathrooms:** 2
**Foundation:** Crawl space
**Materials List Available:** Yes
**Price Category:** D

*Images provided by designer/architect.*

CAD FILE CAD AVAILABLE

Copyright by designer/architect.

MASTER 16/2 X 14/0 + (9' CLG.)

GREAT RM. VAULTED 17/6 X 20/6 (9' CLG.)

DINING 10/6 X 13/0 (9' CLG.)

SHOP / 3RD CAR 12/6 X 19/6

GARAGE 21/0 X 22/6

DEN 11/0 X 10/0 (9' CLG.)

BR. 2 11/0 X 12/6 (9' CLG.)

BR. 3 11/2 X 12/0 (9' CLG.)

51'

70'

Rear Elevation

## Plan #351002

**Dimensions:** 64' W x 45'10" D
**Levels:** 1
**Square Footage:** 1,751
**Bedrooms:** 3
**Bathrooms:** 2
**Foundation:** Crawl space, slab, or basement
**Materials List Available:** Yes
**Price Category:** E

*Images provided by designer/architect.*

CAD FILE CAD AVAILABLE

Garden Tub

M. Bath 15-0 x 10-0

Master Bedroom 14-6 x 16-0 VAULT

Covered Porch 23-0 x 5-0

Kitchen 12-0 x 11-0 Island

Eating 11-0 x 11-0 9-0 Ceiling

Bedroom 2 12-0 x 12-0 9-0 Ceiling

C 8-0 x 6-0

C 7-0 x 6-0

VAULT

Stor. 8-0 x 7-0

Utility 9-6 x 8-0

Entry

Media/ Hobby 9-0 x 8-0

Great Room 23-0 x 16-0

Hall Bath

Hall

Bedroom 3 12-0 x 12-0 9-0 Ceiling

NOTE: ALL DASHED WALLS INDICATE OPTIONAL WALL LOCATIONS IF BASEMENT OPTION IS CHOSEN

2 Car Garage 21-0 x 22-0

Covered Porch 23-0 x 4-0

(OPTIONAL GARAGE EXTENSION NOT INCLUDED IN OVERALL DIMENSIONS)

OPTIONAL EXTENSION OF GARAGE IF BASEMENT OPTION IS CHOSEN

*Copyright by designer/architect.*

**Main Level Floor Plan**

GRILLING PORCH 13'-6" X 5'-8"

DINING 10'-6" X 12'-2"

BREAKFAST ROOM 17'-8" X 8'-2"

GARAGE 20'-4" X 19'-8"

KITCHEN 17'-8" X 13'-6"

LAU. 10'-8" X 7'-2"

M. BATH 16'-10" X 10'-4"

GREAT ROOM 18'-6" X 15'-4"

FOYER 7'-4" X 13'-4"

MASTER SUITE 16'-10" X 13'-2"

8' COLUMNS

6' COVERED PORCH

*Images provided by designer/architect.*

CAD FILE AVAILABLE

## Plan #151189

**Dimensions:** 50' W x 50' D

**Levels:** 1.5

**Square Footage:** 2,196

**Main Level Sq. Ft.:** 1,672

**Upper Level Sq. Ft.:** 524

**Bedrooms:** 3

**Bathrooms:** 2 1/2

**Foundation:** Crawl space or slab; basement or walkout for fee

**CompleteCost List Available:** Yes

**Price Category:** D

**Upper Level Floor Plan**

BONUS 17'-8" X 16'-2"

BATH 11'-10" X 7'-0"

BEDROOM 2 16'-4" X 10'-7"

OPTIONAL BONUS / HOME THEATER 22'-0" X 9'-6"

BEDROOM 3 13'-4" X 10'-7"

*Copyright by designer/architect.*

---

75'-10"

LINE OF ROOF OVERHANG

BED RM.3 12'-0" X 11'-0"

PORCH 16'-0" X 9'-0"

NOOK 11'-0" X 9'-0"

MASTER SUITE 12'-0" X 15'-0"

BATH 1

SHOP AREA

B.2

KITCH. 11' X 11'

10'-0" HIGH CEILING LIVING RM. 15'-0" X 22'-6"

GARAGE 20'-0" X 20'-0"

BED RM.2 12'-0" X 11'-6"

DINING 11'-0" X 12'-0"

UTIL. 12' X 7'

PORCH 31'-6" X 7'-0"

38'-8"

*Copyright by designer/architect.*

## Plan #371072

**Dimensions:** 75'10" W x 38'8" D

**Levels:** 1

**Square Footage:** 1,772

**Bedrooms:** 3

**Bathrooms:** 2

**Foundation:** Crawl space, slab

**Materials List Available:** No

**Price Category:** C

*Images provided by designer/architect.*

CAD FILE AVAILABLE

Rear Elevation

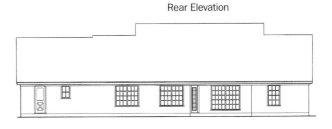

# Plan #131001

**Dimensions:** 72'4" W x 32'4" D
**Levels:** 1
**Square Footage:** 1,615
**Bedrooms:** 3
**Bathrooms:** 2
**Foundation:** Crawl space, slab, basement, or walkout
**Materials List Available:** Yes
**Price Category:** D

Cathedral ceilings and illuminating skylights add drama and beauty to this practical ranch house.

**Features:**

- Ceiling Height: 8 ft.

- Front Porch: Watch the rain in comfort from the covered front porch.

- Foyer: The stone-tiled foyer flows into the living areas.

- Living Room: Oriented towards the front of the house, the living room opens to the dining room and shares a lovely three-sided fireplace with the family room.

- Family Room: Conveniently located to share the fireplace with the living room, this room is bright and cheery thanks to its skylights as well as the sliding glass doors that open onto the rear patio.

- Kitchen: An island makes this sunny room both efficient and attractive.

- Breakfast Nook: Located just off the kitchen, this area can serve double-duty as a spot for kitchen visitors to sit.

- Dining Room: The open design between the dining and living rooms adds to the spacious feeling that the cathedral ceiling creates in this area.

- Laundry Room: This area opens from the kitchen for convenience.

- Master Suite: A walk-in closet makes this room practical, but the master bathroom with a skylight, dual-sink vanity, soaking tub, and separate shower makes it luxurious.

- Bedrooms: The two additional bedrooms share a bathroom.

*Images provided by designer/architect.*

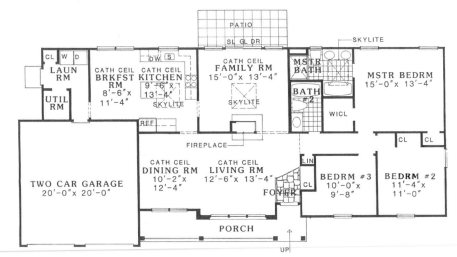

*Copyright by designer/architect.*

## Plan #351038

**Dimensions:** 65' W x 50' D

**Levels:** 1

**Square Footage:** 1,800

**Bedrooms:** 3

**Bathrooms:** 2

**Foundation:** Crawl space, slab, or basement

**Materials List Available:** Yes

**Price Category:** D

This elegant brick home has an excellent floor plan.

**Features:**

• Great Room: This entertainment area, with a vaulted ceiling, has a gas fireplace flanked by built-in cabinets.

• Media Room: This all-purpose room may be used for home schooling or as a computer center, nursery, or hobbies area.

• Master Suite: This impressive area features a vaulted ceiling, his and her closets, a jetted tub, a walk-in shower, and a makeup area.

• Bedrooms: Two secondary bedrooms, located on the opposite side of the home from the master suite, share a common bathroom.

• Garage: This large garage is great storage for four-wheeler ATVs, bikes, lawn mowers, and perhaps a golf cart.

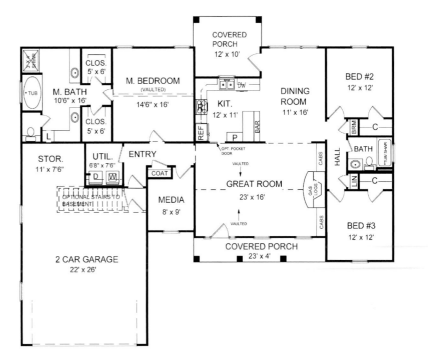

## Plan #301005

**Dimensions:** 71' W x 42' D
**Levels:** 1
**Square Footage:** 1,930
**Bedrooms:** 3
**Bathrooms:** 2
**Foundation:** Crawl space, slab
**Materials List Available:** Yes
**Price Category:** D

This home features an old-fashioned rocking-chair porch that enhances the streetscape.

**Features:**

- Ceiling Height: 8 ft.

- Dining Room: When the weather is warm, guests can step through French doors from this elegant dining room and enjoy a breeze on the rear screened porch.

- Family Room: This family room is a warm and inviting place to gather, with its handsome fireplace and built-in bookcases.

- Kitchen: This kitchen offers plenty of counter space for preparing your favorite recipes. Its U-shape creates a convenient open traffic pattern.

- Master Suite: You'll look forward to retiring at the end of the day in this truly luxurious master suite. The bedroom has a fireplace and opens through French doors to a private rear deck. The bath features a corner spa tub, a walk-in shower, double vanities, and a linen closet.

*Images provided by designer/architect.*

*Copyright by designer/architect.*

## SMARTtip

### Light With Shutters

For the maximum the amount of light coming through shutters, use the largest panel possible on the window. Make sure the shutters have the same number of louvers per panel so that all of the windows in the room look unified. However, don't choose a panel that is over 48 inches high, because the shutter becomes unwieldy. Also, any window that is wider than 96 inches requires extra framing to support the shutters.

## Plan #251004

**Dimensions:** 50'9" W x 42'1" D

**Levels:** 1

**Heated Square Footage:** 1,550

**Bedrooms:** 3

**Bathrooms:** 2

**Foundation:** Crawl space, slab

**Materials List Available:** Yes

**Price Category:** C

Combine the old-fashioned appeal of a country farmhouse with all the comforts of modern living.

**Features:**

• Ceiling Height: 9 ft.

• Foyer: When guests enter this inviting foyer, they will be greeted by a view of the lovely family room.

• Family Room: Usher family and friends into this welcoming family room, where they can warm up in front of the fireplace. The room's 12-ft. ceiling enhances its sense of spaciousness.

• Kitchen: Gather around and keep the cook company at the snack bar in this roomy kitchen. There's still plenty of counter space for food preparation, thanks to the kitchen island.

• Master Bedroom: This elegant master bedroom features a large walk-in closet and a 9-ft. recessed ceiling.

• Master Bath. This master bath includes a double vanity, a tub, and a walk-in shower.

• Garage: This attached garage provides plenty of extra storage space, as well as parking for two cars.

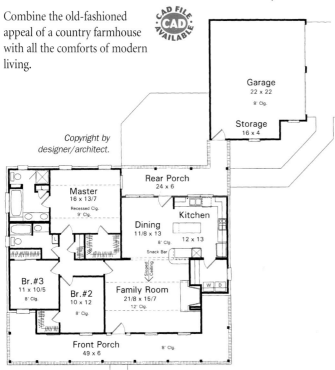

Copyright by designer/architect.

## SMARTtip

### Shaker Style in Your Bathroom

This warm, likable style fits in perfectly with a country home because of its old-fashioned values. But it blends in well with contemporary interiors, too, because of its clean lines and plain geometric shapes. In fact, adding a few Shaker elements can warm up the sometimes cold look of a thoroughly modern room.

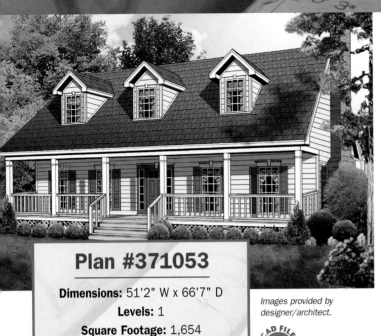

## Plan #371053

**Dimensions:** 51'2" W x 66'7" D

**Levels:** 1

**Square Footage:** 1,654

**Bedrooms:** 3

**Bathrooms:** 2

**Foundation:** Slab

**Materials List Available:** No

**Price Category:** C

*Images provided by designer/architect.*

**CAD FILE AVAILABLE**

---

## Plan #351036

**Dimensions:** 78' W x 46' D

**Levels:** 1

**Square Footage:** 1,799

**Bedrooms:** 3

**Bathrooms:** 2½

**Foundation:** Crawl space or slab

**Materials List Available:** Yes

**Price Category:** E

*Images provided by designer/architect.*

**CAD FILE AVAILABLE**

Rear View

## Plan #341030

**Dimensions:** 52' W x 40' D

**Levels:** 1

**Square Footage:** 1,660

**Bedrooms:** 3

**Bathrooms:** 2

**Foundation:** Crawl space, slab, or basement

**Materials List Available:** Yes

**Price Category:** C

*Images provided by designer/architect.*

CAD FILE AVAILABLE

*Copyright by designer/architect.*

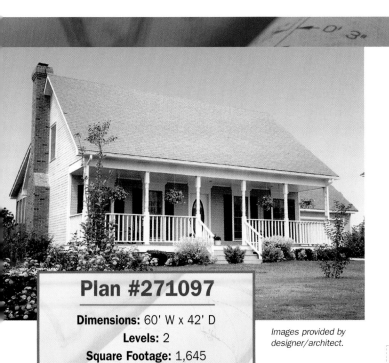

## Plan #271097

**Dimensions:** 60' W x 42' D

**Levels:** 2

**Square Footage:** 1,645

**Main Level Sq. Ft.:** 1,136

**Upper Level Sq. Ft.:** 509

**Bedrooms:** 3

**Bathrooms:** 2

**Foundation:** Basement

**Materials List Available:** No

**Price Category:** C

*Images provided by designer/architect.*

**Main Level Floor Plan**

**Upper Level Floor Plan**

*Copyright by designer/architect.*

# Plan #441006

**Dimensions:** 48' W x 64' D
**Levels:** 1
**Square Footage:** 1,891
**Bedrooms:** 3
**Bathrooms:** 2
**Foundation:** Crawl space;
slab or basement for fee
**Materials List Available:** Yes
**Price Category:** D

If you prefer the look of Craftsman homes, you'll love the details this plan includes. Wide-based columns across the front porch, Mission-style windows, and a balanced mixture of exterior materials add up to true good looks.

**Features:**

- Great Room: A built-in media center and a fireplace in this room make it distinctive.

- Kitchen: A huge skylight over an island eating counter brightens this kitchen. A private office space opens through double doors nearby.

- Dining Room: This room has sliding glass doors opening to the rear patio.

- Bedrooms: Two bedrooms with two bathrooms are located on the right side of the plan. One of the bedrooms is a master suite with a vaulted salon and a bath with a spa tub.

- Garage: You'll be able to reach this two-car garage via a service hallway that contains a laundry room, a walk-in pantry, and a closet.

*Images provided by designer/architect.*

*Copyright by designer/architect.*

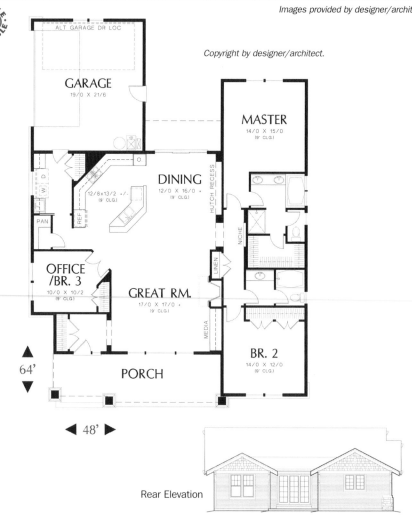

Rear Elevation

# Plan #131043

**Dimensions:** 65'8" W x 43'10" D
**Levels:** 1.5
**Square Footage:** 1,945
**Main Level Sq. Ft.:** 1,375
**Upper Level Sq. Ft.:** 570
**Bedrooms:** 3
**Bathrooms:** 2½
**Foundation:** Crawl space, slab, or basement
**Materials List Available:** Yes
**Price Category:** E

*Images provided by designer/architect.*

This home will delight you with its three dormers and half-round transom windows, which give a nostalgic appearance, and its amenities and conveniences that are certainly contemporary.

**Features:**

- Porch: This covered porch forms the entryway.
- Great Room: Enjoy the fireplace in this large, comfortable room, which is open to the dining area. A French door here leads to the

covered porch at the rear of the house.

- Kitchen: This large, country-style kitchen has a bayed nook, and oversized breakfast bar, and pass-through to the rear porch to simplify serving and make entertaining a pleasure.
- Master Suite: A tray ceiling sets an elegant tone for this room, and the bay window adds to it. The large walk-in closet is convenient, and the bath is sumptuous.
- Bedrooms: These comfortable rooms have convenient access to a bath.

## Main Level Floor Plan

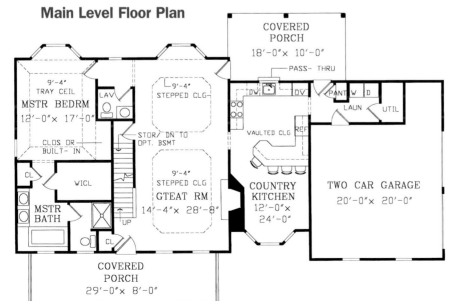

## Upper Level Floor Plan

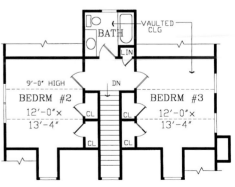

*Copyright by designer/architect.*

## Plan #351001

**Dimensions:** 72'8" W x 51' D
**Levels:** 1
**Square Footage:** 1,855
**Bedrooms:** 3
**Bathrooms:** 2½
**Foundation:** Crawl space, slab, or basement
**Materials List Available:** Yes
**Price Category:** D

From the lovely arched windows on the front to the front and back covered porches, this home is as comfortable as it is beautiful.

**Features:**

- **Great Room:** Come into this room with 12-ft. ceilings, and you're sure to admire the corner gas fireplace and three windows overlooking the porch.

- **Dining Room:** Set off from the open design, this room is designed to be used formally or not.

- **Kitchen:** You'll love the practical walk-in pantry, broom closet, and angled snack bar here.

- **Breakfast Room:** Brightly lit and leading to the covered porch, this room will be a favorite spot.

- **Bonus Room:** Develop a playroom or study in this area.

- **Master Suite:** The large bedroom is complemented by the private bath with garden tub, separate shower, double vanity, and spacious walk-in closet.

*Images provided by designer/architect.*

CAD FILE AVAILABLE

*Copyright by designer/architect.*

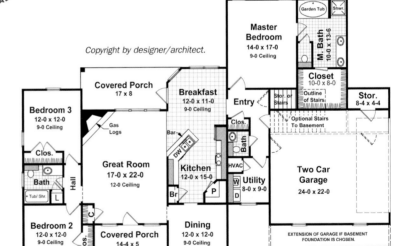

Kitchen

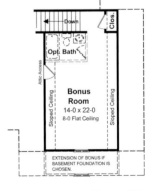

**Bonus Area Floor Plan**

# Plan #371012

**Dimensions:** 56'4" W x 52'10" D

**Levels:** 1

**Square Footage:** 1,720

**Bedrooms:** 3

**Bathrooms:** 2

**Foundation:** Slab

**Materials List Available:** No

**Price Category:** C

The beautifully designed front of this traditional brick home makes it special from the start.

**Features:**

- Living Room: 10-ft.-high ceilings and a cozy fireplace make this large gathering area special.

- Dining Room: Truly grand, this formal room has 10-ft.-high ceilings.

- Kitchen: This kitchen has a raised bar and a breakfast nook that is open to the porch.

- Master Suite: This private area boasts a luxurious bathroom with a marble tub, a glass shower, and two walk-in closets.

- Bedrooms: The two secondary bedrooms share a private bathroom with a powder room.

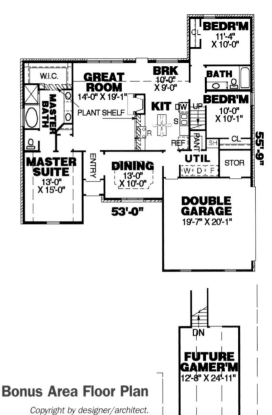

## Plan #241005

**Dimensions:** 53' W x 55'9" D

**Levels:** 1

**Square Footage:** 1,670

**Bedrooms:** 3

**Bathrooms:** 2

**Foundation:** Crawl space or slab; basement option for fee

**Materials List Available:** No

**Price Category:** C

*Images provided by designer/architect.*

**Bonus Area Floor Plan**

*Copyright by designer/architect.*

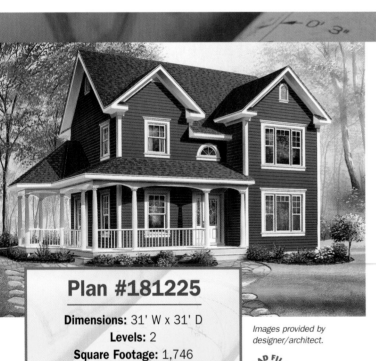

**Main Level Floor Plan**

## Plan #181225

**Dimensions:** 31' W x 31' D

**Levels:** 2

**Square Footage:** 1,746

**Main Level Sq. Ft.:** 873

**Upper Level Sq. Ft.:** 873

**Bedrooms:** 3

**Bathrooms:** 1½

**Foundation:** Basement

**Materials List Available:** Yes

**Price Category:** C

*Images provided by designer/architect.*

**Upper Level Floor Plan**

*Copyright by designer/architect.*

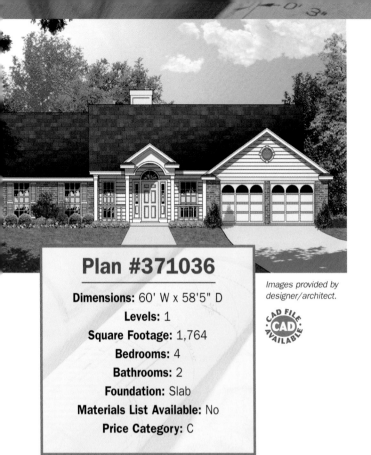

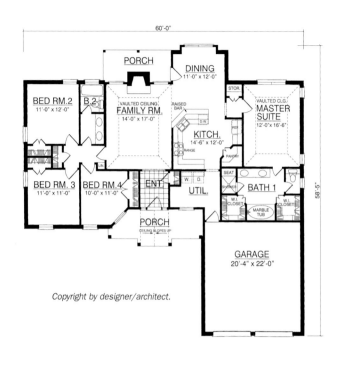

## Plan #371036

**Dimensions:** 60' W x 58'5" D

**Levels:** 1

**Square Footage:** 1,764

**Bedrooms:** 4

**Bathrooms:** 2

**Foundation:** Slab

**Materials List Available:** No

**Price Category:** C

*Images provided by designer/architect.*

CAD FILE AVAILABLE

*Copyright by designer/architect.*

## Plan #121331

**Dimensions:** 62' W x 48' D

**Levels:** 1

**Heated Square Footage:** 1,763

**Bedrooms:** 3

**Bathrooms:** 2½

**Foundation:** Basement

**Materials List Available:** Yes

**Price Category:** G

*Images provided by designer/architect.*

CAD FILE AVAILABLE

*Copyright by designer/architect.*

## Plan #131047

**Dimensions:** 69'10" W x 51'8" D
**Levels:** 1
**Square Footage:** 1,793
**Bedrooms:** 3
**Bathrooms:** 2
**Foundation:** Crawl space, slab, or basement
**Materials List Available:** Yes
**Price Category:** D

The country charm of this well-designed home is mixed with the convenience and luxury normally reserved for more contemporary plans.

**Features:**

• Great Room: The spaciousness of this great room is enhanced by the 11-ft. stepped ceiling. A fireplace makes it cozy on cool evenings or on chilly winter days, and two sets of French sliding glass doors open to the back porch.

• Kitchen: In addition to the convenient layout of this design, you'll also love its bright, airy position. It includes an old-fashioned pantry,

a sink under a window, and a sunny breakfast area that opens to the wraparound porch.

• Master Suite: You'll find 11-ft. ceilings in both the master bedroom and the bayed sitting area that the suite includes. In the bath, the circular spa tub is surrounded by a glass-block wall.

• Bonus Space: A permanent staircase leads to an unfinished bonus space on the upper level.

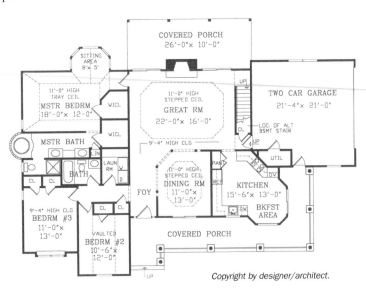

Rear Elevation

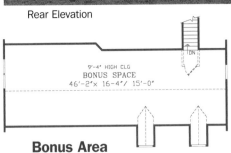

**Bonus Area**

## Plan #191003

**Dimensions:** 56' W x 42' D

**Levels:** 1

**Square Footage:** 1,785

**Bedrooms:** 3

**Bathrooms:** 3

**Foundation:** Crawl space, slab, or basement

**Materials List Available:** No

**Price Category:** C

Images provided by designer/architect.

Enjoy the amenities you'll find in this gracious home, with its traditional Southern appearance.

**Features:**

• Great Room: This expansive room is so versatile that everyone will gather here. A built-in entertainment area with desk makes a great lounging spot, and the French doors topped by transoms open onto the lovely rear porch.

• Dining Room: An arched entry to this room helps to create the open feeling in this home.

• Kitchen: Another arched entryway leads to this fabulous kitchen, which has been designed with the cook's comfort in mind. It features a downdraft range, many cabinets, a snack bar, and a sunny breakfast area, where the family is sure to gather.

• Laundry: A sink, shower, toilet area, and cabinets galore give total convenience in this room.

• Master Suite: Enjoy the walk-in closet and bath with toilet room, tub, and shower.

Copyright by designer/architect.

**56'-0" Width**

## Plan #351006

**Dimensions:** 64' W x 39' D

**Levels:** 1

**Square Footage:** 1,638

**Bedrooms:** 3

**Bathrooms:** 2

**Foundation:** Crawl space, slab, or basement

**Materials List Available:** Yes

**Price Category:** D

This arched window and three-bedroom brick home offers traditional styling featuring an open floor plan.

### Features:

- **Great Room:** This room, with its 10-ft.-high ceiling, features a fireplace and two large glass doors that provide access to the rear covered porch.

- **Dining Room:** Located just off the entry, this room has a view of the front yard.

- **Kitchen:** This kitchen has a raised bar and is open to the breakfast area.

- **Master Suite:** This private area, located on the opposite side of the home from the secondary bedrooms, features a master bath and walk-in closet.

- **Bedrooms:** Two bedrooms with large closets share a hallway bathroom.

*Images provided by designer/architect.*

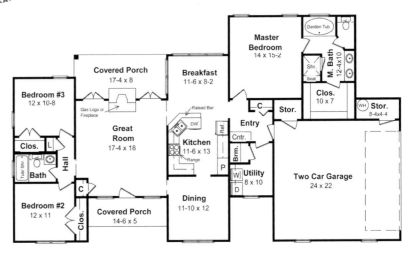

**Stair Location for Basement Option**

*Copyright by designer/architect.*

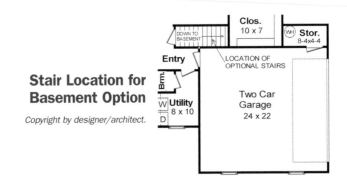

# Plan #351039

**Dimensions:** 78' W x 46' D

**Levels:** 1

**Square Footage:** 1,800

**Bedrooms:** 3

**Bathrooms:** 2½

**Foundation:** Crawl space or slab

**Material List Available:** Yes

**Price Category:** E

*Images provided by designer/architect.*

This home's farmhouse styling is sure to appeal to many people.

## Features:

- Great Room: Enjoy both the fireplace in this room and the view out to the grilling porch and yard. The vaulted ceiling creates the feeling of a large space.

- Kitchen: This Country kitchen with island and raised bar will keep family and friends close but out of the work triangle.

- Master Suite: This master suite is well appointed with a jet tub, dual sinks, separate walk-in shower, and large closets.

- Bonus Room: This bonus room over the garage may serve as a fourth bedroom, a game room, or an office.

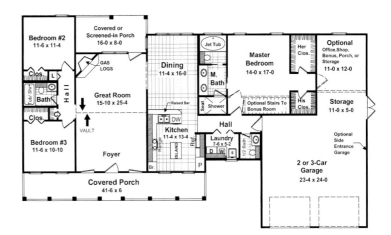

**Bonus Area Floor Plan**

*Copyright by designer/architect.*

**BONUS ROOM**

# Plan #111044

**Dimensions:** 43' W x 47' D

**Levels:** 2

**Square Footage:** 1,819

**Main Level Sq. Ft.:** 1,242

**Upper Level Sq. Ft.:** 577

**Bedrooms:** 3

**Bathrooms:** 2½

**Foundation:** Pier

**Materials List Available:** No

**Price Category:** E

*Images provided by designer/architect.*

Front View

**Main Level Floor Plan**

*Copyright by designer/architect.*

Deck

Breakfast 10'10"x 16'

Dining 13'x 12'

Kitchen 14'6"x 10'2"

Utility

Bath

1/2 Bath

WIC

Living 13'x 20'

Bedroom 12'x 15'

Porch

**Upper Level Floor Plan**

WIC

Bath

WIC

Bedroom 13'x 11'

Bedroom 12'x 11'

Open to Below

---

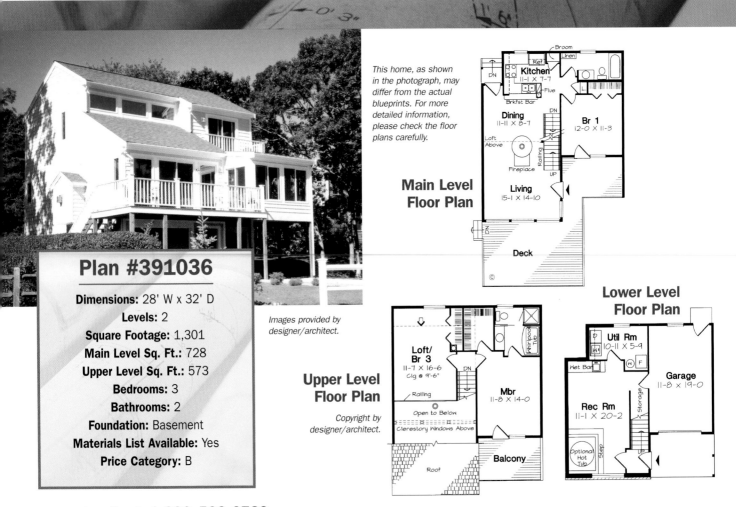

# Plan #391036

**Dimensions:** 28' W x 32' D

**Levels:** 2

**Square Footage:** 1,301

**Main Level Sq. Ft.:** 728

**Upper Level Sq. Ft.:** 573

**Bedrooms:** 3

**Bathrooms:** 2

**Foundation:** Basement

**Materials List Available:** Yes

**Price Category:** B

*Images provided by designer/architect.*

This home, as shown in the photograph, may differ from the actual blueprints. For more detailed information, please check the floor plans carefully.

**Main Level Floor Plan**

Kitchen 11-1 X 7-7

Broom
Linen

DN

Ref
Flue

Brkfst Bar

Dining 11-11 X 8-7

DN

Br 1 12-0 X 11-3

Loft Above

Fireplace

Railing

UP

Living 15-1 X 14-10

DN

Deck

**Upper Level Floor Plan**

*Copyright by designer/architect.*

Whirlpool Tub

Loft/ Br 3 11-7 X 16-6 Clg @ 9'-6"

DN

Railing

Mbr 11-8 X 14-0

Open to Below

Clerestory Windows Above

Roof

Balcony

**Lower Level Floor Plan**

Util Rm 10-11 X 5-9

Wet Bar

F

Garage 11-8 X 19-0

Storage

Rec Rm 11-1 X 20-2

Optional Hot Tub

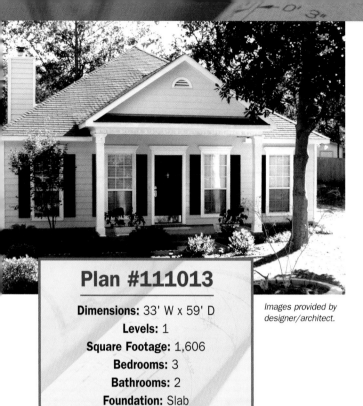

## Plan #111013

**Dimensions:** 33' W x 59' D

**Levels:** 1

**Square Footage:** 1,606

**Bedrooms:** 3

**Bathrooms:** 2

**Foundation:** Slab

**Materials List Available:** No

**Price Category:** D

*Images provided by designer/architect.*

Copyright by designer/architect.

## Plan #151195

**Dimensions:** 52'6" W x 55'6" D

**Levels:** 1.5

**Square Footage:** 1,710

**Bedrooms:** 3

**Bathrooms:** 2

**Foundation:** Crawl space or slab; basement or walkout for fee

**CompleteCost List Available:** Yes

**Price Category:** C

*Images provided by designer/architect.*

CAD FILE AVAILABLE

**Main Level Floor Plan**

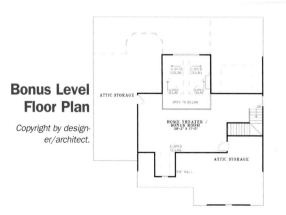

**Bonus Level Floor Plan**

Copyright by designer/architect.

## Plan #401029

**Dimensions:** 37'6" W x 48'4" D

**Levels:** 2

**Square Footage:** 2,163

**Main Level Sq. Ft.:** 832

**Upper Level Sq. Ft.:** 1,331

**Bedrooms:** 3

**Bathrooms:** 2½

**Foundation:** Basement

**Materials List Available:** Yes

**Price Category:** D

This two-level plan has a bonus—a roof deck with hot tub! A variety of additional outdoor spaces makes this one wonderful plan.

**Features:**

- First Level: Family bedrooms, a full bath room, and a cozy den are on the first level, along with a two-car garage.

- Living Area: The living spaces are on the second floor and include a living/dining room combination with a deck and fireplace. The dining room has buffet space.

- Family Room: Featuring a fireplace and a built-in entertainment center, the gathering area is open to the breakfast room and sky lighted kitchen.

- Master Bedroom: This room features a private bath with a whirlpool tub and two-person shower, a walk-in closet, and access to still another deck.

### Upper Level Floor Plan

**CAD FILE AVAILABLE**

*Copyright by designer/architect.*

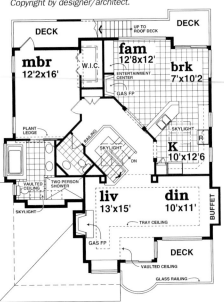

Rear Elevation

Dining Room/Kitchen

### Main Level Floor Plan

# Plan #371081

**Dimensions:** 54'6" W x 41'10" D

**Levels:** 2

**Square Footage:** 2,143

**Main Level Sq. Ft.:** 1,535

**Upper Level Sq. Ft.:** 608

**Bedrooms:** 4

**Bathrooms:** 3

**Foundation:** Slab or basement

**Materials List Available:** No

**Price Category:** D

The cozy wraparound front porch of this beautiful country home invites you to stay awhile.

CAD FILE AVAILABLE — CAD

*Images provided by designer/architect.*

**Features:**

- **Family Room:** This large gathering area features a wonderful fireplace and is open to the dining room.

- **Kitchen:** The island cabinet in this fully functional kitchen brings an open feel to this room and the adjoining dining room.

- **Master Suite:** Mom and Dad can relax downstairs in this spacious master suite, with their luxurious master bathroom, which has double walk-in closets and a marble tub.

- **Bedrooms:** The kids will enjoy these two large secondary bedrooms and the study area with bookcases upstairs.

Rear Elevation

## Upper Level Floor Plan

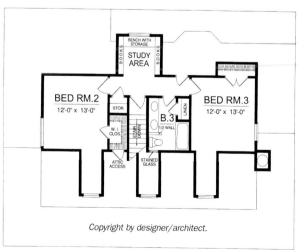

*Copyright by designer/architect.*

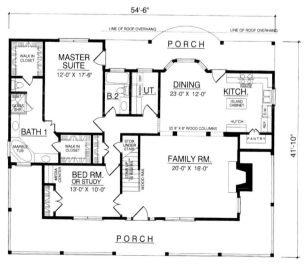

**Main Level Floor Plan**

## Plan #401039

**Dimensions:** 69'8" W x 46' D

**Levels:** 2

**Square Footage:** 2,462

**Main Level Sq. Ft.:** 1,333

**Upper Level Sq. Ft.:** 1,129

**Bedrooms:** 4

**Bathrooms:** 2½

**Foundation:** Basement

**Materials List Available:** Yes

**Price Category:** E

*Images provided by designer/architect.*

A large wraparound porch graces the exterior of this home and gives it great outdoor livability.

**Features:**

• Foyer: This raised foyer spills into a hearth-warmed living room and the bay-windowed dining room beyond; French doors open from the breakfast and dining rooms to the spacious porch.

• Family Room: Built-ins surround a second hearth in this cozy gathering room.

• Study: Located in the front, this room is adorned by a beamed ceiling and, like the family room, features built-ins.

• Bedrooms: You'll find three family bedrooms on the second floor.

• Master Suite: This restful area, located on the second floor, features a walk-in closet and private bath.

• Garage: Don't miss the workshop area in this garage.

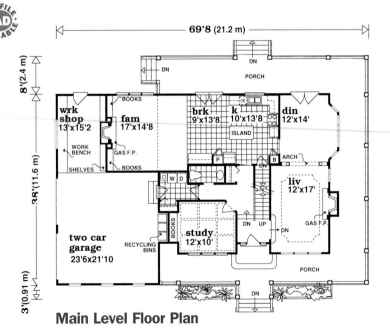

**Main Level Floor Plan**

## Upper Level Floor Plan

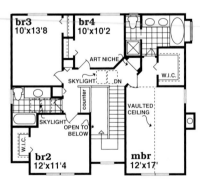

*Copyright by designer/architect.*

## Plan #121123

**Dimensions:** 54' W x 52' D
**Levels:** 1.5
**Square Footage:** 2,277
**Main Level Sq. Ft.:** 1,570
**Upper Level Sq. Ft.:** 707
**Bedrooms:** 4
**Bathrooms:** 2½
**Foundation:** Basement; crawl space for fee
**Material List Available:** Yes
**Price Category:** E

*Images provided by designer/architect.*

This country-style home, with its classic wraparound porch, is just the plan you have been searching for.

**Features:**

- Entry: This two-story entry gives an open and airy feeling when you enter the home. A view into the dining room and great room adds to the open feeling.

- Great Room: This grand gathering area with cathedral ceiling is ready for your friends and family to come and visit. The fireplace, flanked by large windows, adds a cozy feeling to the space.

- Kitchen: The chef in the family will love how efficiently this island kitchen was designed. An abundance of cabinets and counter space is always a plus.

- Master Suite: This main level oasis will help you relieve all the stresses from the day. The master bath boasts dual vanities and a large walk-in closet.

- Secondary Bedrooms: Three generously sized bedrooms occupy the upper level. The full bathroom is located for easy access to all three bedrooms.

**Main Level Floor Plan**

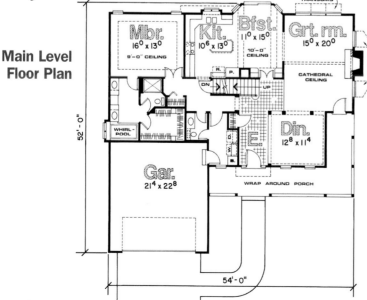

**Upper Level Floor Plan**

*Copyright by designer/architect.*

**Main Level Floor Plan**

*Images provided by designer/architect.*

## Plan #121212

**Dimensions:** 54' W x 44' D

**Levels:** 2

**Square Footage:** 2,219

**Main Level Sq. Ft.:** 1,132

**Upper Level Sq. Ft.:** 1,087

**Bedrooms:** 4

**Bathrooms:** 2½

**Foundation:** Basement; crawl space for fee

**Material List Available:** Yes

**Price Category:** E

**Upper Level Floor Plan**

*Copyright by designer/architect.*

---

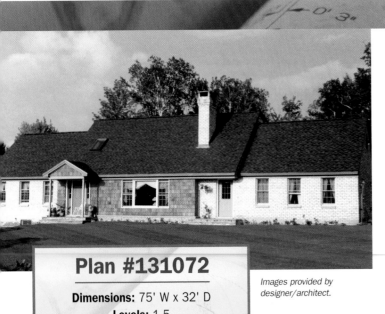

**Main Level Floor Plan**

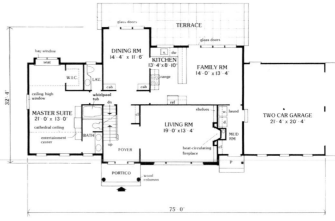

*Images provided by designer/architect.*

## Plan #131072

**Dimensions:** 75' W x 32' D

**Levels:** 1.5

**Square Footage:** 2,053

**Main Floor Sq. Ft.:** 1,440

**Upper Level Sq. Ft.:** 613

**Bedrooms:** 3

**Bathrooms:** 2½

**Foundation:** Crawl space, slab, or basement

**Material List Available:** Yes

**Price Category:** E

**Upper Level Floor Plan**

*Copyright by designer/architect.*

## Plan #181630

**Dimensions:** 38' W x 31'4" D
**Levels:** 2
**Square Footage:** 2,098
**Main Level Sq. Ft.:** 1,092
**Upper Level Sq. Ft.:** 1,006
**Bedrooms:** 3
**Bathrooms:** 1½
**Foundation:** Basement
**Material List Available:** Yes
**Price Category:** D

*Images provided by designer/architect.*

**CAD FILE AVAILABLE**

**Main Level Floor Plan**

**Upper Level Floor Plan**
*Copyright by designer/architect.*

---

## Plan #271062

**Dimensions:** 54' W x 45' D
**Levels:** 2
**Square Footage:** 2,356
**Main Level Sq. Ft.:** 1,222
**Upper Level Sq. Ft.:** 1,134
**Bedrooms:** 4
**Bathrooms:** 2½
**Foundation:** Daylight basement
**Materials List Available:** No
**Price Category:** E

*Images provided by designer/architect.*

**Main Level Floor Plan**

**Upper Level Floor Plan**
*Copyright by designer/architect.*

## Plan #181228

**Dimensions:** 68' W x 36' D

**Levels:** 2

**Square Footage:** 2,393

**Main Level Sq. Ft.:** 1,279

**Upper Level Sq. Ft.:** 1,114

**Bedrooms:** 4

**Bathrooms:** 2

**Foundation:** Slab

**Materials List Available:** Yes

**Price Category:** E

*Images provided by designer/architect.*

Come home to this fine home, and relax on the front or rear porch.

**Features:**

- **Living Room:** This large, open entertaining area has a cozy fireplace and is flooded with natural light.

- **Kitchen:** This fully equipped kitchen has an abundance of cabinets and counter space. Access the rear porch is through a glass door.

- **Laundry Room:** Located on the main level, this laundry area also has space for storage.

- **Upper Level:** Climb the U-shaped staircase, and you'll find four large bedrooms that share a common bathroom.

**Main Level Floor Plan**

*Copyright by designer/architect.*

**Upper Level Floor Plan**

Rear View

Dining Room

Living Room

Living Room

Kitchen

Master Bath

# A Kitchen with Country in Mind

North Americans have always combined comfortable traditions with current inventiveness in the kitchen. Country colors, finishes, and patterns seem especially right here. As the busiest room in the house, the kitchen serves many daily needs. But it also carries symbolic weight as the place where we share work and food among familiar things and friendly faces. It's the room that most clearly says "home."

The earliest settlers recalled the kitchens of their native countries. The English colonists created rooms that glowed with wood paneling, which they painted rich red, grayed teal, and deep green. German and Dutch colonists in the New World tended toward bright colors, with high-contrast decorative painting.

## An Evolving Style

The earliest North American kitchens focused on a wide fireplace. While we romantically picture a roaring fire, a skilled open-hearth cook would manage her fuel carefully, often scooping a hot pile of coals out onto the brick hearth floor to make a separate "burner." For the weekly baking, she might fire up the back oven, which was built into the fireplace wall.

Hot, laborious open-hearth cooking inspired many ingenious devices: revolving toasters, waffle irons, long-handled "spider" skillets, and Dutch ovens, with flanged lids to hold coals scooped on top. Early North Americans used a ratchet to raise and lower the large cooking pots that slow-simmered meat. Crude reflector ovens held meat on a revolving spit until it was "done to a turn." While metalwares were treasured purchases, most cooks also had a supply of homemade "treen," or wooden spoons, cups, and ladles, made by any handy whittler. Such simple early kitchenwares are evocative collectibles today.

In the mid-1800s, only the romanticists sighed over the demise of open-hearth cooking, as households quickly embraced the cast-iron cookstove that burned wood or coal. A prototype gas range appeared at the Great Exhibition of 1851 in London and at the first electric kitchen at the 1893 Chicago World's Fair. But it was well into the 1930s before these appliances came home. At that time, refrigerators arrived and by the late 1940s were considered as fundamental as the modern range and running water.

## Modern Kitchen Charm

The purist, with a sufficient budget, can convincingly conceal modern appliances with specialized cabinetry. Dishwashers, microwaves, trash compactors, and refrigerators can disappear completely behind cabinet doors, perhaps with some decorative fretwork for ventilation. Some new and expensive refrigerators and freezers are modular and are installed much like drawers in various work zones instead of standing as one large unit. Dishwashers, too, are available as compact modular units. In a

**This Country kitchen,** above, uses the most modern appliances and fixtures.

**Inviting morning sunlight** floods this charming Country-style breakfast nook, opposite.

large kitchen, you can locate one near the main sink and another near a secondary bar or island sink.

For less rigorous disguise, matching-panel fronts on the major appliances help blend them into the cabinetry. Appliances can even be concealed with a colorful, washable curtain attached to the counter's overhang. In a colorful kitchen, appliances painted at a local auto body shop in sky blue or geranium red can become whimsical additions. Or apply a stenciled design or a faux finish to appliance fronts. Several manufacturers also offer modern gas and electric ranges styled like old wood-burning stoves. But to contemporary eyes, standard appliances tend to be unobtrusive. If your kitchen is rich with colors, textures, and collectibles, most observers will skim over the appliances as expected background. Appliances in standard, simple designs work best for this strategy.

## The "Unfitted" Look

The informal Country-style family kitchen wasn't designed but evolved along functional lines. Individual pieces of furniture—a table, a cupboard, shelves, a hutch, or an armoire, sometimes retired from the finer "company" rooms—were added as needed. This loose, unfitted look is a hallmark of a humble Country kitchen.

Amid the current design-world hoopla about the "return of the unfitted kitchen," look critically at such plans, particularly if you're an enthusiastic cook. While unfitted designs can provide a handsome Country look, they may lack the workspace or convenient configurations that make a room a pleasure to work in.

Many Country enthusiasts find a middle ground in loosening up modern kitchen planning with selected, character-rich pieces and accessories, open shelving, and eye-catching finishes. A spacious floor plan allows leeway for idiosyncratic touches. In a large kitchen, an island styled differently from the wall cabinets or even a big farmhouse table with baskets underneath will add usable workspace with a casual, random look.

## Storage Strategies

Many unsatisfactory kitchen designs spring from a lack of storage space, as appliances and ingredients proliferate and strain the capacity. When you're designing, remember that while a down-home kitchen may charmingly suggest endless bounty, bulging clutter is less appealing. There are some steps you can take to ensure efficient storage in a Country kitchen.

## Zero In on Necessities

Before declaring your storage inadequate, make sure that every item is pulling its weight. If you use a fish poacher, cake decorator, and turkey platter twice a year, store them elsewhere. Watch out for needless duplication. Don't give prime storage to dozens of glasses or stacks of mixing bowls when you typically use only a few.

**Great rooms,** left, are typical of Country-style kitchens. Furniture that uses beadboard, above, fits right in with Country decorating.

**Translucent-glass-fronted cabinets,**
above, provide attractive, stylish storage.
Reproduction furniture, right, makes for
excellent auxiliary storage.

## Plan Point-of-Use Storage

Put the baking spices within reach of
the mixer and the savory spices near the
stove. Targeting storage may even free
up room for other things such as baskets, tins, or an extra freestanding corner cabinet or work cart.

## Let Practical Wares Double as Decoration

The yellowed plastic spatulas can stay in
the drawer, but wooden spoons, the old
sifter, canisters, skeins of herbs or garlic,
or earthenware bowls can all give a
room a friendly bustle while providing a
useful function.

## Use Open Storage Strategically

It makes sense to reserve open storage for items that you use frequently. That way they don't just gather grimy dust. Be wary of the hanging pot rack directly over the cooktop, where pots can quickly get grubby from spattering grease and liquids.

## Cabinetry

Cabinetry usually costs more than any other item in a kitchen renovation, and it has the biggest impact on the room's style. Before junking existing cabinets, consider whether refinishing, perhaps with a personality-rich faux effect, or refacing with new doors can reclaim basically sound units.

Today's cabinets run a gamut of Country styles: rustic planked fronts, more formal cathedral-arched panels, or classic square panels, recessed or raised. The range of woods from which to choose is equally wide. Oak, with its rugged grain, is the most popular, adaptable choice.

Kitchen cabinet fashions oscillate between very light and very dark stain treatments, so a midtone wood is less likely to become dated in just a few short years.

If you incline toward dark, cozy woods, make sure the kitchen is well lit, and keep other elements on the light side. White-enameled cabinetry can have a cottage-fresh appeal but will require some upkeep. Among bolder choices is a color-stain or a painted finish in a Shaker blue or Nantucket green, perhaps with a distressed or antiqued finish, for example. Stenciling or free-hand painting can add still more individuality to cabinet fronts, but only if you do it sparingly.

Glass-fronted cabinets and open shelves break up the monolithic banks of cabinetry while showing off the wares inside. But don't install them if you can't make a pleasing arrangement of the contents and keep them neat.

**This Country kitchen,** above, with lots of work space and an eat-in area, is open and roomy.

**The choice of fabrics** and accessories gives this kitchen, opposite, a distinctly Country feeling.

## Counter Forces

Counters can be great places for showcasing interesting collections. But unless you've got a spacious kitchen, it's more practical to keep counters clutter-free and reserve these surfaces for work. Place countertop and hand-held appliances in a convenient location where they'll be easy to retrieve, perhaps in a corner storage garage. A swing-up tray for a heavy stand mixer is a nice luxury, but it will consume considerable interior cabinet space.

**Plastic Laminate.** In a Country kitchen, countertop materials should appear natural or, barring that, unobtrusive. Plastic laminate is reasonably priced and easy to install or replace. High-quality plastic laminate is durable, though prone to chipping that can't be repaired, scorching, and water-infiltration at sink-side seams. More expensive solid-core laminates eliminate the dark joints and offer fancy multihued edge treatments. But in a Country setting, laminates are perhaps best presented in low-key, unfussy forms, in simple neutral colors.

**Solid-Surfacing Material.** The same applies to solid-surfacing material, a synthetic made from polyester or acrylic, sometimes mixed with ground stone. It generally costs three to five times as much as standard plastic laminate but is hard-wearing, repairable, and good-looking. It's offered now in a rainbow of choices and faux looks, including some convincing stone impressions. Skilled professional installers can create decorative inlay effects.

**Wood.** Wood has natural country warmth, but as a countertop is subject to water damage and warping. You may want to limit wood to a chopping surface. Durable eastern sugar maple is common for laminated butcher-block tops. Wood countertops must be meticulously cleaned and require periodic maintenance.

**Natural Stone.** Stone tends to be the most expensive countertop. Marble is relatively soft and porous and requires rigorous care in a kitchen setting. Slate and soapstone are sometimes used for countertops, but the most popular choice is granite. Durable and easy to maintain, granite may suit a country mood better in a matte rather than a polished finish. Porous stone requires sealing.

**Ceramic Tile.** Durable, nonabsorbent glazed ceramic tile resists stains, heat, and fading, and spans the greatest range of color and pattern, from dainty florals to bold, rustic squares. But the material is unforgiving to items that are easily breakable. The grout is a weak point for tile. It's easier to maintain if the joint is tight and flush to the surface. Use a grout that's made of an impervious epoxy or a latex-modified formulation. Tiles with a rustic, handmade look may require a wider, sanded grout joint, which you should periodically seal against stains and bacteria. It's also a good idea to clean any countertop regularly with a nonabrasive antibacterial cleanser. Tile that is well maintained will last a lifetime.

Tile spans a wide price range, and the cost has to include skilled installation on a firmly reinforced backing. Countertop tiles should be specified as scratch- and acid-resistant. The countertop edge can be finished with rounded bullnose trim pieces or wood edging.

## Country Kitchen Flooring

No floor takes more abuse than the kitchen's, which is subject to high traffic, dropped kitchenware, spills, grease, water, and harsh cleansers. Yet it's still expected to make a stylish contribution to the room's overall design. In any material, light-colored floors add an airy look but will require more scrupulous housekeeping. A floor that is dark tends to be less demanding, visually and logistically, but it may make a small room feel confining. You'll have to weigh your choice against how much time you have for upkeep and the actual size of the space. Whatever your circumstances, here are the most popular flooring products today.

**Wood.** Classic hardwood flooring and newer wood-look laminate floors evoke a Country feeling in any room. For kitchen use, wood must be particularly well sealed to avoid moisture damage. Pine and fir are the less expensive options, but they aren't as durable as costlier maple, birch, oak, and ash. Color stains or stenciled patterns may be appropriate, especially in a rustic Country kitchen.

Authentic wood floors will probably take a beating in a busy kitchen. That means refinishing periodically—sanding and recoating with a tough polyurethane, for example. Laminate products are easy to keep clean, using a damp mop. But they won't hold up as long as a well-maintained real wood floor.

**Vinyl.** For kitchens, resilient vinyl flooring is a standard choice. It's cost effective, comfortable underfoot, potentially more merciful on dropped breakables, and available in myriad designs. Though easy to maintain with a damp mop, most resilients will eventually need a liquid polish if you want a floor that shines. Vinyl products simulating wood, brick, stone, or tile aren't necessarily going to fool anyone, but they feature easy-to-live-with, dirt-hiding patterns with a pleasant Country attitude. Abstract or speckled patterns can add visual texture.

**Ceramic Tile.** Beyond its countertop applications, ceramic tile makes a long-lasting, easy-to-keep floor with a handsome aura of authenticity and history. Like any hard floor, however, it is cold and tiring to stand on, echoes noise, and is unkind to a dropped teacup. Some judiciously placed rugs can help overcome these disadvantages. Unglazed tiles are simply the hard-fired clay body, the same natural color throughout, from pale sand to deep umber or tinted with minerals.

The more highly fired the product, the denser, harder, and less absorbent it becomes. Low-fired earthenware terra-

cotta tiles are rugged and rustic but porous. They require frequent sealing and extra maintenance in a kitchen setting. Higher-fired stoneware quarry tiles still provide a handsome, earthy look and bear up to heavy use if well sealed. Most highly fired and more expensive tiles are smooth, impervious porcelain pavers, which require no sealing.

To enliven unglazed tiles without losing their neutral earthiness, lay them in intriguing overall patterns, such as octagons, squares, herringbones, or basket weaves. Standard floor mosaics, usually with porcelain bodies, can be factory mounted on mesh sheets in custom patterns. Plain mosaics have a charming retro flair.

Glazed tiles, permanently sealed with a thin, impervious glasslike layer, open up even more decorative possibilities. Tile industry organizations test and rate glazes for durability, so make sure your choice is specified for a demanding floor application, particularly if the kitchen has an exterior entrance.

## Finishing Touches

After assembling the kitchen's working parts, add the flourishes that make the whole less workaday. Paint is often the cheapest form of embellishment. Wainscoting, applied with precut tongue-and-groove planks or scored panels, can effectively dress walls, too. Of course, wallpaper is the easiest way to add pattern and print to your kitchen. You can choose from florals, checks, plaids, ticking stripes, or themed motifs, or look for designs that reinforce your Country decorating style. Many manufacturers carry different lines that might include American, English, French, Italian, or Swedish Country style, as well as Victorian, Shaker, and Arts and Crafts motifs, among others.

**Light-colored wood cabinets** and natural-finish pine table and benches, opposite, shout Country.

**The Modern Country look** is sustained by a copper-finish faucet and solid-wood cabinets, top and bottom right.

## Plan #181151

**Dimensions:** 50' W x 46' D
**Levels:** 2
**Square Footage:** 2,283
**Main Level Sq. Ft.:** 1,274
**Second Level Sq. Ft.:** 1,009
**Bedrooms:** 3
**Bathrooms:** 2½
**Foundation:** Basement
**Materials List Available:** Yes
**Price Category:** F

*Images provided by designer/architect.*

- Kitchen: This efficient and well-designed kitchen has double sinks and offers a separate eating area for those impromptu family meals.

- Master Suite: This master retreat has a walk-in closet and its own sumptuous bath.

- Home Office: Whether you work at home or just need a place for the family computer and keeping track of family finances, this home office fills the bill.

*Front View*

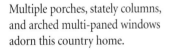

Multiple porches, stately columns, and arched multi-paned windows adorn this country home.

### Features:

- Ceiling Height: 8 ft. unless otherwise noted.

- Great Room: The second-floor mezzanine overlooks this great room. With its soaring ceiling, this dramatic room is the centerpiece of a spacious and flowing design that is just as suited to entertaining as it is to family life.

- Dining Area: Guests will naturally flow into this dining area when it is time to eat. After dinner they can step directly out onto the porch to enjoy coffee and dessert when the weather is fair.

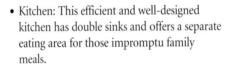

## Main Level Floor Plan

21'-0" X 20'-8"
6,30 X 6,20

46'-0"
13,8 m

17'-0" X 11'-8"
5,10 X 3,50

9'-8" X 8'-8"
2,90 X 2,60

9'-0" X 10'-0"
2,70 X 3,00

10'-0" X 12'-0"
3,00 X 3,60

9'-8" X 9'-4"
2,90 X 2,80

12'-0" X 20'-8"
3,60 X 6,20

50'-0"
15,0 m

## Upper Level Floor Plan

13'-4" X 10'-0"
4,00 X 3,00

17'-0" X 13'-0"
5,10 X 3,90

14'-0" X 10'-0"
4,20 X 3,00

*Copyright by designer/architect.*

# SMARTtip

## Coping Chair Rails

If the teeth of your rasp tend to break out thin edges of the cope, try wrapping the rasp with sandpaper to make fine adjustments.

Dining Room

Living Room

Master Bath

## Plan #181081

**Dimensions:** 58' W x 33' D

**Levels:** 2

**Square Footage:** 2,350

**Main Level Sq. Ft.:** 1,107

**Second Level Sq. Ft.:** 1,243

**Bedrooms:** 3

**Bathrooms:** 2½

**Foundation:** Basement

**Materials List Available:** Yes

**Price Category:** F

*Images provided by designer/architect.*

CAD FILE AVAILABLE

This traditional country home features a wrap-around porch and a second-floor balcony.

**Features:**

- Ceiling Height: 8 ft. unless otherwise noted.
- Family Room: Double French doors and a fireplace in this inviting front room enhance the beauty and warmth of the home's open floor plan.
- Kitchen: You'll love working in this bright and convenient kitchen. The breakfast bar is the perfect place to gather for informal meals.

- Master Suite: You'll look forward to retiring to this elegant upstairs suite at the end of a busy day. The suite features a private bath with separate shower and tub, as well as dual vanities.
- Secondary Bedrooms: Two family bedrooms share a full bath with a third room that opens onto the balcony.
- Basement: An unfinished full basement provides plenty of storage and the potential to add additional finished living space.

## Main Level Floor Plan

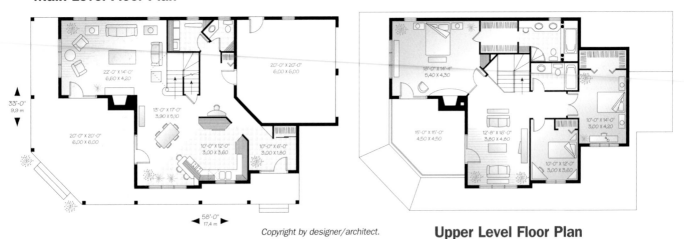

*Copyright by designer/architect.*

**Upper Level Floor Plan**

## Plan #241007

**Dimensions:** 58'10" W x 59'1" D

**Levels:** 1

**Square Footage:** 2,036

**Bedrooms:** 3

**Bathrooms:** 2

**Foundation:** Crawl space, slab

**Materials List Available:** No

**Price Category:** D

Images provided by designer/architect.

Enjoy summer breezes while relaxing on the large front porch of this charming country cottage.

**Features:**

• Great Room: Whether you enter from the front door or from the kitchen, you will feel welcome in this comfortable great room, which features a corner fireplace.

• Kitchen: This well-designed kitchen with extensive counter space offers a delightful eating bar, perfect for quick or informal meals.

• Master Suite: This luxurious master suite, located on the first floor for privacy, features his and her walk-in closets, separate vanities, a deluxe corner tub, a linen closet, and a walk-in shower.

• Additional Bedrooms: Two secondary bedrooms and an optional, large game room —well suited for a growing family—are located on the second floor.

**Bonus Area Floor Plan**

Copyright by designer/architect.

## Plan #321030

**Dimensions:** 61' W x 51' D

**Levels:** 1

**Square Footage:** 2,029

**Bedrooms:** 4

**Bathrooms:** 2

**Foundation:** Crawl space, slab, basement, or walkout

**Materials List Available:** Yes

**Price Category:** F

*Images provided by designer/architect.*

Two covered porches and a rear patio make this lovely home fit right into a site with a view.

### Features:

- Great Room: Boxed entryway columns, a vaulted ceiling, corner fireplace, widowed wall, and door to the patio are highlights in this spacious room.

- Study: Tucked into the back of the house for privacy, the study also opens to the rear patio.

- Dining Area: The windowed alcove lets natural light flow into this room, which adjoins the kitchen.

- Kitchen: A central island, deep pantry, and ample counter area make this room a cook's delight.

- Master Suite: You'll love the two walk-in closets, decorative bedroom window, and double doors opening to the private porch. The bath includes a garden tub, a separate shower, and two vanities.

- Additional Bedrooms: Both bedrooms have a walk-in closet.

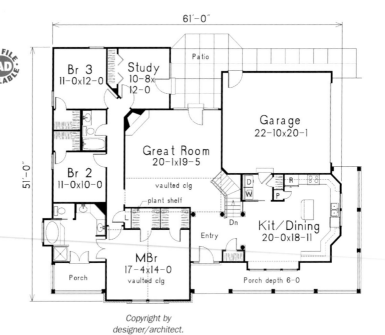

*Copyright by designer/architect.*

## Plan #321019

**Dimensions:** 70'8" W x 70' D

**Levels:** 1

**Square Footage:** 2,452

**Bedrooms:** 4

**Bathrooms:** 2½

**Foundation:** Basement

**Materials List Available:** Yes

**Price Category:** E

This gorgeous, glowing home is as warm and welcoming inside as it looks on the outside.

**Features:**

- Kitchen: This efficient layout features a walk-in pantry, a central island with cooktop, and a snack bar. Transition easily at mealtime from the kitchen to the breakfast room, dining room, or even the back deck.

- Home Office: A separate entrance makes this home office perfect for telecommuting. If you don't work from home, use this space to do the work of the home-the bills and schedules-or just to escape.

- Master Suite: Away from the more bustling areas of the home, this restful space boasts a vast walk-in closet, whirlpool tub flanked with windows, separate shower, and his and her vanities.

- Secondary Bedrooms: Two additional bedrooms have ample closet space and access to a shared full bathroom.

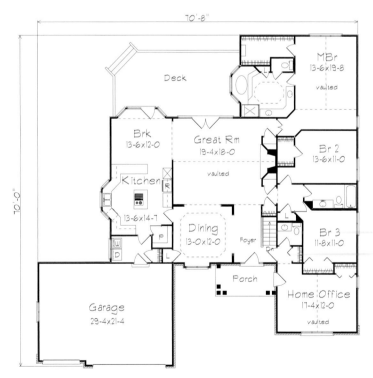

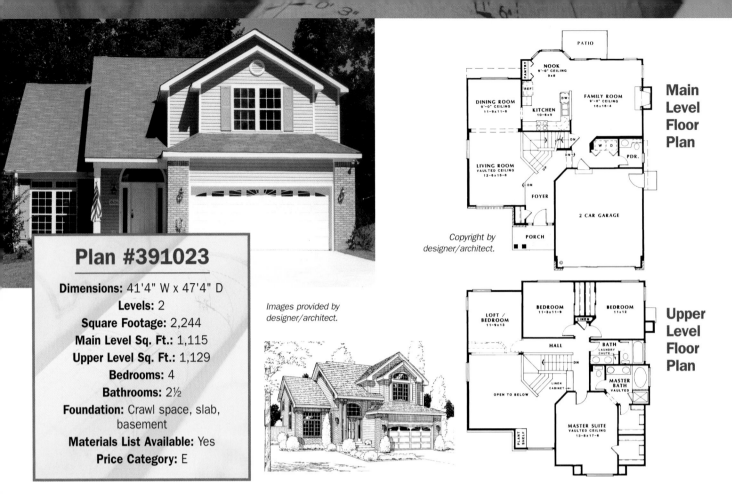

### Main Level Floor Plan

PATIO

NOOK
9'-0" CEILING
9x8

PANTRY

REF

DINING ROOM
9'-0" CEILING
11-9x11-6

KITCHEN
10-0x9

DW

FAMILY ROOM
9'-0" CEILING
16x16-4

UP

LIVING ROOM
VAULTED CEILING
12-8x15-8

DN

DN

W D

PDR.

FOYER

DN

2 CAR GARAGE

PORCH

*Copyright by designer/architect.*

*Images provided by designer/architect.*

### Upper Level Floor Plan

LOFT / BEDROOM
11-9x13

BEDROOM
11-3x11-9

BEDROOM
11x12

LINEN

HALL

BATH

BATH
LAUNDRY
CHUTE

OPEN TO BELOW

LINEN
CABINET

DN

MASTER
BATH
VAULTED

PLANT
SHELF

MASTER SUITE
VAULTED CEILING
13-8x17-6

## Plan #391023

**Dimensions:** 41'4" W x 47'4" D
**Levels:** 2
**Square Footage:** 2,244
**Main Level Sq. Ft.:** 1,115
**Upper Level Sq. Ft.:** 1,129
**Bedrooms:** 4
**Bathrooms:** 2½
**Foundation:** Crawl space, slab, basement
**Materials List Available:** Yes
**Price Category:** E

---

Garage
20-4x21-4

M.Bath
17-8x10-6

Porch
22-0x12-0

1/2
Bath
5-0x6-1

Stor.
5-0x6-1

Master
Bedroom
19-2x13-7

Greatroom
22-0x15-2

Laun.
8-4x5-8

Kitchen
12-8x12-0

Bath

Bedroom
10-8x12-0

Bedroom
11-6x11-0

Foyer

Dining
11-6x13-6

Breakfast
12-8x9-10

Porch
30-8x6-0

*Images provided by designer/architect.*

### Bonus Area Floor Plan

Future
14-0x12-0

Future
29-4x16-0

Future
12-8x12-0

## Plan #311016

**Dimensions:** 63'10" W x 64'7" D
**Levels:** 1
**Square Footage:** 2,089
**Bedrooms:** 3
**Bathrooms:** 2½
**Foundation:** Crawl space, slab, or basement
**Materials List Available:** Yes
**Price Category:** D

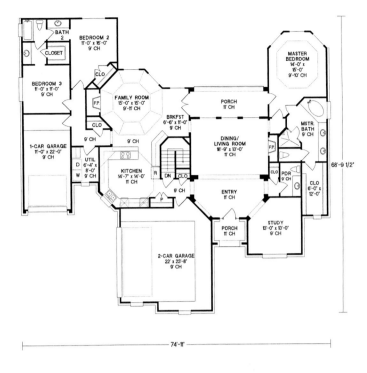

## Plan #121164

**Dimensions:** 74'11" W x 68'9½" D

**Levels:** 1

**Square Footage:** 2,331

**Bedrooms:** 3

**Bathrooms:** 2½

**Foundation:** Slab; basement for fee

**Material List Available:** Yes

**Price Category:** E

**Main Level Floor Plan**

**Upper Level Floor Plan**

## Plan #331002

**Dimensions:** 62'2" W x 66'8" D

**Levels:** 2

**Square Footage:** 2,299

**Main Level Sq. Ft.:** 1,517

**Upper Level Sq. Ft.:** 782

**Bedrooms:** 3

**Bathrooms:** 2½

**Foundation:** Crawl space, slab, or basement

**Materials List Available:** No

**Price Category:** E

## Plan #441048

**Dimensions:** 48' W x 40' D
**Levels:** 2
**Square Footage:** 2,453
**Main Level Sq. Ft.:** 1,118
**Upper Level Sq. Ft.:** 1,335
**Bedrooms:** 4
**Bathrooms:** 2½
**Foundation:** Crawl space
**Materials List Available:** Yes
**Price Category:** E

The perfect-size plan and a pretty facade add up to a great home for your family. The combination of wood siding and stone complements a carriage-style garage door and cedar-shingle detailing on the outside of this home.

**CAD FILE AVAILABLE**

*Images provided by designer/architect.*

**Features:**

- Entry: The interior opens though this angled front entry, with the den on the left and a half-bathroom on the right. The den has a comfortable window seat for dreaming and gazing.

- Kitchen: The dining area adjoins this island kitchen, which has a roomy pantry and built-in desk.

- Master Suite: This vaulted suite features a spa bath, walk-in closet with window seat, and separate tub and shower.

- Upper Level: All bedrooms are located on this level. Bedroom 3 has a walk-in closet. The laundry area is also located here to make wash day trouble free.

Rear Elevation

*Copyright by designer/architect.*

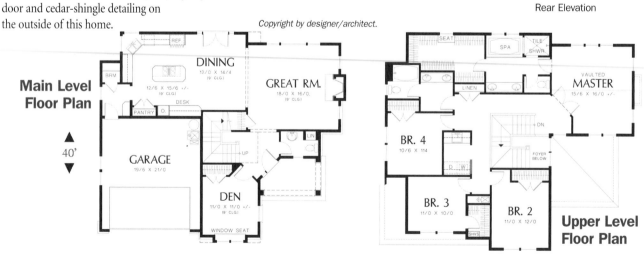

## Plan #161115

**Dimensions:** 79'8" W x 44'2" D
**Levels:** 1
**Heated Square Footage:** 2,253
**Bedrooms:** 4
**Bathrooms:** 3
**Foundation:** Walkout basement
**Material List Available:** Yes
**Price Category:** E

*Images provided by designer/architect.*

This one-level home offers a beautiful exterior of brick and stone with shake siding.

**Features:**

- Great Room: This open gathering area features an 11-foot-high ceiling and access to the rear yard. Turn on the corner gas fireplace, and fill the room with warmth and charm.

- Kitchen: This peninsula kitchen with built-in pantry and counter seating offers easy access to both formal and informal dining. The laundry facilities and the garage are just a few steps away. A magnificent bay window decorates the breakfast room and brings natural light into the area.

- Master Suite: This retreat offers a furniture alcove in the sleeping area and a walk-in closet. The private bath features a double-bowl vanity and a whirlpool tub.

- Guest Suite: This private bedroom suite is located behind the three-car garage and offers a welcoming environment for your overnight guests.

- Basement: This full walkout basement expands the living space of the delightful home.

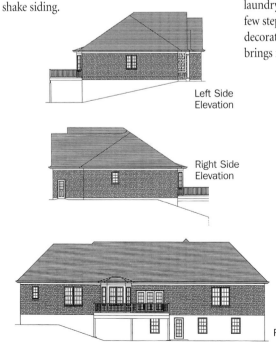

Left Side Elevation

Right Side Elevation

Rear Elevation

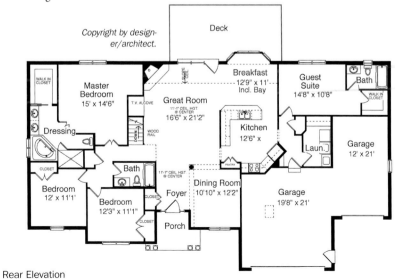

*Copyright by designer/architect.*

## Plan #121021

**Dimensions:** 46' W x 48' D
**Levels:** 2
**Square Footage:** 2,270
**Main Level Sq. Ft.:** 1,150
**Upper Level Sq. Ft.:** 1,120
**Bedrooms:** 4
**Bathrooms:** 2½
**Foundation:** Basement
**Materials List Available:** Yes
**Price Category:** E

*Images provided by designer/architect.*

With its wraparound porch, this home evokes the charm of a traditional home.

**Features:**

• Ceiling Height: 8 ft.

• Foyer: The dramatic two-story entry enjoys views of the formal dining room and great room. A second floor balcony overlooks the entry and a plant shelf.

• Formal Dining Room: This gracious room is perfect for family holiday gatherings and for more formal dinner parties.

• Great Room: All the family will want to gather in this comfortable, informal room which features bay windows, an entertainment center, and a see-through fireplace.

• Breakfast Area: Conveniently located just off the great room, the bayed breakfast area features a built-in desk for household bills and access to the backyard.

• Kitchen: An island is the centerpiece of this kitchen. Its intelligent design makes food preparation a pleasure.

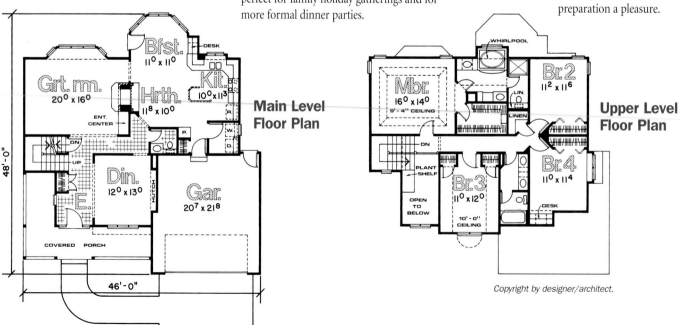

*Copyright by designer/architect.*

## Plan #181094

**Dimensions:** 50' W x 39' D
**Levels:** 2
**Square Footage:** 2,099
**Main Level Sq. Ft.:** 1,060
**Upper Level Sq. Ft.:** 1,039
**Bedrooms:** 4
**Bathrooms:** 2½
**Foundation:** Basement
**Materials List Available:** Yes
**Price Category:** D

The curved covered porch makes this is a great place to come home to.

**CAD FILE AVAILABLE • CAD •**

**Features:**

- **Entry:** This air-lock entry area with closet will help keep energy costs down.

- **Family Room:** This gathering area features a fireplace and is open to the kitchen and the dining area.

- **Kitchen:** U-shaped and boasting an island and a walk-in pantry, this kitchen is open to the dining area.

- **Master Suite:** This large retreat features a fireplace and a walk-in closet. The master bath has dual vanities, a separate shower, and a large tub.

- **Bedrooms:** Located upstairs with the master suite are three additional bedrooms. They share a common bathroom, and each has a large closet.

*Images provided by designer/architect.*

Rear View

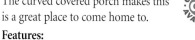

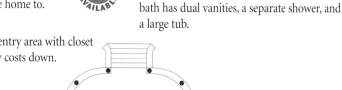

**Main Level Floor Plan**

**Upper Level Floor Plan**

*Copyright by designer/architect.*

## Plan #151113

**Dimensions:** 62'10" W x 91'4" D

**Levels:** 1

**Square Footage:** 2,186

**Bedrooms:** 4

**Bathrooms:** 3

**Foundation:** Crawl space, slab, or basement

**CompleteCost List Available:** Yes

**Price Category:** D

*Images provided by designer/architect.*

**CAD FILE AVAILABLE**

### Optional Bonus Area Floor Plan

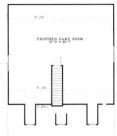

*Copyright by designer/architect.*

---

## Plan #441041

**Dimensions:** 49' W x 45' D

**Levels:** 2

**Square Footage:** 2,164

**Main Level Sq. Ft.:** 1,171

**Upper Level Sq. Ft.:** 993

**Bedrooms:** 3

**Bathrooms:** 2½

**Foundation:** Crawl space; slab or basement for fee

**Material List Available:** Yes

**Price Category:** D

*Images provided by designer/architect.*

**CAD FILE AVAILABLE**

### Main Level Floor Plan

*Copyright by designer/architect.*

### Upper Level Floor Plan

Rear Elevation

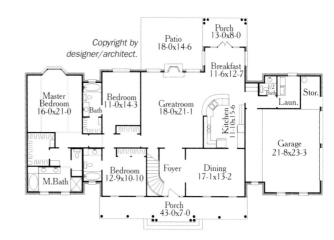

# Plan #311005

**Dimensions:** 87' W x 57'3" D

**Levels:** 1

**Square Footage:** 2,497

**Bedrooms:** 3

**Bathrooms:** 2½

**Foundation:** Crawl space, slab, or basement

**Materials List Available:** Yes

**Price Category:** E

*Images provided by designer/architect.*

## Bonus Area Floor Plan

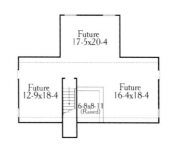

# Plan #151835

**Dimensions:** 76' W x 50'6" D

**Levels:** 2

**Square Footage:** 2,458

**Main Level Sq. Ft.:** 1,804

**Upper Level Sq. Ft.:** 654

**Bedrooms:** 4

**Bathrooms:** 3

**Foundation:** Crawl space or slab; basement or walkout for fee

**CompleteCost List Available:** Yes

**Price Category:** E

*Images provided by designer/architect.*

## Main Level Floor Plan

## Upper Level Floor Plan

# Plan #121038

**Dimensions:** 54' W x 52' D

**Levels:** 2

**Square Footage:** 2,332

**Main Level Sq. Ft.:** 1,597

**Upper Level Sq. Ft.:** 735

**Bedrooms:** 4

**Bathrooms:** 3½

**Foundation:** Basement

**Materials List Available:** Yes

**Price Category:** E

Offering plenty of architectural style, this home is designed with the busy modern lifestyle in mind.

**Features:**

- Ceiling Height: 8 ft. unless otherwise noted.

- Family Room: The visual spaciousness of this stylish family room is enhanced by a cathedral ceiling and light streaming through stacked windows.

- Kitchen: This is sure to be a popular informal gathering place. The kitchen features a convenient center island with a snack bar, pantry, and planning desk. The breakfast area is perfect for quick family meals.

- Master Suite: This peaceful retreat is thoughtfully located apart from the rest of the house. It includes a walk-in closet and a private bath.

- Bedrooms: Bedroom 2 has its own walk-in closet and private bath. Bedrooms 3 and 4 share a full bath.

**CAD FILE AVAILABLE**

## Main Level Floor Plan

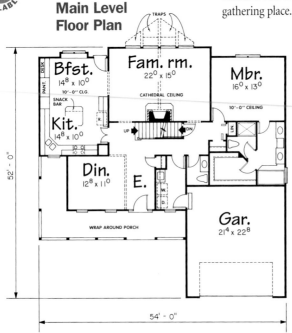

## Upper Level Floor Plan

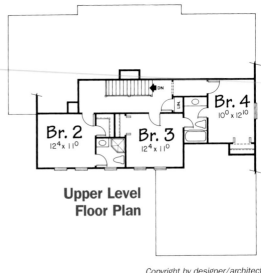

# Plan #161034

**Dimensions:** 56' W x 53' D
**Levels:** 2
**Square Footage:** 2,156
**Main Level Sq. Ft.:** 1,605
**Upper Level Sq. Ft.:** 551
**Bedrooms:** 3
**Bathrooms:** 2½
**Foundation:** Basement
**Materials List Available:** No
**Price Category:** D

*Images provided by designer/architect.*

Multiple gables, a covered porch, and circle-topped windows combine to enhance the attractiveness of this exciting home.

**Features:**

- Great Room: A raised foyer introduces this open combined great room and dining room. Enjoy the efficiency of a dual-sided fireplace that warms both the great room and kitchen.

- Kitchen: The kitchen, designed for easy traffic patterns, offers an abundance of counter space and features a cooktop island.

- Master Suite: This first-floor master suite, separated for privacy, includes twin vanities and a walk-in closet. A deluxe corner bath and walk-in shower complete its luxurious detail.

- Additional Rooms: Two additional bedrooms lead to the second-floor balcony, which overlooks the great room. You can use the optional bonus room as a den or office.

*Copyright by designer/architect.*

**Main Level Floor Plan**

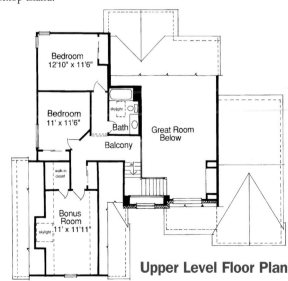

**Upper Level Floor Plan**

## Plan #351069

**Dimensions:** 78' W x 49'6" D

**Levels:** 1

**Heated Square Footage:** 2,008

**Bedrooms:** 3

**Bathrooms:** 2½

**Foundation:** Crawl space or slab

**Materials List Available:** No

**Price Category:** F

*Images provided by designer/architect.*

This is a great house with a functional split-floor-plan layout.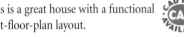

### Features:

- **Entertaining Areas:** A large dining area for those family get-togethers and an expansive great room with a gas log fireplace and vaulted ceiling will make entertaining easy.

- **Master Suite:** This expansive suite has a large sitting area, his and her walk-in closets, a jetted tub, and a walk-in shower.

- **Storage Areas:** The home features plenty of storage space; a large utility room will help stow away your odds and ends.

- **Expansion:** Flex space can be used as a home office/study, playroom, and/or entertainment center. There is even a bonus room above the garage.

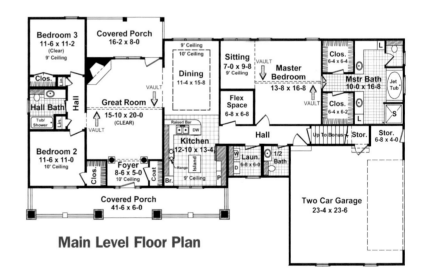

**Main Level Floor Plan**

**Upper Level Floor Plan**

*Copyright by designer/architect.*

## Plan #311003

**Dimensions:** 70'10" W x 65'4" D
**Levels:** 2
**Square Footage:** 2,428
**Main Level Sq. Ft.:** 2,348
**Upper Level Sq. Ft.:** 80
**Bedrooms:** 3
**Bathrooms:** 2½
**Foundation:** Crawl space, slab
**Materials List Available:** Y
**Price Category:** E

*Images provided by designer/architect.*

If you admire the gracious colonnaded porch, curved brick steps, and stunning front windows, you'll fall in love with the interior of this home.

**Features:**

• Great Room: Enjoy the vaulted ceiling, balcony from the upper level, and fireplace with flanking windows that let you look out to the patio.

• Dining Room: Columns define this formal room, which is adjacent to the breakfast room.

• Kitchen: A bayed sink area and extensive curved bar provide visual interest in this well-designed kitchen, which every cook will love.

• Breakfast Room: Huge windows let the sun shine into this room, which is open to the kitchen.

• Master Suite: The sitting area is open to the rear porch for a special touch in this gorgeous suite. Two walk-in closets and a vaulted ceiling and double vanity in the bath will make you feel completely pampered.

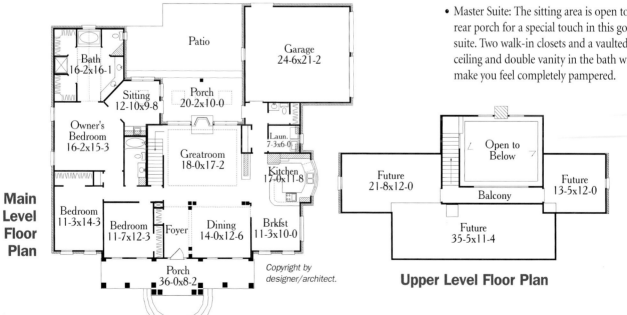

**Main Level Floor Plan**

Bath 16-2x16-1
Sitting 12-10x9-8
Patio
Porch 20-2x10-0
Garage 24-6x21-2
Owner's Bedroom 16-2x15-3
Greatroom 18-0x17-2
Laun. 7-3x6-0
Kitchen 17-0x11-8
Bedroom 11-3x14-3
Bedroom 11-7x12-3
Foyer
Dining 14-0x12-6
Brkfst 11-3x10-0
Porch 36-0x8-2

*Copyright by designer/architect.*

**Upper Level Floor Plan**

Open to Below
Future 21-8x12-0
Future 13-5x12-0
Balcony
Future 35-5x11-4

## Plan #421044

**Dimensions:** 70'8" W x 53' D
**Levels:** 2
**Square Footage:** 2,302
**Main Level Sq. Ft.:** 1,570
**Upper Level Sq. Ft.:** 732
**Bedrooms:** 4
**Bathrooms:** 2½
**Foundation:** Crawl space, slab or basement
**Material List Available:** Yes
**Price Category:** E

*Images provided by designer/architect.*

**Main Level Floor Plan**

*Copyright by designer/architect.*

**Upper Level Floor Plan**

## Plan #131009

**Dimensions:** 64'10" W x 57'8" D
**Levels:** 1
**Square Footage:** 2,018
**Bedrooms:** 3
**Bathrooms:** 2
**Foundation:** Crawl space, slab, or basement
**Materials List Available:** Yes
**Price Category:** E

*Images provided by designer/architect.*

*Copyright by designer/architect.*

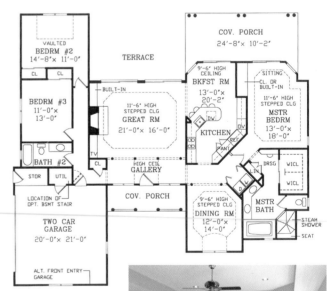

Great Room

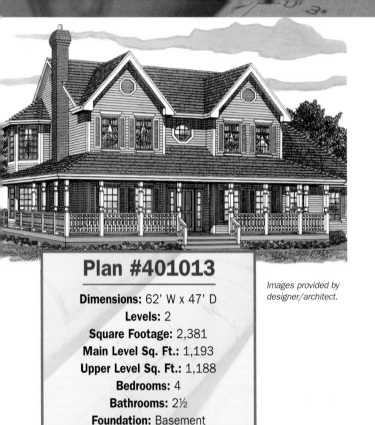

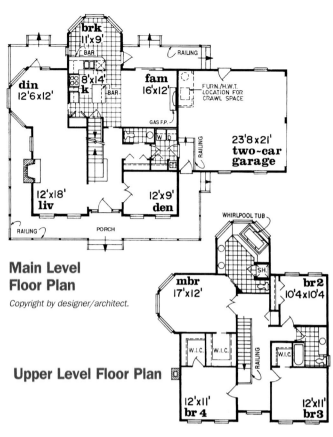

## Plan #401013

**Dimensions:** 62' W x 47' D

**Levels:** 2

**Square Footage:** 2,381

**Main Level Sq. Ft.:** 1,193

**Upper Level Sq. Ft.:** 1,188

**Bedrooms:** 4

**Bathrooms:** 2½

**Foundation:** Basement

**Materials List Available:** Yes

**Price Category:** E

*Images provided by designer/architect.*

**Main Level Floor Plan**

*Copyright by designer/architect.*

**Upper Level Floor Plan**

---

## Plan #371127

**Dimensions:** 85'2" W x 42'4 1/2" D

**Levels:** 2

**Square Footage:** 2,427

**Main Level Sq. Ft.:** 1,788

**Upper Level Sq. Ft.:** 639

**Bedrooms:** 4

**Bathrooms:** 3

**Foundation:** Crawl space, slab, or basement

**Material List Available:** No

**Price Category:** E

*Images provided by designer/architect.*

**CAD FILE AVAILABLE**

**Upper Level Floor Plan**

**Main Level Floor Plan**

*Copyright by designer/architect.*

## Plan #131022

**Dimensions:** 54'8" W x 43' D

**Levels:** 2

**Square Footage:** 2,092

**Main Level Sq. Ft.:** 1,152

**Upper Level Sq. Ft.:** 940

**Bedrooms:** 4

**Bathrooms:** 2½

**Foundation:** Crawl space, slab, or basement

**Materials List Available:** Yes

**Price Category:** E

*This home, as shown in the photograph, may differ from the actual blueprints. For more detailed information, please check the floor plans carefully.*

You'll love the way this charming home reminds you of an old-fashioned farmhouse.

**Features:**

• Ceiling Height: 8 ft.

• Living Room: This large living room can be used as guest quarters when the need arises.

• Dining Room: This bayed, informal room is large enough for all your dining and entertaining needs. It could also double as an office or den.

• Garage: An expandable loft over the garage offers an ideal playroom or fourth bedroom.

*Images provided by designer/architect.*

Rear Elevation

## Main Level Floor Plan

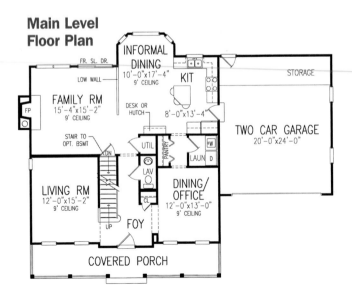

## Upper Level Floor Plan

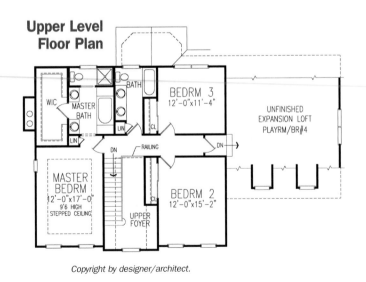

*Copyright by designer/architect.*

## Plan #131046

**Dimensions:** 68' W x 57'6" D
**Levels:** 2
**Square Footage:** 2,245
**Main Level Sq. Ft.:** 1,720
**Upper Level Sq. Ft.:** 525
**Bedrooms:** 3
**Bathrooms:** 2½
**Foundation:** Crawl space, slab, or basement
**Materials List Available:** Yes
**Price Category:** F

*Images provided by designer/architect.*

You'll love the mixture of country charm and contemporary amenities in this lovely home.

**Features:**

- Porch: The covered wraparound porch spells comfort, and the arched windows spell style.

- Great Room: Look up at the 18-ft. vaulted ceiling and the balcony that looks over this room from the upper level, and then notice the wall of windows and the fireplace that's set into a media wall for decorating ease.

- Kitchen: This roomy kitchen is also designed for convenience, thanks to its ample counter space and work island.

- Breakfast Room: The kitchen looks out to this lovely room, with its vaulted ceiling and sliding French doors that open to the rear covered porch.

- Master Bedroom: A 10-ft-ceiling and a dramatic bay window give character to this charming room.

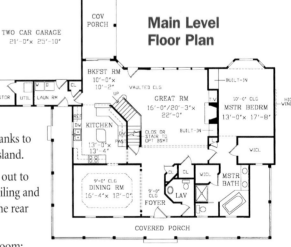

**Main Level
Floor Plan**

**Upper Level
Floor Plan**

*Copyright by designer/architect.*

## Plan #161026

**Dimensions:** 67'6" W x 63'6" D
**Levels:** 1
**Heated Square Footage:** 2,041
**Bedrooms:** 3
**Bathrooms:** 2
**Foundation:** Basement
**Materials List Available:** No
**Price Category:** D

You'll love the special features of this home, which has been designed for efficiency and comfort.

**CAD FILE AVAILABLE** CAD

*Images provided by designer/architect.*

**Features:**

- **Foyer:** This raised foyer offers a view through the great room and beyond it to the covered deck.

- **Great Room:** Elegant windows allow versatility — decorate casually or more formally.

- **Kitchen:** You'll find ample counter space and cabinets in this spacious room, which adjoins the dining room and opens onto the rear yard.

- **Library:** Curl up on the window seat that wraps around the tower in this quiet spot.

- **Laundry Room:** A tub makes this large room practical for crafts as well as laundry.

- **Master Suite:** A vaulted ceiling gives grace to the sitting area, and the garden bath with a walk-in closet and whirlpool tub adds luxury.

Rear Elevation

## Main Level Floor Plan

## Lower Level Floor Plan

*Copyright by designer/architect.*

# Plan #391002

**Dimensions:** 76'4" W x 45'10" D
**Levels:** 2
**Square Footage:** 2,281
**Main Level Sq. Ft.:** 1,260
**Upper Level Sq. Ft.:** 1,021
**Bedrooms:** 3
**Bathrooms:** 2½
**Foundation:** Crawl space, slab, or basement
**Materials List Available:** Yes
**Price Category:** E

*Images provided by designer/architect.*

The luxurious amenities in this compact, well designed home are sure to delight everyone in the family.

**Features:**

- Ceiling Height: 9-ft. ceilings add to the spacious feeling created by the open design.

- Family Room: A vaulted ceiling and large window area add elegance to this comfortable room, which will be the heart of this home.

- Dining Area: Adjoining the kitchen, this room features a large bayed area as well as French doors that open onto the back deck.

- Kitchen: This step-saving design will make cooking a joy for everyone in the family.

- Utility Room: Near the kitchen, this room includes cabinets and shelves for extra storage space.

- Master Suite: A triple window, tray ceiling, walk-in closet, and luxurious bath make this area a treat.

## Main Level Floor Plan

*Copyright by designer/architect.*

## Alternate Crawl Space/Slab

Alternate Crawl/Slab

## Upper Level Floor Plan

SMARTtip

## Creating Depth with Wall Frames

Wall frames create an illusion of depth and density because 1) they are three-dimensional and 2) they divide the wall area into smaller, denser segments. The three-dimensional quality of wall frames is fundamentally different from that of the alternative treatment: raised panels. Despite the name, raised panels actually produce a concave-like, or receding, effect whereas wall frames are more convex, protruding outward. In terms of sculpture, concave units create negative space while convex units create positive space. Raised panels, therefore, deliver a uniform sense of volume, mass, and density, while wall frames create a higher level of tension and dramatic interest.

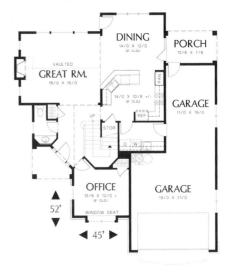

## Main Level Floor Plan

DINING
14/0 X 12/0
(9' CLG)

PORCH
12/6 X 7/6

VAULTED
GREAT RM.
18/0 X 15/0

14/0 X 10/8 +/-
(9' CLG)

PAN

REF

GARAGE
11/0 X 19/0

UP

STOR

D W

OFFICE
12/6 X 10/0 +
(9' CLG)

GARAGE
19/0 X 21/0

WINDOW SEAT

52'

45'

**Main Level Floor Plan**

Rear View

Images provided by designer/architect.

VAULTED
MASTER
14/0 X 17/6

SPA

DN

SHELVES

LINEN

BR. 2
11/2 X 10/4

PLANT
SHELF

BR. 3
11/10 X 10/2

**Upper Level Floor Plan**

Copyright by designer/architect.

## Plan #441040

**Dimensions:** 45' W x 52' D

**Levels:** 2

**Square Footage:** 2,079

**Main Level Sq. Ft.:** 1,109

**Upper Level Sq. Ft.:** 970

**Bedrooms:** 3

**Bathrooms:** 2½

**Foundation:** Crawl space; slab or basement for fee

**Materials List Available:** No

**Price Category:** D

---

## Main Level Floor Plan

PORCH

MEDIA CENTER

LIVING RM.
16'-0" X 21'-0"

PORCH

MASTER SUITE
15'-0" X 13'-0"

DINING
12'-0" X 14'-0"

GARAGE
24'-0" X 23'-0"

CEILING
SLOPES

COUNTRY KITCHEN

RAISED BAR

STOR. UNDER STAIR

GLASS
SHOWER

WALK IN
CLOSET

BATH 1

STOR.
UNDER

KITCHEN
14'-0" X 14'-0"

MARBLE
TUB

WALK IN
CLOSET

B.2

ENTRY

WINDOW
SEAT

WALK IN
PANTRY

UTIL.

W. D.

P O R C H

Copyright by designer/architect.

## Upper Level Floor Plan

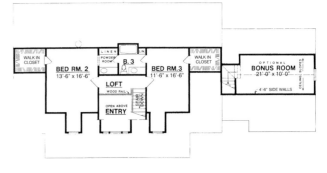

WALK IN
CLOSET

LINEN

POWDER
ROOM

LIN

WALK IN
CLOSET

OPTIONAL
BONUS ROOM
21'-0" x 10'-0"

BED RM. 2
13'-6" x 16'-6"

B.3

BED RM.3
11'-6" x 16'-6"

CEILING SLOPES

4'-6" SIDE WALLS

LOFT

WOOD RAIL

STAIR DOWN

OPEN ABOVE
ENTRY

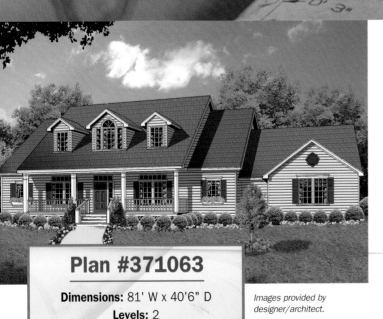

## Plan #371063

**Dimensions:** 81' W x 40'6" D

**Levels:** 2

**Square Footage:** 2,330

**Main Level Sq. Ft.:** 1,605

**Upper Level Sq. Ft.:** 725

**Bedrooms:** 3

**Bathrooms:** 2½

**Foundation:** Slab

**Materials List Available:** No

**Price Category:** E

Images provided by designer/architect.

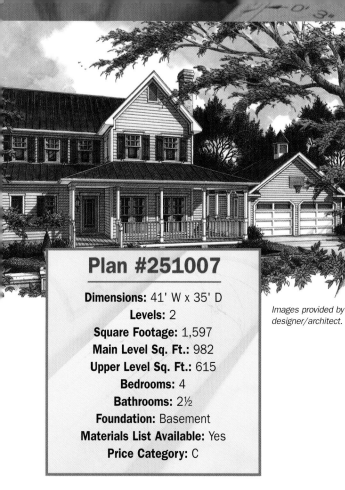

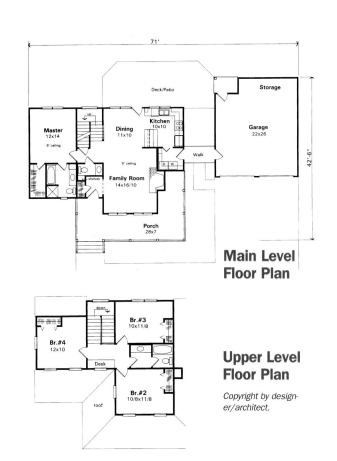

**Main Level
Floor Plan**

*Images provided by
designer/architect.*

**Upper Level
Floor Plan**

*Copyright by designer/architect.*

## Plan #251007

**Dimensions:** 41' W x 35' D

**Levels:** 2

**Square Footage:** 1,597

**Main Level Sq. Ft.:** 982

**Upper Level Sq. Ft.:** 615

**Bedrooms:** 4

**Bathrooms:** 2½

**Foundation:** Basement

**Materials List Available:** Yes

**Price Category:** C

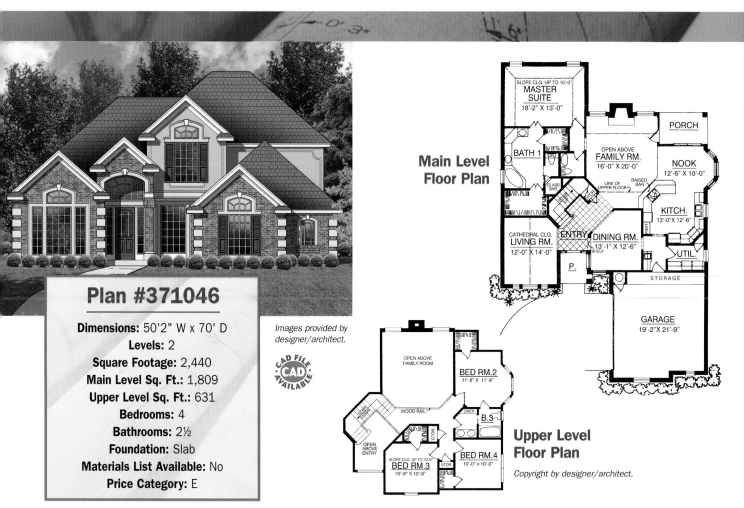

**Main Level
Floor Plan**

**Upper Level
Floor Plan**

*Images provided by
designer/architect.*

*Copyright by designer/architect.*

## Plan #371046

**Dimensions:** 50'2" W x 70' D

**Levels:** 2

**Square Footage:** 2,440

**Main Level Sq. Ft.:** 1,809

**Upper Level Sq. Ft.:** 631

**Bedrooms:** 4

**Bathrooms:** 2½

**Foundation:** Slab

**Materials List Available:** No

**Price Category:** E

## Plan #131051

**Dimensions:** 64'4" W x 53'4" D
**Levels:** 2
**Square Footage:** 2,431
**Main Level Sq. Ft.:** 1,293
**Upper Level Sq. Ft.:** 1,138
**Bedrooms:** 4
**Bathrooms:** 2½
**Foundation:** Crawl space, slab, or basement
**Materials List Available:** Yes
**Price Category:** F

Gracious and charming with a wraparound front porch and a backyard terrace, this home also has a ready-to-finish third floor all-purpose room and a full bath.

**Features:**

• Main Level Ceiling Height: 8 ft.

• Family Room: A comfortable space for the entire family to gather, this delightful room can be warmed by a heat-circulating fireplace.

• Dining Room: A cozy dinette boasts a sliding glass door with access to a gorgeous backyard terrace with an optional calm reflecting pool.

• Kitchen: Adjoining the dining area, the kitchen offers plenty of storage and counter space. The laundry room and half-bath are nearby for convenience.

• Garage: The garage is tucked way back to keep it from intruding into the traditional facade.

**Main Level Floor Plan**

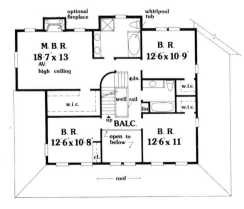

*Images provided by designer/architect.*

*This home, as shown in the photograph, may differ from the actual blueprints. For more detailed information, please check the floor plans carefully.*

Rear Elevation

**Upper Level Floor Plan**

**Optional 3rd Level Floor Plan**

*Copyright by designer/architect.*

## Plan #171011

**Dimensions:** 70' W x 58' D
**Levels:** 1
**Square Footage:** 2,069
**Bedrooms:** 3
**Bathrooms:** 2½
**Foundation:** Crawl space, slab
**Materials List Available:** Yes
**Price Category:** D

This home combines the charm of a country cottage with all the modern amenities.

*Images provided by designer/architect.*

**Features:**

- Ceiling Height: 9 ft. unless otherwise noted.
- Front Porch: Watch the sun set, read a book, or just relax on this spacious front porch.
- Foyer: This gracious foyer has two closets and opens to the formal dining room and the study.
- Dining Room: This big dining room works just as well for family Sunday dinner as it does for entertaining guests on Saturday night.

- Family Room: This inviting family room features an 11-ft. ceiling, a paddle fan, and a corner fireplace.
- Kitchen: This smart kitchen includes lots of counter space, a built in desk, and a breakfast bar.
- Master Bedroom: This master bedroom is separate from the other bedrooms for added privacy. It includes a paddle fan.
- Master Bath: This master bath has two vanities, walk-in closets, a deluxe tub, and a walk-in shower.

*Copyright by designer/architect.*

## SMARTtip

### Types of Paintbrush Bristles

**Nylon Bristles.** These are most suitable for latex paint, although they can also be used with solvent-based paint.

**Natural Bristles.** Also called "China bristle," natural bristle brushes are preferred for use with solvent-based paints and varnishes because they tend to hold more paint and generally brush out to a smoother looking finish. Natural bristle brushes should not be used with latex paint. The water in the paint will cause the bristles to expand and ruin the brush.

**Choosing Brushes.** When buying a brush, check for thick, resilient bristles that are firmly held in place. Be sure, also, to get the proper type brush for the job.

## Plan #271082

**Dimensions:** 71' W x 62' D

**Levels:** 1

**Square Footage:** 2,074

**Bedrooms:** 4

**Bathrooms:** 2

**Foundation:** Crawl space or slab

**Materials List Available:** No

**Price Category:** D

*Images provided by designer/architect.*

Magnificent pillars and a huge transom window add stature to the impressive entry of this traditional home.

**Features:**

• Living Room: A corner fireplace warms this spacious room, which shares a 12-ft. ceiling with the dining room and the kitchen.

• Backyard: A French door provides direct access to a covered porch, which in turn flows into a wide deck and a sunny patio.

• Master Suite: A cathedral ceiling enhances the master bedroom, which offers a large walk-in closet. The private bath is certainly luxurious, with its whirlpool tub and two vanities

*Copyright by designer/architect.*

## SMARTtip

### Making a Cornice

Any new cornice or cornice shelf includes mounting hardware and directions for its installation. But you'll probably need to purchase mounting brackets to install older or homemade cornices. If you're not comfortable with the idea of working on a ladder, especially while handling the cornice and various tools, call a pro. A professional installer will charge a flat rate for coming to your house plus an additional fee for each treatment. Prices vary, but your location, the size of the treatment (measured by the foot), and the difficulty of the job will determine its price.

## Plan #271070

**Dimensions:** 70'3" W x 60' D

**Levels:** 2

**Square Footage:** 2,144

**Main Level Sq. Ft.:** 1,156

**Upper Level Sq. Ft.:** 988

**Bedrooms:** 4

**Bathrooms:** 2½

**Foundation:** Basement, crawl space

**Materials List Available:** No

**Price Category:** D

*Images provided by designer/architect.*

A nice example of a country farmhouse design on the outside, this home is thoroughly modern on the inside.

**Features:**

- Living Room: To the left of the foyer, this secluded space offers a moment of peace and quiet after a long day at the office.

- Dining Room: An interesting ceiling treatment makes this elegant room even more sophisticated.

- Kitchen: You won't find a more well-appointed space than this! You'll love the central work island, this useful menu desk

and nearby pantry. The adjacent dinette hosts casual meals and offers outdoor access via sliding glass doors.

- Family Room: A handsome fireplace sets the mood in this expansive area.

- Master Suite: A vaulted ceiling presides over the sleeping room, while a walk-in closet organizes your entire wardrobe. The private bath boasts a refreshing shower and a linen closet.

**Main Level Floor Plan**

**Upper Level Floor Plan**

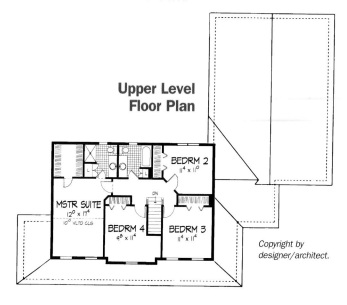

## Main Level Floor Plan

PORCH

LIVING RM.
16'-0" X 18'-0"

MORNING ROOM
12'-0" X 12'-0"

MASTER SUITE
13'-6" X 16'-0"

BATH 1

KITCH.
13'-0" X 12'-0"

ENT.

DINING RM.
11'-6" X 15'-6"

UT.

STORAGE

PORCH

GARAGE
22'-6" X 23'-0"

*Copyright by designer/architect.*

BED RM.3
12'-6" X 10'-4"

OPEN ABOVE LIVING RM.

BONUS RM.
17'-6" X 13'-6"

B.4

BRIDGE

BED RM.4
12'-6" X 10'-4"

BED RM.2
11'-0" X 11'-6"

B.3

## Upper Level Floor Plan

## Plan #371021

**Dimensions:** 53' W x 48'10" D
**Levels:** 2
**Square Footage:** 2,384
**Main Level Sq. Ft.:** 1,542
**Upper Level Sq. Ft.:** 842
**Bedrooms:** 4
**Bathrooms:** 3½
**Foundation:** Slab
**Materials List Available:** No
**Price Category:** E

*Images provided by designer/architect.*

CAD FILE CAD AVAILABLE

---

Covered Porch
23-0 x 8-0

Outdoor Kitchen

Patio

Garden Tub

M. Bath
15-4 x 9-6

9-0 Ceiling
10-0 Ceiling

Master Bedroom
14-0 x 15-6

Kitchen
11-6 x 15-6

Eating
11-2 x 15-6
9-0 Ceiling

Bedroom 2
13-4 x 11-6
9-0 Ceiling

Clos.
7-6 x 5-8

Clos.
7-6 x 5-8

Island

Pantry

Hall Bath

Stor.
8-5 x 7-4

Utility
8-3 x 7-2

Entry

9-0 Ceiling
10-0 Ceiling

Great Room
22-8 x 15-6
(Clear)

Gas Logs

Hall

Lin.

Bedroom 3
13-4 x 11-6
9-0 Ceiling

Half Bath

Media/ Hobby
8-0 x 7-10

Sloped Clg.

2 Car Garage
23-4 x 23-10

Covered Porch
23-0 x 5-0

## Plan #351105

**Dimensions:** 69' W x 59'10" D
**Levels:** 1
**Square Footage:** 2,000
**Bedrooms:** 3
**Bathrooms:** 2½
**Foundation:** Crawl space or slab
**Material List Available:** Yes
**Price Category:** E

*Images provided by designer/architect.*

CAD FILE CAD AVAILABLE

Unfinished Bonus Room
14-0 x 23-10
(Clear)
8-0 Clg. Ht.

## Bonus Area Floor Plan

*Copyright by designer/architect.*

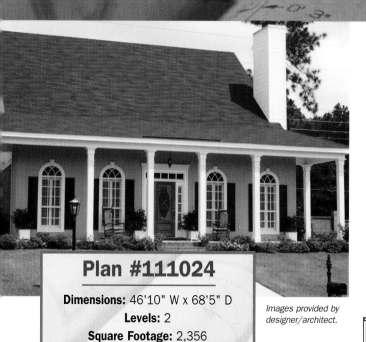

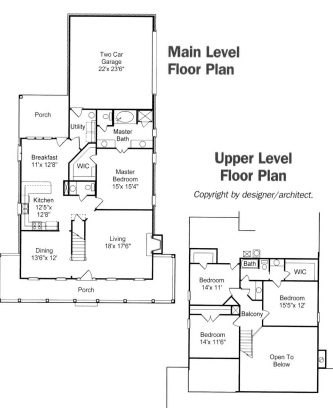

## Main Level Floor Plan

## Upper Level Floor Plan

*Copyright by designer/architect.*

*Images provided by designer/architect.*

# Plan #111024

**Dimensions:** 46'10" W x 68'5" D

**Levels:** 2

**Square Footage:** 2,356

**Main Level Sq. Ft.:** 1,516

**Upper Level Sq. Ft.:** 840

**Bedrooms:** 4

**Bathrooms:** 2½

**Foundation:** Slab

**Materials List Available:** No

**Price Category:** F

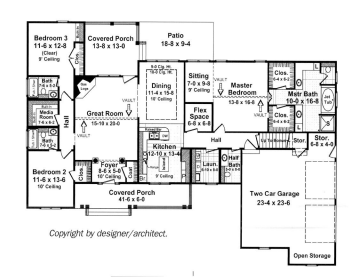

*Copyright by designer/architect.*

## Bonus Area Floor Plan

# Plan #351067

**Dimensions:** 78' W x 58'6" D

**Levels:** 1

**Square Footage:** 2,200

**Bedrooms:** 3

**Bathrooms:** 3½

**Foundation:** Crawl space or slab

**Material List Available:** Yes

**Price Category:** F

*Images provided by designer/architect.*

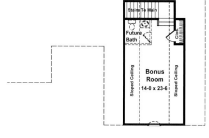

CAD FILE AVAILABLE

## Plan #121037

**Dimensions:** 46' W x 47'10" D

**Levels:** 2

**Square Footage:** 2,292

**Main Level Sq. Ft.:** 1,158

**Upper Level Sq. Ft.:** 1,134

**Bedrooms:** 4

**Bathrooms:** 2½

**Foundation:** Basement

**Materials List Available:** Yes

**Price Category:** E

*Images provided by designer/architect.*

This convenient and comfortable home is filled with architectural features that set it apart.

**Features:**

- Ceiling Height: 8 ft. unless otherwise noted.

- Foyer: You'll know you have arrived when you enter this two-story area highlighted by a decorative plant shelf and a balcony.

- Great Room: Just beyond the entry is the great room where the warmth of the two-sided fireplace will attract family and friends to gather. A bay window offers a more intimate place to sit and converse.

- Hearth Room: At the other side of the fireplace, the hearth offers a cozy spot for smaller gatherings or a place to sit alone and enjoy a book by the fire.

- Breakfast Area: With sunlight streaming into its bay window, the breakfast area offers the perfect spot for informal family meals.

- Master Suite: This private retreat is made more convenient by a walk-in closet. It features its own tub and shower.

**Main Level Floor Plan**

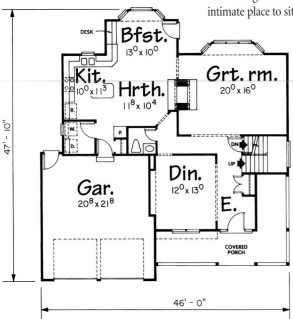

**Upper Level Floor Plan**

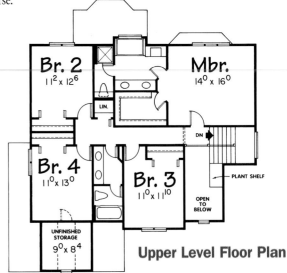

*Copyright by designer/architect.*

# Plan #181085

**Dimensions:** 56'4" W x 44' D

**Levels:** 2

**Square Footage:** 2,183

**Main Level Sq. Ft.:** 1,232

**Second Level Sq. Ft.:** 951

**Bedrooms:** 3

**Bathrooms:** 2½

**Foundation:** Basement

**Materials List Available:** Yes

**Price Category:** E

This country home features an inviting front porch and a layout designed for modern living.

*Images provided by designer/architect.*

**Features:**

- Ceiling Height: 8 ft.
- Solarium: Sunlight streams through the windows of this solarium at the front of the house.
- Living Room: Walk through French doors, and you will enter this inviting living room. Family and friends will be drawn to the corner fireplace.
- Formal Dining Room: Usher your guests directly from the living room into this formal dining room. The kitchen is located on the other side of the dining room for convenient service.
- Kitchen: This generously sized kitchen is a delight, it offers a center island, separate eat-in area, and access to the back deck.
- Bonus Room: This room just off the entry hall can become a family room, a bedroom, or an office.
- Master Suite: Curl up by the corner fireplace in this master retreat, with its walk-in closet and lavish bath with separate shower and tub.

## Main Level Floor Plan

## Upper Level Floor Plan

*Copyright by designer/architect.*

## Plan #171015

**Dimensions:** 79' W x 46' D

**Levels:** 1

**Square Footage:** 2,089

**Bedrooms:** 3

**Bathrooms:** 2½

**Foundation:** Crawl space or slab

**Materials List Available:** Yes

**Price Category:** D

*Images provided by designer/architect.*

This lovely three-bedroom country home, with a bonus room above the garage, is a perfect family home.

**Features:**

• Dining Room: This formal room and the great room form a large gathering space with a 12-ft.-high ceiling.

• Kitchen: The raised bar defines this kitchen and offers additional seating.

• Master Suite: This suite, located on the opposite side of the home from the secondary bedrooms, enjoys a luxurious bath with his and her walk-in closets.

• Bedrooms: Two secondary bedrooms have large closets and share a hall bathroom.

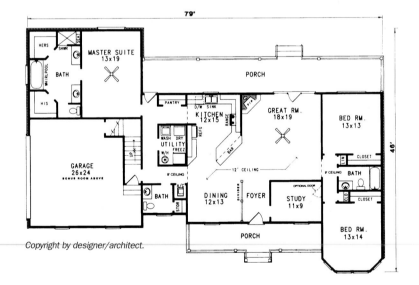

*Copyright by designer/architect.*

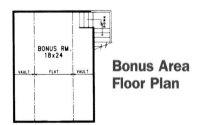

**Bonus Area
Floor Plan**

# Plan #151027

**Dimensions:** 37' W x 73' D

**Levels:** 2

**Square Footage:** 2,323

**Main Level Sq. Ft.:** 1,713

**Upper Level Sq. Ft.:** 619

**Bedrooms:** 3

**Bathrooms:** 3

**Foundation:** Crawl space, slab; basement option for fee

**CompleteCost List Available:** Yes

**Price Category:** E

A traditional design with a covered front porch and high ceilings in many rooms gives this home all the space and comfort you'll ever need.

### Features:

- **Foyer:** A formal foyer with 8-in. wood columns will lead you to an elegant dining area.

- **Great Room:** This wonderful gathering room has 10-ft. boxed ceilings, a built-in media center, and an atrium door leading to a rear grilling porch.

- **Kitchen:** Functional yet cozy, this kitchen opens to the breakfast area with built-in computer desk and is open to the great room as well.

- **Master Suite:** Pamper yourself in this luxurious bedroom with 10-ft. boxed ceilings, large walk-in closets, and a bath area with a whirlpool tub, shower, and double vanity.

- **Second Level:** A game room and two bedrooms with walk-thru baths make this floor special.

*Images provided by designer/architect.*

**CAD FILE AVAILABLE**

## Main Level Floor Plan

## Upper Level Floor Plan

*Copyright by designer/architect.*

## Plan #151279

**Dimensions:** 51'6" W x 49' D
**Levels:** 1
**Square Footage:** 1,485
**Bedrooms:** 3
**Bathrooms:** 2
**Foundation:** Crawl space, slab, basement or walkout
**CompleteCost List Available:** Yes
**Price Category:** B

**CAD FILE AVAILABLE**

*Images provided by designer/architect.*

**Main Level Floor Pl**

DINING ROOM 11'-0" X 9'-4"

BREAKFAST ROOM 10'-0" X 7'-8"

M.BATH 15'-8" X 10'-8"

KITCHEN 15'-2" X 10'-8"

GREAT ROOM 13'-6" X 19'-8"

MASTER SUITE 15'-8" X 12'-0"

BATH

BEDROOM 2 10'-2" X 10'-8"

BEDROOM 3 10'-0" X 10'-8"

FOYER 6'-6" X 7'-0"

GARAGE 20'-10" X 20'-0"

PORCH 16'-5" X 5'-0"

*Copyright by designer/architect.*

---

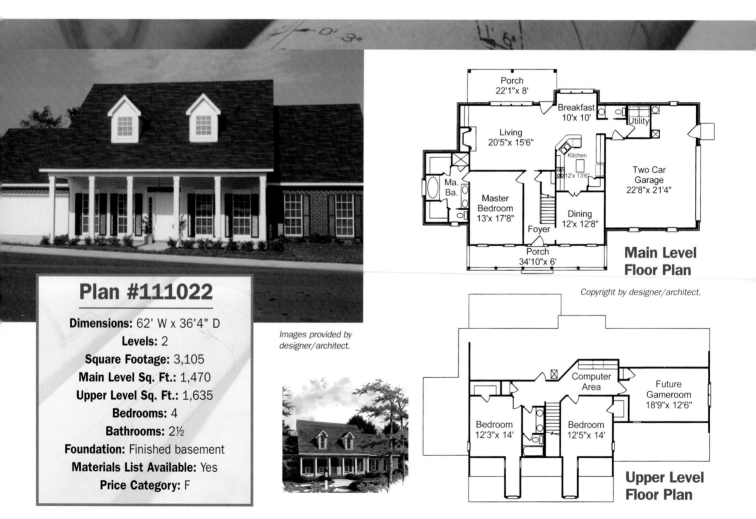

## Plan #111022

**Dimensions:** 62' W x 36'4" D
**Levels:** 2
**Square Footage:** 3,105
**Main Level Sq. Ft.:** 1,470
**Upper Level Sq. Ft.:** 1,635
**Bedrooms:** 4
**Bathrooms:** 2½
**Foundation:** Finished basement
**Materials List Available:** Yes
**Price Category:** F

*Images provided by designer/architect.*

Porch 22'1"x 8'

Breakfast 10'x 10'

Utility

Living 20'5"x 15'6"

Kitchen 12'x 13'6"

Two Car Garage 22'8"x 21'4"

Ma. Ba.

Master Bedroom 13'x 17'8"

Foyer

Dining 12'x 12'8"

Porch 34'10"x 6'

**Main Level Floor Plan**

*Copyright by designer/architect.*

Computer Area

Future Gameroom 18'9"x 12'6"

Bedroom 12'3"x 14'

Bedroom 12'5"x 14'

**Upper Level Floor Plan**

## Plan #151743

**Dimensions:** 42'10" W x 69'6" D
**Levels:** 2
**Square Footage:** 2,457
**Main Level Sq. Ft.:** 1,623
**Upper Level Sq. Ft.:** 834
**Bedrooms:** 3
**Bathrooms:** 2½
**Foundation:** Crawl space or slab
**CompleteCost List Available:** Yes
**Price Category:** E

*Images provided by designer/architect.*

**CAD FILE AVAILABLE**

### Main Level Floor Plan

### Upper Level Floor Plan

*Copyright by designer/architect.*

## Plan #521017

**Dimensions:** 94'11" W x 94'10" D
**Levels:** 1
**Square Footage:** 2,359
**Bedrooms:** 3
**Bathrooms:** 3
**Foundation:** Slab
**Material List Available:** No
**Price Category:** E

*Images provided by designer/architect.*

**CAD FILE AVAILABLE**

*Copyright by designer/architect.*

Rear View

## Plan #121087

**Dimensions:** 50' W x 40' D
**Levels:** 2
**Square Footage:** 2,103
**Main Level Sq. Ft.:** 1,082
**Upper Level Sq. Ft.:** 1,021
**Bedrooms:** 4
**Bathrooms:** 2½
**Foundation:** Basement
**Materials List Available:** Yes
**Price Category:** D

*Images provided by designer/architect.*

You'll love the comfort and the unusual design details you'll find in this home.

**Features:**

- **Entry:** A T-shaped staircase frames this two-story entry, giving both visual interest and convenience.

- **Family Room:** Bookcases frame the lovely fireplace here, so you won't be amiss by decorating to create a special reading nook.

- **Breakfast Area:** Pass through the cased opening between the family room and this breakfast area for convenience.

- **Kitchen:** Combined with the breakfast area, this kitchen features an island, pantry, and desk.

- **Master Suite:** On the upper floor, this suite has a walk-in closet and a bath with sunlit whirlpool tub, separate shower, and double vanity. A window seat makes the bedroom especially cozy, no matter what the outside weather.

### Main Level Floor Plan

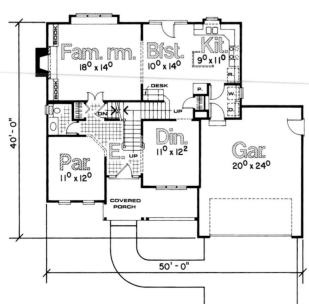

### Upper Level Floor Plan

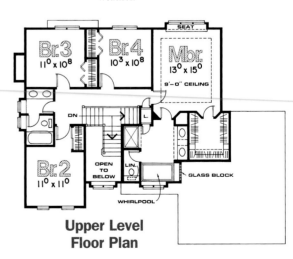

*Copyright by designer/architect.*

# Plan #351007

**Dimensions:** 73'8"W x 53'2" D

**Levels:** 1

**Square Footage:** 2,251

**Bedrooms:** 3

**Bathrooms:** 2½

**Foundation:** Crawl space, slab, or basement

**Materials List Available:** Yes

**Price Category:** E

*Images provided by designer/architect.*

This three-bedroom brick home with arched window offers traditional styling that features an open floor plan.

**Features:**

- **Great Room:** This room has a 12-ft.-high ceiling and a corner fireplace.

- **Kitchen:** This kitchen boasts a built-in pantry and a raised bar open to the breakfast area.

- **Dining Room:** This area features a vaulted ceiling and a view of the front yard.

- **Master Bedroom:** This private room has an office and access to the rear porch.

- **Master Bath:** This bathroom has a double vanity, large walk-in closet, and soaking tub.

**Bonus Room**

*Copyright by designer/architect.*

# Plan #351008

**Dimensions:** 64'6" W x 61'4" D

**Levels:** 1

**Square Footage:** 2,002

**Bedrooms:** 3

**Bathrooms:** 2

**Foundation:** Crawl space or basement

**Materials List Available:** Yes

**Price Category:** E

*Images provided by designer/architect.*

This home has the charming appeal of a quaint cottage that you might find in an old village in the English countryside. It's a unique design that maximizes every inch of its usable space.

## Features:

- **Great Room:** This room has a vaulted ceiling and built-in units on each side of the fireplace.

- **Kitchen:** This kitchen boasts a raised bar open to the breakfast area; the room is also open to the dining room.

- **Master Suite:** This bedroom retreat features a raised ceiling and a walk-in closet. The bathroom has a double vanity, large walk-in closet, and soaking tub.

- **Bedrooms:** Two bedrooms share a common bathroom and have large closets.

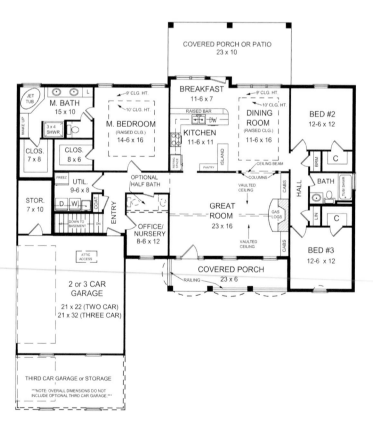

*Copyright by designer/architect.*

## Plan #121080

**Dimensions:** 56' W x 49' D

**Levels:** 2

**Square Footage:** 2,384

**Main Level Sq. Ft.:** 1,616

**Upper Level Sq. Ft.:** 768

**Bedrooms:** 4

**Bathrooms:** 2½

**Foundation:** Slab

**Materials List Available:** Yes

**Price Category:** E

*This home, as shown in the photograph, may differ from the actual blueprints.   Images provided by designer/architect. For more detailed information, please check the floor plans carefully.*

This design is ideal if you want a generously sized home now and room to expand later.

**Features:**

• Living Room: Your eyes will be drawn towards the ceiling as soon as you enter this lovely room. The ceiling is vaulted, giving a sense of grandeur, and a graceful balcony from the second floor adds extra interest to this room.

• Kitchen: Designed with lots of counter space to make your work convenient, this kitchen also shares an eating bar with the breakfast nook.

• Breakfast Nook: Eat here or go out to the adjoining private porch where you can enjoy your meal in the morning sunshine.

• Master Suite: The bayed area in the bedroom makes a picturesque sitting area. French doors in the bedroom open to a private bath that's fitted with a bathtub, separate shower, two vanities, and a walk-in closet.

## Main Level Floor Plan

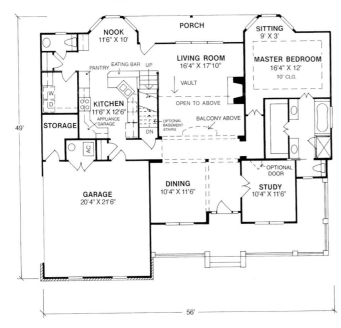

## Upper Level Floor Plan

*Copyright by designer/architect.*

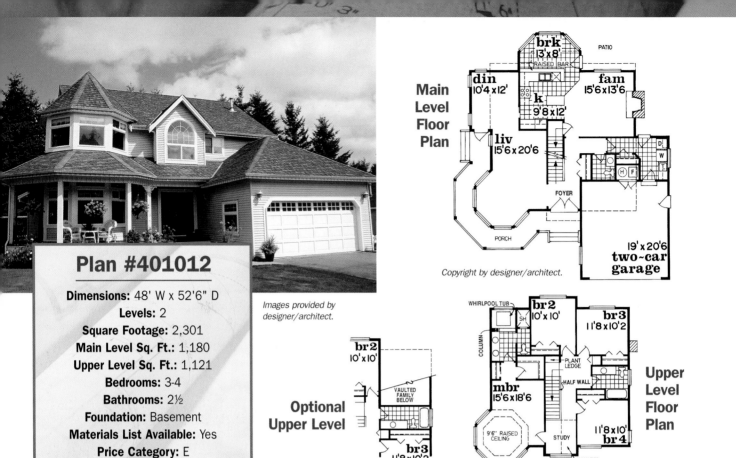

# Plan #401012

**Dimensions:** 48' W x 52'6" D

**Levels:** 2

**Square Footage:** 2,301

**Main Level Sq. Ft.:** 1,180

**Upper Level Sq. Ft.:** 1,121

**Bedrooms:** 3-4

**Bathrooms:** 2½

**Foundation:** Basement

**Materials List Available:** Yes

**Price Category:** E

*Images provided by designer/architect.*

**Main Level Floor Plan**

brk 13'x8'
RAISED BAR
PATIO

din 10'4 x12'
k 9'8 x12'
fam 15'6 x13'6

liv 15'6 x 20'6

FOYER

PORCH

19' x 20'6 two-car garage

D W T
H F

*Copyright by designer/architect.*

**Optional Upper Level**

br2 10' x 10'
VAULTED FAMILY BELOW

br3 11'8 x10'2

**Upper Level Floor Plan**

WHIRLPOOL TUB
COLUMN
SH

br2 10' x 10'
br3 11'8 x10'2

PLANT LEDGE
HALF WALL

mbr 15'6 x18'6

9'6" RAISED CEILING

STUDY

br4 11'8 x10'

VAULTED

---

# Plan #151491

**Dimensions:** 66'10" W x 73'4" D

**Levels:** 1.5

**Square Footage:** 2,379

**Bedrooms:** 5

**Bathrooms:** 4

**Foundation:** Crawl space or slab; basement or walkout for fee

**CompleteCost List Available:** Yes

**Price Category:** E

*Images provided by designer/architect.*

**Main Level Floor Plan**

GRILLING PORCH

M. BATH
MASTER SUITE
GREAT ROOM
BREAKFAST ROOM
HEARTH ROOM
W.I.C.
BATH
KITCHEN
LAU.
FOYER
BEDROOM 3
BEDROOM 2 / STUDY
DINING ROOM
TEENAGE GUEST ROOM
COVERED PORCH
BATH
STRG.
GARAGE

**Upper Level Floor Plan**

GUEST ROOM
ATTIC STORAGE
GAME ROOM / MEDIA ROOM
ATTIC STORAGE

*Copyright by designer/architect.*

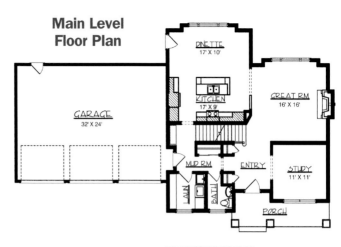

## Main Level Floor Plan

DINETTE
17' X 10'

KITCHEN
17' X 9'

GARAGE
32' X 24'

GREAT RM
16' X 16'

MUD RM

ENTRY

STUDY
11' X 11'

LAUN

BATH

PORCH

*Images provided by designer/architect.*

## Upper Level Floor Plan

BED RM
11' X 12'

BATH

OWNER'S SUITE
16' X 15'

BONUS RM
32' X 14'

HALL

BED RM
13' X 11'

W.I.C.

BATH

*Copyright by designer/architect.*

# Plan #271057

**Dimensions:** 66' W x 41' D
**Levels:** 2
**Square Footage:** 2,195
**Main Level Sq. Ft.:** 1,095
**Upper Level Sq. Ft.:** 1,100
**Bedrooms:** 3
**Bathrooms:** 2½
**Foundation:** Daylight basement
**Materials List Available:** No
**Price Category:** D

---

# Plan #351044

**Dimensions:** 68' W x 55'8" D
**Levels:** 1
**Square Footage:** 2,00
**Bedrooms:** 4
**Bathrooms:** 2½
**Foundation:** Crawl space, slab or basement
**Material List Available:** Yes
**Price Category:** F

*Images provided by designer/architect.*

**CAD FILE AVAILABLE**

M. BATH
14-4 x 9-6

5' X 5' JET TUB

M. BEDROOM
14 x 15-6

COVERED PORCH
11 x 9-4

SCREENED PORCH
11-8 x 9

BED #4
11-4 x 11-6

KITCHEN
11-2 x 11-6

DINING
11-6 x 11-6

CLOS.
7-4 x 5-8

CLOS.
6-8 x 5-8

3' X 4' SHWR

BATH

STOR.
6-8 x 7-4

LAUNDRY
9-2 x 7-2

ENTRY

HALF BATH

GREAT ROOM
22-8 x 15-6

BED #3/
GAME ROOM/
DEN
11-8 x 11-6

HOBBY/
OFFICE
8 x 8-2

VAULT

GAS LOGS

OPTIONAL STAIRS TO BASEMENT

2 CAR GARAGE
20-4 x 26-2

COVERED PORCH
23' X 6'

BED #2
11-4 x 11-6

HALL

*Copyright by designer/architect.*

# Plan #151028

**Dimensions:** 36' W X 69' D

**Levels:** 2

**Square Footage:** 2,252

**Main Level Sq. Ft.:** 1,694

**Upper Level Sq. Ft.:** 558

**Bedrooms:** 3

**Bathrooms:** 3

**Foundation:** Crawl space, slab; basement for fee

**CompleteCost List Available:** Yes

**Price Category:** E

*Images provided by designer/architect.*

You'll love entertaining in this elegant home with its large covered front porch, grilling porch off the kitchen and breakfast room, and great room with a gas fireplace and media center.

**Features:**

- Foyer: A wonderful open staircase from the foyer leads you to the second floor.

- Guest Room/Study: A private bath makes this room truly versatile.

- Dining Room: Attached to the great room, this dining room features 8-in. wooden columns that you can highlight for a formal atmosphere.

- Kitchen: This cleverly laid-out kitchen with access to the breakfast room is ideal for informal gatherings as well as family meals.

- Master Suite: French doors here open to the bath, with its large walk-in closet, double vanities, corner whirlpool tub, and corner shower.

## Main Level Floor Plan

36'-0"

GRILLING PORCH
16'-6" X 7'-8"

GARAGE
18'-10" X 20'-0"

BREAKFAST ROOM
16'-2" X 8'-0"

BENCH W/ HANGING & STORAGE BINS

KITCHEN
11'-8" X 12'-2"

WHP TUB

DW

M. BATH
13'-0" X 13'-2"

KID'S NOOK

RG

REF.

PANTRY

W. LAU. D

KNEE SPACE

DINING RM.
11'-4" X 10'-6"

69'-0"

COMPUTER DESK

8" COLUMNS

MASTER SUITE
13'-0" X 15'-0"

GREAT RM.
18'-0" X 18'-4"

MEDIA CENTER

FOYER

COVERED PORCH
20'-0" X 8'-0"

GUEST RM. / STUDY
13'-0" X 11'-0"

## Upper Level Floor Plan

ATTIC STRG.

LIN

BED RM. 3
14'-10" X 12'-0"

BED RM. 2
13'-0" X 12'-0"

*Copyright by designer/architect.*

## Plan #101011

**Dimensions:** 71'2" W x 58'1" D

**Levels:** 1

**Square Footage:** 2,184

**Bedrooms:** 3

**Bathrooms:** 3

**Foundation:** Crawl space, slab, basement, or walkout

**Materials List Available:** Yes

**Price Category:** E

*Images provided by designer/architect.*

A classic design and spacious interior add up to a flexible design suitable to any modern lifestyle.

**Features:**

- Ceiling Height: 9 ft. unless otherwise noted.
- Dining Room: A decorative square column and a tray ceiling adorn this elegant dining room.

- Screened Porch: Enjoy summer breezes in style by stepping out of the French doors into this vaulted screened porch.
- Kitchen: Does everyone want to hang out in the kitchen while you are cooking? No problem. True to the home's country style, this huge 14-ft.-3-in. x 22-ft.-6-in. has plenty of room for helpers. This area is open to the vaulted family room.

- Patio or Deck: This pleasant outdoor area is accessible from both the screened porch and the master bedroom.
- Master Suite: This luxurious suite includes a double tray ceiling, a sitting area, two walk-in closets, and an exquisite bath.

Kitchen

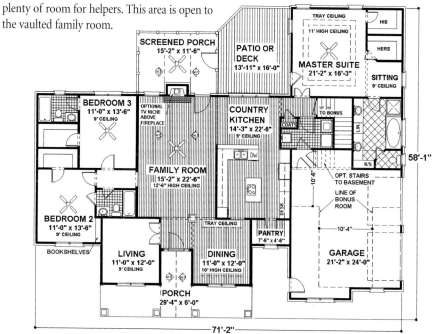

*Copyright by designer/architect.*

## Plan #151171

**Dimensions:** 63'10" W x 72'2" D
**Levels:** 1
**Square Footage:** 2,131
**Bedrooms:** 3
**Bathrooms:** 2½
**Foundation:** Crawl space, slab; basement or daylight basement for fee
**CompleteCost List Available:** Yes
**Price Category:** D

This home has everything an active family could possibly want—beauty, luxury, and plenty of space to relax and entertain, both inside and out.

### Features:

- **Great Room:** Skylights in the vaulted ceiling, a fireplace, and the door to the rear screened porch make this a favorite place to spend time.

- **Dining Area:** Bay windows let light flood the area.

- **Kitchen:** The central island and snack bar, pantry, computer center, and ample counter and cabinet space make a great working area.

- **Storm Shelter:** You'll be happy to have this room, and even happier not to have to use it.

- **Master Suite:** The vaulted ceiling, door to the grilling patio, two walk-in closets, and luxury bath combine to create a suite you'll love.

- **Additional Bedrooms:** A window seat in one room is a child's dream, and you'll love the big closets.

# Plan #271049

**Dimensions:** 74' W x 44' D

**Levels:** 2

**Square Footage:** 2,464

**Main Level Sq. Ft.:** 1,288

**Upper Level Sq. Ft.:** 1,176

**Bedrooms:** 4

**Bathrooms:** 2½

**Foundation:** Basement, crawl space

**Materials List Available:** Yes

**Price Category:** E

*Images provided by designer/architect.*

This classic farmhouse design features a wraparound porch for enjoying conversation on warm afternoons.

**Features:**

- Living Room: A central fireplace warms this spacious gathering place, while French doors offer porch access.

- Dining Room: On formal occasions, this room is perfect for hosting elegant meals.

- Country Kitchen: An island workstation and a handy pantry keep the family chef organized and productive.

- Family Room: The home's second fireplace warms this cozy area, which is really an extension of the kitchen. Set up a kitchen table here, and enjoy casual meals near the crackling fire.

- Master Suite: The master bedroom is certainly vast. The walk-in closet is large as well. The private, compartmentalized bath offers a sit-down shower and a separate dressing area.

## Main Level Floor Plan

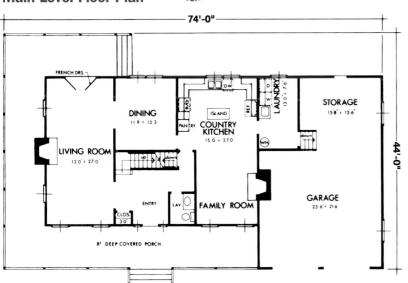

## Upper Level Floor Plan

*Copyright by designer/architect.*

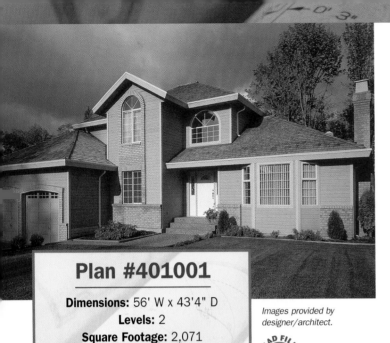

**Main Level Floor Plan**

*Images provided by designer/architect.*

**Upper Level Floor Plan**

*Copyright by designer/architect.*

## Plan #401001

**Dimensions:** 56' W x 43'4" D
**Levels:** 2
**Square Footage:** 2,071
**Main Level Sq. Ft.:** 1,204
**Upper Level Sq. Ft.:** 867
**Bedrooms:** 3
**Bathrooms:** 2½
**Foundation:** Basement
**Materials List Available:** Yes
**Price Category:** D

**Main Level Floor Plan**

*Images provided by designer/architect.*

**Upper Level Floor Plan**

*Copyright by designer/architect.*

## Plan #441039

**Dimensions:** 50' W x 56' D
**Levels:** 2
**Square Footage:** 2,120
**Main Level Sq. Ft.:** 1,603
**Upper Level Sq. Ft.:** 517
**Bedrooms:** 3
**Bathrooms:** 2½
**Foundation:** Crawl space; slab
or basement for fee
**Materials List Available:** Yes
**Price Category:** D

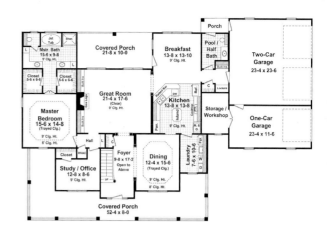

**Main Level Floor Plan**

*Images provided by designer/architect.*

**CAD FILE AVAILABLE**

**Upper Level Floor Plan**

*Copyright by designer/architect.*

# Plan #351179

**Dimensions:** 83'10" W x 56' D

**Levels:** 2

**Square Footage:** 3,000

**Main Level Sq. Ft.:** 2,109

**Upper Level Sq. Ft.:** 891

**Bedrooms:** 4

**Bathrooms:** 3½

**Foundation:** Crawl space or slab

**Materials List Available:** Yes

**Price Category:** G

**Main Level Floor Plan**

*Images provided by designer/architect.*

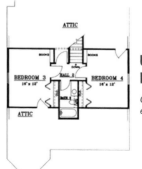

**Upper Level Floor Plan**

*Copyright by designer/architect.*

# Plan #171005

**Dimensions:** 56' W x 58' D

**Levels:** 2

**Square Footage:** 2,276

**Main Level Sq. Ft.:** 1,748

**Upper Level Sq. Ft.:** 528

**Bedrooms:** 4

**Bathrooms:** 3

**Foundation:** Crawl space, slab

**Materials List Available:** Yes

**Price Category:** E

## Plan #131030

**Dimensions:** 51' W x 41'10" D

**Levels:** 2

**Square Footage:** 2,470

**Main Level Sq. Ft.:** 1,290

**Upper Level Sq. Ft.:** 1,180

**Bedrooms:** 4

**Bathrooms:** 2½

**Foundation:** Crawl space, slab, basement, or walkout

**Materials List Available:** Yes

**Price Category:** F

*This home, as shown in the photograph, may differ from the actual blueprints. For more detailed information, please check the floor plans carefully.*

*Images provided by designer/architect.*

If high ceilings and spacious rooms make you happy, you'll love this gorgeous home.

**Features:**

• Family Room: An 18-ft. vaulted ceiling that's open to the balcony above, a corner fireplace, and a wall of windows make this room feel special.

• Dining Room: This formal room, which flows into the living room, also opens to the front porch and optional backyard deck.

• Kitchen: A bright breakfast room joins with this kitchen and opens to the backyard deck.

• Master Suite: You'll smile when you see the 11-ft. vaulted ceiling, stunning arched window, and two walk-in closets in the bedroom. A skylight lets natural light into the private bath, with its spa tub, separate shower, and dual-sink vanity.

• Bedrooms: To reach these three charming bedrooms, you'll admire the view into the family room below as you walk along the balcony hall.

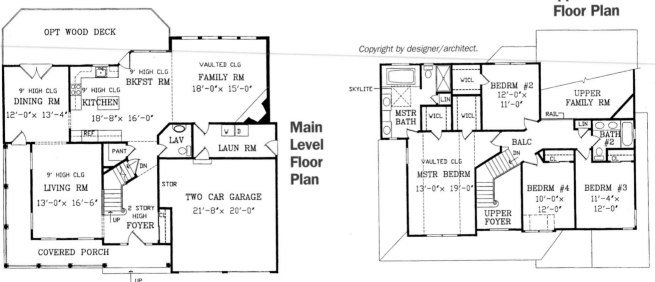

**Main Level Floor Plan**

**Upper Level Floor Plan**

*Copyright by designer/architect.*

## Plan #321041

**Dimensions:** 64' W x 34' D
**Levels:** 2
**Square Footage:** 2,286
**Main Level Sq. Ft.:** 1,283
**Upper Level Sq. Ft.:** 1,003
**Bedrooms:** 4
**Bathrooms:** 2½
**Foundation:** Crawl space, slab, or basement
**Materials List Available:** No
**Price Category:** E

*Images provided by designer/architect.*

If you love the way these gorgeous windows look from the outside, you'll be thrilled with the equally gracious interior of this home.

**Features:**

- Entryway: This two-story entryway shows off the fine woodworking on the railing and balustrades.

- Living Room: The large front windows form a glamorous background in this spacious room.

- Family Room: A handsome fireplace and a sliding glass door to the backyard enhance the open design of this room.

- Breakfast Room: Large enough for a crowd, this room makes a perfect dining area.

- Kitchen: The angled bar and separate pantry are highlights in this step-saving design.

- Master Suite: Enjoy this suite's huge walk-in closet, vaulted ceiling, and private bath, which features a double vanity, tub, and shower stall.

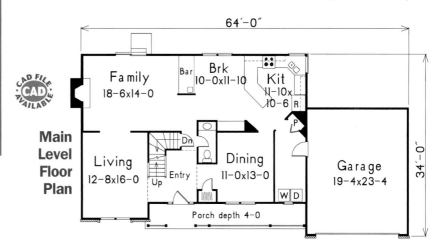

**Upper Level Floor Plan**

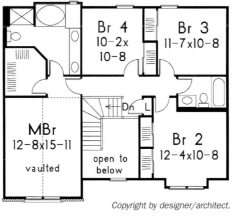

Front View

*Copyright by designer/architect.*

## Plan #341014

**Dimensions:** 57'9" W x 40' D

**Levels:** 2

**Square Footage:** 2,128

**Main Level Sq. Ft.:** 1,064

**Upper Level Sq. Ft.:** 1,064

**Bedrooms:** 3

**Bathrooms:** 2½

**Foundation:** Crawl space, slab, or basement

**Materials List Available:** Yes

**Price Category:** D

*Images provided by designer/architect.*

You'll love the serene appearance of this traditionally styled home, with its romantic front porch and practical backyard deck.

**Features:**

- Foyer: Look onto this two-story foyer from the sunlit upper floor balcony.
- Dining Room: A tray ceiling sets the formal tone for this lovely room.
- Living Room: A fireplace, built-in cabinets or shelves, and generous windows make this room as practical as it is welcoming.

- Kitchen: A pantry and a work island make this an ideal kitchen for all the cooks in the family.
- Master Suite: A walk-in closet and private bath with double vanities, garden tub, and separate shower make this suite a pleasure.
- Bonus Room: Use this room however you wish — as a study, media room, or play space.

CAD FILE AVAILABLE

### Main Level Floor Plan

### Upper Level Floor Plan

*Copyright by designer/architect.*

## Plan #271074

**Dimensions:** 68' W x 86' D
**Levels:** 1
**Square Footage:** 2,400
**Bedrooms:** 4
**Bathrooms:** 3
**Foundation:** Crawl space or slab
**Materials List Available:** No
**Price Category:** E

*Images provided by designer/architect.*

Perfect for families with aging relatives or boomerang children, this home includes a completely separate suite at the rear.

**Features:**

• Living Room: A corner fireplace casts a friendly glow over this gathering space.

• Kitchen: This efficient space offers a serving bar that extends toward the eating nook and the formal dining room.

• Master Suite: A cathedral ceiling presides over this deluxe suite, which boasts a whirlpool tub, dual-sink vanity, and walk-in closet.

• In-law Suite: This separate wing has its own vaulted living room, plus a kitchen, a dining room, and a bedroom suite.

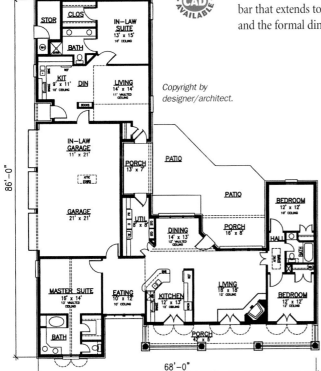

*Copyright by designer/architect.*

## SMARTtip

### Adding Professional Flair to Window Treatments

You can give your window treatment designs a professional look by using decorator tricks to customize readymades or dress your own home-sewn designs. These could include contrast linings, tassels, cording, ribbons, or couture trimmings such as buttons, coins, or bows applied to edges. Another trick is to sew a fine wire into the hem of curtains or valances to create a pliable edge that you can shape yourself. Small weights that you can sew into the hem of drapery panels or jabots will make them hang better. For more inspiration look at fashion magazines and visit showrooms.

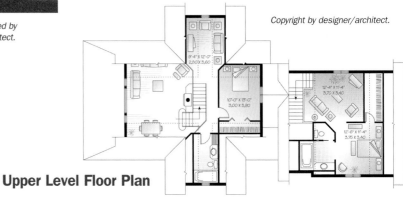

**Main Level Floor Plan**

*Copyright by designer/architect.*

# Plan #181243

**Dimensions:** 67' W x 40' D
**Levels:** 2
**Square Footage:** 2,219
**Main Level Sq. Ft.:** 1,232
**Upper Level Sq. Ft.:** 987
**Bedrooms:** 3
**Bathrooms:** 3½
**Foundation:** Basement
**Materials List Available:** Yes
**Price Category:** E

*Images provided by designer/architect.*

**CAD FILE AVAILABLE**

**Upper Level Floor Plan**

# Plan #111026

**Dimensions:** 66' W x 65' D
**Levels:** 2
**Square Footage:** 2,406
**Main Level Sq. Ft.:** 1,796
**Upper Level Sq. Ft.:** 610
**Bedrooms:** 4
**Bathrooms:** 3½
**Foundation:** Crawlspace
**Materials List Available:** No
**Price Category:** F

*Images provided by designer/architect.*

**Main Level Floor Plan**

Two Car Garage 21'2"x 21'1"

Patio

Porch

½ Ba  Storage

Master Bedroom 15'x 15'

WIC

Breakfast 13'8"x 10'7"

Living 19'4"x 17'1"

Bath

WIC

Kitchen 10'8"x 12'3"

Ma. Bath

Bedroom 12'x 11'7"

Dining 12'x 13'6"

Utility

Porch

**Upper Level Floor Plan**

Open to Below

Bath

Balcony

Bedroom 12'x 11'7"

Bedroom 12'x 13'

*Copyright by designer/architect.*

*Images provided by designer/architect.*

*Copyright by designer/architect.*

## Plan #351102

**Dimensions:** 67' W x 56' D

**Levels:** 1

**Square Footage:** 2,000

**Bedrooms:** 3

**Bathrooms:** 2½

**Foundation:** Basement, crawl space, slab

**Materials List Available:** Yes

**Price Category:** F

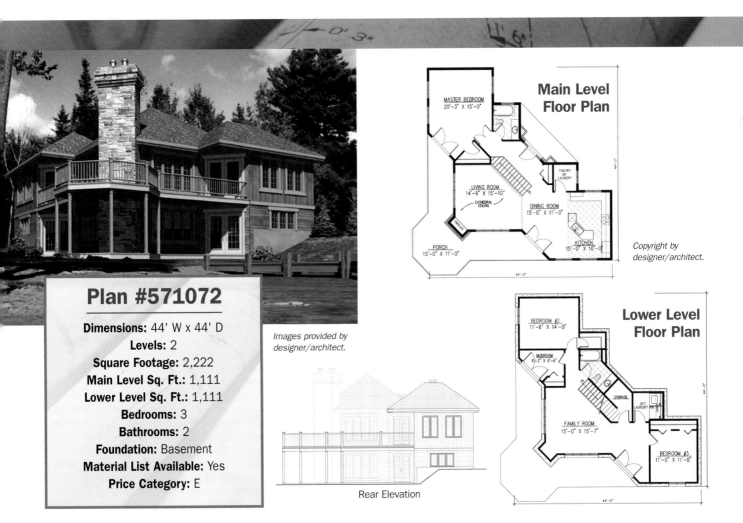

*Images provided by designer/architect.*

*Copyright by designer/architect.*

Rear Elevation

## Plan #571072

**Dimensions:** 44' W x 44' D

**Levels:** 2

**Square Footage:** 2,222

**Main Level Sq. Ft.:** 1,111

**Lower Level Sq. Ft.:** 1,111

**Bedrooms:** 3

**Bathrooms:** 2

**Foundation:** Basement

**Material List Available:** Yes

**Price Category:** E

## Plan #391007

**Dimensions:** 74' W x 41'6" D
**Levels:** 2
**Square Footage:** 2,083
**Main Level Sq. Ft.:** 1,113
**Upper Level Sq. Ft.:** 970
**Bedrooms:** 3
**Bathrooms:** 2½
**Foundation:** Crawl space, slab, or basement
**Materials List Available:** Yes
**Price Category:** D

With a wide-wrapping porch and a pretty Palladian window peeking from a sky-high dormer, this charming home is cheerfully reminiscent of the good old days.

*Images provided by designer/architect.*

**Features:**

• Dining and Living Rooms: Over the threshold, this dining room engages one side of the staircase and the living room with fireplace occupies the other to maintain balance.

• Kitchen: One section of this functional kitchen looks out at the deck, feeds into the breakfast area, and flows into the great-sized family room while the other leads to the laundry area, half bath, mudroom, and garage.

• Master Suite: The second level delivers the master suite, with its wide walk-in closet and a full bath with separate shower and tub areas, double sinks, and a bright window.

• Bedrooms: Each of the two equally spacious secondary bedrooms with wall-length closets and large windows shares a full-size bath uniquely outfitted with double sinks so that no one has to wait to primp.

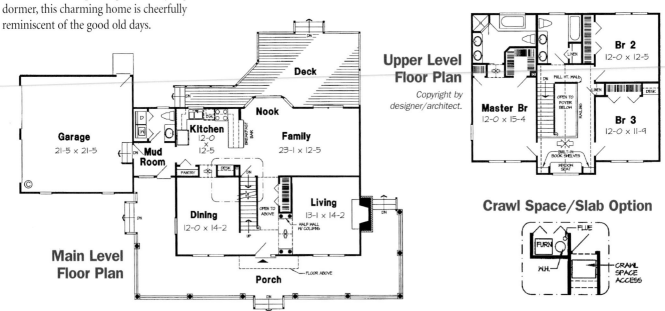

**Upper Level Floor Plan**

*Copyright by designer/architect.*

**Main Level Floor Plan**

**Crawl Space/Slab Option**

Rear View

Rear View

Loft Area

Front Porch

Master Bedroom

# Plans and Ideas for Your Landscape

Landscapes change over the years. As plants grow, the overall look evolves from sparse to lush. Trees cast cool shade where the sun used to shine. Shrubs and hedges grow tall and dense enough to provide privacy. Perennials and ground covers spread to form colorful patches of foliage and flowers. Meanwhile, paths, arbors, fences, and other structures gain the patina of age.

Constant change over the years—sometimes rapid and dramatic, sometimes slow and subtle—is one of the joys of landscaping. It is also one of the challenges. Anticipating how fast plants will grow and how big they will eventually get is difficult, even for professional designers, and was a major concern in formulating the designs for this book.

To illustrate the kinds of changes to expect in a planting, these pages show a landscape design at three different "ages." Even though a new planting may look sparse at first, it will soon fill in. And because of careful spacing, the planting will look as good in 10 to 15 years as it does after 3 to 5. It will, of course, look different, but that's part of the fun.

**At Planting**

Crape myrtle

Carolina jasmine or clematis

Spirea

Bluebeard

Barberry

Annuals

Mondo grass

**Three to Five Years**

Crape myrtle

Carolina jasmine or clematis

Spirea

Barberry

Mondo grass

**At Planting**—Here's how a corner planting might appear in spring immediately after planting. The fence and mulch look conspicuously fresh, new, and unweathered. The crape myrtle is only 4 to 5 ft. tall, with trunks no thicker than broomsticks. It hasn't leafed out yet. The spirea and barberries are 12 to 18 in. tall and wide, and the Carolina jasmine (or clematis) just reaches the bottom rail of the fence. Evenly spaced tufts of mondo grass edge the sidewalk. The bluebeards are stubby now but will grow 2 to 3 ft. tall by late summer, when they bloom. Annuals such as vinca and ageratum start flowering right away and soon form solid patches of color. The first year after planting, be sure to water during dry spells, and to pull or spray any weeds that pop through the mulch.

**Three to Five Years**—Shown in summer now, the planting has begun to mature. The mondo grass has spread to make a continuous, weed-proof patch. The Carolina jasmine (or clematis) reaches partway along the fence. The spirea and barberries have grown into bushy, rounded specimens. From now on, they'll get wider but not much taller. The crape myrtle will keep growing about 1 ft. taller every year, and its crown will broaden. As you continue replacing the annuals twice a year, keep adding compost or organic matter to the soil and spreading fresh mulch on top.

**Ten to Fifteen Years**—As shown here in late summer, the crape myrtle is now a fine specimen, about 15 ft. tall, with a handsome silhouette, beautiful flowers, and colorful bark on its trunks. The bluebeards recover from an annual spring pruning to form bushy mounds covered with blooms. The Carolina jasmine, (or clematis) spirea, and barberry have reached their mature size. Keep them neat and healthy by pruning out old, weak, or dead stems every spring. If you get tired of replanting annuals, substitute low-growing perennials or shrubs in those positions.

### Ten to Fifteen Years

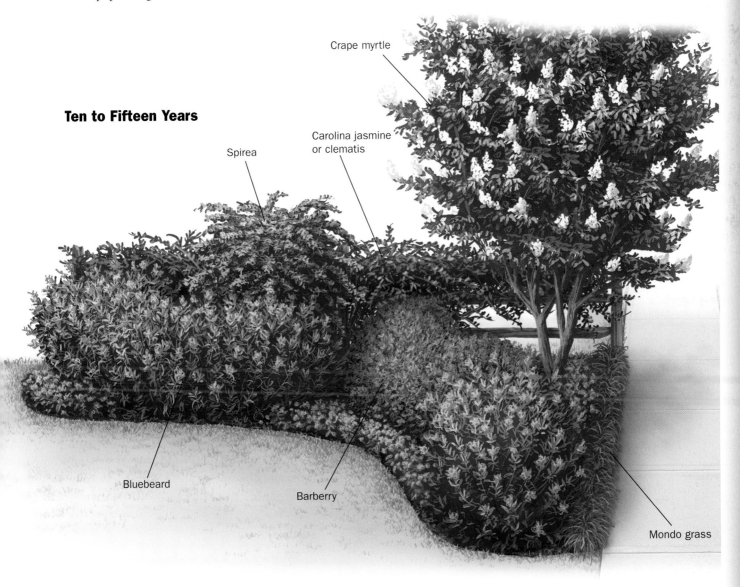

Crape myrtle

Carolina jasmine or clematis

Spirea

Bluebeard

Barberry

Mondo grass

# "Around Back"

## Dress Up the Area between the House and a Detached Garage

When people think of landscaping the entrance to their home, the public entry at the front of the house comes immediately to mind. It's easy to forget that the back door often gets more use. If you make the journey between back door and driveway or garage many times each day, why not make it as pleasant a trip as possible? For many properties, a simple planting can transform the space bounded by the house, garage, and driveway, making it at once more inviting and more functional.

In a high-traffic area frequented by ball-bouncing, bicycle-riding children as well as busy adults, delicate, fussy plants have no place. The design shown here employs a few types of tough low-care plants, all of which look good year-round. The low yew hedge links the house and the garage and separates the more private backyard from the busy driveway. The star magnolia is just the right size for its spot. Its early-spring flowers will be a delight whether viewed coming up the driveway or from a window overlooking the backyard. The wide walk makes passage to and from the car easy—even with your arms full of groceries.

*Note: All plants are appropriate for USDA Hardiness Zones 5, 6, and 7.*

**A** Star magnolia

See site plan for **F**

**Site:** Sunny
**Season:** Summer
**Concept:** A planting to raise spirits when weighed down by shopping bags and to separate activities in the backyard from the driveway.

**C** 'Steeds' Japanese holly

**B** 'Hicksii' hybrid yew

**D** 'Hidcote' hypericum

**E** 'Big Blue' lilyturf

**G** Walkway

**E** 'Big Blue' lilyturf

# Plants & Projects

The watchword in this planting is evergreen. Except for the magnolia, all the plants here are fully evergreen or are nearly so. Spring and summer see lovely flowers from the magnolia and hypericum, and the carpet of lilyturf turns a handsome blue in August. For a bigger splash in spring, underplant the lilyturf with daffodils. Choose a single variety for uniform color, or select several varieties for a mix of colors and bloom times. Other than shearing the hedge, the only maintenance required is cutting back the lilyturf and hypericum in late winter.

**A** **Star magnolia** *Magnolia stellata* (use 1 plant)
Lovely white flowers cover this small deciduous tree before the leaves appear. Starlike blooms, slightly fragrant and sometimes tinged with pink, appear in early spring and last up to two weeks. In summer, the dense leafy crown of dark green leaves helps provide privacy in the backyard. A multi-trunked specimen will fill the space better and display more of the interesting winter bark.

**B** **'Hicksii' hybrid yew** *Taxus x media* (use 9)
A fast-growing evergreen shrub is ideal for this 3-ft.-tall, neatly sheared hedge. Needles are glossy dark green and soft, not prickly. Eight plants form the L-shaped portion, while a single sheared plant extends the hedge on the other side of the walk connecting it to the house. (If the hedge needs to play a part in confining a family pet, you could easily set posts either side of the walk and add a gate.)

**C** **'Steeds' Japanese holly** *Ilex crenata* (use 3 or more)
Several of these dense, upright evergreen shrubs can be grouped at the corner as specimen plants or to tie into an existing foundation planting. You could also extend them along the house to create a foundation planting, as shown here. The small dark green leaves are thick and leathery and have tiny spines. Plants attain a pleasing form when left to their own devices. Resist the urge to shear them; just prune to control size if necessary.

**D** **'Hidcote' hypericum** *Hypericum* (use 1)
All summer long, clusters of large golden flowers cover the arching stems of this tidy semievergreen shrub, brightening the entrance to the backyard.

**E** **'Big Blue' lilyturf** *Liriope muscari* (use 40 or more)
Grasslike evergreen clumps of this perennial ground cover grow together to carpet the ground flanking the driveway and walk. (Extend the planting as far down the drive as you like.) Slim spires of tiny blue flowers rise above the dark green leaves in June. Lilyturf doesn't stand up to repeated tromping. If the drive is also a basketball court, substitute periwinkle (*Vinca minor*) a tough ground cover with late-spring lilac flowers.

**F** **Stinking hellebor** *Helleborus foetidus* (use 5 or more) This clump-forming perennial is ideal for filling the space between the walk and house on the backyard side of the hedge. (You might also consider extending the planting along the L-shaped side of the hedge.) Its pale green flowers are among the first to bloom in the spring and continue for many weeks; dark green leaves are attractive year-round.

**G** **Walkway**
Precast concrete pavers, 2 ft. by 2 ft., replace an existing walk or form a new one.

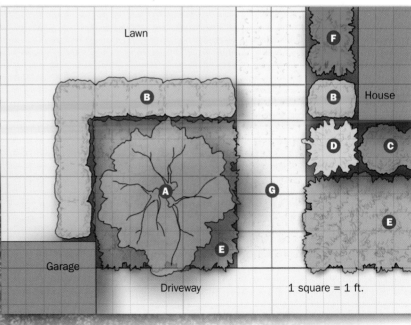

# Beautify Your Garden Shed

Just as you enhance your living room by hanging paintings on the walls, you can decorate blank walls in your outdoor "living rooms." The design shown here transforms a nondescript shed wall into a living fresco, showcasing lovely plants in a framework of roses and flowering vines. Instead of a view of peeling paint, imagine gazing at this scene from a nearby patio, deck, or kitchen window.

This symmetrical composition frames two crape myrtles between arched latticework trellises. Handsome multitrunked shrubs, the crape myrtles perform year-round, providing sumptuous pink flowers in summer, orange-red foliage in fall, and attractive bark in winter. On either side of the crape myrtles, roses and clematis scramble over the trellis in a profusion of yellow and purple flowers.

A tidy low boxwood hedge sets off a shallow border of shrubs and perennials at the bottom of the "frame." Cheerful long-blooming daylilies and asters, airy Russian sage, and elegant daphne make sure that the ground-level attractions hold their own with the aerial performers covering the wall above. The flowers hew to a color scheme of yellows, pinks, blues, and purples.

Wider or narrower walls can be accommodated by expanding the design to include additional "panels," or by reducing it to one central panel. To set off the plants, consider painting or staining the wall and trellises in an off-white, an earth tone, or a light gray color.

Jackman clematis

'Golden Showers' rose

'Carol Mackie' daphne **F**    'Happy Returns' daylily **H**    'Green Beauty' littleleaf boxwood **E**

## Plants and Projects

These plants will all do well in the hot, dry conditions often found near a wall with a sunny exposure. Other than training and pruning the vines, roses, and hedge, maintenance involves little more than fall and spring cleanup. The trellises, supported by 4x4 posts and attached to the garage, are well within the reach of average do-it-yourselfers.

**A** **'Hopi' crape myrtle** *Lagerstroemia indica* (use 2 plants) Large multitrunked deciduous shrubs produce papery pink flowers for weeks in summer. They also contribute colorful fall foliage and attractive flaky bark for winter interest.

**B** **'Golden Showers' rose** *Rosa* (use 3) Tied to each trellis, the long canes of these climbers dis-

play large, fragrant, double yellow flowers in abundance all summer long.

**C** **Golden clematis** *Clematis tangutica* (use 1) Twining up through the rose canes, this deciduous vine adds masses of small yellow flowers to the larger, more elaborate roses all summer. Feathery silver seed heads in fall.

**D** **Jackman clematis** *Clematis x jackmanii* (use 2) These deciduous vines clamber among the rose canes at the corners of the wall. The combination of their large but simple purple flowers and the double yellow roses is spectacular.

**E** **'Green Beauty' littleleaf boxwood** *Buxus microphylla* (use 15) Small evergreen leaves make this an ideal shrub for this

neat hedge. The leaves stay bright green all winter. Trim it about 12 to 18 in. high so it won't obscure the plants behind.

**F** **'Carol Mackie' daphne** *Daphne x burkwoodii* (use 2) This small rounded shrub marks the far end of the bed with year-round green-and-cream variegated foliage. In spring, pale pink flowers fill the yard with their perfume.

**G** **Russian sage** *Perovskia atriplicifolia* (use 7) Silver-green foliage and tiers of tiny blue flowers create a light airy effect in the center of the design from midsummer until fall. Cut stems back partway in early summer to control the size and spread of this tall perennial.

**H** **'Happy Returns' daylily** *Hemerocallis* (use 6) These compact grassy-leaved

perennials provide yellow trumpet-shaped flowers from early June to frost. A striking combination of color and texture with the Russian sage behind.

**I** **'Monch' aster** *Aster x frikartii* (use 4) Pale purple daisylike flowers bloom gaily from June until frost on these knee-high perennials. Cut stems partway back in midsummer if they start to flop over the hedge.

**J** **Trellis** Simple panels of wooden lattice frame the crape myrtles while supporting the roses and clematis.

**K** **Steppingstones** Rectangular flagstone slabs provide a place to stand while pruning and tying nearby shrubs and vines.

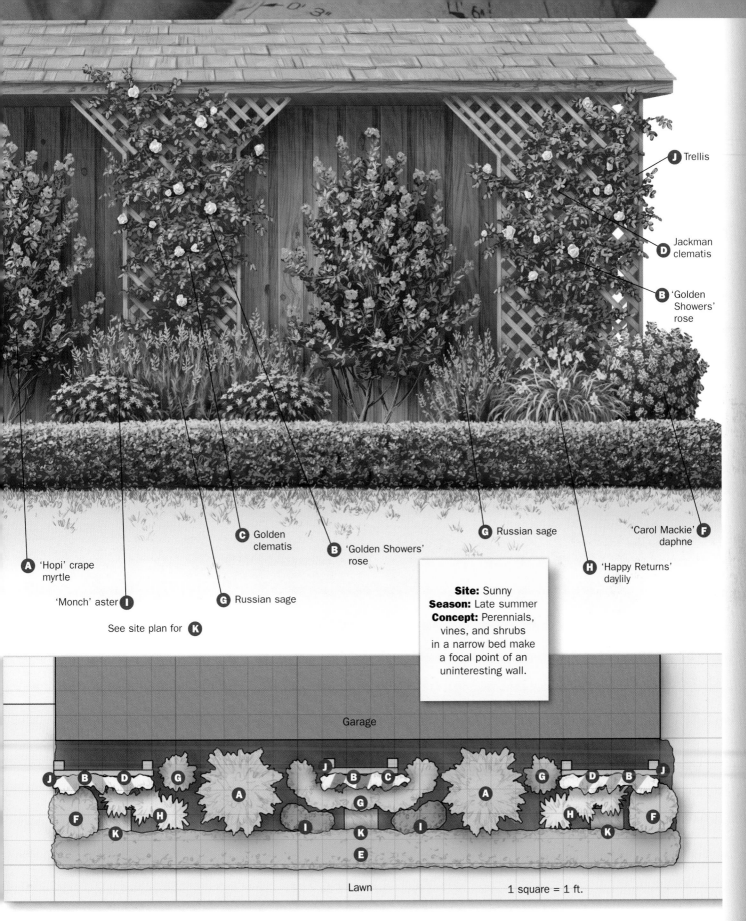

**J** Trellis

**D** Jackman clematis

**B** 'Golden Showers' rose

**C** Golden clematis

**B** 'Golden Showers' rose

**G** Russian sage

**G** Russian sage

**'Carol Mackie' daphne** **F**

**A** 'Hopi' crape myrtle

'Monch' aster **I**

**G** Russian sage

**H** 'Happy Returns' daylily

See site plan for **K**

**Site:** Sunny
**Season:** Late summer
**Concept:** Perennials, vines, and shrubs in a narrow bed make a focal point of an uninteresting wall.

Garage

Lawn

1 square = 1 ft.

*Note: All plants are appropriate for USDA Hardiness Zones 5, 6, and 7.*

# Pleasing Passage to a Garden Landscape

Entrances are an important part of any landscape. They can welcome visitors onto your property; highlight a special feature, such as a rose garden; or mark passage between two areas with different character or function. The design shown here can serve in any of these situations. A picket fence and perennial plantings create a friendly, attractive barrier, just enough to signal the confines of the front yard or contain the family dog. The vine-covered arbor provides welcoming access.

The design combines uncomplicated elements imaginatively, creating interesting details to catch the eye and a slightly formal but comfortable overall effect. Picketed enclosures and compact evergreen shrubs broaden the arbor, giving it greater presence. The wide flagstone apron, flanked by neat deciduous shrubs, reinforces this effect and frames the entrance. Massed perennial plantings lend substance to the fence, which serves as a backdrop to their handsome foliage and colorful flowers.

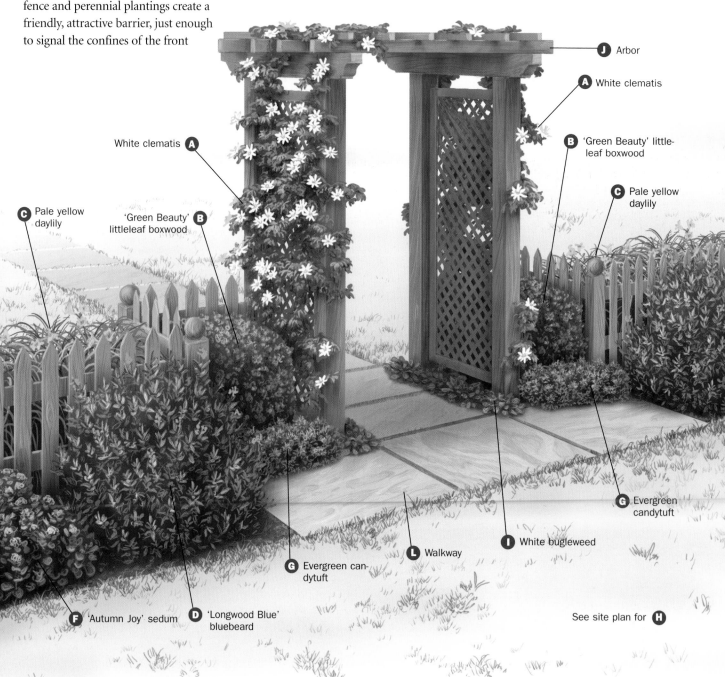

J Arbor

A White clematis

White clematis A

B 'Green Beauty' littleleaf boxwood

C Pale yellow daylily

C Pale yellow daylily

'Green Beauty' littleleaf boxwood B

G Evergreen candytuft

I White bugleweed

L Walkway

G Evergreen candytuft

F 'Autumn Joy' sedum

D 'Longwood Blue' bluebeard

See site plan for H

*Note: All plants are appropriate for USDA Hardiness Zones 5, 6, and 7.*

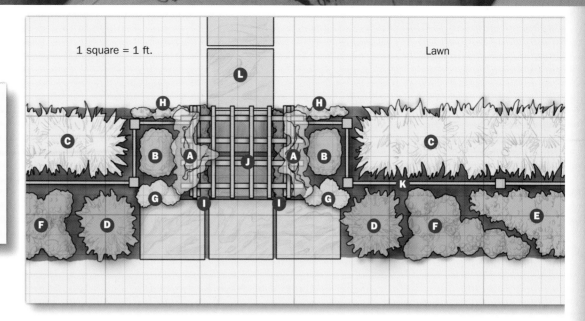

**Site:** Sunny
**Season:** Late summer
**Concept:** Perennials, and flowering vines accent traditional fence entry and arbor.

**K** Picket fence

**E** 'Wargrave Pink' geranium

**F** 'Autumn Joy' sedum

**D** 'Longwood Blue' bluebeard

## Plants and Projects

For many people, a picket fence and vine-covered arbor represent old-fashioned "Cottage" style. The plantings here further encourage this feeling.

Pretty white flowers cover the arbor for much of the summer. Massed plantings of daylilies, geraniums, and sedums along the fence produce wide swaths of flowers and attractive foliage from early summer to fall. Plant drifts of snowdrops in these beds; their late-winter flowers are a welcome sign that spring will soon come.

The structures and plantings are easy to build, install, and care for. You can extend the fence and plantings as needed. To use an existing concrete walk, just pour pads either side to create the wide apron in front of the arbor.

**A** **White clematis** *Clematis* (use 4 plants)
Four of these deciduous climbing vines, one at each post, will cover the arbor in a few years. For large white flowers, try the cultivar 'Henryi', which blooms in early and late summer.

**B** **'Green Beauty' littleleaf boxwood** *Buxus microphylla* (use 2)
This evergreen shrub forms a neat ball of small bright green

leaves without shearing. It is colorful in winter when the rest of the plants are dormant.

**C** **Pale yellow daylily** *Hemerocallis* (use 24)
A durable perennial whose cheerful trumpet-shaped flowers nod above clumps of arching foliage. Choose from the many yellow-flowered cultivars (some fragrant); mix several to extend the season of bloom.

**D** **'Longwood Blue' bluebeard** *Caryopteris x clandonensis* (use 2)
A pair of these small deciduous shrubs with soft gray foliage frame the entry. Sky blue late-summer flowers cover the plants for weeks.

**E** **'Wargrave Pink' geranium** *Geranium endressii* (use 9)
This perennial produces a mass of bright green leaves and a profusion of pink flowers in early summer. Cut it back in July and it will bloom intermittently until frost.

**F** **'Autumn Joy' sedum** *Sedum* (use 13)
This perennial forms a clump of upright stems with distinctive fleshy foliage. Pale flower buds that appear during summer are followed by pink flowers during fall and rusty seed

heads that stand up in winter.

**G** **Evergreen candytuft** *Iberis sempervirens* (use 12)
A perennial ground cover that spreads to form a small welcome mat at the foot of the boxwoods. White flowers stand out against glossy evergreen leaves in spring.

**H** **Lamb's ears** *Stachys byzantina* (use 6)
Favorites of children, the long woolly gray leaves of this perennial form a soft carpet. In early summer, thick stalks carry scattered purple flowers.

**I** **White bugleweed** *Ajuga reptans 'Alba'* (use 20)
Edging the walk under the arbor, this perennial ground cover has pretty green leaves and, in late spring, short spikes of white flowers.

**J** **Arbor** Thick posts give this simple structure a sturdy visual presence. Paint or stain it, or make it of cedar and let it weather as shown here.

**K** **Picket fence** Low picket fence adds character to the planting; materials and finish should match the arbor.

**L** **Walkway** Flagstone walk can be large pavers, as shown here, or made up of smaller rectangular flags.

## Plan #131027

**Dimensions:** 62'4" W x 53'6" D
**Levels:** 1.5
**Square Footage:** 2,567
**Main Level Sq. Ft.:** 2,017
**Upper Level Sq. Ft.:** 550
**Bedrooms:** 4
**Bathrooms:** 3
**Foundation:** Crawl space, slab, or basement
**Materials List Available:** Yes
**Price Category:** F

*This home, as shown in the photograph, may differ from the actual blueprints. For more detailed information, please check the floor plans carefully.*

*Images provided by designer/architect.*

The features of this home are so good that you may have trouble imagining all of them at once.

**Features:**

- **Great Room:** Imagine a stepped ceiling, corner fireplace, built-media center, and wall of windows with a glass door to the backyard—in one room.

- **Dining Room:** A stepped ceiling and server with a sink add to the elegance of this formal room.

- **Breakfast Room:** Eat at the bar this room shares with the island kitchen, and admire the

12-ft. cathedral ceiling and bayed group of 8- and 9-ft. windows. Or go through the sliding glass door to the covered side porch.

- **Master Suite:** The bedroom has a tray ceiling and cozy sitting area, and a whirlpool tub, shower, and walk-in closet are in the skylighted bath.

- **Optional Study:** The private bath in bedroom 2 makes it ideal for a study or home office.

Breakfast Nook

Rear View

Great Room

## Main Level Floor Plan

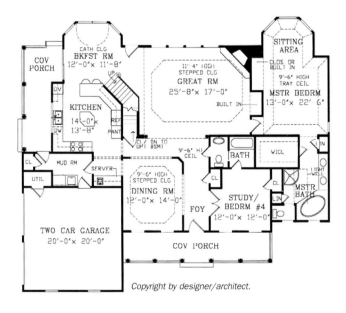

Copyright by designer/architect.

## Upper Level Floor Plan

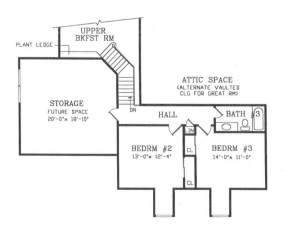

## Painting Tips

As with any skill, there is a right and a wrong way to paint. There is a right way to hold a brush, a right way to maneuver a roller, a right way to spray a wall, etc. Follow these basic professional tips:

**Brushing vs. Rolling.** Some painters insist that only a brush-painted job looks right. However, most painters will "cut in" the edges with a brush, and then finish the main body of a wall or ceiling using a roller. Brushing alone can be time-consuming, and it is typically reserved for architectural woodwork.

**Using the Right Brush.** Use the largest brush with which you are comfortable. Professional painters seldom pick up anything smaller than a 4-inch brush. Most homeowners will achieve good results using a 4-inch brush for "cutting in" and for large surfaces, and an angled 2½- to 3-inch sash brush for trim around windows and doors. Be sure, also, to use brushes that are appropriate for the type of paint being applied. Oil-based paints require a natural bristle (also called "China bristles"), while water-based paints are applied with a synthetic bristle brush.

**Handling a Brush.** Many people grip a paintbrush as if they were shaking someone's hand. It is better to grip a brush more like a pencil, with the fingers and thumb wrapped around the metal ferrule. This grip provides the hand and wrist with a wider range of motion and therefore greater speed and precision. If your hand cramps, switch hands or switch temporarily to the handshake grip.

**Wiping Rags.** Before you begin painting, put a dust rag in your pocket. This is helpful for clearing away cobwebs and dust before painting. It is also handy for wiping off paint drips before they have a chance to dry.

**Paint Hooks.** When working on a ladder, use a good-quality paint hook to secure the paint bucket to your ladder. Avoid makeshift hooks made with wire or coat hangers. Paint hooks are inexpensive and available at virtually all paint and hardware stores.

# Plan #151015

**Dimensions:** 72'4" W x 48'4" D
**Levels:** 2
**Square Footage:** 2,789
**Main Level Sq. Ft.:** 1,977
**Upper Level Sq. Ft.:** 812
**Bedrooms:** 4
**Bathrooms:** 3
**Foundation:** Crawl space, slab, or basement
**CompleteCost List Available:** Yes
**Price Category:** F

*Images provided by designer/architect.*

The spacious kitchen that opens to the breakfast room and the hearth room make this family home ideal for entertaining.

**Features:**

- Great Room: The fireplace will make a cozy winter focal point in this versatile space.

- Hearth Room: Enjoy the built-in entertainment center, built-in shelving, and fireplace here.

- Dining Room: A swing door leading to the kitchen is as attractive as it is practical.

- Study: A private bath and walk-in closet make this room an ideal spot for guests when needed.

- Kitchen: An island work area, a computer desk, and an eat-in bar add convenience and utility.

- Master Suite: Two vanities, two walk-in closets, a shower with a seat, and a whirlpool tub highlight this private space.

## Main Level Floor Plan

*Copyright by designer/architect.*

## Upper Level Floor Plan

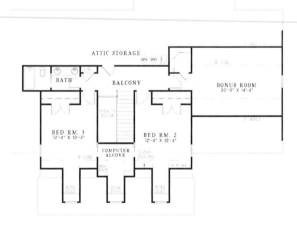

## Plan #321007

**Dimensions:** 76' W x 55'2" D

**Levels:** 1

**Square Footage:** 2,695

**Bedrooms:** 3

**Bathrooms:** 2½

**Foundation:** Basement

**Materials List Available:** Yes

**Price Category:** G

You'll love the way this spacious ranch reminds you of a French country home.

**Features:**

- Foyer: Come into this lovely home's foyer, and be greeted with a view of the gracious staircase and the great room just beyond.

- Great Room: Settle down by the cozy fireplace in cool weather, and reach for a book on the built-in shelves that surround it.

- Kitchen: Designed for efficient work patterns, this large kitchen is open to the great room.

- Breakfast Room: Just off the kitchen, this sunny room will be a family favorite all through the day.

- Master Suite: A bay window, walk-in closet, and shower built for two are highlights of this area.

- Additional Bedrooms: These large bedrooms both have walk-in closets and share a Jack-and-Jill bath for total convenience.

*Images provided by designer/architect.*

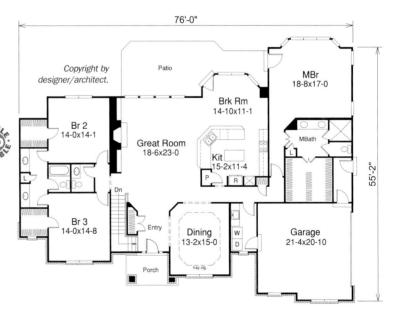

*Copyright by designer/architect.*

SMARTtip

## Decorative Poles

Drapery poles are supported by the brackets fastened to the window frame or wall. The brackets that are provided with the poles generally coordinate and blend in with the pole finish. Brackets can be simple but also decorative. If you opt for a spectacular, attention-grabbing bracket, consider choosing less showy finials for the ends of the pole.

# Plan #101020

**Dimensions:** 55'8" W x 49'2" D

**Levels:** 2

**Square Footage:** 2,972

**Main Level Sq. Ft.:** 1,986

**Upper Level Sq. Ft.:** 986

**Bedrooms:** 4

**Bathrooms:** 3½

**Foundation:** Crawl space, slab, basement or walkout

**Materials List Available:** No

**Price Category:** F

*Images provided by designer/architect.*

This luxurious country home has an open-design main level that maximizes the use of space.

**Features:**

- Ceiling Height: 9 ft. unless otherwise noted.
- Foyer: Guests will be greeted by this grand two-story entry, with its graceful angled staircase.
- Dining Room: At nearly 12 ft. x 15 ft., this elegant dining room has plenty of room for large parties.
- Family Room: Everyone will be drawn to

this 17-ft. x 19-ft. room, with its dramatic two-story ceiling and its handsome fireplace.

- Kitchen: This spacious kitchen is open to the family room and features a breakfast bar and built-in table in the cooktop island.
- Master Suite: This elegant retreat includes a bayed 18-ft.-5-in. x 14-ft.-9-in. bedroom and a beautiful corner his and her bath/closet arrangement.
- Secondary Bedrooms: Upstairs you'll find three spacious bathrooms, one with a private bath and two with access to a shared bath.

**CAD FILE AVAILABLE**

## Main Level Floor Plan

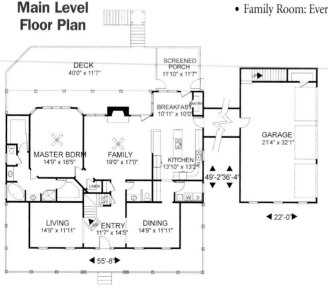

## Upper Level Floor Plan

*Copyright by designer/architect.*

## Plan #101013

**Dimensions:** 72' W x 66' D

**Levels:** 1

**Square Footage:** 2,564

**Bedrooms:** 3

**Bathrooms:** 2½

**Foundation:** Basement; crawl space or slab for fee

**Materials List Available:** Yes

**Price Category:** F

This exciting design combines a striking classic exterior with a highly functional floor plan.

### Features:

• **Ceiling Height:** 9 ft. unless otherwise noted.

• **Family Room:** This warm and inviting room measures 18 ft. x 22 ft. It features a 14-ft. ceiling and a rear wall of windows. French doors lead to an enormous deck.

• **Kitchen:** This unique angled kitchen is open to the hearth room and eating areas, all of which enjoy vaulted ceilings and are surrounded by windows. The hearth room has a TV niche.

• **Master Suite:** This 19-ft. x 18-ft. master suite is truly sumptuous, with its 12-ft. ceiling, sitting area, two walk-in closets, and full-featured bath.

• **Secondary Bedrooms:** Each of the secondary bedrooms measures 11 ft. x 14 ft. and has direct access to a shared bath.

• **Bonus Room:** Just beyond the entry are stairs leading to this bonus room, which measures approximately 12 ft. x 21 ft.—plenty of room for storage or future expansion.

Master Bedroom

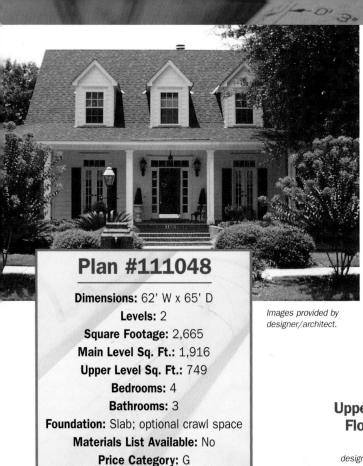

**Main Level Floor Plan**

Two Car Garage 21'4"x 21'4"

Patio

Porch

Utility 12'2"x 7'6"

Breakfast 14'2"x 9'6"

Living 20'2"x 20'

WIC

Master Bedroom 18'x 14'2"

Kitchen 12'2"x 12'

Bath

Dining 11'6' x 15'

Bath

Master Bath

Bedroom 11'6"x 11'4"

Porch

*Images provided by designer/architect.*

**Upper Level Floor Plan**

WIC

Bath

WIC

Bedroom 14'8"x 12'6"

Bedroom 14'8"x 12'6"

*Copyright by designer/architect.*

## Plan #111048

**Dimensions:** 62' W x 65' D

**Levels:** 2

**Square Footage:** 2,665

**Main Level Sq. Ft.:** 1,916

**Upper Level Sq. Ft.:** 749

**Bedrooms:** 4

**Bathrooms:** 3

**Foundation:** Slab; optional crawl space

**Materials List Available:** No

**Price Category:** G

## Plan #211148

**Dimensions:** 74'6" W x 77' D

**Levels:** 1

**Square Footage:** 2,710

**Bedrooms:** 4

**Bathrooms:** 3½

**Foundation:** Crawl space, slab

**Materials List Available:** No

**Price Category:** F

*Images provided by designer/architect.*

CAD FILE AVAILABLE

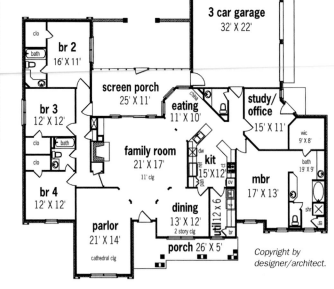

3 car garage 32' X 22'

clo

br 2 16' X 11'

bath

screen porch 25' X 11'

eating 11' X 10'

study/office 15' X 11'

br 3 12' X 12'

clo

bath

family room 21' X 17' 11' clg

wic 9' X 8'

dw

kit 15'X12

bath

clo

mbr 17' X 13'

bath 19' X 9'

br 4 12' X 12'

dining 13' X 12' 2 story clg

util 12 x 6

shr

parlor 21' X 14'

cathedral clg

porch 26' X 5'

*Copyright by designer/architect.*

## Plan #191029

**Dimensions:** 78' W x 67' D

**Levels:** 1

**Square Footage:** 2,726

**Bedrooms:** 4

**Bathrooms:** 3½

**Foundation:** Crawl space, slab, or basement

**Materials List Available:** No

**Price Category:** F

*Images provided by designer/architect.*

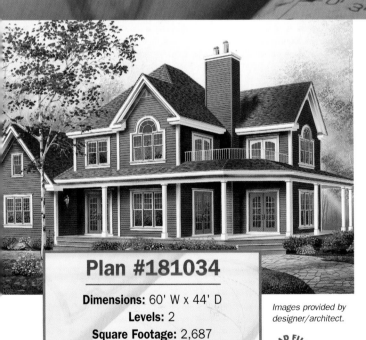

78-0 WIDE X 67-0 DEEP
(INCLUDING PORCHES)

*Copyright by designer/architect.*

---

**Main Level Floor Plan**

**Upper Level Floor Plan**

*Copyright by designer/architect.*

## Plan #181034

**Dimensions:** 60' W x 44' D

**Levels:** 2

**Square Footage:** 2,687

**Main Level Sq. Ft.:** 1,297

**Upper Level Sq. Ft.:** 1,390

**Bedrooms:** 3

**Bathrooms:** 2½

**Foundation:** Full basement

**Materials List Available:** Yes

**Price Category:** F

*Images provided by designer/architect.*

CAD FILE AVAILABLE

## Plan #121083

**Dimensions:** 72' W x 45'4" D
**Levels:** 2
**Square Footage:** 2,695
**Main Level Sq. Ft.:** 1,881
**Upper Level Sq. Ft.:** 814
**Bedrooms:** 4
**Bathrooms:** 3½
**Foundation:** Basement
**Materials List Available:** Yes
**Price Category:** F

*Images provided by designer/architect.*

You'll love this home for its soaring entryway ceiling and well-designed layout.

**Features:**

• Entry: A balcony from the upper level looks down into this two-story entry, which features a decorative plant shelf.

• Great Room: Comfort is guaranteed in this large room, with its built-in bookcases framing a lovely fireplace and trio of transom-topped windows along one wall.

• Living Room: Save both this formal room and the formal dining room, both of which flank the entry, for guests and special occasions.

• Kitchen: This convenient work space includes a gazebo-shaped breakfast area where friends and family will gather at any time of day.

### Main Level Floor Plan

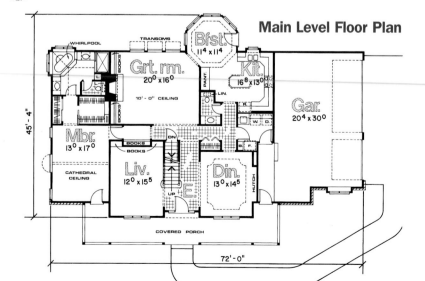

### Upper Level Floor Plan

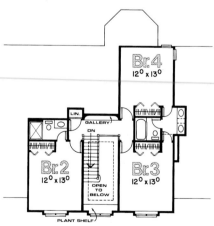

*Copyright by designer/architect.*

# Plan #151144

**Dimensions:** 66'4" W x 64' D

**Levels:** 1

**Square Footage:** 2,624

**Bedrooms:** 4

**Bathrooms:** 3

**Foundation:** Crawl space, slab; basement for fee

**CompleteCost List Available:** Yes

**Price Category:** F

*Images provided by designer/architect.*

The traditional exterior appearance of this home gives way to a surprisingly contemporary interior design and a wealth of lovely amenities.

**Features:**

- Living Room: The 8-inch columns create an elegant feeling in this well-lit room.

- Dining Room: An 11-ft. ceiling makes this room ideal for hosting dinner parties or entertaining a crowd.

- Kitchen: The kitchen features a pass-through to the living room for serving convenience and a snack bar where the kids are sure to gather.

- Breakfast/Hearth Room: The fireplace is the centerpiece in winter, but you'll love the access to the grilling porch when the weather's warm.

- Master Suite: The door to the rear porch is a special feature in this private retreat, and you'll love the bath with a walk-in closet, split vanities, and a glass shower.

**CAD FILE AVAILABLE**

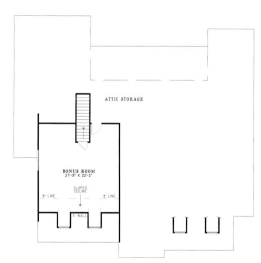

## Bonus Area Floor Plan

*Copyright by designer/architect.*

## Plan #441046

**Dimensions:** 50' W x 42' D
**Levels:** 2
**Square Footage:** 2,606
**Main Level Sq. Ft.:** 1,216
**Upper Level Sq. Ft.:** 1,390
**Bedrooms:** 4
**Bathrooms:** 2½
**Foundation:** Crawl space; slab or basement for fee
**Materials List Available:** Yes
**Price Category:** F

*Images provided by designer/architect.*

Little things mean a lot, and in this design it's the little details that add up to a marvelous plan.

### Features:

- **Great Room:** If you like, you might include a corner media center in this room to complement the fireplace.

- **Den:** This vaulted room lies just off the entry and opens through double doors.

- **Kitchen:** Both formal and casual dining spaces are included and flank this open kitchen, which overlooks the great room.

- **Upper Level:** Sleeping quarters are upstairs and include three family bedrooms and the master suite. Look for a spa tub, separate shower, dual sinks, and a walk-in closet in the master bath. The family bedrooms share the full bathroom, which has double sinks.

**Main Level Floor Plan**

Rear Elevation

**Upper Level Floor Plan**

*Copyright by designer/architect.*

## Plan #121016

**Dimensions:** 56' W x 48' D

**Levels:** 2

**Square Footage:** 2,594

**Main Level Sq. Ft.:** 1,322

**Upper Level Sq. Ft.:** 1,272

**Bedrooms:** 4

**Bathrooms:** 3

**Foundation:** Basement

**Materials List Available:** Yes

**Price Category:** E

A huge wraparound porch gives this home warmth and charm.

**Features:**

- Ceiling Height: 8 ft. except as noted.
- Family Room: This informal sunken room's beamed ceiling and fireplace flanked by windows makes it the perfect place for family gatherings.
- Formal Dining Room: Guests will enjoy gathering in this large elegant room.

- Master Suite: The second-floor master bedroom features its own luxurious bathroom.
- Compartmented Full Bath: This large bathroom serves the three secondary bedrooms on the second floor.
- Optional Play Area: This special space, included in one of the bedrooms, features a cathedral ceiling.
- Kitchen: A large island is the centerpiece of this modern kitchen's well-designed food-preparation area.

**CAD FILE AVAILABLE**

## Main Level Floor Plan

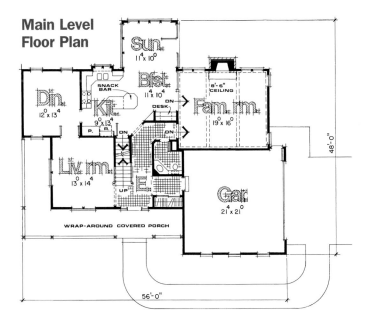

## Upper Level Floor Plan

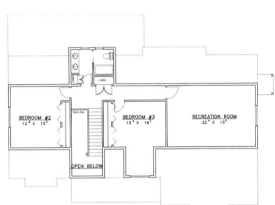

**Main Level Floor Plan**

*Images provided by designer/architect.*

## Plan #451162

**Dimensions:** 62'10" W x 46'10" D

**Levels:** 2

**Square Footage:** 2,565

**Main Level Sq. Ft.:** 1,504

**Upper Level Sq. Ft.:** 1,061

**Bedrooms:** 3

**Bathrooms:** 2½

**Foundation:** Crawl space

**Material List Available:** No

**Price Category:** E

### Upper Level Floor Plan

*Copyright by designer/architect.*

**Main Level Floor Plan**

*Images provided by designer/architect.*

## Plan #421023

**Dimensions:** 72' W x 52'4" D

**Levels:** 2

**Square Footage:** 2,579

**Main Level Sq. Ft.:** 1,399

**Upper Level Sq. Ft.:** 1,180

**Bedrooms:** 4

**Bathrooms:** 2½

**Foundation:** Crawl space, slab or basement

**Material List Available:** Yes

**Price Category:** E

**Upper Level Floor Plan**

*Copyright by designer/architect.*

# Plan #421010

**Dimensions:** 67'6" W x 56' D
**Levels:** 2
**Square Footage:** 2,457
**Main Level Sq. Ft.:** 1,378
**Upper Level Sq. Ft.:** 1,079
**Bedrooms:** 4
**Bathrooms:** 3½
**Foundation:** Crawl space, slab or basement
**Material List Available:** Yes
**Price Category:** E

*Images provided by designer/architect.*

**Main Level Floor Plan**

## Upper Level Floor Plan

*Copyright by designer/architect.*

# Plan #271056

**Dimensions:** 73' W x 52' D
**Levels:** 2
**Square Footage:** 2,850
**Main Level Sq. Ft.:** 1,596
**Upper Level Sq. Ft.:** 1,254
**Bedrooms:** 3
**Bathrooms:** 2½
**Foundation:** Daylight basement
**Materials List Available:** No
**Price Category:** F

*Images provided by designer/architect.*

**Main Level Floor Plan**

*Copyright by designer/architect.*

## Upper Level Floor Plan

# Plan #441009

**Dimensions:** 94' W x 53' D

**Levels:** 1

**Heated Square Footage:** 2,650

**Bedrooms:** 4

**Bathrooms:** 2½

**Foundation:** Crawl space;
slab or basement available for fee

**Materials List Available:** Yes

**Price Category:** F

You'll love to call this plan home. It's large enough for the whole family and has a façade that will make you the envy of the neighborhood.

*This home, as shown in the photograph, may differ from the actual blueprints. For more information, please check the floor plans carefully.*

*Images provided by designer/architect.*

**Features:**

• **Foyer:** The covered porch protects the entry, which has a transom and sidelights to brighten this space.

• **Great Room:** To the left of the foyer, beyond decorative columns, lies this vaulted room, with its fireplace and media center. Additional columns separate the room from the vaulted formal dining room.

• **Kitchen:** A casual nook and this island work center are just around the corner from the great room. The second covered porch can be reached via a door in the nook.

• **Master Suite:** This luxurious space boasts a vaulted salon, a private niche that could be a small study, and a view of the front yard. The master bath features a spa tub, separate shower, compartmented toilet, huge walk-in closet, and access to the laundry room.

• **Bedrooms:** The two additional bedrooms are located at the back of the plan and share the Jack-and-Jill bathroom.

*Copyright by designer/architect.*

## Plan #371087

**Dimensions:** 88'2" W x 62'10" D

**Levels:** 1

**Square Footage:** 2,643

**Bedrooms:** 3

**Bathrooms:** 2½

**Foundation:** Crawl space, slab, or basement

**Materials List Available:** No

**Price Category:** F

This beautiful country home has a warm look that is all its own.

**Features:**

- Dining Room: Once inside you will find a tiled entry that leads into this elegant room, with its 11-ft.-high ceiling.

- Living Room: This large gathering area has a 10-ft.-high ceiling, built-in bookcases, and a country fireplace.

- Kitchen: This island kitchen, with a raised bar, is open to the breakfast nook and meets the garage entrance.

- Master Suite: This suite, located in the rear of the home, features a private bathroom, large walk-in closet, marble tub, and double vanities.

- Bedrooms: Two secondary bedrooms have large closets and share a hall bathroom.

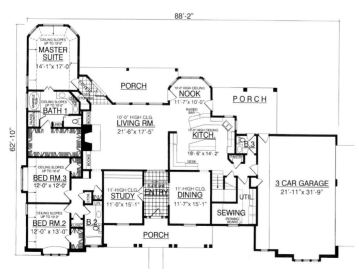

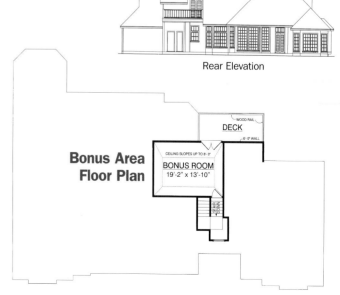

Rear Elevation

**Bonus Area Floor Plan**

## Plan #221042

**Dimensions:** 50' W x 63' D
**Levels:** 2
**Square Footage:** 2,704
**Main Level Sq. Ft.:** 1,797
**Upper Level Sq. Ft.:** 907
**Bedrooms:** 4
**Bathrooms:** 2 full, 2 half
**Foundation:** Basement
**Materials List Available:** No
**Price Category:** F

• Upper Level: Upstairs you'll find a loft with balcony that overlooks the great room below and three additional bedrooms, making this four-bedroom home perfect for just about any size family.

Rear Elevation

Stone and shingle siding and graceful columns adorn the front of this European style two-story home.

**Features:**

• Great Room: Upon entering, you'll be pleased with the sight of a wall of windows in this room, providing a tremendous view of the backyard.

• Kitchen: This kitchen features a breakfast bar overlooking the dining room and providing additional seating for family and friends.

• Master Suite: With its large walk-in closet and spacious bathroom, complete with a Jacuzzi tub, this suite is sure to please.

### Main Level Floor Plan

### Upper Level Floor Plan

*Copyright by designer/architect.*

## Plan #151029

**Dimensions:** 59'4" W x 74'2" D
**Levels:** 1.5
**Square Footage:** 2,777
**Main Level Sq. Ft.:** 2,082
**Upper Level Sq. Ft.:** 695
**Bedrooms:** 4
**Bathrooms:** 2½
**Foundation:** Crawl space, slab; basement for fee
**CompleteCost List Available:** Yes
**Price Category:** F

*Images provided by designer/architect.*

This grand home combines historic Southern charm with modern technology and design. A two-car garage and covered front porch allow for optimum convenience.

**Features:**

- Foyer: This marvelous foyer leads directly to an elegant dining room and comfortable great room.

- Great Room: With high ceilings, a built-in media center, and a fireplace, this will be your favorite room during the chilly fall months.

- Kitchen: An eat-in-bar with an optional island, computer area, and adjoining breakfast room with a bay window make a perfect layout.

- Master Suite: Relax in comfort with a corner whirlpool tub, a separate glass shower, double vanities, and large walk-in closets.

- Upper Level Bedrooms: 2 and 3 both have window seats.

**Main Level Floor Plan**

*Copyright by designer/architect.*

**Upper Level Floor Plan**

**Main Level Floor Plan**

*Images provided by designer/architect.*

CAD FILE AVAILABLE

# Plan #421012

**Dimensions:** 64'4" W x 56'4" D

**Levels:** 2

**Square Footage:** 2,795

**Main Level Sq. Ft.:** 1,787

**Upper Level Sq. Ft.:** 1,008

**Bedrooms:** 4

**Bathrooms:** 3½

**Foundation:** Crawl space, slab, or basement

**Materials List Available:** Yes

**Price Category:** F

**Upper Level Floor Plan**

*Copyright by designer/architect.*

**Main Level Floor Plan**

*Images provided by designer/architect.*

CAD FILE AVAILABLE

# Plan #221080

**Dimensions:** 67'8" W x 63' D

**Levels:** 2

**Square Footage:** 2,772

**Main Level Sq. Ft.:** 1,902

**Upper Level Sq. Ft.:** 870

**Bedrooms:** 4

**Bathrooms:** 3½

**Foundation:** Basement

**Material List Available:** No

**Price Category:** F

**Upper Level Floor Plan**

*Copyright by designer/architect.*

## Main Level Floor Plan

# Plan #341007

**Dimensions:** 87'7" W x 30' D
**Levels:** 2
**Square Footage:** 4,068
**Main Level Sq. Ft.:** 3,218
**Upper Level Sq. Ft.:** 850
**Bedrooms:** 4
**Bathrooms:** 2½
**Foundation:** Crawl space, slab, or basement
**Materials List Available:** Yes
**Price Category:** F

*Images provided by designer/architect.*

CAD FILE AVAILABLE

## Upper Level Floor Plan

*Copyright by designer/architect.*

---

# Plan #441036

**Dimensions:** 60' W x 50' D
**Levels:** 2
**Square Footage:** 2,902
**Main Level Sq. Ft.:** 1,617
**Upper Level Sq. Ft.:** 1,285
**Bedrooms:** 3
**Bathrooms:** 2½
**Foundation:** Crawl space
**Materials List Available:** Yes
**Price Category:** F

*Images provided by designer/architect.*

## Upper Level Floor Plan

## Main Level Floor Plan

*Copyright by designer/architect.*

◄ 60' ►

## Plan #241008

**Dimensions:** 65' W x 56'8" D
**Levels:** 1
**Square Footage:** 2,526
**Bedrooms:** 4
**Bathrooms:** 3
**Foundation:** Crawl space, slab, or basement
**Materials List Available:** No
**Price Category:** E

*Images provided by designer/architect.*

A covered back porch—with access from the master suite and the breakfast area—makes this traditional home ideal for sitting near a golf course or with a backyard pool.

**Features:**

- Great Room: From the foyer, guests enter this spacious and comfortable great room, which features a handsome fireplace.

- Kitchen: This kitchen—the hub of this family-oriented home—is a joy in which to work, thanks to abundant counter space, a pantry, a convenient eating bar, and an adjoining breakfast area and sunroom.

- Master Suite: Enjoy the quiet comfort of this coffered-ceiling master suite, which features dual vanities and separate walk-in closets.

- Additional Bedrooms: Two secondary bedrooms, which share a full bath, are located at the opposite end of the house from the master suite. Bedroom 4—in front of the house—can be converted into a study.

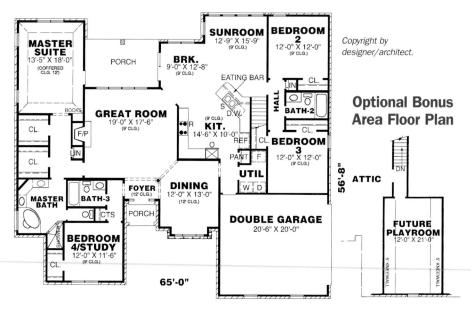

**Optional Bonus Area Floor Plan**

## SMARTtip

### Traditional-Style Kitchen Cabinetry

You can modify stock kitchen cabinetry to enjoy fine furniture-quality details. Prefabricated trims may be purchased at local lumber mills and home centers. For example, crown molding, applied to the top of stock cabinetry and stained or painted to match the door style, may be all you need. Likewise, you can replace hardware with reproduction polished-brass door and drawer knobs or pulls for a finishing touch.

# Plan #441042

**Dimensions:** 52' W x 45' D
**Levels:** 2
**Square Footage:** 2,538
**Main Level Sq. Ft.:** 1,342
**Upper Level Sq. Ft.:** 1,196
**Bedrooms:** 3
**Bathrooms:** 2½
**Foundation:** Crawl space;
slab or basement available for fee
**Materials List Available:** Yes
**Price Category:** E

*Images provided by designer/architect.*

It's never too late to have a happy childhood—or the exact home you want.

**CAD FILE AVAILABLE · CAD**

## Features:

- **Foyer:** This entry soars up two stories with a view to the open hallway above.

- **Family Room:** This large informal gathering area has large windows with a view to the backyard. It also has a two-sided fireplace, which it shares with the den.

- **Kitchen:** This fully equipped island kitchen has a built-in pantry and desk. The nook and family room are open to it.

- **Master Suite:** This private retreat includes a sitting area in the master bedroom that

provides ample space for a comfortable lounge in front of its fireplace. The master bath features a compartmentalized lavatory, spa tub, large shower, and his and her vanities.

- **Bedrooms:** The two additional bedrooms are located on the upper level with the master suite. Both rooms have large closets and share a common bathroom.

Rear Elevation

**Main Level Floor Plan**

◀ 52' ▶

**Upper Level Floor Plan**

*Copyright by designer/architect.*

## Plan #161080

**Dimensions:** 67'4" W x 59'6" D
**Levels:** 2
**Square Footage:** 2,759
**Main Level Sq. Ft.:** 2,007
**Upper Level Sq. Ft.:** 752
**Bedrooms:** 4
**Bathrooms:** 3½
**Foundation:** Basement or walkout
**Material List Available:** Yes
**Price Category:** F

A brick-and-stone exterior with brick quoins and limestone keys decorate the facade of this graceful home.

**Features:**

• Great Room: The foyer slopes upward in transition into this two-story-high great room, which features a gas fireplace and 6-ft.-high windows.

• Kitchen: This spacious area enjoys a snack bar and work island, as well as easy access to a sunny breakfast area and formal dining room. The covered deck is also nearby for meals outside.

• Master Suite: In a space all its own, this master suite boasts ceilings up to 11 ft. and two walk-in closets. The master bath features his and hers vanities, whirlpool tub, and spacious shower.

• Secondary Bedrooms: On the second floor are three additional bedrooms, all with ample closet space and adjacent or private bath rooms.

*Images provided by designer/architect.*

**Main Level Floor Plan**

*Copyright by designer/architect.*

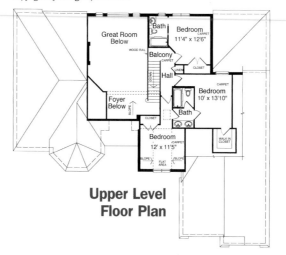

**Upper Level Floor Plan**

Rear Elevation

Left Side Elevation

Right Side Elevation

# Plan #461092

**Dimensions:** 81' W x 54' D
**Levels:** 2
**Square Footage:** 2,844
**Main Level Sq. Ft.:** 2,128
**Upper Level Sq. Ft.:** 716
**Bedrooms:** 4
**Bathrooms:** 4
**Foundation:** Slab or basement; crawl space for fee
**Material List Available:** No
**Price Category:** F

Enjoy country living at its best in this well-designed home.

**Features:**

- Dining Room: Located at the entry, this formal dining room features a nook for your hutch. Pocket doors lead into the foyer, adding the ability for the space to work as a home office.

- Guest Suite: This main-level suite offers your guests privacy while staying connected to what is happening in other parts of the house. The accessible full bathroom is a bonus for the area.

- Master Suite: Located on the main level, this retreat boasts two large walk-in closets. The master bath features a whirlpool tub and a stall shower.

- Upper Level: This level is home to the two secondary bedrooms, each with a walk-in closet. Each bedroom has a private bathroom.

Rear View

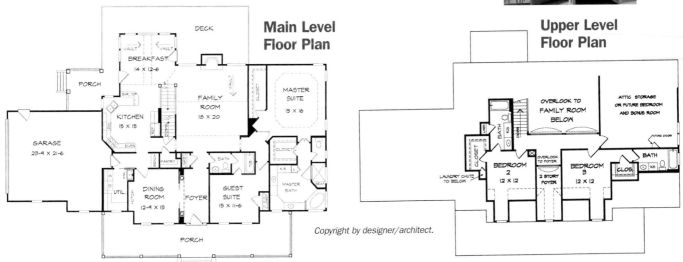

**Main Level Floor Plan**

**Upper Level Floor Plan**

## Plan #131055

**Dimensions:** 62'4" W x 53'6" D
**Levels:** 1.5
**Square Footage:** 2,575
**Main Level Sq. Ft.:** 2,007
**Upper Level Sq. Ft.:** 568
**Bedrooms:** 4
**Bathrooms:** 3
**Foundation:** Crawl space, slab, or basement
**Materials List Available:** Yes
**Price Category:** F

*Images provided by designer/architect.*

**Main Level Floor Plan**

**Upper Level Floor Plan**

*Copyright by designer/architect.*

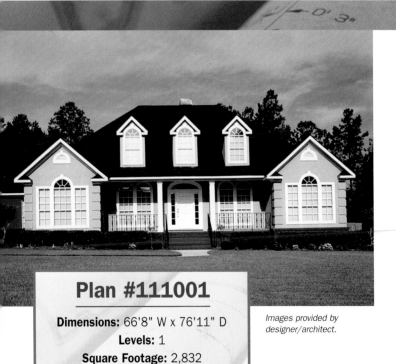

## Plan #111001

**Dimensions:** 66'8" W x 76'11" D
**Levels:** 1
**Square Footage:** 2,832
**Bedrooms:** 4
**Bathrooms:** 2½
**Foundation:** Crawl space or slab
**Materials List Available:** No
**Price Category:** G

*Images provided by designer/architect.*

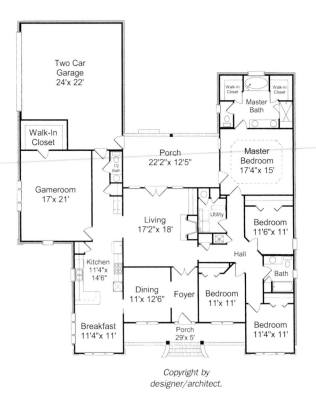

*Copyright by designer/architect.*

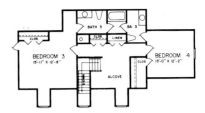

## Upper Level Floor Plan

*Copyright by designer/architect.*

*Images provided by designer/architect.*

## Main Level Floor Plan

## Plan #341006

**Dimensions:** 86'3" W x 35'4" D

**Levels:** 2

**Square Footage:** 2,588

**Main Level Sq. Ft.:** 1,660

**Upper Level Sq. Ft.:** 928

**Bedrooms:** 4

**Bathrooms:** 3½

**Foundation:** Crawl space, slab, or basement

**Materials List Available:** Yes

**Price Category:** E

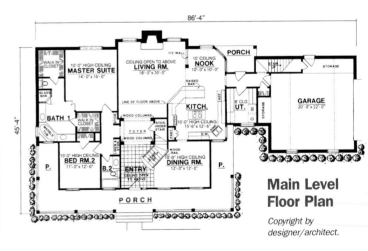

## Main Level Floor Plan

*Copyright by designer/architect.*

*Images provided by designer/architect.*

**CAD FILE AVAILABLE**

## Upper Level Floor Plan

## Plan #371008

**Dimensions:** 86'4" W x 45'4" D

**Levels:** 2

**Square Footage:** 2,656

**Main Level Sq. Ft:** 1,969

**Upper Level Sq. Ft:** 687

**Bedrooms:** 4

**Bathrooms:** 3

**Foundation:** Crawl space, slab, or basement

**Materials List Available:** No

**Price Category:** F

## Plan #271081

**Dimensions:** 86' W x 54' D
**Levels:** 1
**Square Footage:** 2,539
**Bedrooms:** 3
**Bathrooms:** 2
**Foundation:** Slab
**Materials List Available:** No
**Price Category:** E

*Images provided by designer/architect.*

This traditional home is sure to impress your guests and even your neighbors.

**Features:**

- **Living Room:** This quiet space off the foyer is perfect for pleasant conversation.
- **Family Room:** A perfect gathering spot, this room is nicely enhanced by a fireplace.
- **Kitchen:** This room easily serves the bayed morning room and the formal dining room.
- **Master Suite:** The master bedroom overlooks a side patio, and boasts a private bath with a skylight and a whirlpool tub.
- **Library:** This cozy room is perfect for curling up with a good novel. It would also make a great extra bedroom.

Copyright by designer/architect.

## SMARTtip

### Determining Curtain Length

Follow length guidelines for foolproof results, but remember that they're not rules. Go ahead and play with curtain and drapery lengths. Instead of shortening long panels at the hem, for instance, take up excess material by blousing them over tiebacks for a pleasing effect.

## Plan #391050

**Dimensions:** 67' W x 51' D

**Levels:** 2

**Square Footage:** 2,674

**Main Level Sq. Ft.:** 1,511

**Upper Level Sq. Ft.:** 1,163

**Bedrooms:** 3

**Bathrooms:** 2½

**Foundation:** Crawl space, slab, or basement

**Materials List Available:** Yes

**Price Category:** F

*This home, as shown in the photograph, may differ from the actual blueprints. For more detailed information, please check the floor plans carefully.*

*Images provided by designer/architect.*

This home truly transforms tutor styling for today. Charming Old World half-timbering dramatizes exterior dormers and the deeply recessed pillared porch, while New World surprises fill the interior.

**Features:**

• Kitchen: Beyond the living room and study and past the double-entry stairway, this elaborately open-ended kitchen feeds into other important spaces, including the breakfast room, which is bathed in natural light on three sides as it looks out on the patio and three-season porch.

• Family Room: This open family room is also a big draw, with its fireplace, two-story cathedral ceilings, and porch access.

• Master Suite: The second level, enjoying the spacious aura of the vaulted ceiling, high lights this master suite, with its generous windowing, spectacular closeting, and bathroom with tub situated in a wide windowed corner.

• Bedrooms: Two additional bedrooms feature plentiful closeting and pretty front-view windows (one with window seat) and share a second full bath.

### Main Level Floor Plan

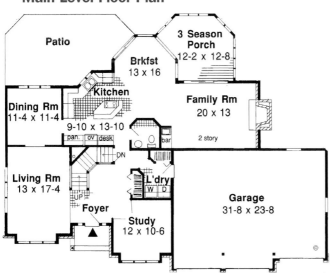

### Upper Level Floor Plan

*Copyright by designer/architect.*

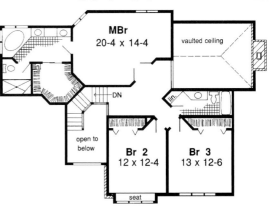

## Plan #121163

**Dimensions:** 65'10" W x 75'6" D
**Levels:** 1
**Square Footage:** 2,679
**Bedrooms:** 4
**Bathrooms:** 3
**Foundation:** Slab; basement for fee
**Material List Available:** Yes
**Price Category:** F

*Images provided by designer/architect.*

Large rooms give this home a spacious feel in a modest footprint.

### Features:

• **Family Room:** This area is the central gathering place in the home. The windows to the rear fill the area with natural light. The fireplace take the chill off on cool winter nights.

• **Kitchen:** This peninsula kitchen with raised bar is open into the family room and the breakfast area. The built-in pantry is a welcomed storage area for today's family.

• **Master Suite:** This secluded area features large windows with a view of the backyard. The master bath boasts a large walk-in closet, his and her vanities and a compartmentalized lavatory area.

• **Secondary Bedrooms:** Bedroom 2 has its own access to the main bathroom, while bedrooms 3 and 4 share a Jack-and-Jill bathroom. All bedrooms feature walk-in closets.

*Copyright by designer/architect.*

# Plan #131050

**Dimensions:** 72'8" W x 47' D
**Levels:** 2
**Square Footage:** 2,874
**Main Level Sq. Ft.:** 2,146
**Upper Level Sq. Ft.:** 728
**Bedrooms:** 4
**Bathrooms:** 3
**Foundation:** Crawl space, slab, or basement
**Materials List Available:** Yes
**Price Category:** G

A gazebo and long covered porch at the entry let you know that this is a spectacular design.

*Images provided by designer/architect.*

**Features:**

• Foyer: This vaulted foyer divides the formal living room and dining room, setting the stage for guests to feel welcome in your home.

• Great Room: This large room is defined by several columns; a corner fireplace and vaulted ceiling add to its drama.

• Kitchen: An island work space separates this area from the bayed breakfast nook.

• Master Suite: You'll have privacy in this main-floor suite, which features two walk-in

closets and a separate toilet room with a dual-sink vanity.

• Upper Level: The two large bedrooms share a bath and a dramatic balcony.

• Bonus Room: Walk down a few steps into this large bonus room over the 3-car garage.

Rear Elevation

**Main Level Floor Plan**

*Copyright by designer/architect.*

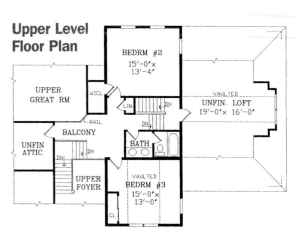

**Upper Level Floor Plan**

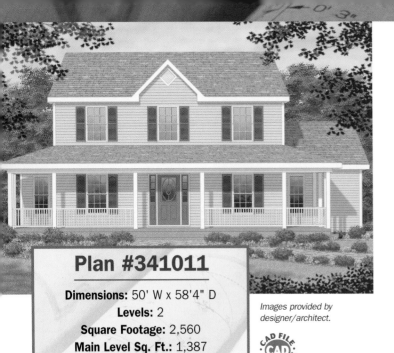

**Main Level Floor Plan**

*Images provided by designer/architect.*

**CAD FILE AVAILABLE**

# Plan #341011

**Dimensions:** 50' W x 58'4" D

**Levels:** 2

**Square Footage:** 2,560

**Main Level Sq. Ft.:** 1,387

**Upper Level Sq. Ft.:** 1,173

**Bedrooms:** 4

**Bathrooms:** 3½

**Foundation:** Crawl space, slab, or basement

**Materials List Available:** Yes

**Price Category:** E

**Upper Level Floor Plan**

*Copyright by designer/architect.*

---

**Main Level Floor Plan**

*Images provided by designer/architect.*

**CAD FILE AVAILABLE**

# Plan #181241

**Dimensions:** 60' W x 44' D

**Levels:** 2

**Square Footage:** 2,687

**Main Level Sq. Ft.:** 1,297

**Upper Level Sq. Ft.:** 1,390

**Bedrooms:** 3

**Bathrooms:** 2½

**Foundation:** Basement

**Materials List Available:** Yes

**Price Category:** F

**Upper Level Floor Plan**

*Copyright by designer/architect.*

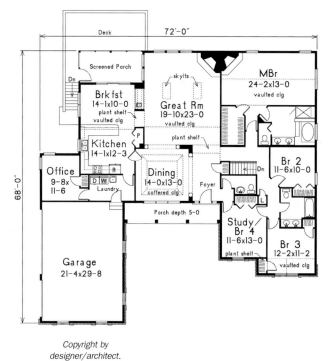

## Plan #321027

**Dimensions:** 72' W x 68' D

**Levels:** 1

**Square Footage:** 2,758

**Bedrooms:** 4

**Bathrooms:** 2½

**Foundation:** Basement

**Materials List Available:** Yes

**Price Category:** F

*Images provided by designer/architect.*

*Copyright by designer/architect.*

## Plan #181039

**Dimensions:** 38' W x 36' D

**Levels:** 2

**Square Footage:** 1,661

**Main Level Sq. Ft.:** 923

**Upper Level Sq. Ft.:** 738

**Bedrooms:** 3

**Bathrooms:** 1½

**Foundation:** Full basement

**Materials List Available:** Yes

**Price Category:** C

*Images provided by designer/architect.*

### Main Level
### Floor Plan

### Upper Level
### Floor Plan

*Copyright by designer/architect.*

## Plan #121028

**Dimensions:** 54'8" W x 42' D

**Levels:** 2

**Square Footage:** 2,644

**Main Level Sq. Ft.:** 1,366

**Upper Level Sq. Ft.:** 1,278

**Bedrooms:** 4

**Bathrooms:** 2½

**Foundation:** Basement

**Materials List Available:** Yes

**Price Category:** F

*Images provided by designer/architect.*

This home is filled with special touches and amenities that add up to gracious living.

**Features:**

• Ceiling Height: 8 ft.

• Formal Living Room: This large, inviting room is the perfect place to entertain guests.

• Family Room: This cozy, comfortable room is accessed through elegant French doors in the living room. It is sure to be the favorite family gathering place with its bay window, see-through fireplace, and bay window.

• Breakfast Area: This area is large enough for the whole family to enjoy a casual meal as they are warmed by the other side of the see-through fireplace. The area features a bay window and built-in bookcase.

• Master Bedroom: Upstairs, enjoy the gracious and practical master bedroom with its boxed ceiling and two walk-in closets.

• Master Bath: Luxuriate in the whirlpool bath as you gaze through the skylight framed by ceiling accents.

## Main Level Floor Plan

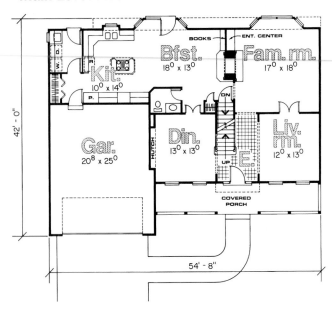

## Upper Level Floor Plan

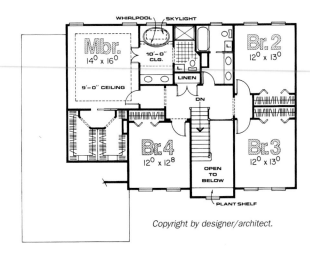

*Copyright by designer/architect.*

## Plan #391030

**Dimensions:** 60" W x 82"6" D
**Levels:** 1
**Square Footage:** 2,662
**Main Level Sq. Ft.:** 2367
**Upper Level Sq. Ft.:** 295
**Bedrooms:** 4
**Bathrooms:** 3
**Foundation:** Basement
**Materials List Available:** Yes
**Price Category:** F

Images provided by designer/architect.

*This home, as shown in the photograph, may differ from the actual blueprints. For more detailed information, please check the floor plans carefully.*

All decked out with rich wood decking that sweeps around the family room to the dining and kitchen areas as well as to the main-floor family room, this home has the feel of living in harmony with nature.

Features:

• Dining Room: A greenhouse window adds exotic flair to this formal dining room.

• Master Suite: This master suite is lavish with amenities--skylight over the tub, double vanity sinks, separate shower, two walk-in closets, a dressing room, and a skylight over the tub.

• Bedroom: Teenagers can appreciate the second bedroom with built-in cabinet and private bath. Plus, it's ideally situated near the kitchen for late night snacking, close to the laundry room for quick wardrobe freshening, and it's only a quick jog to the garage.

• Dramatic Features: The house is outfitted with a massive family-room fireplace, built-in bookshelves, and a soaring loft with study.

**Main Level Floor Plan**

**Lower Level Floor Plan**

Great Room

## Plan #441010

**Dimensions:** 108' W x 59' D

**Levels:** 1

**Square Footage:** 2,973

**Bedrooms:** 4

**Bathrooms:** 4½

**Foundation:** Crawl space; slab or basement available for fee

**Materials List Available:** Yes

**Price Category:** F

Bordering on estate-sized, this plan borrows elements from Norman, Mediterranean, and English architecture.

*Images provided by designer/architect.*

**Features:**

- Great Room: This gathering area features a large bay window and a fireplace flanked with built-ins. The vaulted ceiling adds to the large feel of the area.

- Kitchen: This large island kitchen features a walk-in pantry and a built-in desk. The breakfast nook has access to the patio.

- Master Suite: This retreat features a vaulted ceiling in the sleeping area and access to the patio. The master bath boasts dual vanities, a stand-up shower, a spa tub, and a very large walk-in closet.

- Bedrooms: Two family bedrooms, each with its own private bathroom, have large closets.

CAD FILE AVAILABLE

*Copyright by designer/architect.*

Rear Elevation

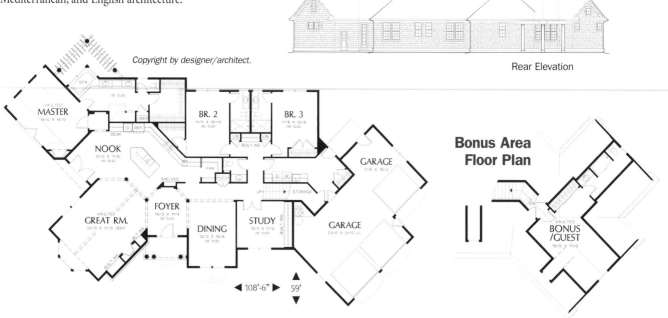

## Plan #151014

**Dimensions:** 70'2" W x 51'4" D

**Levels:** 1.5

**Square Footage:** 2,698

**Main Level Sq. Ft.:** 1,813

**Upper Level Sq. Ft.:** 885

**Bedrooms:** 5

**Bathrooms:** 3

**Foundation:** Crawl space, slab or basement; walk out for fee

**CompleteCost List Available:** Yes

**Price Category:** F

*Images provided by designer/architect.*

A comfortable front porch welcomes you into this home that features a balcony over the great room, a study, and a kitchen designed for gourmet cooks.

**CAD FILE AVAILABLE**

**Features:**

- Ceiling Height: 9 ft.
- Front Porch: Stately 12-in.-wide pillars form the entryway.
- Foyer: Open to upper story.
- Great Room: A fireplace, vaulted 9-ft. ceiling, and balcony from the second floor add character to this lovely room.
- Dining Room: Open to the kitchen for convenience.
- Kitchen: A large walk-in pantry, well-designed work areas, and eat-in bar make this room a treasure.
- Breakfast Room: Enjoy this spot that opens to both the kitchen and a large covered porch at the rear of the house.
- Study: This quiet room has French doors leading to the yard.
- Master Suite: This spacious area has cozy window seats as well as his and her walk-in closets. The master bathroom is fitted with a whirlpool tub, a glass shower, and his and her sinks.

### Upper Level Floor Plan

### Main Level Floor Plan

*Copyright by designer/architect.*

## Main Level Floor Plan

Breakfast 14' x 11'2"
Great Room 16' x 19'6"
Hearth Room 17' x 14'10"
Dressing
Kitchen
Laun.
Foyer
Master Bedroom 14' x 14'1"
Porch
Dining Room 12' x 13'10"
Two-car Garage 21' x 20'4"
Sitting Area 11'2" x 9'4"

63'4"
48'

# Plan #161041

**Dimensions:** 63'4" W x 48' D

**Levels:** 2

**Square Footage:** 2,738

**Main Level Sq. Ft.:** 1,915

**Upper Level Sq. Ft.:** 823

**Bedrooms:** 4

**Bathrooms:** 3½

**Foundation:** Basement

**Materials List Available:** Yes

**Price Category:** F

*Images provided by designer/architect.*

Rear Elevation

Great Room Below
Bedroom 17' x 12'6"
Balcony
Bedroom 10' x 13'10"
Bath
Bedroom 12' x 10'6"
slope ceiling    slope ceiling

## Upper Level Floor Plan

*Copyright by designer/architect.*

STORAGE
BREEZEWAY
PORCH
UTILITY
CARPORT 22x22
DINING 13x11
KITCHEN 16x11
BREAKFAST 11x11
MORNING PORCH
BATH
GREAT ROOM 17x23
MASTER SUITE 14x18
MASTER BATH
PORCH
PORCH
PORCH

## Main Level Floor Plan

# Plan #171017

**Dimensions:** 84' W x 54' D

**Levels:** 2

**Square Footage:** 2,558

**Main Level Sq. Ft.:** 1,577

**Upper Level Sq. Ft.:** 981

**Bedrooms:** 4

**Bathrooms:** 2½

**Foundation:** Slab, crawl space

**Materials List Available:** Yes

**Price Category:** E

*Images provided by designer/architect.*

GAME RM./ BEDRM. 17x13
BEDRM. 14x17
LANDING
BATH
OPEN TO GREAT RM
BEDRM. 14x13

## Upper Level Floor Plan

*Copyright by designer/architect.*

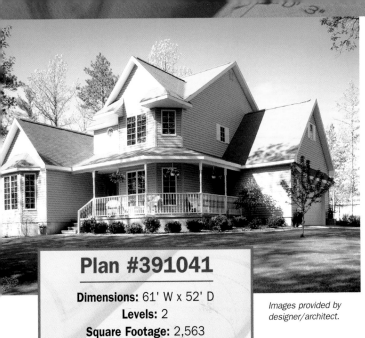

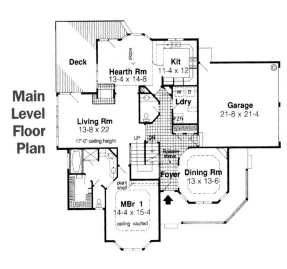

**Main Level Floor Plan**

Deck

Hearth Rm
13-4 x 14-8

Kit
11-4 x 12

slope

Living Rm
13-8 x 22
17'-0" ceiling height

Ldry

W D

FZR

Garage
21-8 x 21-4

UP DN

Foyer

Dining Rm
13 x 13-6

plant shelf

MBr 1
14-4 x 15-4
ceiling vaulted

*Images provided by designer/architect.*

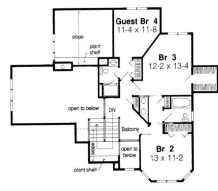

**Upper Level Floor Plan**

*Copyright by designer/architect.*

slope

plant shelf

Guest Br 4
11-4 x 11-8

Br 3
12-2 x 13-4

open to below

DN

linen

linen

Balcony

open to below

slope

plant shelf

Br 2
13 x 11-2

## Plan #391041

**Dimensions:** 61' W x 52' D

**Levels:** 2

**Square Footage:** 2,563

**Main Level Sq. Ft.:** 1,737

**Upper Level Sq. Ft.:** 826

**Bedrooms:** 4

**Bathrooms:** 3½

**Foundation:** Basement

**Materials List Available:** No

**Price Category:** E

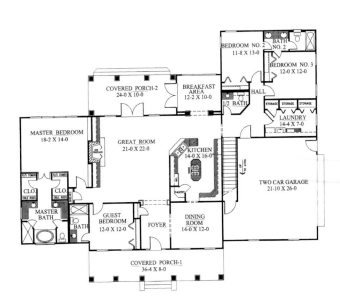

COVERED PORCH-2
24-0 X 10-0

BREAKFAST AREA
12-2 X 10-0

BEDROOM NO. 2
11-8 X 13-0

BATH NO. 2

BEDROOM NO. 3
12-0 X 12-0

HALL

1/2 BATH

STORAGE

STORAGE

MASTER BEDROOM
18-2 X 14-0

GREAT ROOM
21-0 X 22-0

KITCHEN
14-0 X 16-0

LAUNDRY
14-4 X 7-0

TWO CAR GARAGE
21-10 X 26-0

CLO.

CLO.

PANTRY

MASTER BATH

BATH

GUEST BEDROOM
12-0 X 12-0

FOYER

DINING ROOM
14-0 X 12-0

COVERED PORCH-1
36-4 X 8-0

*Images provided by designer/architect.*

*Copyright by designer/architect.*

## Plan #191028

**Dimensions:** 80' W x 63' D

**Levels:** 1

**Square Footage:** 2,669

**Bedrooms:** 4

**Bathrooms:** 3½

**Foundation:** Slab or basement

**Materials List Available:** No

**Price Category:** F

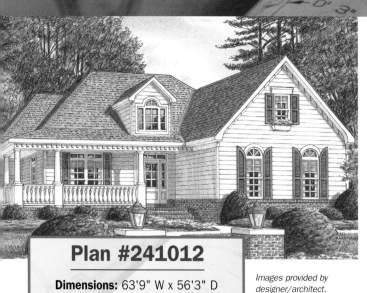

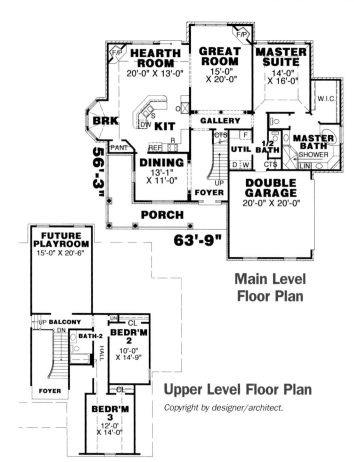

**Main Level Floor Plan**

## Plan #241012

Dimensions: 63'9" W x 56'3" D

Levels: 2

Square Footage: 2,743

Main Level Sq. Ft.: 2,153

Upper Level Sq. Ft.: 590

Bedrooms: 3

Bathrooms: 2½

Foundation: Slab

Materials List Available: No

Price Category: E

*Images provided by designer/architect.*

**Upper Level Floor Plan**

*Copyright by designer/architect.*

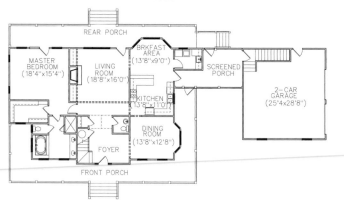

**Main Level Floor Plan**

## Plan #521006

Dimensions: 99'2" W x 47'5" D

Levels: 1.5

Square Footage: 2,818

Main Level Sq. Ft.: 1,787

Upper Level Sq. Ft.: 1,031

Bedrooms: 4

Bathrooms: 3½

Foundation: Crawl space

Material List Available: No

Price Category: F

*Images provided by designer/architect.*

**Upper Level Floor Plan**

*Copyright by designer/architect.*

## Plan #441313

**Dimensions:** 53' W x 77' D

**Levels:** 2

**Square Footage:** 2,998

**Main Level Sq. Ft.:** 1,618

**Upper Level Sq. Ft.:** 1,380

**Bedrooms:** 4

**Bathrooms:** 2½

**Foundation:** Crawl space

**Materials List Available:** No

**Price Category:** F

*Images provided by designer/architect.*

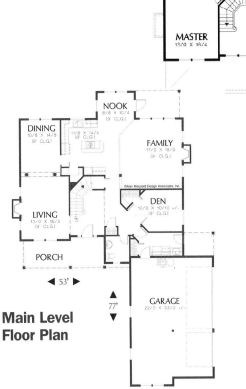

**Upper Level Floor Plan**

**Main Level Floor Plan**

## Plan #151174

**Dimensions:** 57'4" W x 55'10" D

**Levels:** 2

**Square Footage:** 2,815

**Main Level Sq. Ft.:** 2,142

**Upper Level Sq. Ft.:** 673

**Bedrooms:** 4

**Bathrooms:** 3

**Foundation:** Crawl space, slab; basement or walkout for fee

**CompleteCost List Available:** Yes

**Price Category:** F

*Images provided by designer/architect.*

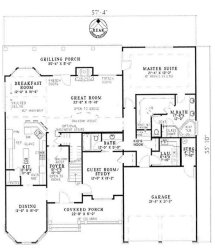

**Main Level Floor Plan**

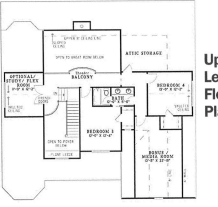

**Upper Level Floor Plan**

*Copyright by designer/architect.*

## Plan #121030

**Dimensions:** 58' W x 45' D

**Levels:** 2

**Square Footage:** 2,613

**Main Level Sq. Ft.:** 1,333

**Upper Level Sq. Ft.:** 1,280

**Bedrooms:** 4

**Bathrooms:** 2½

**Foundation:** Basement

**Materials List Available:** Yes

**Price Category:** F

*Images provided by designer/architect.*

This home is packed with all the amenities you need for a gracious and comfortable lifestyle.

**Features:**

- Ceiling Height: 8 ft. unless otherwise noted.

- Foyer: The elegant entry opens into the living room and formal dining room.

- Adaptable Space: An area linking the formal living room and the family room would make a great area for the family computer. Alternately, it can become a wet bar with window seat.

- Breakfast Area: The family will enjoy informal meals in this sun-bathed area.

- Snack Bar: Perfect for a quick bite, this angled area joins the kitchen to the breakfast area.

- Master Suite: Two walk-in closets make this suite convenient as well as luxurious. The bayed whirlpool tub under a cathedral ceiling invites you to unwind and relax.

- Bonus Room: The second level includes a large room that could become an extra bedroom, a guest room, or a home office.

**CAD FILE AVAILABLE**

## Main Level Floor Plan

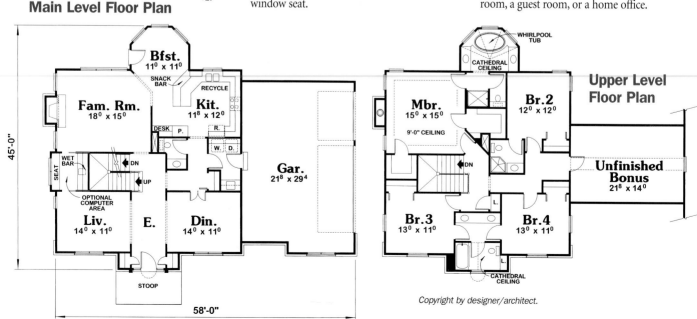

*Copyright by designer/architect.*

# Plan #351068

**Dimensions:** 84' W x 54' D

**Levels:** 1

**Square Footage:** 2,501

**Bedrooms:** 4

**Bathrooms:** 3

**Foundation:** Crawl space or slab

**Materials List Available:** Yes

**Price Category:** G

This beautiful home includes an open floor plan with four spacious bedrooms, three baths, a split bedroom layout, and several other unique features.

**Features:**

- Porches: Large front and rear covered porches complement the livability of the home.

- Great Room: This expansive room features a vaulted ceiling and a gas log fireplace.

- Kitchen: Fully equipped with a wraparound raised bar, a walk-in pantry, and a large adjoining laundry, this kitchen is luxurious yet functional.

- Master Suite: This suite includes a raised ceiling in the master bedroom, two large walk-in closets, a jetted tub, and an oversized shower.

*Images provided by designer/architect.*

## Main Level Floor Plan

## Bonus Area Floor Plan

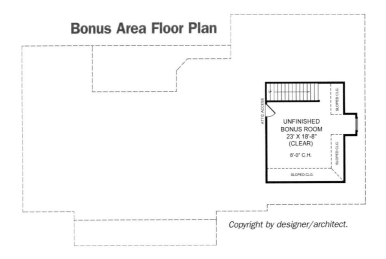

*Copyright by designer/architect.*

## Plan #391056

**Dimensions:** 73'10" W x 53'4" D
**Levels:** 2
**Square Footage:** 2,607
**Main Level Sq. Ft.:** 1,429
**Upper Level Sq. Ft.:** 1,178
**Bedrooms:** 3
**Bathrooms:** 2½
**Foundation:** Basement
**Materials List Available:** No
**Price Category:** F

*Images provided by designer/architect.*

The spectacular pavilion front with Palladian window creates a dramatic picture indoors and out.

**Features:**

- Walk up the steps, onto the porch, and then through the front door with sidelights, this entry opens into a two-story space and feels light and airy. The nearby coat closet is a convenient asset.

- Living Room: This "sunken" room features a cozy fireplace flanked by two doors, allowing access to the wraparound deck. The dining room is open to the area, creating a nice flow between the two spaces.

- Family Room: This casual relaxing area is one step down from the kitchen; it boasts another fireplace and access to the large wraparound deck.

- Kitchen: This island kitchen features plenty of cabinet and counter space and is waiting for the chef in the family to take control. The breakfast area with bay window is the perfect place to start the day.

- Upper Level: This area is dedicated to the master suite with full master bath and two family bedrooms. Enjoy the dramatic view as you look down into the entry.

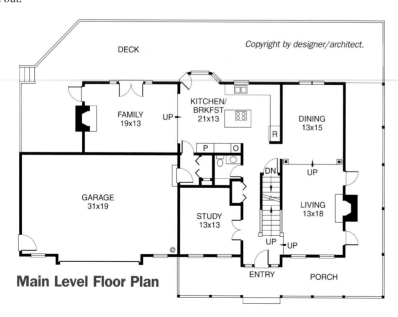

**Main Level Floor Plan**

**Upper Level Floor Plan**

## Plan #271054

**Dimensions:** 63' W x 49' D

**Levels:** 2

**Square Footage:** 2,654

**Main Level Sq. Ft.:** 1,384

**Upper Level Sq. Ft.:** 1,270

**Bedrooms:** 4

**Bathrooms:** 2½

**Foundation:** Daylight basement

**Materials List Available:** No

**Price Category:** F

This updated farmhouse attracts comments from passersby with its shuttered windows and welcoming wraparound porch.

**CAD FILE AVAILABLE** CAD

### Features:

- **Great Room:** This popular gathering spot includes a fireplace flanked by a media center and abundant shelves, and a wall of windows.

- **Dining Room:** This formal dining room is closed off with a pocket door for peace and quiet during meals. The bayed window facing the front is a nice touch.

- **Kitchen:** This thoroughly modern kitchen boasts an island with two sinks, a good-sized pantry, and a bayed dinette with sliding doors to the backyard.

- **Sun Porch:** Accessed via double doors from the dinette, this warm getaway spot flaunts a wood floor, ample angled windows, and a French door to the backyard.

- **Owner's Suite:** This master bedroom has a gorgeous tray ceiling in the sleeping chamber, plus a private bath with a corner whirlpool tub, a separate shower, and an endless walk-in closet.

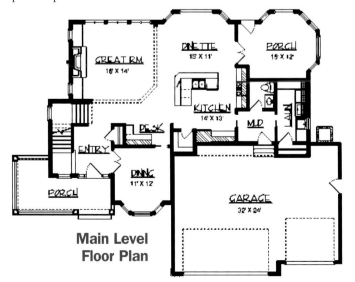

**Main Level Floor Plan**

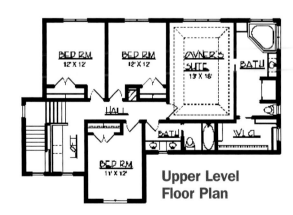

**Upper Level Floor Plan**

*Copyright by designer/architect.*

## Main Level Floor Plan

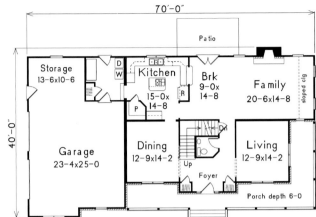

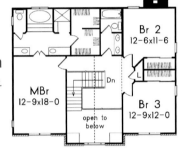

### Upper Level Floor Plan

*Copyright by designer/architect.*

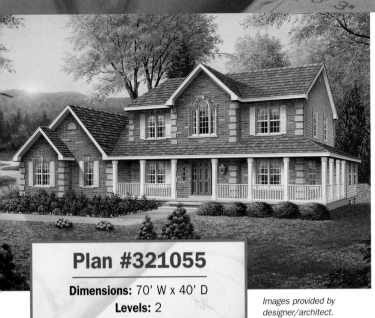

## Plan #321055

**Dimensions:** 70' W x 40' D

**Levels:** 2

**Square Footage:** 2,505

**Main Level Sq. Ft.:** 1,436

**Upper Level Sq. Ft.:** 1,069

**Bedrooms:** 3

**Bathrooms:** 2½

**Foundation:** Basement

**Materials List Available:** Yes

**Price Category:** E

*Images provided by designer/architect.*

## Plan #401018

**Dimensions:** 80' W x 44' D

**Levels:** 2

**Square Footage:** 2,797

**Main Level Sq. Ft.:** 1,639

**Upper Level Sq. Ft.:** 1,158

**Bedrooms:** 4

**Bathrooms:** 3

**Foundation:** Crawl space

**Materials List Available:** Yes

**Price Category:** G

*Images provided by designer/architect.*

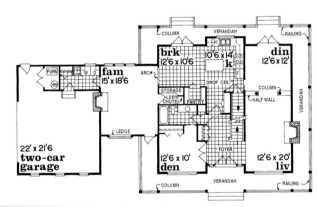

### Main Level Floor Plan

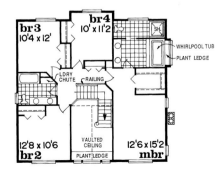

### Upper Level Floor Plan

*Copyright by designer/architect.*

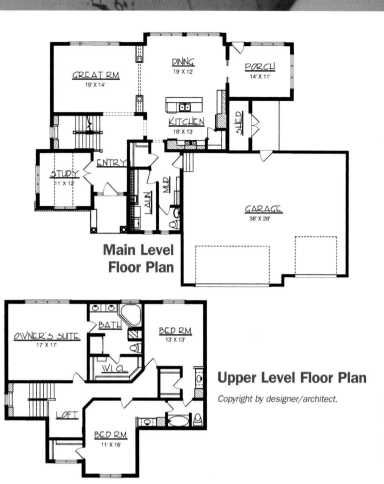

## Main Level Floor Plan

GREAT RM
19' X 14'

DINING
19' X 12'

PORCH
14' X 11'

KITCHEN
18' X 13'

MUD

STUDY
11' X 12'

ENTRY

LAUN

GARAGE
36' X 28'

*Images provided by designer/architect.*

OWNER'S SUITE
17' X 17'

BATH

BED RM
13' X 13'

W I CL

LOFT

BED RM
11' X 16'

## Upper Level Floor Plan

*Copyright by designer/architect.*

## Plan #271058

**Dimensions:** 68' W x 53' D

**Levels:** 2

**Square Footage:** 2,924

**Main Level Sq. Ft.:** 1,579

**Upper Level Sq. Ft.:** 1,345

**Bedrooms:** 3

**Bathrooms:** 2½

**Foundation:** Daylight basement

**Materials List Available:** No

**Price Category:** F

---

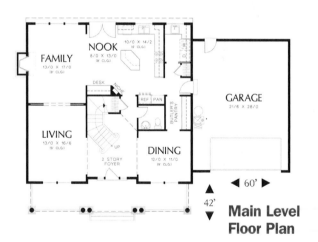

FAMILY
13/0 X 17/0
(9' CLG)

NOOK
8/0 X 13/0
(9' CLG)

10/0 X 14/2
(9' CLG)

GARAGE
21/6 X 28/0

DESK

REF PAN

BUTLER'S PANTRY

LIVING
13/0 X 16/6
(9' CLG)

UP

2 STORY FOYER

DINING
12/0 X 11/0
(9' CLG)

◄ 60' ►

42'

## Main Level Floor Plan

*Images provided by designer/architect.*

VAULTED
MASTER
13/0 X 17/0

DEN/
BR. 4
10/0 X 12/4
(9' CLG)

BR. 3
11/0 X 13/6
(9' CLG)

BONUS RM.
16/0 X 16/0
(8' CLG)

DN

SPA

FOYER BELOW

BR. 2
12/0 X 10/0
(9' CLG)

LIN

## Upper Level Floor Plan

*Copyright by designer/architect.*

## Plan #441023

**Dimensions:** 60' W x 42' D

**Levels:** 2

**Square Footage:** 2,500

**Main Level Sq. Ft.:** 1,319

**Upper Level Sq. Ft:** 1,181

**Bedrooms:** 4

**Bathrooms:** 2½

**Foundation:** Crawl space; slab or basement for fee

**Materials List Available:** Yes

**Price Category:** E

CAD FILE AVAILABLE

## Plan #121079

**Dimensions:** 50' W x 60' D

**Levels:** 2

**Square Footage:** 2,688

**Main Level Sq. Ft.:** 1,650

**Upper Level Sq. Ft.:** 1,038

**Bedrooms:** 4

**Bathrooms:** 3½

**Foundation:** Slab

**Materials List Available:** Yes

**Price Category:** F

You'll love this open design if you're looking for a home that gives a spacious feeling while also providing private areas.

**Features:**

• Entry: The cased openings and corner columns here give an attractive view into the dining room.

• Living Room: Another cased opening defines the entry to this living room but lets traffic flow into it.

• Kitchen: This well-designed kitchen is built around a center island that gives you extra work space. A snack bar makes an easy, open transition between the sunny dining nook and the kitchen.

• Master Suite: An 11-ft. ceiling sets the tone for this private space. With a walk-in closet and adjoining full bath, it will delight you.

*Images provided by designer/architect.*

*This home, as shown in the photograph, may differ from the actual blueprints. For more detailed information, please check the floor plans carefully.*

*Copyright by designer/architect.*

# Plan #371024

**Dimensions:** 54'4" W x 47'8" D
**Levels:** 2
**Square Footage:** 2,843
**Main Level Sq. Ft.:** 1,810
**Upper Level Sq. Ft.:** 1,033
**Bedrooms:** 5
**Bathrooms:** 3½
**Foundation:** Slab
**Materials List Available:** No
**Price Category:** F

You're sure to find all the room you could ever want in this five-bedroom two-story home.

**Features:**

- **Family Room:** The fireplace and built-in bookshelves in this enormous room make it perfect for entertaining.

- **Living Room:** This large formal room has a bay window looking onto the front yard.

- **Kitchen:** Cabinet- and counter-filled, this kitchen has a raised bar and is open to the family room and the breakfast nook.

- **Master Suite:** This large area, located on the first floor, has two walk-in closets and a luxurious private bath.

- **Bedrooms:** Four additional bedrooms are located upstairs and share two full bathrooms.

## Main Level Floor Plan

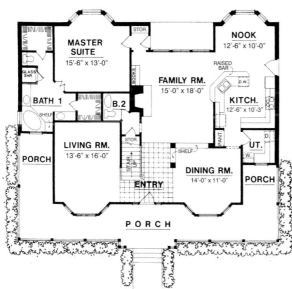

## Upper Level Floor Plan

*Copyright by designer/architect.*

## Plan #441011

**Dimensions:** 67' W x 46' D
**Levels:** 1
**Square Footage:** 2,898
**Main Level Sq. Ft.:** 1,744
**Basement Level Sq. Ft.:** 1,154
**Bedrooms:** 3
**Bathrooms:** 2½
**Foundation:** Walkout basement
**Materials List Available:** Yes
**Price Category:** F

*Images provided by designer/architect.*

**Features:**

- Dining Room: Box beams and columns define this formal space, which is just off the foyer.

- Kitchen: This fully equipped kitchen has everything the chef in the family could want. Nearby is the breakfast nook with sliding glass doors to the deck, which acts as the roof for the patio below.

- Master Suite: This suite is located on the right side of the main level. The master bath is replete with a spa tub, compartmented toilet, separate shower, and dual lavatories.

- Lower Level: The two extra bedrooms, full bathroom, and games room are on this lower floor, which adds to the great livability of the home. The wet bar in the games room is a bonus.

Think one-story, then think again— it's a hillside home designed to make the best use of a sloping lot. Elegant in exterior appeal, this home uses high arches and a hipped room to promote a sense of style.

**CAD FILE AVAILABLE** CAD

Rear Elevation

### Main Level Floor Plan

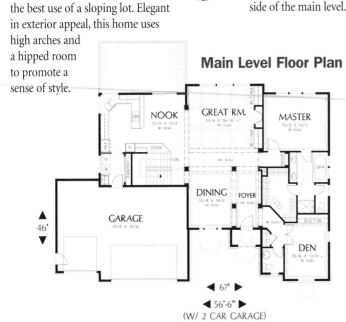

### Basement Level Floor Plan

*Copyright by designer/architect.*

## Plan #391057

**Dimensions:** 62'8" W x 50' D
**Levels:** 2
**Square Footage:** 2,851
**Main Level Sq. Ft.:** 1,933
**Upper Level Sq. Ft.:** 918
**Bedrooms:** 4
**Bathrooms:** 2½
**Foundation:** Crawl space or basement
**Material List Available:** Yes
**Price Category:** F

*Images provided by designer/architect.*

Modernity meets classic style in this contemporary home.

**Features:**

• Library: An element of interest to this home's design is the library/parlor area, which boasts 11-ft.-high ceilings and a bookcase that covers an entire wall.

• Kitchen: This spacious kitchen features a snack bar and breakfast nook. Large skylights let you enjoy the sunrise indoors.

• Master Suite: This master bed and bath are luxuriously spacious with elements of comfort and practicality.

Enjoy dual vanity sinks, whirlpool tub, and separate shower. An eye-catching recessed ceiling completes the design.

• Secondary: The secondary bedrooms feature access to a dramatic balcony and shared full bath with a gorgeous skylight.

Right Side Elevation

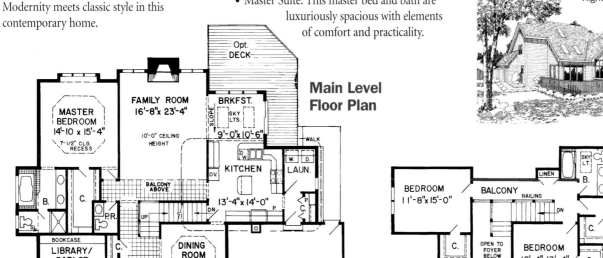

**Upper Level Floor Plan**

*Copyright by designer/architect.*

**Main Level Floor Plan**

## Plan #331003

**Dimensions:** 68'8" W x 75' D

**Levels:** 2

**Square Footage:** 2,661

**Main Level Sq. Ft.:** 2,000

**Upper Level Sq. Ft.:** 660

**Bedrooms:** 4

**Bathrooms:** 3

**Foundation:** Crawl space, slab or basement

**Materials List Available:** No

**Price Category:** F

*Images provided by designer/architect.*

**Upper Level Floor Plan**

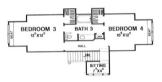

*Copyright by designer/architect.*

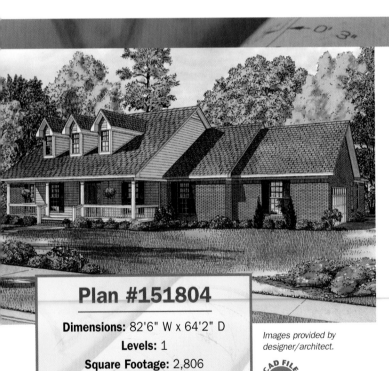

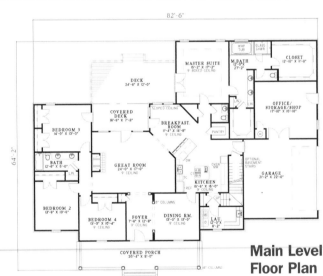

**Main Level Floor Plan**

## Plan #151804

**Dimensions:** 82'6" W x 64'2" D

**Levels:** 1

**Square Footage:** 2,806

**Bedrooms:** 4

**Bathrooms:** 2½

**Foundation:** Crawl space or slab

**CompleteCost List Available:** Yes

**Price Category:** F

*Images provided by designer/architect.*

CAD FILE AVAILABLE

**Upper Level Floor Plan**

*Copyright by designer/architect.*

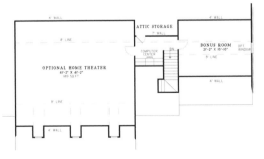

# Plan #351088

**Dimensions:** 66'8" W x 73'2" D

**Levels:** 1

**Square Footage:** 2,500

**Bedrooms:** 4

**Bathrooms:** 3

**Foundation:** Crawl space or slab

**Material List Available:** Yes

**Price Category:** G

*Images provided by designer/architect.*

CAD FILE AVAILABLE

Rear Elevation

**Bonus Area Floor Plan**

Bedroom 3
12-0 x 12-0
9-0 Clg. Ht.

Covered Porch
18-0 x 7-6

Keeping /
Breakfast
12-0 x 17-4
9-0 Clg. Ht.

*Copyright by designer/architect.*

Master Bath
14-4 x 13-10

Closet
6-1 x 6-6

Master
Bedroom
14-6 x 15-6
(Trayed)
10-0 Clg. Ht.
9-0 Clg. Ht.

Closet
8-2 x 8-2

Bath 2
8-0 x 7-7

Hall 1

Great Room
17-8 x 17-0
(Clear)

Office /
Nursery
7-6 x 7-8
9-0 Clg. Ht.

Bedroom 4
11-2 x 11-10
9-0 Clg. Ht.

Hall 2

Kitchen
12-0 x 12-8

Hall 3

Bath 3
8-10 x 5-0

Laun.
7-2 x 9-2

Stor.

Bedroom 2
12-0 x 12-0
9-0 Clg. Ht.

Foyer
5-8 x 12-10
10-0 Clg. Ht.

Dining
12-0 x 12-6
10-0 Clg. Ht.

Two Car Garage
23-0 x 22-2

Covered Porch
31-0 x 6-0

Unfinished
Bonus Room
13-0 x 22-2
8-0 Clg. Ht.

---

# Plan #391024

**Dimensions:** 71' W x 45' D

**Levels:** 1.5

**Square Footage:** 2,647

**Main Level Sq. Ft.:** 1,378

**Upper Level Sq. Ft.:** 1,269

**Bedrooms:** 3

**Bathrooms:** 3

**Foundation:** Crawl space, slab, or basement

**Materials List Available:** Yes

**Price Category:** F

*Images provided by designer/architect.*

Rear View

**Main Level Floor Plan**

71'-0"

45'-0"

Family Rm
21-4 x 15-1

Brkfst
10-6 x 15-1

Kit.
4-6 x 15-1

Shop
14-5 x 15-5

Study/Guest
11-8 x 14-0

Foyer

Dining Rm
11-8 x 14-0

Garage
21-5 x 22-0

Porch

**Upper Level Floor Plan**

*Copyright by designer/architect.*

Mstr Bath

Br 2
15-5 x 11-4

Master Br
14-0 x 17-9

Sitting Area
12-2 x 10-9

Br 3
11-8 x 13-6

Copyright by designer/architect.

## Plan #351089

**Dimensions:** 79'4" W x 53'6" D
**Levels:** 1
**Square Footage:** 2,505
**Bedrooms:** 3
**Bathrooms:** 3
**Foundation:** Crawl space or slab
**Material List Available:** Yes
**Price Category:** G

Images provided by designer/architect.

CAD FILE AVAILABLE

### Bonus Area Floor Plan

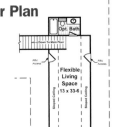

Rear View

---

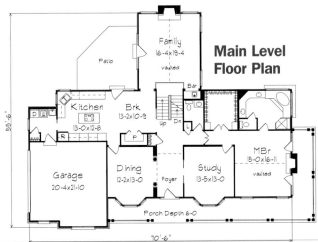

**Main Level Floor Plan**

## Plan #321054

**Dimensions:** 70'6" W x 55'6" D
**Levels:** 2
**Square Footage:** 2,828
**Main Level Sq. Ft.:** 2,006
**Upper Level Sq. Ft.:** 822
**Bedrooms:** 5
**Bathrooms:** 3½
**Foundation:** Basement
**Materials List Available:** Yes
**Price Category:** F

Images provided by designer/architect.

CAD FILE AVAILABLE

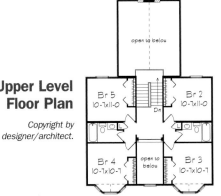

**Upper Level Floor Plan**

Copyright by designer/architect.

**Main Level Floor Plan**

*Images provided by designer/architect.*

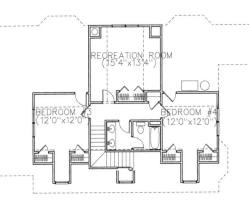

## Plan #521011

**Dimensions:** 58'8" W x 51' D

**Levels:** 2

**Square Footage:** 2,605

**Main Level Sq. Ft.:** 1,809

**Upper Level Sq. Ft.:** 796

**Bedrooms:** 4

**Bathrooms:** 3

**Foundation:** Crawl space

**Material List Available:** No

**Price Category:** F

**Upper Level Floor Plan**

*Copyright by designer/architect.*

**Main Level Floor Plan**

*Images provided by designer/architect.*

## Plan #521009

**Dimensions:** 62' W x 48' D

**Levels:** 2

**Square Footage:** 2,741

**Main Level Sq. Ft.:** 1,876

**Upper Level Sq. Ft.:** 865

**Bedrooms:** 3

**Bathrooms:** 2½

**Foundation:** Crawl space

**Material List Available:** No

**Price Category:** F

**Upper Level Floor Plan**

*Copyright by designer/architect.*

# Plan #121048

**Dimensions:** 67'5" W x 59'9½" D
**Levels:** 2
**Square Footage:** 2,975
**Main Level Sq. Ft.:** 1,548
**Upper Level Sq. Ft.:** 1,427
**Bedrooms:** 4
**Bathrooms:** 3½
**Foundation:** Slab
**Materials List Available:** Yes
**Price Category:** F

*Images provided by designer/architect.*

The classic good looks on the exterior of this impressive home are matched by an interior that's as beautiful as it is comfortable.

**Features:**

• Dining Room: A built-in hutch adds elegance to this formal dining room.

• Library: Shut the doors to this large room, and you'll make it into a quiet retreat.

• Family Room: A fireplace and a wall of windows highlight this spacious, open room.

• Breakfast Room: This room features a door to the rear covered porch and large window area.

• Kitchen: The angled bar adds convenience to this well-planned kitchen.

• Master Suite: Enjoy this suite's fireplace, which is open to the bedroom and the bath. A large tub, separate shower, and two vanities highlight the bathroom, and a huge walk-in closet completes the area.

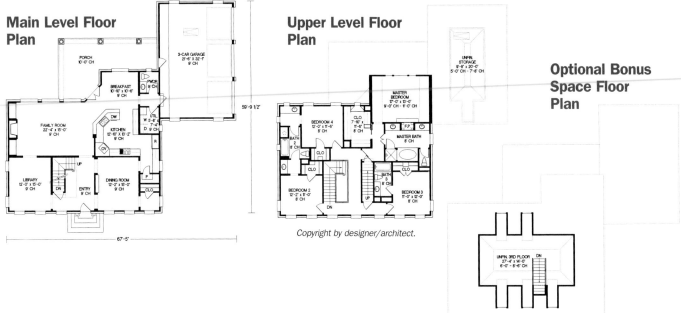

**Main Level Floor Plan**

**Upper Level Floor Plan**

**Optional Bonus Space Floor Plan**

*Copyright by designer/architect.*

## Plan #391061

**Dimensions:** 59'8" W x 55'8" D
**Levels:** 2
**Square Footage:** 2,541
**Main Level Sq. Ft.:** 1,625
**Upper Level Sq. Ft.:** 916
**Bedrooms:** 4
**Bathrooms:** 3½
**Foundation:** Basement
**Material List Available:** Yes
**Price Category:** E

*Images provided by designer/architect.*

Victorian appeal gives way to modern floor plan.

**Features:**

- **Kitchen:** This angular kitchen is unusually cozy thanks to the bright breakfast bay and the hearth room with fireplace.
- **Living Room:** This living room's soaring ceiling, skylight, and deck access elevate the atmosphere of the space.
- **Master Suite:** Located on the main level for convenience and privacy, this master suite has it all. The master bath features a large walk-in closet, dual vanities, and an oversize shower.
- **Secondary Bedrooms:** Three bedrooms over look the upstairs balcony, and two full baths add convenience to everyday life.

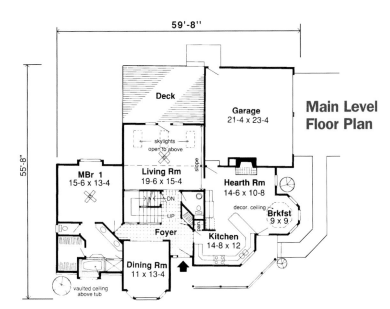

**Main Level Floor Plan**

## Upper Level Floor Plan

*Copyright by designer/architect.*

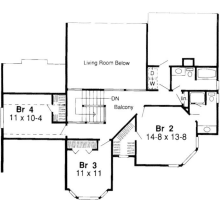

# Plan #401009

**Dimensions:** 70'8" W x 54' D
**Levels:** 2
**Square Footage:** 2,750
**Main Level Sq. Ft.:** 1,462
**Upper Level Sq. Ft.:** 1,288
**Bedrooms:** 4
**Bathrooms:** 2½
**Foundation:** Basement
**Materials List Available:** Yes
**Price Category:** F

*Images provided by designer/architect.*

*This home, as shown in the photograph, may differ from the actual blueprints. For more detailed information, please check the floor plans carefully.*

A touch of Victoriana, including a turret roof over a wraparound porch with turned wood spindles, enhances the facade of this home.

**Features:**

• Living Room: This octagonal gathering area features a tray ceiling and a fireplace. An abundance of windows allows natural light to flood the room.

• Kitchen: The breakfast room is attached to this country kitchen, which features a built-in pantry. The fireplace located in the breakfast room adds warmth to the kitchen.

• Master Suite: This retreat features an octagonal sleeping area with a decorative ceiling. The master bath features a walk-in closet and a whirlpool tub.

• Secondary Bedrooms: Three additional bedrooms and a full bathroom share the upper level with the master suite.

## Main Level Floor Plan

*Copyright by designer/architect.*

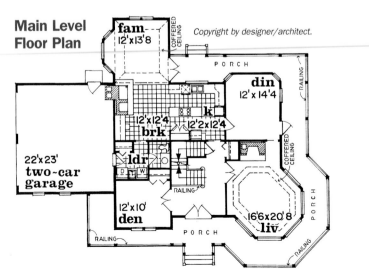

## Upper Level Floor Plan

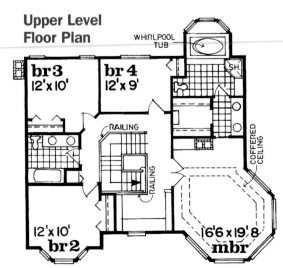

## Plan #271099

**Dimensions:** 71' W x 74'2" D

**Levels:** 2

**Square Footage:** 2,949

**Main Level Sq. Ft.:** 2,000

**Upper Level Sq. Ft.:** 949

**Bedrooms:** 3

**Bathrooms:** 2½

**Foundation:** Crawl space

**Materials List Available:** No

**Price Category:** F

*Images provided by designer/architect.*

Gracious symmetry highlights the lovely facade of this traditional two-story home.

**Features:**

- Foyer: With a high ceiling and a curved staircase, this foyer gives a warm welcome to arriving guests.

- Family Room: At the center of the home, this room will host gatherings of all kinds. A fireplace adds just the right touch.

- Kitchen: An expansive island with a cooktop anchors this space, which easily serves the adjoining nook and the nearby dining room.

- Master Suite: A cozy sitting room with a fireplace is certainly the highlight here. The private bath is also amazing, with its whirlpool tub, separate shower, dual vanities, and walk-in closet.

- Bonus Room: This generous space above the garage could serve as an art studio or as a place for your teenagers to play their electric guitars.

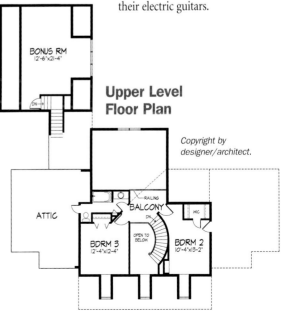

*Copyright by designer/architect.*

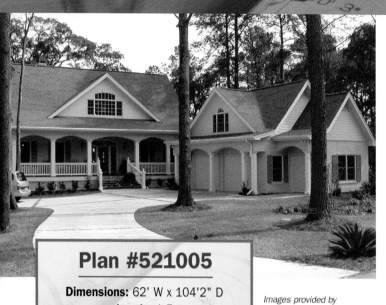

## Main Level
## Floor Plan

*Copyright by designer/architect.*

*Images provided by designer/architect.*

## Plan #521005

**Dimensions:** 62' W x 104'2" D
**Levels:** 1.5
**Square Footage:** 2,932
**Main Level Sq. Ft.:** 2,026
**Upper Level Sq. Ft.:** 906
**Bedrooms:** 3
**Bathrooms:** 3½
**Foundation:** Crawl space
**Material List Available:** No
**Price Category:** F

## Upper Level
## Floor Plan

## Bonus
## Area
## Floor
## Plan

## Main Level
## Floor Plan

*Copyright by designer/architect.*

## Plan #111009

**Dimensions:** 56' W x 49' D
**Levels:** 2
**Square Footage:** 2,514
**Main Level Sq. Ft.:** 1,630
**Upper Level Sq. Ft.:** 884
**Bedrooms:** 4
**Bathrooms:** 3½
**Foundation:** Basement
**Materials List Available:** No
**Price Category:** F

*Images provided by designer/architect.*

## Upper Level
## Floor Plan

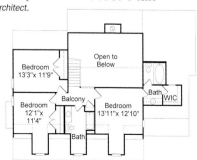

## Basement
## Level Floor
## Plan

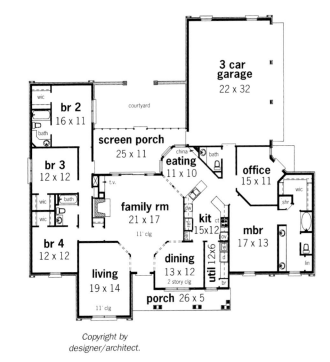

## Plan #211062

**Dimensions:** 96'6" W x 43' D

**Levels:** 1

**Square Footage:** 2,719

**Bedrooms:** 4

**Bathrooms:** 2½

**Foundation:** Slab

**Materials List Available:** Yes

**Price Category:** F

*Images provided by designer/architect.*

*Copyright by designer/architect.*

## Plan #281032

**Dimensions:** 66' W x 49' D

**Levels:** 2

**Square Footage:** 2,904

**Main Level Sq. Ft.:** 1,494

**Upper Level Sq. Ft.:** 1,410

**Bedrooms:** 4

**Bathrooms:** 2½

**Foundation:** Basement

**Material List Available:** Yes

**Price Category:** F

*Images provided by designer/architect.*

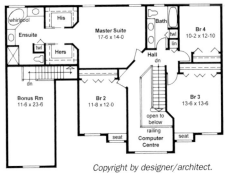

Rear Elevation

*Copyright by designer/architect.*

## Plan #131029

**Dimensions:** 56'4" W x 46'6" D
**Levels:** 2
**Square Footage:** 2,936
**Main Level Sq. Ft.:** 1,680
**Upper Level Sq. Ft.:** 1,256
**Bedrooms:** 4
**Bathrooms:** 2½
**Foundation:** Crawl space, slab, or basement
**Materials List Available:** Yes
**Price Category:** G

*Images provided by designer/architect.*

This home, as shown in the photograph, may differ from the actual blueprints. For more detailed information, please check the floor plans carefully.

This home is ideal if you love the look of a country-style farmhouse.

**Features:**

- Foyer: Walk across the large wraparound porch that defines this home to enter this two-story foyer.

- Living Room: French doors from the foyer lead into this living room.

- Family Room: The whole family will love this room, with its vaulted ceiling, fireplace, and sliding glass doors that open to the wooden rear deck.

- Kitchen: A beautiful sit-down center island opens to the family room. There's also a breakfast nook with a lovely bay window.

- Master Suite: Luxury abounds with vaulted ceilings, walk-in closets, private bath with whirlpool tub, separate shower, and dual sinks.

- Loft: A special place with vaulted ceiling and view into the family room below.

**Main Level Floor Plan**

*Copyright by designer/architect.*

**Upper Level Floor Plan**

Rear Elevation

Dining Room

Breakfast Area

Kitchen Island

Kitchen

Master Bathroom

CRE**A**TIVE
HOMEOWNER

# Porches and Sunrooms

PLANNING AND
REMODELING IDEAS

This article was reprinted from *Porches &
Sunrooms* (Creative Homeowner 2006).

# Porches and Three-Season Rooms

**A**t its simplest, a three-season room or sunroom is a porch modified to keep the weather out. A three-season room protects you from wind, rain, and snow, but it isn't heated or cooled. A sunroom not only keeps the elements out, it offers a heated and cooled environment similar to any other room in your house. If you're looking for a protected spot to get some fresh air, and you don't mind what temperature that air is, consider a three-season room. If you're a sun lover who'd rather not brave freezing cold or oppressive heat to bask in the sunlight, think about a sunroom. In this article we'll look at what goes into creating each of these rooms.

**Traditional-style sunrooms,** opposite, are often made with standard windows rather than floor-to-ceiling glass.

**This manufactured addition** could be either a three-season room or a sunroom, depending on the type of glass chosen.

## Room Options

You can convert an existing porch to a three-season room by installing glass and screen panels and a storm door between posts or columns. Or you can build a new three-season addition with floor-to-ceiling window-and-screen panels.

Because it is uninsulated and unheated, a three-season room won't get much winter use in cold climates. But on those late fall or early spring days when a porch would be uncomfortably chilly, a three-season room can warm up nicely as radiant heat from the sun is captured in the enclosed space. Where winters are warm, the off season may be the summer, when the uninsulated, unairconditioned space may get too toasty.

Sunrooms are by definition habitable in all seasons, though the demands of insulation, heating, and cooling make them more expensive than three-season rooms. They may be conversions of porches, patios, or decks. They can be custom-

made from the ground up. Or they can be manufactured and installed in a matter of days.

Many sunrooms are highly finished and indistinguishable in style, detail, and furnishings from other rooms in the house. Or they may have a distinctive style all their own.

Whether they are conversions, custom built, or factory made, three-season rooms and sunrooms have many similarities. Their basic structures are often the same. Replace single-pane glass with insulated glass and add insulation to the walls, floors, and roof, and add a source of heating and cooling, and a three-season room becomes a sunroom.

## Porch Conversions

Many open-air porches can be converted to three-season rooms. How easily this can be done depends a great deal on how ornate the porch is. It's relatively simple to install window and screen units and a door on a porch that has rectilinear posts and simple railings. Adding windows and a door to a

A **manufactured room** was cleverly adapted to convert this porch to a three-season room, above and below.

# Framing a Porch for Windows

If an opening on a porch is already rectangular and is plumb and level, you can size a custom-built window and frame to fit in that opening, attaching it to the posts, deck or railing, and top beam. Or you can frame new openings to fit standard-size manufactured windows or custom windows of a size you desire. Windows for porch conversions are often housed in wood frames because a carpenter can often make them on site. You can also have aluminum frames custom-built with individual windows and screens made to fit.

If porch openings are irregularly shaped, it's usually more cost-effective to modify the openings than to build oddly shaped windows. This is especially true for windows with moving parts, such as sashes or louvers. Porches with round or molded columns, sloped floors, or elaborate brackets can be framed to accept rectilinear windows, as shown in the drawings at night. Porch decks usually slope away from the house. Openings for windows added along the slope are best framed to create a level bottom because rectilinear windows are much cheaper than trapezoidal ones. Also, glass that rests less than 18 inches above the deck is required by code to be tempered, which will increase the cost. You can frame the opening higher to accommodate standard glass.

## Simple Framing for Porch Windows

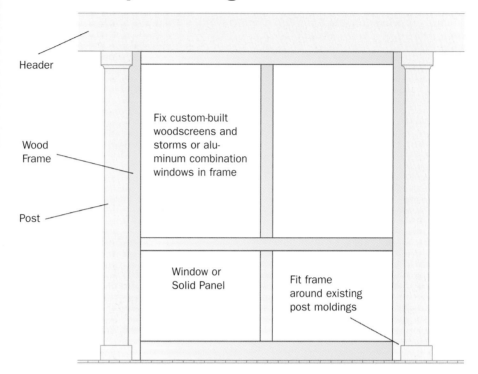

Header

Wood Frame

Post

Fix custom-built woodscreens and storms or aluminum combination windows in frame

Window or Solid Panel

Fit frame around existing post moldings

## Scribed Framing for Porch Windows

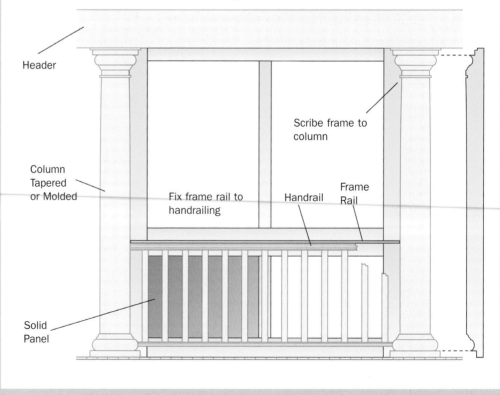

Header

Column Tapered or Molded

Scribe frame to column

Fix frame rail to handrailing

Handrail

Frame Rail

Solid Panel

**A window frame** has been carefully scribed to the Ionic capital and base and the gentle curve of the column shaft in the conversion shown above.

porch that has tapered or heavily molded columns, elaborate brackets, and complex or curved railings requires more thought, more construction skills, and usually more money. (See "Framing a Porch for Windows," left.)

Door, window, and screen units are often much the same for simple and complicated installations alike. The extra cost and installation finesse comes from figuring out how to fill in between rectangular door, window, and screen units and the existing curved and filigreed porch columns and railings.

Converting a porch to a sunroom is a bit more difficult and expensive. Insulated windows and doors are more costly than those with single-pane glass. Insulating an existing porch floor and roof isn't necessarily expensive or difficult, but it may not be terribly effective, either. Nevertheless, charming sunrooms have been made from porches.

Before you consider how to convert an existing porch, make sure it is structurally sound. Check for good footings and foundations; no rotting or deteriorating posts, joists, floor boards, or roof members; and no leaning or tilting. If it's going to cost a lot of money to fix the structure before you convert the space, you should probably tear off the existing porch and build from scratch.

## Converting a Deck

A deck is often an ideal site for a three-season room or sunroom addition. Decks are usually located where sun, shade, and wind conditions on your property are optimal. They are usually adjacent to a room in the house that is desirable for connection to a three-season room or sunroom. They may already have a door or sliding door suitable for access to the new room. And they can provide, at the least, a ready-made floor or subfloor.

Before you convert a deck, you'll need to check its footings to see if they are large enough to carry the additional load of walls and roof. A contractor or codes department can help you with the calculations. If the footings are insufficient, you may be able to enlarge them with additional concrete. Or you may need to build temporary supports, tear out the existing footings, and re-pour.

**Straight columns** are relatively easy to fill in to enclose a porch, right. Turned columns and a railing, far right, make enclosing a porch a more complicated project.

**Traditional wooden storm windows** and screens enclose this three-season porch conversion, below.

**Embedded in the wall,** the original porch columns are a striking feature of this converted sunroom, opposite.

## Plan #161061

**Dimensions:** 90' W x 69'10" D
**Levels:** 2
**Square Footage:** 3,816
**Main Level Sq. Ft.:** 2,725
**Upper Level Sq. Ft.:** 1,091
**Bedrooms:** 4
**Bathrooms:** 3½
**Foundation:** Basement, walkout basement
**Materials List Available:** No
**Price Category:** H

*Images provided by designer/architect.*

Luxurious amenities make living in this spacious home a true pleasure for the whole family.

**Features:**

- Great Room: A fireplace, flanking built-in shelves, a balcony above, and three lovely windows create a luxurious room that's always comfortable.

- Hearth Room: Another fireplace with surrounding built-ins and double doors to the outside deck (with its own fireplace) highlight this room.

- Kitchen: A butler's pantry, laundry room, and mudroom with a window seat and two walk-in closets complement this large kitchen.

- Library: Situated for privacy and quiet, this spacious room with a large window area may be reached from the master bedroom as well as the foyer.

- Master Suite: A sloped ceiling and windows on three walls create a lovely bedroom, and the huge walk-in closet, dressing room, and luxurious bath add up to total comfort.

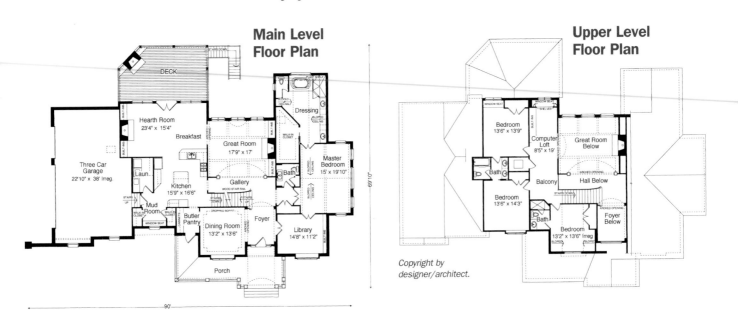

**Main Level Floor Plan**

**Upper Level Floor Plan**

*Copyright by designer/architect.*

Rear Elevation

Right Side Elevation

Left Side Elevation

Great Room

Hearth Room

Kitchen

Dining Room

Library

## Plan #331005

**Dimensions:** 85'11" W x 55'7" D
**Levels:** 2
**Square Footage:** 3,585
**Main Level Sq. Ft.:** 2,691
**Upper Level Sq. Ft.:** 894
**Bedrooms:** 4
**Bathrooms:** 3½
**Foundation:** Crawl space, slab, or basement
**Materials List Available:** No
**Price Category:** H

*Images provided by designer/architect.*

You'll love the stately, traditional exterior design and the contemporary, casual interior layout as they are combined in this elegant home.

**Features:**

- Foyer: The highlight of this spacious area is the curved stairway to the balcony overhead.
- Family Room: The two-story ceiling and second-floor balcony overlooking this room add to its spacious feeling, but you can decorate around the fireplace to create a cozy, intimate area.
- Study: Use this versatile room as a guest room, home office or media room.
- Kitchen: Designed for the modern cook, this kitchen features a step-saving design, an island for added work space, and ample storage space.
- Master Suite: Step out to the rear deck from the bedroom to admire the moonlit scenery or bask in the morning sun. The luxurious bath makes an ideal place to relax in privacy.

Rear View

### Main Level Floor Plan

*Copyright by designer/architect.*

### Upper Level Floor Plan

## Plan #321048

**Dimensions:** 77'6" W x 30' D
**Levels:** 2
**Square Footage:** 3,216
**Main Level Sq. Ft.:** 1,834
**Upper Level Sq. Ft.:** 1,382
**Bedrooms:** 4
**Bathrooms:** 4½
**Foundation:** Basement
**Materials List Available:** Yes
**Price Category:** G

*Images provided by designer/architect.*

You'll love the columns and well-proportioned dormers that grace the exterior of this home, which is as spacious as it is comfortable.

**Features:**

- **Family Room:** This large room, featuring a graceful bay window and a wet bar, is sure to be the heart of your home. On chilly evenings, the whole family will gather around the fireplace.

- **Dining Room:** Whether you're serving a family dinner or hosting a formal dinner party, everyone will feel at home in this lovely room.

- **Kitchen:** The family cooks will appreciate the thought that went into designing this kitchen, which includes ample work and storage space. A breakfast room adjoins the kitchen.

- **Hearth Room:** This room also adjoins the kitchen, creating a large area for informal entertaining.

- **Bedrooms:** Each bedroom is really a suite, because it includes a private, full bath.

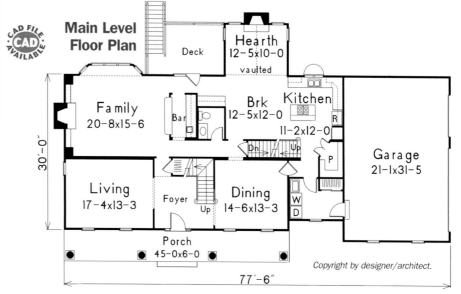

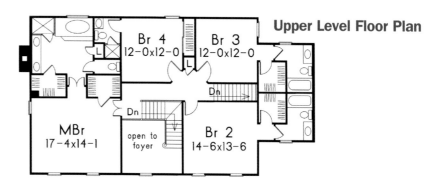

## Plan #441028

**Dimensions:** 53'6" W x 73' D
**Levels:** 2
**Square Footage:** 3,165
**Main Level Sq. Ft.:** 1,268
**Upper Level Sq. Ft.:** 931
**Lower Level Sq. Ft.:** 966
**Bedrooms:** 4
**Bathrooms:** 3½
**Foundation:** Slab
**Materials List Available:** Yes
**Price Category:** G

*Images provided by designer/architect.*

Arts and Crafts style meets hillside design. The result is this stunning design, which fits perfectly on a sloped site.

**CAD FILE AVAILABLE**

**Features:**

- Porch: This covered porch introduces the front entry but also allows access to a mudroom and the three-car garage beyond.

- Great Room: This room is vaulted and has a fireplace, media center, and window seat in a corner window area—a cozy place to read or relax.

- Dining Room: The recess in this room is ideal for a hutch, and the double French doors open to the wide lower deck.

- Upper Level: This floor holds the two family bedrooms with walk-in closets, the shared bathroom, and the master suite. A spa tub and vaulted salon with private deck appoint the suite.

- Lower Level: This floor features another bedroom, with its full bathroom; the recreation room, which has a fireplace and wet bar; and the wine cellar.

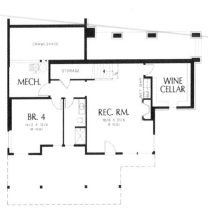

**Lower Level Floor Plan**
*Copyright by designer/architect.*

**Main Level Floor Plan**

**Upper Level Floor Plan**

## Plan #131021

**Dimensions:** 60' W x 52'4" D

**Levels:** 2

**Square Footage:** 3,110

**Main Level Sq. Ft.:** 1,818

**Upper Level Sq. Ft.:** 1,292

**Bedrooms:** 5

**Bathrooms:** 2½

**Foundation:** Crawl space, slab, or basement

**Materials List Available:** Yes

**Price Category:** H

*This home, as shown in the photograph, may differ from the actual blueprints. For more detailed information, please check the floor plans carefully.*

*Images provided by designer/architect.*

Amenities abound in this luxurious two-story beauty with a cozy gazebo on one corner of the spectacular wraparound front porch. Comfort, functionality, and spaciousness characterize this home.

**Features:**

- Ceiling Height: 8 ft.

- Foyer: This two-story high foyer is breathtaking.

- Family Room: Roomy with open views of the kitchen, the family room has a vaulted ceiling and boasts a functional fireplace and a built-in entertainment center.

- Dining Room: Formal yet comfortable, this spacious dining room is perfect for entertaining family and friends.

- Kitchen: Perfectly located with access to a breakfast room and the family room, this U-shaped kitchen with large center island is charming as well as efficient.

- Master Suite: Enjoy this sizable room with a vaulted ceiling, two large walk-in closets, and a lovely compartmented bath.

**Main Level Floor Plan**

**Upper Level Floor Plan**

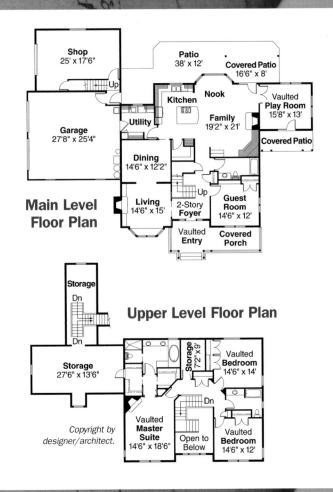

# Plan #361484

**Dimensions:** 86' W x 67' D

**Levels:** 2

**Square Footage:** 3,303

**Main Level Sq. Ft.:** 1,996

**Upper Level Sq. Ft.:** 1,307

**Bedrooms:** 4

**Bathrooms:** 3

**Foundation:** Crawl space

**Material List Available:** No

**Price Category:** G

*Images provided by designer/architect.*

**Main Level Floor Plan**

- Shop 25' x 17'6"
- Garage 27'8" x 25'4"
- Patio 38' x 12'
- Covered Patio 16'6" x 8'
- Kitchen
- Nook
- Utility
- Family 19'2" x 21'
- Vaulted Play Room 15'8" x 13'
- Covered Patio
- Dining 14'6" x 12'2"
- Living 14'6" x 15'
- 2-Story Foyer
- Up
- Guest Room 14'6" x 12'
- Vaulted Entry
- Covered Porch

**Upper Level Floor Plan**

- Storage
- Dn
- Dn
- Storage 27'6" x 13'6"
- Storage 7'2" x 9'
- Vaulted Bedroom 14'6" x 14'
- Vaulted Master Suite 14'6" x 18'6"
- Open to Below
- Dn
- Vaulted Bedroom 14'6" x 12'

*Copyright by designer/architect.*

---

# Plan #641001

**Dimensions:** 61'6" W x 56' D

**Levels:** 2

**Square Footage:** 3,034

**Main Level Sq. Ft.:** 1,323

**Upper Level Sq. Ft.:** 1,711

**Bedrooms:** 4

**Bathrooms:** 2½

**Foundation:** Basement or walkout; crawl space or slab for fee

**Material List Available:** No

**Price Category:** G

*Images provided by designer/architect.*

**Main Level Floor Plan**

**Upper Level Floor Plan**

*Copyright by designer/architect.*

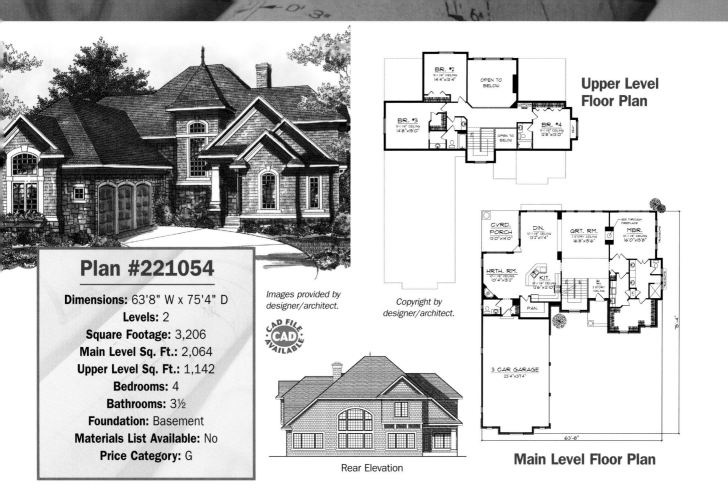

# Plan #221054

**Dimensions:** 63'8" W x 75'4" D

**Levels:** 2

**Square Footage:** 3,206

**Main Level Sq. Ft.:** 2,064

**Upper Level Sq. Ft.:** 1,142

**Bedrooms:** 4

**Bathrooms:** 3½

**Foundation:** Basement

**Materials List Available:** No

**Price Category:** G

*Images provided by designer/architect.*

*Copyright by designer/architect.*

**CAD FILE AVAILABLE**

Rear Elevation

**Upper Level Floor Plan**

**Main Level Floor Plan**

# Plan #211072

**Dimensions:** 62' W x 86' D

**Levels:** 2

**Square Footage:** 3,012

**Main Level Sq. Ft.:** 2,202

**Upper Level Sq. Ft.:** 810

**Bedrooms:** 4

**Bathrooms:** 3½

**Foundation:** Crawl space, optional basement

**Materials List Available:** Yes

**Price Category:** G

*Images provided by designer/architect.*

**CAD FILE AVAILABLE**

**Main Level Floor Plan**

**Upper Level Floor Plan**

*Copyright by designer/architect.*

## Main Level Floor Plan

Images provided by designer/architect.

## Plan #441026

**Dimensions:** 60' W x 52' D

**Levels:** 2

**Square Footage:** 3,623

**Main Level Sq. Ft.:** 1,835

**Upper Level Sq. Ft.:** 1,788

**Bedrooms:** 4

**Bathrooms:** 2½

**Foundation:** Crawl space

**Materials List Available:** Yes

**Price Category:** H

### Upper Level Floor Plan

Copyright by designer/architect.

---

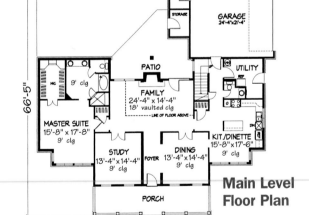

## Main Level Floor Plan

## Plan #271100

**Dimensions:** 69'10" W x 66'5" D

**Levels:** 2

**Square Footage:** 3,263

**Main Level Sq. Ft.:** 2,017

**Upper Level Sq. Ft.:** 1,246

**Bedrooms:** 4

**Bathrooms:** 2½

**Foundation:** Basement

**Material List Available:** No

**Price Category:** G

Images provided by designer/architect.

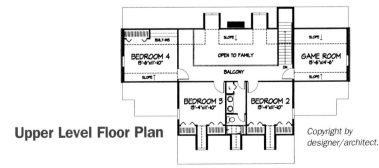

### Upper Level Floor Plan

Copyright by designer/architect.

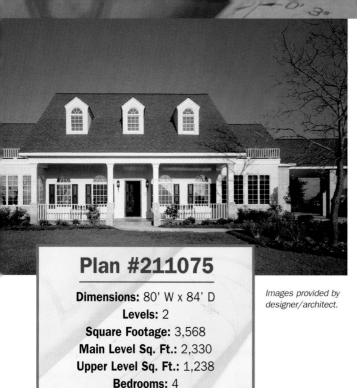

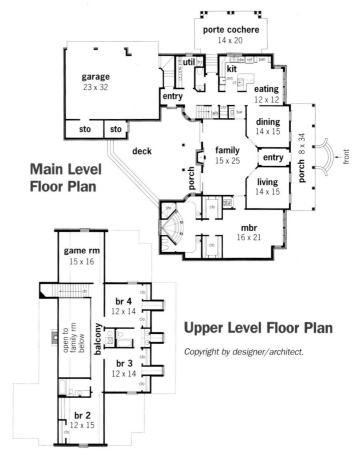

**Main Level Floor Plan**

porte cochere
14 x 20

garage
23 x 32

util

kit

entry

eating
12 x 12

dining
14 x 15

deck

family
15 x 25

entry

porch

living
14 x 15

porch 8 x 34

front

mbr
16 x 21

game rm
15 x 16

open to family rm below

balcony

br 4
12 x 14

br 3
12 x 14

br 2
12 x 15

**Upper Level Floor Plan**

*Copyright by designer/architect.*

## Plan #211075

**Dimensions:** 80' W x 84' D

**Levels:** 2

**Square Footage:** 3,568

**Main Level Sq. Ft.:** 2,330

**Upper Level Sq. Ft.:** 1,238

**Bedrooms:** 4

**Bathrooms:** 3½

**Foundation:** Crawl space

**Materials List Available:** Yes

**Price Category:** H

*Images provided by designer/architect.*

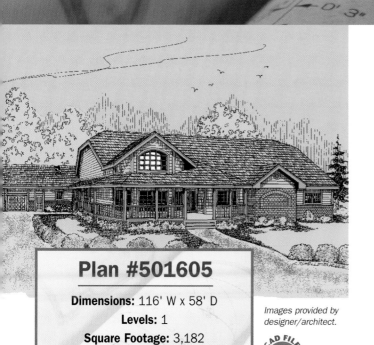

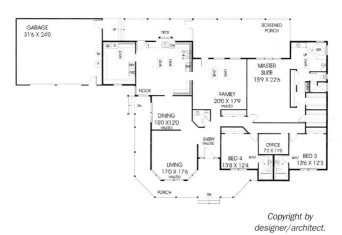

GARAGE
31'6 X 24'0

DECK

SCREENED PORCH

NOOK

MASTER SUITE
15'9 X 22'6

DINING
15'0 X 12'0
VAULTED

FAMILY
20'0 X 17'9
VAULTED

ENTRY
VAULTED

OFFICE
7'2 X 11'0

BED 4
13'8 X 12'4

BED 3
13'6 X 12'3

LIVING
17'0 X 17'6
VAULTED

PORCH

## Plan #501605

**Dimensions:** 116' W x 58' D

**Levels:** 1

**Square Footage:** 3,182

**Bedrooms:** 3

**Bathrooms:** 3½

**Foundation:** Crawl space

**Material List Available:** Yes

**Price Category:** G

*Images provided by designer/architect.*

CAD FILE AVAILABLE

*Copyright by designer/architect.*

# Plan #121047

**Dimensions:** 67'8" W x 57' D

**Levels:** 2

**Square Footage:** 3,072

**Main Level Sq. Ft.:** 2,116

**Upper Level Sq. Ft.:** 956

**Bedrooms:** 4

**Bathrooms:** 3½

**Foundation:** Slab

**Materials List Available:** Yes

**Price Category:** G

*Images provided by designer/architect.*

A long porch and a trio of roof dormers give this gracious home a sophisticated country look.

**Features:**

• Ceiling Height: 8 ft. unless otherwise noted.

• Balcony: This balcony overlooks the entry and the staircase hall.

• Dining Room: Columns and a cased opening lend elegance, making this the perfect venue for stylish dinner parties.

• Family Room: A cathedral ceiling gives this room a light and airy feel. The handsome fireplace framed by windows is sure to become a favorite family gathering place.

• Master Suite: This architecturally distinctive bedroom features a bayed sitting area and a tray ceiling.

• Bedrooms: One of the bedrooms enjoys a private bath, making it a perfect guest room. Other bedrooms feature walk-in closets.

**CAD FILE AVAILABLE**

## Main Level Floor Plan

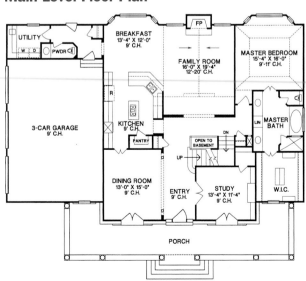

## Upper Level Floor Plan

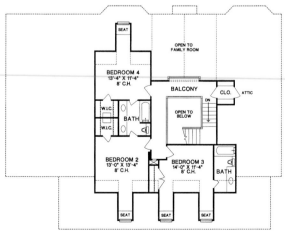

*Copyright by designer/architect.*

## Plan #241013

**Dimensions:** 68' W x 46' D

**Levels:** 2

**Square Footage:** 3,033

**Main Level Sq. Ft.:** 1,918

**Upper Level Sq. Ft.:** 1,115

**Bedrooms:** 4

**Bathrooms:** 3½

**Foundation:** Crawl space, slab, or walkout

**Materials List Available:** No

**Price Category:** G

*Images provided by designer/architect.*

The generous front porch and balcony of this home signal its beauty and comfortable design.

**Features:**

- Great Room: A large fireplace is the focal point of this spacious room, which opens from the foyer.

- Kitchen: Open to the dining room and breakfast room, the kitchen is designed for convenience.

- Sunroom: A fireplace and tray ceiling highlight this room that's just off the breakfast room.

- Study: Positioned for privacy, the study is ideal for quiet time alone.

- Master Suite: You'll love the decorative drop ceiling, huge walk-in closet, and bath with two vanities, a tub, and separate shower.

- Playroom: This enormous space gives ample room for play on rainy afternoons. Set up a media center here when the children have outgrown the need for a playroom.

**Main Level Floor Plan**

*Copyright by designer/architect.*

**Upper Level Floor Plan**

## Plan #441030

**Dimensions:** 117'6" W x 63'6" D
**Levels:** 2
**Square Footage:** 5,180
**Main Level Sq. Ft.:** 3,030
**Upper Level Sq. Ft.:** 2,150
**Bedrooms:** 6
**Bathrooms:** 5
**Foundation:** Crawl space;
slab or basement available for fee
**Materials List Available:** Yes
**Price Category:** J

*Images provided by designer/architect.*

There's no doubt, this home plan is pure luxury. The plan incorporates a wealth of space on two levels, plus every amenity a family could desire.

**CAD FILE AVAILABLE**

### Features:

• **Great Room:** Defined by columns, this room with fireplace and built-in cabinet has an 11-ft.-high ceiling. There is access to the rear patio through French doors.

• **Kitchen:** Furnished with multiple work-stations, this kitchen can accommodate a cook and helpers. The island is equipped with a sink and dishwasher. The secondary sink occupies the half-wall facing the family room. The walk-in pantry beside the dining room supplements storage.

• **Main Level:** The main level is host to rooms devoted to special interests-the office, complete with storage units and a French door to the front porch, and the crafts or hobby room, furnished with an L-shaped work surface.

• **Upper Level:** The upper level of the home accommodates three bedrooms, two bathrooms, the full-service laundry room, and the master suite, which is a dream come true. The master bedroom is divided into sitting and sleeping areas. French doors open it to a private deck. A two-sided fireplace warms both the sitting area and the master bath. The highlight of the spacious bath is the oval tub, which is tucked beneath a bay window.

*Rear View*

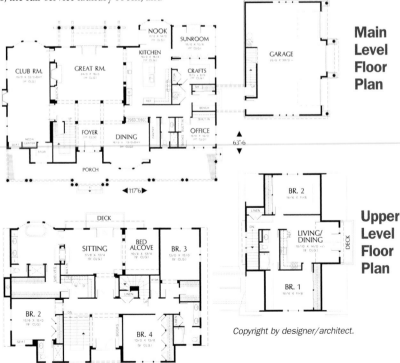

**Main Level Floor Plan**

**Upper Level Floor Plan**

*Copyright by designer/architect.*

# Plan #121065

**Dimensions:** 62' W x 55'4" D

**Levels:** 2

**Square Footage:** 3,407

**Main Level Sq. Ft.:** 1,719

**Upper Level Sq. Ft.:** 1,688

**Bedrooms:** 4

**Bathrooms:** 2½

**Foundation:** Basement

**Materials List Available:** Yes

**Price Category:** G

*Images provided by designer/architect.*

If you love contemporary design, the unusual shapes of the rooms in this home will delight you.

**Features:**

- Entry: You'll see a balcony from the upper level that overlooks this entryway, as well as the lovely curved staircase to this floor.

- Great Room: This room is sunken to set it apart. A fireplace, wet bar, spider-beamed ceiling, and row of arched windows give it character.

- Dining Room: Columns define this lovely octagon room, where you'll love to entertain guests or create lavish family dinners.

- Master Suite: A multi-tiered ceiling adds a note of grace, while the fireplace and private library create a real retreat. The gracious bath features a gazebo ceiling and a skylight.

## Main Level Floor Plan

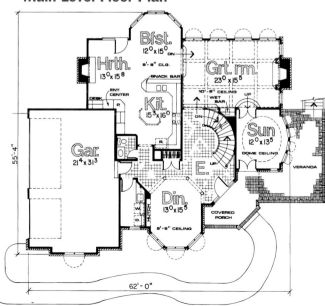

## Upper Level Floor Plan

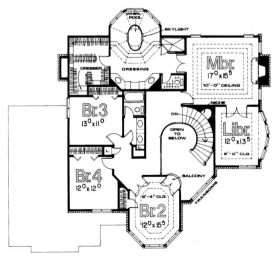

*Copyright by designer/architect.*

**Main Level Floor Plan**

# Plan #151207

**Dimensions:** 72'8" W x 44' D

**Levels:** 2

**Square Footage:** 3,099

**Main Level Sq. Ft.:** 1,603

**Upper Level Sq. Ft.:** 1,496

**Bedrooms:** 4

**Bathrooms:** 3½

**Foundation:** Crawl space or slab

**CompleteCost List Available:** Yes

**Price Category:** G

*Images provided by designer/architect.*

**Upper Level Floor Plan**

*Copyright by designer/architect.*

---

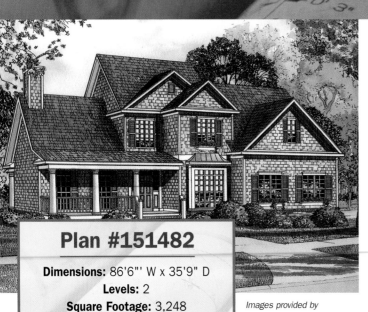

# Plan #151482

**Dimensions:** 86'6"' W x 35'9" D

**Levels:** 2

**Square Footage:** 3,248

**Main Level Sq. Ft.:** 2,021

**Upper Level Sq. Ft.:** 1,227

**Bedrooms:** 5

**Bathrooms:** 3

**Foundation:** Crawl space or slab; basement or walkout for fee

**CompleteCost List Available:** Yes

**Price Category:** G

*Images provided by designer/architect.*

**Main Level Floor Plan**

**Upper Level Floor Plan**

*Copyright by designer/architect.*

## Upper Level Floor Plan

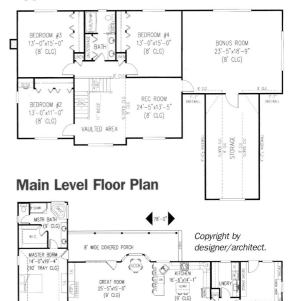

## Main Level Floor Plan

# Plan #421028

**Dimensions:** 78' W x 61' D
**Levels:** 2
**Square Footage:** 3,005
**Main Level Sq. Ft.:** 1,874
**Upper Level Sq. Ft.:** 1,131
**Bedrooms:** 5
**Bathrooms:** 2½
**Foundation:** Crawl space, slab or basement
**Material List Available:** Yes
**Price Category:** G

*Images provided by designer/architect.*

*Copyright by designer/architect.*

## Optional Stair Location

## Main Level Floor Plan

# Plan #441025

**Dimensions:** 70' W x 100'6" D
**Levels:** 2
**Square Footage:** 3,457
**Main Level Sq. Ft.:** 2,222
**Upper Level Sq. Ft.:** 1,235
**Bedrooms:** 4
**Bathrooms:** 3 full, 2 half
**Foundation:** Crawl space; slab or basement for fee
**Materials List Available:** Yes
**Price Category:** G

*Images provided by designer/architect.*

## Upper Level Floor Plan

*Copyright by designer/architect.*

## Plan #391031

**Dimensions:** 78' W x 64' D
**Levels:** 2
**Square Footage:** 3,176
**Main Level Sq. Ft.:** 2,310
**Upper Level Sq. Ft.:** 866
**Bedrooms:** 3
**Bathrooms:** 3½
**Foundation:** Crawl space, slab, or basement
**Materials List Available:** Yes
**Price Category:** G

You can almost feel this home's architectural philosophy of only the best will do the moment you enter its two-story gallery.

### Features:

- **Family Room:** This room is a showstopper, with its three large windows, fireplace, and vaulted ceilings.

- **Kitchen:** This G-Shaped kitchen glides to the breakfast nook, which in turn drifts to the outdoor patio.

- **Utility Area:** The laundry room and sewing workroom meet the garage entrance.

- **Dining Room:** This room with floor-to-ceiling windows maintains formality and aligns with an exterior porch.

- **Living Room:** This highly formal room is along the opposite side of the house from the family room.

- **Study:** This impressive study features atrium doors and clerestory windows.

- **Master Suite:** The first-floor master suite boasts a sit-down vanity, enormous closet, and spa-style tub.

**Main Level Floor Plan**

*Copyright by designer/architect.*

**Upper Level Floor Plan**

Rear View

Stairs

## Plan #171013

**Dimensions:** 74' W x 72' D

**Levels:** 1

**Square Footage:** 3,084

**Bedrooms:** 4

**Bathrooms:** 3½

**Foundation:** Crawl space or slab

**Materials List Available:** Yes

**Price Category:** G

*Images provided by designer/architect.*

Impressive porch columns add to the country charm of this amenity-filled family home.

**Features:**

- Ceiling Height: 10 ft.

- Foyer: The sense of style continues from the front porch into this foyer, which opens to the formal dining room and the living room.

- Dining Room: Two handsome support columns accentuate the elegance of this dining room.

- Living Room: This living room features a cozy corner fireplace and plenty of room for the entire family to gather and relax.

- Kitchen: You'll be inspired to new culinary heights in this kitchen, which offers plenty of counter space, a snack bar, a built-in pantry, and a china closet.

- Master Suite: The bedroom of this master suite has a fireplace and overlooks a rear courtyard. The bath has two vanities a large walk-in closet, a deluxe tub, a walk-in shower, and a skylight.

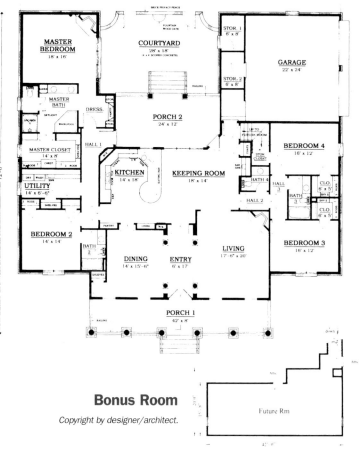

**Bonus Room**

*Copyright by designer/architect.*

## Plan #121023

**Dimensions:** 85'5" W x 74'8" D
**Levels:** 2
**Square Footage:** 3,904
**Main Level Sq. Ft.:** 2,813
**Upper Level Sq. Ft.:** 1,091
**Bedrooms:** 4
**Bathrooms:** 3½
**Foundation:** Basement
**Materials List Available:** Yes
**Price Category:** H

CAD FILE AVAILABLE

*Images provided by designer/architect.*

Spacious and gracious, here are all the amenities you expect in a fine home.

**Features:**

- Ceiling Height: 8 ft. except as noted.

- Foyer: This magnificent entry features a graceful curved staircase with balcony above.

- Sunken Living Room: This sunken room is filled with light from a row of bowed windows. It's the perfect place for social gatherings both large and small.

- Den: French doors open into this truly distinctive den with its 11-ft. ceiling and built-in bookcases.

- Formal Dining Room: Entertain guests with style and grace in this dining room with corner column.

- Master Suite: Another set of French doors leads to this suite that features two walk-in closets, a tub flanked by vanities, and a private sitting room with built-in bookcases.

**Main Level Floor Plan**

**Upper Level Floor Plan**

*Copyright by designer/architect.*

# Plan #151022

**Dimensions:** 79' W x 77'8" D
**Levels:** 2
**Square Footage:** 3,059
**Main Level Sq. Ft.:** 2,650
**Upper Level Sq. Ft.:** 409
**Bedrooms:** 4
**Bathrooms:** 4
**Foundation:** Crawl space, slab, or basement
**CompleteCost List Available:** Yes
**Price Category:** G

*Images provided by designer/architect.*

The two front porches, a rear covered porch, and a huge rear deck are your first clues to the comfort you'll enjoy in this home.

**Features:**

• Great Room: This versatile room with a 10-ft. ceiling has a gas fireplace, built-in shelves and entertainment center, a place for an optional staircase, and access to the rear covered porch.

• Dining Room: The 10-ft. ceiling lets you decorate for formal dining but still allows a casual feeling.

• Breakfast Room: This bright space is open to the kitchen, so you can enjoy it at any time of day.

• Hobby Room: Use this space just off the garage for almost any activity.

• Master Suite: Enjoy the 10-ft. boxed ceiling, built-in cabinets, and access to the rear covered porch. The split design gives privacy. The bath has a corner whirlpool tub, separate glass shower, and split vanities.

**Main Level Floor Plan**

## Upper Level Floor Plan

*Copyright by designer/architect.*

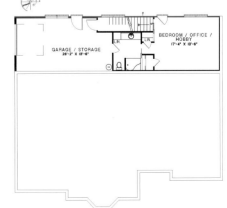

Rear View

Copyright by designer/architect.

## Plan #321009

**Dimensions:** 55'8" W x 46'4" D

**Levels:** 1

**Heated Square Footage:** 1,684

**Bedrooms:** 3

**Bathrooms:** 2

**Foundation:** Walkout

**Materials List Available:** Yes

**Price Category:** E

*Images provided by designer/architect.*

**CAD FILE AVAILABLE**

### Optional Lower Level Floor Plan

**Main Level Floor Plan**

**Lower Level Floor Plan**

**Upper Level Floor Plan**

*Images provided by designer/architect.*

Copyright by designer/architect.

## Plan #451330

**Dimensions:** 65' W x 40' D

**Levels:** 2

**Square Footage:** 3,288

**Main Level Sq. Ft.:** 1,743

**Upper Level Sq. Ft.:** 338

**Lower Level Sq. Ft.:** 1,207

**Bedrooms:** 3

**Bathrooms:** 2½

**Foundation:** Walkout – insulated concrete form

**Material List Available:** No

**Price Category:** G

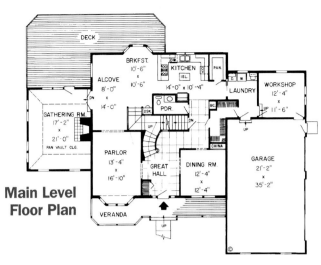

**Main Level Floor Plan**

**Upper Level Floor Plan**

*Copyright by designer/architect.*

# Plan #391055

**Dimensions:** 76'6" W x 55' D

**Levels:** 2

**Square Footage:** 4,217

**Main Level Sq. Ft.:** 2,108

**Upper Level Sq. Ft.:** 2,109

**Bedrooms:** 4

**Bathrooms:** 2½

**Foundation:** Basement

**Material List Available:** Yes

**Price Category:** I

*Images provided by designer/architect.*

*This home, as shown in the photograph, may differ from the actual blueprints. For more detailed information, please check the floor plans carefully.*

**Main Level Floor Plan**

**Upper Level Floor Plan**

*Copyright by designer/architect.*

# Plan #381159

**Dimensions:** 81' W x 41' D

**Levels:** 2

**Square Footage:** 3,230

**Main Level Sq. Ft.:** 1,835

**Upper Level Sq. Ft.:** 1,395

**Bedrooms:** 5

**Bathrooms:** 4½

**Foundation:** Crawl space or basement

**Material List Available:** Yes

**Price Category:** G

*Images provided by designer/architect.*

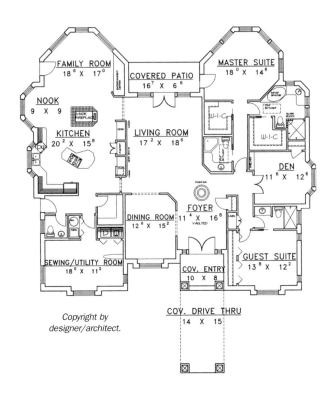

## Plan #451069

**Dimensions:** 68' W x 76' D

**Levels:** 1

**Square Footage:** 3,109

**Bedrooms:** 2

**Bathrooms:** 3½

**Foundation:** Slab – insulated concrete form

**Material List Available:** No

**Price Category:** F

*Images provided by designer/architect.*

CAD FILE AVAILABLE

*Copyright by designer/architect.*

## Plan #331004

**Dimensions:** 81' W x 49'10" D

**Levels:** 2

**Square Footage:** 3,146

**Main Level Sq. Ft.:** 2,150

**Upper Level Sq. Ft.:** 996

**Bedrooms:** 4

**Bathrooms:** 3½

**Foundation:** Crawl space, slab, or basement

**Materials List Available:** No

**Price Category:** G

*Images provided by designer/architect.*

*This home, as shown in the photograph, may differ from the actual blueprints. For more detailed information, please check the floor plans carefully.*

**Main Level Floor Plan**

**Upper Level Floor Plan**

*Copyright by designer/architect.*

# Plan #371155

**Dimensions:** 82' W x 81'2" D

**Levels:** 1

**Square Footage:** 3,304

**Bedrooms:** 4

**Bathrooms:** 3½

**Foundation:** Crawl space or slab

**Material List Available:** No

**Price Category:** G

*Images provided by designer/architect.*

*Copyright by designer/architect.*

# Plan #391425

**Dimensions:** 82' W x 62' D

**Levels:** 2

**Square Footage:** 3,947

**Main Level Sq. Ft.:** 1,533

**Lower Level Sq. Ft.:** 2,414

**Bedrooms:** 4

**Bathrooms:** 2½

**Foundation:** Basement

**Material List Available:** Yes

**Price Category:** H

*Images provided by designer/architect.*

**Main Level Floor Plan**

**Lower Level Floor Plan**

Rear View

*Copyright by designer/architect.*

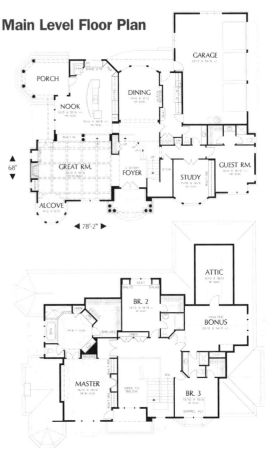

## Main Level Floor Plan

*Images provided by designer/architect.*

## Upper Level Floor Plan

*Copyright by designer/architect.*

# Plan #441031

**Dimensions:** 78'2" W x 68' D

**Levels:** 2

**Square Footage:** 4,150

**Main Level Sq. Ft.:** 2,572

**Upper Level Sq. Ft.:** 1,578

**Bedrooms:** 4

**Bathrooms:** 4½

**Foundation:** Crawl space; slab or basement for fee

**Materials List Available:** Yes

**Price Category:** I

---

## Main Level Floor Plan

*Images provided by designer/architect.*

## Upper Level Floor Plan

*Copyright by designer/architect.*

### Front Elevation

# Plan #551195

**Dimensions:** 85' W x 61' D

**Levels:** 2

**Square Footage:** 4,720

**Main Level Sq. Ft.:** 2,240

**Lower Level Sq. Ft.:** 2,480

**Bedrooms:** 4

**Bathrooms:** 3½

**Foundation:** Crawl space; slab, basement or walkout for fee

**Material List Available:** No

**Price Category:** G

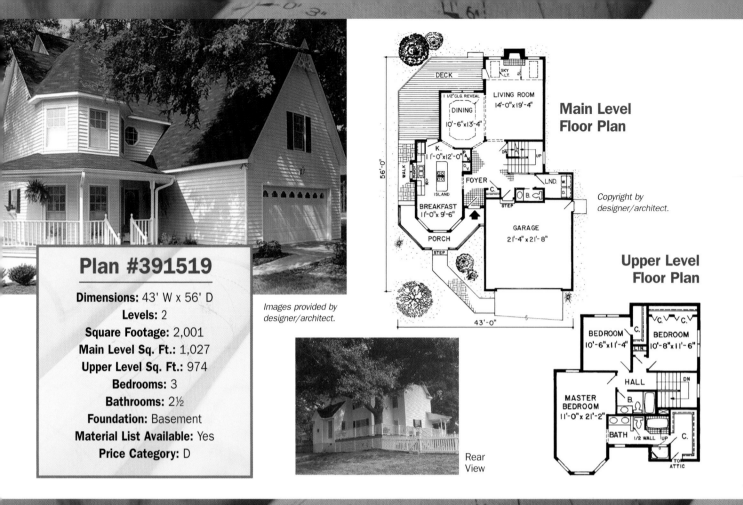

## Plan #391519

**Dimensions:** 43' W x 56' D
**Levels:** 2
**Square Footage:** 2,001
**Main Level Sq. Ft.:** 1,027
**Upper Level Sq. Ft.:** 974
**Bedrooms:** 3
**Bathrooms:** 2½
**Foundation:** Basement
**Material List Available:** Yes
**Price Category:** D

*Images provided by designer/architect.*

**Main Level Floor Plan**

*Copyright by designer/architect.*

**Upper Level Floor Plan**

Rear View

---

## Plan #441013

**Dimensions:** 69' W x 59' D
**Levels:** 2
**Square Footage:** 3,317
**Main Level Sq. Ft.:** 2,657
**Lower Level Sq. Ft.:** 660
**Bedrooms:** 4
**Bathrooms:** 3½
**Foundation:** Slab
**Materials List Available:** Yes
**Price Category:** G

*Images provided by designer/architect.*

CAD FILE AVAILABLE

**Main Level Floor Plan**

**Lower Level Floor Plan**

*Copyright by designer/architect.*

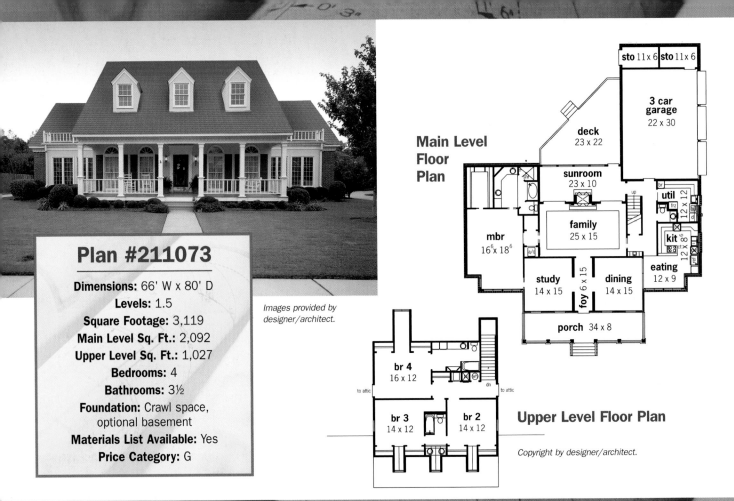

# Plan #211073

**Dimensions:** 66' W x 80' D

**Levels:** 1.5

**Square Footage:** 3,119

**Main Level Sq. Ft.:** 2,092

**Upper Level Sq. Ft.:** 1,027

**Bedrooms:** 4

**Bathrooms:** 3½

**Foundation:** Crawl space, optional basement

**Materials List Available:** Yes

**Price Category:** G

*Images provided by designer/architect.*

**Main Level Floor Plan**

sto 11x 6  sto 11x 6

3 car garage 22 x 30

deck 23 x 22

sunroom 23 x 10

util 12 x 12

family 25 x 15

up

br

kit 12 x 8⁶

mbr 16⁶ x 18⁶

eating 12 x 9

study 14 x 15

foy 6 x 15

dining 14 x 15

porch 34 x 8

br 4 16 x 12

to attic

dn

to attic

br 3 14 x 12

br 2 14 x 12

**Upper Level Floor Plan**

*Copyright by designer/architect.*

---

# Plan #661210

**Dimensions:** 91'4" W x 77'4" D

**Levels:** 2

**Square Footage:** 3,338

**Main Level Sq. Ft.:** 2,854

**Upper Level Sq. Ft.:** 484

**Bedrooms:** 4

**Bathrooms:** 3½

**Foundation:** Slab

**Material List Available:** No

**Price Category:** G

*Images provided by designer/architect.*

**CAD FILE AVAILABLE**

Front Elevation

**Main Level Floor Plan**

Master Bath

Master Bedroom 15' - 28'

Patio

Living 14' · 14'

Patio

Master Bath

W.C.

Foyer

Entry

Family 19' · 17'

Dining 13' · 15'

Kitchen

Decorative Wall

Courtyard

Breakfast

Bath

Utility

Bath

Bedroom 2/ Home Office 13' · 15'

Entry Gate

2 Car Garage

**Upper Level Floor Plan**

*Copyright by designer/architect.*

Bedroom 3 13⁰ · 11⁰

Bath

Bedroom 4 11⁰ · 11²

down

Terrace

## Main Level Floor Plan

*Copyright by designer/architect.*

*Images provided by designer/architect.*

Rear Elevation

## Lower Level Floor Plan

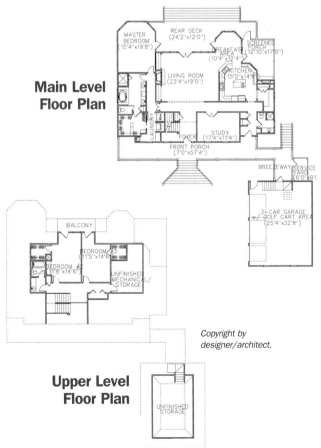

# Plan #161102

**Dimensions:** 99'6" W x 84'2" D

**Levels:** 1

**Square Footage:** 6,659

**Main Level Sq. Ft.:** 3,990

**Lower Level Sq. Ft.:** 2,669

**Bedrooms:** 4

**Bathrooms:** 4 full, 2 half

**Foundation:** Walkout; basement for fee

**Material List Available:** Yes

**Price Category:** K

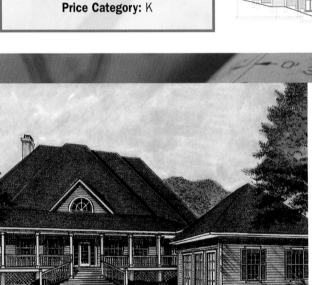

# Plan #521004

**Dimensions:** 79'6" W x 95'8" D

**Levels:** 2

**Square Footage:** 3,131

**Main Level Sq. Ft.:** 2,357

**Upper Level Sq. Ft.:** 774

**Bedrooms:** 3

**Bathrooms:** 3

**Foundation:** Crawl space

**Material List Available:** No

**Price Category:** G

*Images provided by designer/architect.*

CAD FILE AVAILABLE

## Main Level Floor Plan

*Copyright by designer/architect.*

## Upper Level Floor Plan

# Plan #531020

**Dimensions:** 74' W x 97' D

**Levels:** 1.5

**Square Footage:** 4,271

**Main Level Sq. Ft.:** 3,371

**Upper Level Sq. Ft.:** 540

**Bedrooms:** 4

**Bathrooms:** 3½

**Foundation:** Slab

**Material List Available:** No

**Price Category:** I

*Images provided by designer/architect.*

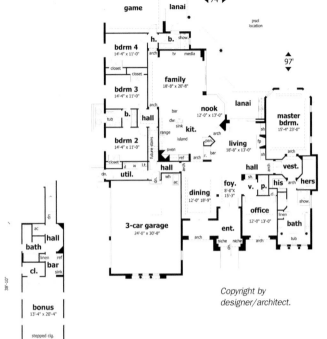

**Bonus Area Floor Plan**

*Copyright by designer/architect.*

# Plan #541042

**Dimensions:** 85'6" W x 57'6" D

**Levels:** 1

**Square Footage:** 4,012

**Main Level Sq. Ft.:** 2,302

**Lower Level Sq. Ft.:** 1,710

**Bedrooms:** 4

**Bathrooms:** 3 full. 2 half

**Foundation:** Walkout

**Material List Available:** No

**Price Category:** I

*Images provided by designer/architect.*

**Main Level Floor Plan**

**Lower Level Floor Plan**

*Copyright by designer/architect.*

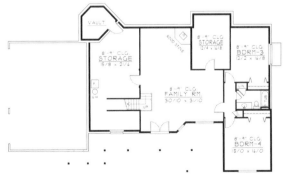

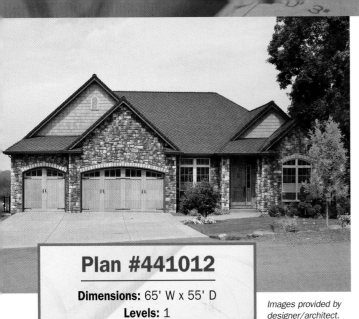

## Main Level Floor Plan

## Basement Level Floor Plan

*Images provided by designer/architect.*

CAD FILE AVAILABLE

Rear Elevation

*Copyright by designer/architect.*

## Plan #441012

**Dimensions:** 65' W x 55' D
**Levels:** 1
**Square Footage:** 3,682
**Main Level Sq. Ft.:** 2,192
**Basement Level Sq. Ft.:** 1,490
**Bedrooms:** 4
**Bathrooms:** 4
**Foundation:** Walkout
**Materials List Available:** Yes
**Price Category:** H

## Upper Level Floor Plan

*Copyright by designer/architect.*

## Main Level Floor Plan

*Images provided by designer/architect.*

## Plan #241020

**Dimensions:** 82'6" W x 78'7" D
**Levels:** 2
**Square Footage:** 4,058
**Main Level Sq. Ft.:** 2,570
**Upper Level Sq. Ft.:** 1,488
**Bedrooms:** 4
**Bathrooms:** 3 full, 2 half
**Foundation:** Slab
**Materials List Available:** No
**Price Category:** I

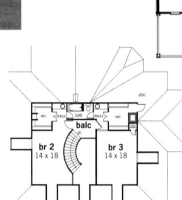

## Main Level Floor Plan

garage
22 x 22

pool storage
10 x 12

sto
8x12

guest rm
14 x 16
9' clg

sun rm
9x14
vault

porch

deck

eating
9' clg

por
6x8

bath

clo

util
8x8
ct

kit

cab
shvs

ref
pan

wet bar

living
18 x 20
9' clg

bath

shv clo

clo shv

mbr
15 x 21
9' clg

sitting

foy
11x15

dining
12 x 14
9' clg

porch 56 x 10

## Plan #211074

**Dimensions:** 64' W x 89' D

**Levels:** 2

**Square Footage:** 3,486

**Main Level Sq. Ft.:** 2,575

**Upper Level Sq. Ft.:** 911

**Bedrooms:** 4

**Bathrooms:** 3

**Foundation:** Crawl space

**Materials List Available:** Yes

**Price Category:** G

*Images provided by designer/architect.*

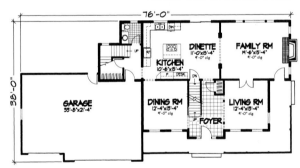

### Upper Level Floor Plan

wic

dress

bath

dress

wic

attic

balc
dn

br 2
14 x 18

br 3
14 x 18

*Copyright by designer/architect.*

---

## Main Level Floor Plan

76'-0"

38'-0"

GARAGE
35'-8"x21'-4"

KITCHEN
10'-6"x15'-4"

DINETTE
11'-0"x15'-4"
8'-0" clg

FAMILY RM
14'-6"x15'-4"
8'-0" clg

DESK

DINING RM
12'-4"x15'-4"
8'-0" clg

LIVING RM
12'-4"x15'-4"
8'-0" clg

FOYER

## Plan #271072

**Dimensions:** 76' W x 38' D

**Levels:** 2

**Square Footage:** 3,081

**Main Level Sq. Ft.:** 1,358

**Upper Level Sq. Ft.:** 1,723

**Bedrooms:** 3

**Bathrooms:** 2½

**Foundation:** Crawl space or basement

**Materials List Available:** No

**Price Category:** G

*Images provided by designer/architect.*

CAD FILE AVAILABLE

### Upper Level Floor Plan

BDRM 3
14'-2"x11'-4"

BONUS ROOM
21'-0"x15'-0"

BOOKS

BDRM 2
12'-4"x11'-4"

MSTR SUITE
12'-4"x17'-4"
10'-4" tray clg

BONUS
11'-0"x11'-6"

(OPEN TO FOYER)

*Copyright by designer/architect.*

# Let Us Help You
## Plan Your Dream Home

**Whether you've always dreamed of building your own home** or you can't find the right house from among the dozens you've toured, our collection of affordable plans can help you achieve the home of your dreams. You could have an architect create a one-of-a-kind home for you, but the design services alone could end up costing up to 15 percent of the cost of construction—a hefty premium for any building project. Isn't it a better idea to select from among the hundreds of unique designs shown in our collection for a fraction of the cost?

### What does Creative Homeowner Offer?

In this book, Creative Homeowner provides hundreds of home plans from the country's best architects and designers. Our designs are among the most popular available. Whether your taste runs from traditional to contemporary, Victorian to early American, you are sure to find the best house design for you and your family. Our plans packages include detailed drawings to help you or your builder construct your dream house. **(See page 374.)**

### Can I Make Changes to the Plans?

Creative Homeowner offers three ways to help you achieve a truly unique home design. Our customizing service allows for extensive changes to our designs. **(See page 375.)** We also provide reverse images of our plans, or we can give you and your builder the tools for making minor changes on your own. **(See page 378.)**

### Can You Help Me Manage My Costs?

To help you stay within your budget, Creative Homeowner has teamed up with the leading estimating company to provide one of the most accurate, complete, and reliable building material take-offs in the industry. **(See page 376.)** If that is too much detail for you, we can provide you with general construction costs based on your zip code. **(See page 378.)** Also, many of our plans come with the option of buying detailed materials lists to help you price out construction costs.

### How Can I Begin the Building Process?

To get started building your dream home, fill out the order form on page 379, call our order department at 1-800-523-6789, or visit ultimateplans.com. If you plan on doing all or part of the work yourself, or want to keep tabs on your builder, we offer best-selling building and design books available at www.creativehomeowner.com.

# Our Plans Packages Offer:

"Square footage" refers to the total "heated square feet" of this plan. This number does not include the garage, porches, or unfinished areas. All of our home plans are the result of many hours of work by leading architects and professional designers. Most of our home plans include each of the following:

## Frontal Sheet

This artist's rendering of the front of the house gives you an idea of how the house will look once it is completed and the property landscaped.

## Detailed Floor Plans

These plans show the size and layout of the rooms. They also provide the locations of doors, windows, fireplaces, closets, stairs, and electrical outlets and switches.

## Foundation Plan

A foundation plan gives the dimensions of basements, walk-out basements, crawl spaces, pier foundations, and slab construction. Each house design lists the type of foundation included. If the plan you choose does not have the foundation type you require, our customer service department can help you customize the plan to meet your needs.

## Roof Plan

In addition to providing the pitch of the roof, these plans also show the locations of dormers, skylights, and other elements.

## Exterior Elevations

These drawings show the front, rear, and sides of the house as if you were looking at it head on. Elevations also provide information about architectural features and finish materials.

## Interior Elevations and Details

Interior elevations show specific details of such elements as fireplaces, kitchen and bathroom cabinets, built-ins, and other unique features of the design.

## Sections

These show the structure as if it were sliced to reveal construction requirements, such as insulation, flooring, and roofing details.

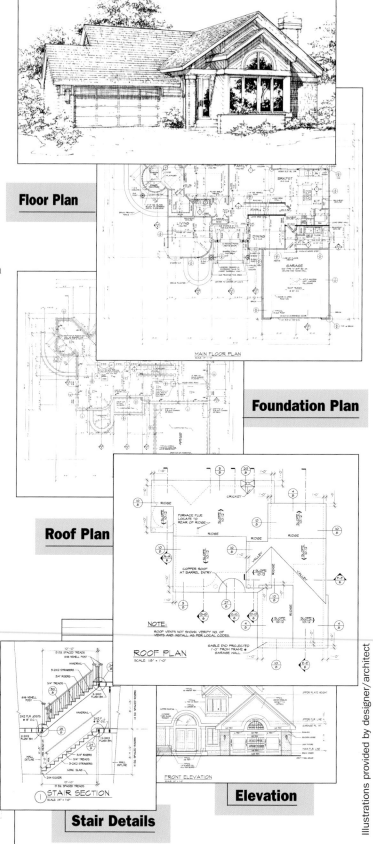

Frontal Sheet

Floor Plan

Foundation Plan

Roof Plan

Cross Sections

Stair Details

Elevation

Illustrations provided by designer/architect

# Customize Your Plans in 4 Easy Steps

**1** **Select the home plan** that most closely meets your needs. Purchase of a reproducible master, PDF files or CAD files is necessary in order to make changes to a plan.

**2** **Call 1-800-523-6789 to place your order.** Tell our sales representative you are interested in customizing your plan, and provide your contact information. Within a day or two you will be contacted (via phone or email) to provide a list or sketch of the changes requested to one of our plans. There is no consultation fee for this service.

**3** **Within three business days** of receipt of your request, a detailed cost estimate will be provided to you.

**4** **Once you approve the estimate,** you will purchase either the reproducible master, PDF files, or CAD files, and customization work will begin. During all phases of the project, you will receive progress prints by fax or email. On average, the project will be completed in two or three weeks. After completion of the work, modified plans will be shipped. You will receive one set of blueprints in addition to a reproducible master or CAD files, depending on which package you purchased.

## Modification Pricing Guide

| Categories | Average Cost For Modification |
|---|---|
| Add or remove living space | Quote required |
| Bathroom layout redesign | Starting at $200 |
| Kitchen layout redesign | Starting at $200 |
| Garage: add or remove | Starting at $400 |
| Garage: front entry to side load or vice versa | Starting at $300 |
| Foundation changes | Starting at $200 |
| Exterior building materials change | Starting at $200 |
| Exterior openings: add, move, or remove | $65 per opening |
| Roof line changes | Starting at $360 |
| Ceiling height adjustments | Starting at $280 |
| Fireplace: add or remove | Starting at $90 |
| Screened porch: add | Starting at $280 |
| Wall framing change from 2x4 to 2x6 | Starting at $200 |
| Bearing and/or exterior walls changes | Quote required |
| Non-bearing wall or room changes | $65 per room |
| Metric conversion of home plan | Starting at $400 |
| Adjust plan for handicapped accessibility | Quote required |
| Adapt plans for local building code requirements | Quote required |
| Engineering stamping only | Quote required |
| Any other engineering services | Quote required |
| Interactive illustrations (choices of exterior materials) | Quote required |

**Note:** *Any home plan can be customized to accommodate your desired changes. The average prices above are provided only as examples of the most commonly requested changes, and are subject to change without notice. Prices for changes will vary according to the number of modifications requested, plan size, style, and method of design used by the original designer. To obtain a detailed cost estimate, please contact us.*

**Before Customization**

**After**

# Turn your dream home into reality with

# a **Material Take-off** and

When purchasing a home plan with Creative Homeowner, we recommend
you order one of the most complete materials lists in the industry.

## 1 | What comes with a Material Take-off?

### Quote

- Basis of the entire estimate.

- Detailed list of all the framing materials needed to build your project, listed from the bottom up, in the order that each one will actually be used.

### Comments

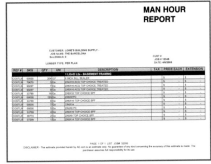

- Details pertinent information beyond the cost of materials.

- Includes any notes from our estimates.

### Express List

- A combined version of the Quote with SKUs listed for purchasing the items at your local Lowe's.

- Your Lowe's Commercial Sales Specialist can then price out the materials list.

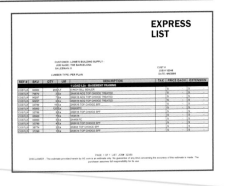

### Construction-Ready Framing Diagrams

- Your "map" to exact roof and floor framing.

### Millwork Report

- A complete count of the windows, doors, molding, and trim.

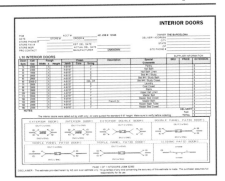

### Man-Hour Report

- Calculates labor on a line-by-line basis for all items quoted and presented in man-hours.

**CRE\TIVE**
**HOMEOWNER**®

**2** ## Why a Material Take-off?

**Accurate.** Professional estimators break down each individual item from the blueprints using advanced software, techniques, and equipment.

**Timely.** You will be able to start your home-building project quickly— knowing the exact framing materials you need and how to get them with Lowe's.

**Detailed.** Work with your Lowe's associate to select the remaining products needed for your new home and get a final, acurate quote.

**3** ## So how much does it cost?

Pricing is determined by the total square feet of the home plan—including living area, garages, decks, porches, finished basements, and finished attics.

| Square Feet Range | MT Tier* | Price |
|---|---|---|
| **Up to 5,000 total square feet** | **XB** | **$345.00** |
| **5,001 to 10,000 total square feet** | **XC** | **$545.00** |

*Please see the Plan Index to determine your plan's Material Take-off Tier (MT Tier).
Note: All prices subject to change.

Call our toll-free number (800-523-6789), or visit ultimateplans.com to order your Material Take-off (also called Ultimate Estimate online).

**4** ## What else do I need to know?

When you purchase your products from Lowe's you may receive a gift card for the amount of your **Material Take-off.** Please go to **UltimatePlans.com** and select **Ultimate Estimate** located under "Quick Links" for complete details of the program.

**The Lowe's Advantage:**

What's more is you can save an **additional 10%** (up to $500.00) on your first building material purchase.* You will receive details on this program with your order.

# Turn your dream home into reality.

*Good for a single purchase of any in-stock or Special Order merchandise only up to $5,000 (maximum discount $500). Not valid on previous sales, service or installation fees, the purchase of gift cards, or any products by Fisher & Paykel, Electrolux, John Deere, or Weber.

# Decide What Type of Plan Package You Need

## How many Plans Should You Order?

**Standard 8-Set Package.** We've found that our 8-set package is the best value for someone who is ready to start building. The 8-set package provides plans for you, your builder, the subcontractors, mortgage lender, and the building department.

**Minimum 5-Set Package.** If you are in the bidding process, you may want to order only five sets for the bidding round and reorder additional sets as needed.

**1-Set Study Package.** The 1-set package allows you to review your home plan in detail. The plan will be marked as a study print, and it is illegal to build a house from a study print alone. It is a violation of copyright law to reproduce a blueprint without permission.

**Buying Additional Sets.** If you require additional copies of blueprints for your home construction, you can order additional sets within 60 days of the original order date at a reduced price. The cost is $35.00 for each additional set. For more information, contact customer service.

## Reproducible Masters

If you plan to make minor changes to one of our home plans, you can purchase reproducible masters. These plans are printed on bond or vellum paper that is easy to alter. They clearly indicate your right to modify, copy, or reproduce the plans. Reproducible masters allow an architect, designer, or builder to alter our plans to give you a customized home design. This package allows you to print as many copies of the modified plans as you need for the construction of one home.

## PDF Files

PDF files are a complete set of home plans in electronic file format sent to you via email. These files cannot be altered electronically, once printed changes can be hand drawn. A PDF file gives you the license to modify the plans to fit your needs and build one home. Not available for all plans. Please contact our order department or visit our Web site to check the availability of PDF files for your plan.

## CAD (Computer-Aided Design) Files

CAD files are the complete set of home plans in an electronic file format. Choose this option if there are multiple changes you wish made to the home plans and you have a local design professional able to make the changes. Not available for all plans. Please contact our order department or visit our Web site to check the availability of CAD files for your plan.

## Mirror-Reverse Sets/Right-Reading Reverse

Plans can be printed in mirror-reverse—we can "flip" plans to create a mirror image of the design. This is useful when the house would fit your site or personal preferences if all the rooms were on the opposite side than shown. As the image is reversed, the lettering and dimensions will also be reversed, meaning they will read backwards. Therefore, when ordering mirror-reverse drawings, you must order at least one set of the original plan unreversed. A $50.00 fee per plan order will be charged for mirror-reverse (regardless of the number of mirror-reverse sets ordered). Some plans are available in right-reading reverse; this feature will show the plan in reverse, but the writing on the plan will be readable. A $150.00 fee per plan order will be charged for right-reading reverse (regardless of the number of right-reading reverse sets ordered). Please contact our order department or visit our website to check the availibility of this feature for your chosen plan.

## EZ Quote: Home Cost Estimator

EZ Quote is our response to a frequently asked question we hear from customers: "How much will the house cost me to build?" EZ Quote: Home Cost Estimator will enable you to obtain a calculated building cost to construct your home, based on labor rates and building material costs within your zip code area. This summary is useful for those who want to get an idea of the total construction costs before purchasing sets of home plans. It will also provide a level of comfort when you begin soliciting bids. The cost is $29.95 for the first EZ Quote and $19.95 for each additional one in the same order. Available only in the U.S. and Canada.

## Materials List

Available for most of our plans, the Materials List provides you an invaluable resource in planning and estimating the cost of your home. Each Materials List outlines the quantity, dimensions, and type of materials needed to build your home (with the exception of mechanical systems). You will get faster, more-accurate bids from your contractors and building suppliers. A Materials List may only be ordered with the purchase of at least five sets of home plans.

## CompleteCost Estimator

CompleteCost Estimator is a valuable tool for use in planning and constructing your new home. It provides more detail than a materials list and will act as a checklist for all items you will need to select or coordinate during your building process. CompleteCost Estimator is only available for certain plans (please see Plan Index) and may only be ordered with the purchase of at least five sets of home plans. The cost is $125.00 for CompleteCost Estimator

## Material Take-off (See page 376.)

---

**Order Toll Free by Phone**
**1-800-523-6789**
By Fax: 201-760-2431

Orders received 3PM ET, will be processed and shipped within two business days.

**Order Online**
**www.ultimateplans.com**
**Mail Your Order**
Creative Homeowner
Attn: Home Plans
24 Park Way
Upper Saddle River, NJ 07458

**Canadian Customers**
**Order Toll Free 1-800-393-1883**
**Mail Your Order (Canada)**
Creative Homeowner Canada
Attn: Home Plans
113-437 Martin St., Ste. 215
Penticton, BC V2A 5L1

# Before You Order

## Our Exchange Policy

Blueprints are nonrefundable. However, should you find that the plan you have purchased does not fit your needs, you may exchange that plan for another plan in our collection within 60 days from the date of your original order. The entire content of your original order must be returned before an exchange will be processed. You will be charged a processing fee of 20% of the amount of the original order, the cost difference between the new plan set and the original plan set (if applicable), and all related shipping costs for the new plans. Contact our order department for more information. Please note: reproducible masters may only be exchanged if the package is unopened. PDF files and CAD files cannot be exchanged and are nonrefundable.

## Building Codes and Requirements

All plans offered for sale in this book and on our website (www.ultimateplans.com) are continually updated to meet the latest International Residential Code (IRC). Because building codes vary from area to area, some drawing modifications and/or the assistance of a professional designer or architect may be necessary to comply with your local codes or to accommodate specific building site conditions. We strongly advise you to consult with your local building official for information regarding codes governing your area.

## Multiple Plan Discount

Purchase 3 different home plans in the **same order** and receive **5% off** the plan price.

Purchase 5 or more different home plans in the **same order** and receive **10% off** the plan price. (Please Note: Study sets do not apply.)

## Blueprint Price Schedule

| Price Code | 1 Set | 5 Sets | 8 Sets | Reproducible Masters or PDF Files | CAD | Materials List |
|---|---|---|---|---|---|---|
| A | $410 | $470 | $545 | $660 | $1,125 | $85 |
| B | $465 | $540 | $615 | $740 | $1,310 | $85 |
| C | $525 | $620 | $695 | $820 | $1,475 | $85 |
| D | $575 | $670 | $745 | $870 | $1,575 | $95 |
| E | $625 | $730 | $805 | $925 | $1,675 | $95 |
| F | $690 | $790 | $865 | $990 | $1,800 | $95 |
| G | $720 | $820 | $895 | $1,020 | $1,845 | $95 |
| H | $730 | $830 | $905 | $1,045 | $1,900 | $95 |
| I | $995 | $1,095 | $1,170 | $1,290 | $2,110 | $105 |
| J | $1,190 | $1,290 | $1,365 | $1,490 | $2,300 | $105 |
| K | $1,195 | $1,295 | $1,370 | $1,495 | $2,300 | $105 |
| L | $1,240 | $1,335 | $1,410 | $1,535 | $2,400 | $105 |

Note: All prices subject to change

## Lowe's Material Take-off (MT Tier)

| MT Tier* | Price | |
|---|---|---|
| XB | $345 | * Please see the Plan Index to determine your |
| XC | $545 | plan's Lowe's Material Take-off (MT Tier). |

## Shipping & Handling

| | 1–4 Sets | 5–7 Sets | 8+ Sets or Reproducibles | CAD |
|---|---|---|---|---|
| **US Regular** (7–10 business days) | $18 | $20 | $25 | $25 |
| **US Priority** (3–5 business days) | $25 | $30 | $35 | $35 |
| **US Express** (1–2 business days) | $40 | $45 | $50 | $50 |
| **Canada Express** (3–4 business days) | $100 | $100 | $100 | $100 |
| **Worldwide Express** (3–5 business days) | ** Quote Required ** | | | |

Note: All delivery times are from date the blueprint package is shipped (typically within 1-2 days of placing order).

---

# Order Form Please send me the following:

**Plan Number:** _____ **Price Code:** _____ (See Plan Index.)

Indicate Foundation Type: (Select ONE. See plan page for availability.)

❏ Slab   ❏ Crawl space   ❏ Basement   ❏ Walk-out basement

❏ Optional Foundation for Fee _____ $_____
*(Please enter foundation here)*

*Please call all our order department or visit our website for optional foundation fee

**Basic Blueprint Package**                                    Cost

❏ CAD Files                                          $_____
❏ PDF Files                                          $_____
❏ Reproducible Masters                               $_____
❏ 8-Set Plan Package                                 $_____
❏ 5-Set Plan Package                                 $_____
❏ 1-Set Study Package                                $_____
❏ Additional plan sets:
   ___ sets at $50.00 per set                        $_____
❏ Print in mirror-reverse: $50.00 per order          $_____
   *Please call all our order department
    or visit our website for availibility
❏ Print in right-reading reverse: $150.00 per order  $_____
   *Please call all our order department
    or visit our website for availibility

**Important Extras**

❏ Lowe's Material Take-off (See Price Tier above.)   $_____
❏ Materials List                                     $_____
❏ CompleteCost Materials Report at $125.00           $_____
   Zip Code of Home/Building Site _____
❏ EZ Quote for Plan #_____ at $29.95           $_____
❏ Additional EZ Quotes for Plan #s_____        $_____
   at $19.95 each
**Shipping** (see chart above)                       $_____
**SUBTOTAL**                                         $_____
**Sales Tax** (NJ residents only, add 7%)            $_____
**TOTAL**                                            $_____

Order Toll Free: 1-800-523-6789   By Fax: 201-760-2431
Creative Homeowner (Home Plans Order Dept.)
24 Park Way
Upper Saddle River, NJ 07458

Name _____
*(Please print or type)*

Street _____
*(Please do not use a P.O. Box)*

City _____ State _____

Country _____ Zip _____

Daytime telephone ( ___ )_____

Fax ( ___ )_____
*(Required for reproducible orders)*

E-Mail _____

**Payment**   ❏ Bank check/money order. No personal checks.
*Make checks payable to Creative Homeowner*

❏ VISA      ❏ MasterCard      ❏ American Express Cards      ❏ Discover

Credit card number _____

Expiration date (mm/yy) _____

Signature _____

*Please check the appropriate box:*
❏ Building home for myself   ❏ Building home for someone else

SOURCE CODE | LE501

# Copyright Notice

All home plans sold through this publication are protected by copyright. Reproduction of these home plans, either in whole or in part, including any form and/or preparation of derivative works thereof, for any reason without prior written permission is strictly prohibited. The purchase of a set of home plans in no way transfers any copyright or other ownership interest in it to the buyer except for a limited license to use that set of home plans for the construction of one, and only one, dwelling unit. The purchase of additional sets of the home plans at a reduced price from the original set or as a part of a multiple-set package does not convey to the buyer a license to construct more than one dwelling.

Similarly, the purchase of reproducible home plans (sepias, mylars) carries the same copyright protection as mentioned above. It is generally allowed to make up to a maximum of 10 copies for the construction of a single dwelling only. To use any plans more than once, and to avoid any copyright license infringement, it is necessary to contact the plan designer to receive a release and license for any extended use. Whereas a purchaser of reproducible plans is granted a license to make copies, it should be noted that because blueprints are copyrighted, making photocopies from them is illegal.

Copyright and licensing of home plans for construction exist to protect all parties. Copyright respects and supports the intellectual property of the original architect or designer. Copyright law has been reinforced over the past few years. Willful infringement could cause settlements for statutory damages to $150,000.00 plus attorney fees, damages, and loss of profits.

---

**CREATIVE HOMEOWNER®**

**ultimateplans.com**

### Order online by visiting our Web site.

### Open 24 hours a day, 7 days a week.

*Still haven't found your perfect home?*
With thousands of plans online at ultimateplans.com, there are plenty more to choose from. Using our automated search tools, we make the process even easier. Just enter your ideal home criteria, and let our search tools find the plans for you!

Other great benefits for many plans at ultimateplans.com include:

- **More photos of both the exterior and interior of many of our most popular homes**
- **More side and rear elevations**
- **More data and information about each particular plan**

In addition, you will find more information about the building process and even free step-by-step DIY projects you can do!

# Index

For pricing, see page 379.

# Index

*For pricing, see page 379.*

| Plan # | Price Code | Page | Total Finished Area Square Feet | Materials List Available | Complete Cost | MT Tier |
|---|---|---|---|---|---|---|
| 361340 | B | 62 | 1331 | N | N | XB |
| 361448 | C | 164 | 1634 | N | N | XB |
| 361484 | G | 348 | 3303 | N | N | XC |
| 371002 | C | 110 | 1590 | N | N | XB |
| 371004 | D | 105 | 1815 | N | N | XB |
| 371007 | D | 104 | 1944 | N | N | XB |
| 371008 | F | 297 | 2656 | N | N | XC |
| 371012 | C | 181 | 1720 | N | N | XB |
| 371021 | E | 236 | 2384 | N | N | XB |
| 371024 | F | 319 | 2843 | N | N | XB |
| 371030 | B | 35 | 1434 | N | N | XB |
| 371036 | C | 183 | 1764 | N | N | XB |
| 371046 | E | 231 | 2440 | N | N | XC |
| 371049 | B | 53 | 1440 | N | N | XB |
| 371053 | C | 176 | 1654 | N | N | XB |
| 371063 | E | 230 | 2330 | N | N | XC |
| 371072 | C | 171 | 1772 | N | N | XC |
| 371081 | D | 191 | 2143 | N | N | XB |
| 371087 | F | 287 | 2643 | N | N | XC |
| 371125 | C | 164 | 1746 | N | N | XC |
| 371127 | E | 225 | 2427 | N | N | XC |
| 371155 | G | 365 | 3304 | N | N | XB |
| 381003 | D | 81 | 1925 | Y | N | XB |
| 381010 | E | 85 | 1905 | Y | N | XB |
| 381029 | B | 63 | 1200 | Y | N | XB |
| 381045 | B | 15 | 1015 | Y | N | XB |
| 381048 | A | 15 | 895 | Y | N | XB |
| 381131 | D | 51 | 2190 | Y | N | XB |
| 381159 | G | 363 | 3230 | Y | N | XB |
| 391002 | E | 229 | 2281 | Y | N | XB |
| 391007 | D | 262 | 2083 | Y | N | XB |
| 391007 | D | 263 | 2083 | Y | N | XB |
| 391023 | E | 212 | 2244 | Y | N | XB |
| 391024 | F | 323 | 2647 | Y | N | XB |
| 391026 | B | 62 | 1470 | Y | N | XB |
| 391030 | F | 305 | 2662 | N | N | XB |
| 391031 | G | 358 | 3176 | Y | N | XB |
| 391036 | C | 188 | 1710 | Y | N | XB |
| 391041 | E | 309 | 2563 | N | N | XB |
| 391050 | F | 299 | 2674 | Y | N | XB |
| 391055 | I | 363 | 4217 | Y | N | XC |
| 391056 | F | 314 | 2607 | N | N | XB |
| 391057 | F | 321 | 2851 | Y | N | XC |
| 391060 | B | 14 | 1359 | Y | N | XB |
| 391061 | E | 327 | 2541 | Y | N | XB |
| 391068 | D | 84 | 1855 | N | N | XB |
| 391070 | D | 92 | 1960 | Y | N | XB |
| 391211 | B | 40 | 1461 | Y | N | XB |
| 391328 | A | 50 | 988 | Y | N | XB |
| 391373 | C | 80 | 1554 | Y | N | XB |
| 391425 | H | 365 | 3947 | Y | N | XB |
| 391459 | B | 20 | 1341 | Y | N | XB |
| 391478 | D | 103 | 1945 | Y | N | XB |
| 391489 | B | 26 | 1328 | Y | N | XB |
| 391504 | C | 146 | 1763 | Y | N | XB |
| 391519 | D | 367 | 2001 | Y | N | XB |
| 401001 | D | 254 | 2071 | Y | N | XB |
| 401008 | C | 83 | 1541 | Y | N | XB |
| 401009 | F | 328 | 2750 | Y | N | XC |
| 401012 | E | 248 | 2301 | Y | N | XB |
| 401013 | E | 225 | 2381 | Y | N | XB |
| 401018 | G | 316 | 5699 | Y | N | XC |
| 401024 | B | 60 | 3384 | Y | N | XB |
| 401029 | D | 190 | 2163 | Y | N | XB |
| 401031 | B | 11 | 1260 | Y | N | XB |
| 401036 | C | 125 | 1583 | Y | N | XB |
| 401037 | D | 167 | 1924 | Y | N | XB |
| 401039 | E | 192 | 2462 | Y | N | XC |
| 401044 | C | 77 | 1568 | Y | N | XB |
| 401047 | B | 41 | 1064 | Y | N | XB |
| 421005 | C | 158 | 1784 | Y | N | XB |
| 421010 | E | 285 | 2457 | Y | N | XC |
| 421012 | F | 290 | 2795 | Y | N | XC |
| 421023 | E | 284 | 2579 | Y | N | XC |
| 421028 | G | 357 | 3005 | Y | N | XC |
| 421044 | E | 224 | 2302 | Y | N | XC |
| 431002 | C | 153 | 1680 | Y | N | XB |
| 441002 | D | 170 | 1873 | Y | N | XB |
| 441003 | C | 165 | 1580 | Y | N | XB |
| 441004 | C | 127 | 1728 | Y | N | XB |
| 441006 | D | 178 | 1891 | Y | N | XB |
| 441009 | F | 286 | 2650 | Y | N | XB |
| 441010 | F | 306 | 2973 | Y | N | XB |
| 441011 | F | 320 | 2898 | Y | N | XB |
| 441012 | H | 371 | 3682 | Y | N | XC |
| 441013 | G | 367 | 3317 | Y | N | XB |
| 441021 | C | 93 | 1760 | N | N | XB |
| 441023 | E | 317 | 2500 | Y | N | XB |
| 441026 | G | 357 | 3457 | Y | N | XB |
| 441026 | H | 350 | 3623 | Y | N | XB |
| 441028 | G | 346 | 3165 | Y | N | XB |
| 441030 | J | 354 | 5180 | Y | N | XC |
| 441031 | I | 366 | 4150 | Y | N | XB |
| 441032 | D | 76 | 1944 | Y | N | XB |
| 441036 | F | 291 | 2902 | Y | N | XB |
| 441039 | D | 254 | 2120 | Y | N | XB |
| 441040 | D | 230 | 2079 | N | N | XB |
| 441041 | D | 218 | 2164 | Y | N | XB |
| 441042 | E | 293 | 2538 | Y | N | XB |
| 441046 | F | 282 | 2606 | Y | N | XB |
| 441048 | E | 214 | 2453 | Y | N | XB |
| 441032 | D | 76 | 1944 | Y | N | XB |
| 441313 | F | 311 | 3588 | N | N | XB |
| 451162 | E | 284 | 2565 | N | N | XB |
| 451330 | G | 362 | 3288 | N | N | XB |
| 461092 | F | 295 | 2844 | N | N | XB |
| 491004 | B | 56 | 1154 | Y | N | XB |
| 491005 | B | 45 | 1333 | Y | N | XB |
| 491006 | B | 32 | 1470 | Y | N | XB |
| 501593 | B | 39 | 1490 | Y | N | XB |
| 501605 | G | 351 | 3182 | Y | N | XB |
| 511012 | C | 99 | 1573 | N | N | XB |
| 521004 | G | 369 | 3131 | N | N | XB |
| 521005 | F | 330 | 2932 | N | N | XB |
| 521006 | F | 310 | 2818 | N | N | XB |
| 521009 | F | 325 | 2741 | N | N | XB |
| 521011 | F | 325 | 2605 | N | N | XB |
| 521017 | E | 243 | 2359 | N | N | XB |
| 521030 | C | 122 | 1944 | N | N | XB |
| 521036 | C | 80 | 1578 | N | N | XB |
| 521040 | C | 115 | 1555 | N | N | XB |
| 521042 | C | 129 | 1552 | N | N | XB |
| 521043 | C | 104 | 1536 | N | N | XB |
| 521056 | B | 44 | 1400 | N | N | XB |
| 521063 | B | 33 | 1229 | N | N | XB |
| 531020 | I | 370 | 4271 | N | N | XC |
| 541042 | I | 370 | 4012 | N | N | XC |
| 551195 | G | 366 | 5610 | N | N | XC |
| 571004 | B | 39 | 1021 | Y | N | XB |
| 571029 | A | 50 | 844 | Y | N | XB |
| 571056 | C | 122 | 1559 | Y | N | XB |
| 571072 | E | 261 | 2222 | Y | N | XB |
| 571078 | D | 128 | 1945 | Y | N | XB |
| 571078 | D | 120 | 1870 | Y | N | XB |
| 631065 | C | 128 | 1682 | Y | N | XB |
| 641001 | G | 348 | 3034 | N | N | XB |
| 651026 | B | 10 | 1145 | N | N | XB |
| 651079 | E | 98 | 2207 | N | N | XB |
| 661210 | G | 368 | 5193 | N | N | XC |

# Material Take-off

## The fastest way to get started building your dream home